JN410145

Translation, Transculturation, and Transformation of Modernity in East Asia

Editors

Ewha Institute for Humanities, Ewha Womans University

The Ewha Institute for the Humanities(EIH) has been established as a research institute at Ewha Womans University to overcome the crisis of the humanities and deal with the changes in knowledge, technology, and culture in the 21st century. It is developing itself into a hub for devising a new paradigm to guide the humanities in line with Ewha's tradition of excellence in the humanities. Reflecting on the specificity of Korean humanistic knowledge, the future of humanity, and posthuman conditions, The EIH is leading the theorization and globalization of Trans-Humanities with its focus on posthumanism and trans-boundary knowledge.

Graduate School of Integrated Sciences for Global Society, Kyushu University

Graduate School of Integrated Sciences for Global Society (ISGS) was established in 2014, it is the newest graduate school of Kyushu University. The challenges facing humankind are interrelated in diverse and complex ways. Determining challenges and resolving problems requires a truly integrated interdiscipline transcending the frameworks of the humanities and sciences via interdisciplinary partnerships in various fields of research. The Graduate School's educational objective is to pursue education and research from the perspective of global society and envisioning a human society coexisting with other living things on the planet.

Translation, Transculturation, and Transformation of Modernity in East Asia

Published by Somyong Publishing co.
6-gil 15, Seocho Joongang-ro, Seocho-gu, Seoul, Korea
Tel. 02-585-7840 Fax. 02-585-7848
somyungbooks@daum.net
http ://somyong.co.kr

ISBN 979-11-5905-228-6 93910
₩30,000

This work was supported by the National Research Foundation of Korea Grant
funded by the Korea Government. (NRF-2007-361-AL0015)

Ewha Institute for Humanities Humanistic Knowledge Series 07

Translation, Transculturation, and Transformation of Modernity in East Asia

Edited by
Ewha Institute for Humanities &
Graduate School of Integrated Sciences for Global Society, Kyushu University

Somyong Publishing

•• Introduction ••

Between the late 19th century and the early 20th century, East Asia including Japan, Korea and China was experiencing the modern age more intensely than any other place on the earth. Western powers were intent on colonizing the region through distorted capitalism, and the three countries, which had been struggling with one another in traditional historic relationships, attempted to self-strengthen and promote national prosperity and military power according to their respective situations in admiration of the glory of the West's modern development. Since the early 20th century, a pessimistic view was raised by some scholars criticizing East Asia for passively imitating and mimicking Western modernity, faced with the overwhelming accumulation of cultural and intellectual outcomes of the West. However, as mentioned above, the modern age in East Asia was extremely intense. There must have been a cultural drive from external influences, but East Asia was a melting pot of modern thought created by crossing between tradition and modernity, East and West, and humanities and scientific knowledge, through the integration of global cultures and interdisciplinary crossover of knowledges. We do not believe that Western modern thought influenced East Asia unilaterally in its fixed form. Modern cultures and philosophies flow like organisms, interact with other cultures/bodies of knowledge, and evolve into new cultures/thought. East Asia's modern thought and cultures have existed on these dynamic modern fields of knowledge that we are still embracing.

With this awareness as a point of departure, the Ewha Institute for Humanities of Ewha Womans University and the Graduate School of Integrated Sciences for Global Society of Kyushu University intended to examine the processes of change and reconstruction of modern East Asian fields of knowledge in this book. The implications and value of the East Asian modern age are reconsidered based on the knowledge discourses of the 21st century, and its modernity, which traversed the 20th century and is heading towards the 21st century, is materialized concretely. In this process, it is attempted to promote the creation of new historic relationships, academic exchange, and knowledge discourses of the 21st century from the traditional historic relationships and knowledge discourses based on the fundamental question of 'What is East Asian thought knowledge?' Although oppositions and conflicts are increasing among peoples of different countries, ethnic cultures and languages, East Asia is the most critical region for living in harmony, pursuing coexistence and creating new knowledge in the 21st century. It is our hope that this book will mark the beginning of these efforts.

The book consists of three chapters. The first chapter "Translation of modernity" explores the transformation of Western literary works in the process of their translation into East Asian languages and the significance of formation of East Asian modern literature and knowledges. The second chapter "Transculturation in East Asia" looks into cultural interaction at the time of the encounter between Western modern culture and East Asia and its transformation into new modern culture (literature) in East Asia. Various aspects of the transculturation of East Asian modern culture, which is created anew by crossing over the boundaries between East and West, tradition and modernity, literature and visual media, are examined. The third chapter "Transformation of knowledge" examines the influences of modern Western knowledge on East Asian intellectuals and the possibility of modern social transformation.

The Ewha Institute for Humanities and the Graduate School of Integrated Sciences for Global Society have maintained academic exchange and held workshops and international conferences to study the global universality and paradigm shift of modern thought since 2014. The passion for deep contemplation on the true nature of knowledge and the value of human existence amid the global changes in the 21st century has summoned us back to 100 years ago to study the nature and value of modernity together. Now we conclude the work, hoping that this will provide the beginning for reconsideration of the true nature of knowledge in the 21st century and the value of East Asia. Publication of this book does not mean the end of the joint research by the Ewha Institute for Humanities and the Graduate School of Integrated Sciences for Global Society. Recalling the phrase of 'East Asia in dynamic interaction,' we pledge to continue to plan and carry out joint research to intensify the East Asian knowledge discourses heading into the 100 years ahead of us.

There are many that we need to thank for helping in the book's publication. First of all, We would like to express our gratitude to Professor Jin-hee Kim, who has a critical mind and deep insights on East Asian modernity; Professor Namigata Tsuyoshi, who tried to deliver messages related to the publication to the professors on the Japanese side and let us know their answers; and Professor Dongju Seo, who liaised between the Korean and Japanese scholars and played an essential role for the joint research for the book. We would also like to express thanks to our colleagues who joined in writing the research papers and the staff at Somyung Publishing which assisted in the publication.

August 15, 2017
Ewha Institute for Humanities, Ewha Womans University &
Gradate School of Integrated Sciences for Global Society, Kyushu University

Tsuyoshi Namigata (Kyushu University)
Dongju Seo (Seoul University)

This book contains the accomplishments achieved through the many academic exchanges made between Ewha Institute for the Humanities of Ewha Womans University and Graduate School of Integrated Sciences for Global Society of Kyushu University since 2014. More specifically, this book is the result of three years of joint researches through various exchanges between the Transboundary Knowledge Team consisted of scholars of Korean, Japanese, and Chinese Studies within the trans boundary knowledge team of Ewha Institute for the Humanities, and Interdisciplinary Research Team of Kyushu University that aims for a new creation of scholarship named "Knowledge fabrication"

The Transboundary Knowledge Team of Ewha Institute for the Humanities took notice of the 21st century composition of knowledge creation through diverse methods of rapid communication and crossings, and studies the historical identity and future mappings of Korean humanities knowledge. In order to create new discourses of Korean humanities knowledge the team need reflective reexamination and empirical analysis of the histories of humanities knowledge in the modern times. The Transboundary Knowledge Team has concentrated on viewing the 'now' of East Asian humanities knowledge that is being reorganized through globalization, and on examining the landscape of knowledge of Korea, China, and Japan in the context of Modern East Asia.

On the one hand, Interdisciplinary Research Team which study Knowledge fabrication research commenced with the critical viewing of wanting to secure a new point of view on the historical fact of Japan having been the 'bridge of knowledge,' and showing an outstanding ability of 'Processing trade of knowledge'. Here, Knowledge fabrication means the accepting of various advanced knowledge, exploring its principals, applying the accomplishments made by innovation and improvement of accepted knowledge into society on various levels, and the series of processes included for the universal utilization. The team conducted its research through collaborations of various scholarships with the aim to elucidate the process and methods of advanced culture, technology, thinking, acceptance of system, fabrication, and transmittance caused by Japan.

The academic exchanges between the two research teams started on July, 2014 when a member of the Transboundary Knowledge Team visited Kyushu University and attended a meeting. The meeting was arranged with Kyushu University Professor Namigata Tsuyoshi's efforts, and two research teams shared their research contents, and decided to seek the possibilities of joint-researches through the exchanges of visits. To realize what has been discussed, Ewha Institute for the Humanities created a new academic conference called "East Asia Humanities Knowledge Forum" to promote research exchanges.

The first "East Asia Humanities Forum' was held in Ewha Womans University on November 2014 under the topic of "Transference of Knowledge : Between Locality and Globality". As stated in the title, the aim of the first forum was to examine not only the aspects of the acceptance of Western knowledge in East Asia on a national level, but also to consider the transference that happens within the region of East Asia. In the first Forum, Professor Andrew Hall from Kyushu University presented on "Bucking Colonial Education Trends in Machukoku," and Professor Jin-hee Kim from Ewha Institute for the Humanities presented on "Text on the Boundary Between Imperial and Colonial : Late 1930s Writers Bound for Manchuria, before and after". These presentations focused on the third reference — 'Manchuria' — and relativized the role of Japan in the formation of modern knowledge of East Asia, and demonstrated the transference of knowledge within East Asia from all angles.

The exchange between the two research teams continued through the third "East Asia Humanities Forum" held on March 2015. Under the Forum's topic, "Modern Times and Modernism in East Asia" Professor Namigata Tsuyoshi presented on "Exotic Modern : Japanese Literature and Cultural Translation in the Early Showa Period," introducing the translation acceptance of 'modern' in 1920-30s Japan. Especially in the third forum, Professor

Liang Luo from Kentucky University in the U.S. and Professor John Treat who East Asian Viterature Scholar from Yale University in U.S. presented on "Hong Shen, Tian Han, and Intermedial Art and Activism" and "The Queer Career of Yi Sang and Telling Time in an Empire," providing discussion opportunities on the modernization aspects of Knowledge of Japan, China, and Korea, which was in a state of Colonization at the time.

Through such academic exchanges the two research teams found the need for a direct communication and discussions for a full-scale joint-research as well as the need for an interdisciplinary research that integrates the processes of the formation of knowledge in East Asia. Therefore, to deepen the understanding on each other's research and information, joint-workshop at Kyushu University's Ito Campus on August, 2015 under the theme of "Transference/ Production of Knowledge in Modern East Asia" The joint-workshop began with Professor Dongju Seo from Ewha Institute for the Humanities and Professor Se Terahisa from Kyushu University introducing the researches of each team and the publication accomplishments, followed by round-table discussions joined by the members of both teams. In the round-table discussions, both teams saw similar issues, but on the other hand various opinions were exchanged to find the intersecting point of research in identifying Korean humanities knowledge and Japanese traits of knowledge acceptance. Moreover, the workshop provided an opportunity for the Korean, Japan, and Chinese researchers to self-objectify by examining the similarities and differences in practically and theoretically on matters of the role of translation, and the formation of knowledge from modern to present.

Both teams spent some time to substantially strengthen their researches after the joint-workshop, and held the joint-international symposium on July 2016 to sum up the accomplishments of research exchanges made over the past two years. Kyushu University hosted the symposium under the title, "Translation, Transculturation, and Transformation of Modernity in East Asia." In this symposium, Professor Noriko Matsunaga from Kyushu University presented a paper on "Japan's 'Production of Knowledge' in the Aspect of Process of Formation of Modern Vocabulary", Professor Matsumoto Tsunehiko presented a paper on "Japanese Modern Literature and Body Schema," and Professor Namigata Tsuyoshi presented on "Another 'Paris of the Orient' : Overlapping Exoticism in Japanese Modernism around 1930." From the Ewha Institute for the Humanities Transboundary Knowledge Team, Professor Jin-hee Kim presented a paper on "Rethinking 1930s Korean Modernism : Kim Kirim and 'New Artist Group in Japan," Professor Sun-hee Kim presented on "Jeong Yak-yong and Hirata Atsutane : One Route of Accepting Western Learning in Joseon and Japan," and Professor Byeong-jin Kim presented on "Reconsidering of Accepting Socialism in 1920s Joseon : Centered on Osugi Sakae." Likewise, the symposium included premodern and modern into its sight, and proceeded dense presentations and discussions on the aspects of accepting Western knowledge unfolding in various directions of literature, thinking, idea, and representation of East Asia region.

Looking back, we remember many participants being surprised including myself, by how similar our research directions were in the joint-workshop held on August 2015. The reason being was that there were no direct contact or exchanges of any sort, though our issues were so similar. Korean and Japanese Research institutes that did not have any relations prior, conducting group research on similar issues and at similar times was in fact a wonderful coincidence. However, on the other hand, it may not be so surprising taking into account the reality that many East Asian Humanities scholars are interested in the history of transnational exchange of knowledge. What's for certain are that each individual scholar of East Asia in both institutions was connecting their research interests to the contemporary trend of knowledge, and that they exists as part of the bigger network. Furthermore, they have matured such similar issues in the different knowledge environment they were in. In this sense, this book demonstrates its value as a modern case of new exchange of knowledge and at the same time academic accomplishment of creative reproduction.

Chapter 3 : Transformation of knowledge

Translation of Modernity

Towards a Transcultural Supernatural

Poe's "The Black Cat" and Western Gothic Tales in the Early Meiji Era

Daniel J. Wyatt (Kyushu University)

1. Introduction

Japan has a long and particularly rich tradition of narratives that depict stories of *kami* [神, Shinto deities], *oni* [鬼, Buddhist demons], *yōkai* [妖怪, monsters], *bakemono* [化け物, shape-shifting foxes, cats, badgers, etc.] and a myriad of other fantastic creatures, including spirits of both the living and the dead, in great abundance. Such stories date as far back as the collection of Buddhist *setsuwa* tales, the *Nihon ryōiki* [日本霊異記, lit. 'Ghostly Records of Japan'] circa 822, and continued to maintain a strong presence throughout history. Other notable works include the collections, *Konjaku monogatari* [今昔物語], *Uji shūi monogatari* [宇拾遺語], *Kokon chomonjū* [古今著聞集], and 'otogizōshi' [御伽草子] prose narratives from the classical and medieval periods; *Tonoigusa* [宿直草] (1660), *Inga monogatari* [因果語] (1661), *Otogi bōko* [御伽婢子] (1666), *Ugetsu monogatari* [雨月物語] (1776), *Nansō satomi hakkenden* [南総里見八犬伝] (1814-1842), as well as countless works of *kanazōshi* [仮名草子] picture books throughout the Edo period (1603-1868) before eventually permeating through to all forms of literature, art and theatre, and viably inoculating *kaidan* [怪談, ghost stories and tales relating to the supernatural] as a genre in its own right.

Studies have indicated a relationship between the prevalence of symbols of monstrosity and periods of social, economic and or political "times of crisis."[1] Accordingly, the popularity of bakemono and yōkai in the Edo period extended beyond literature and art, as supernatural motifs were also as a means of protest by discontented factions in various manners of carnivalesque practices, parody, and protest.[2] With the Meiji Restoration and introduction of a new government in 1868, however, Japan opened its doors to the West and sought to homogenize modern ideology through an emphasis on science and Western thought. As such, all aspects and affiliations with 'uncivilized' culture that were seen to contradict modern discourse — including yōkai, bakemono and belief in the supernatural — came to be denounced as '*meishin*' [迷信, superstition] and seen as an impediment to Japan's efforts towards becoming a modern state. Traditional Buddhist practices were also closely related to the supernatural realm,[3] and under the *shinbutsu bunri* [神仏分離, division of Shinto and Buddhism] and *haibutsu kishaku* [廃仏毀釈, lit. 'Abolish Buddha, destroy

1. See : Komatsu, *Oni ga tsukutta kuni, nihon, rekishi wo ugokashitekita "kurayami" no chikara to wa* [鬼がつくった国・日本・歴史を動かしてきた「暗闇」の力とは], 2002; Figal, *Civilization and Monsters : Spirits of Modernity in Meiji Japan*, 1999.

2 Such as the so-called "monster riots" [妖怪騒動, *yōkai sōdo*] in Osaka, and the "goblin riots" [天狗騒動, tengu sōdo] in present day Ibaraki [茨城] and Chiba [千葉] prefectures. See : Koschmann, "Action as Text : Ideology in the Tengu Insurrection," in *Conflict in Modern Japanese History : The Neglected Tradition*, 1982, 83.

3 'Hungry ghosts' [餓鬼, *gaki*], demons [鬼, *oni*] and magic [魔, *ma*] where integral aspects of Buddhism, both in canonical texts and in daily practices (which included performing exorcisms and spells for various purposes).

Shakyamuni'] movements, Buddhism too came to be stigmatized as a cult that perpetuated these so-called 'superstitions.'[4] Philosopher Inoue Enryō (井上円了, 1858-1919) was a key participant to the deconstruction and subsequent reconstruction of Buddhism from 'superstition' to 'proper religion,'[5] but it was also his establishment of '*yōkaigaku*' [妖怪学, lit. 'monsterology'], under the guise of which he set out to debunk all manner of supernatural entities and beliefs, that proceeded to have a profound impact on kaidan as a genre in the years to come.

Through all the attempts to denounce belief in the supernatural, the first twenty years of the era (1868-1888) certainly represents a decline in popularity of written texts of a fantastic nature, however, the subject matter never truly disappeared from the public sphere entirely. Ironically, it was through academic practices like reading, writing and translation — all modern pursuits — that allowed the supernatural to haunt the imagination of the Japanese public once more. Stories of strange happenings, ghosts and shape-shifting animals were a regular feature of Meiji newspapers,[6] and the supernatural also served as prolific subject matter in the *jidaimono* [時代物, period plays], *sewamono* [世話物, contemporary plays] and *buyōgeki* [舞踊劇, dance dramas] of Kawatake Mokuami (河竹黙阿弥, 1816-1893), and the development of *sokki* (速記) transcription practices even-

4 See : Kashiwahara, *Nihon bukkyōshi : Kindai* [日本仏教史<近代>], 1990, 20-42.

5 His book *Meishin to shūkyō* [迷信と宗教, Superstition and Religion] (1916) was fundamental to this process. Enryō does not provide a clear definition of what "superstition" is, but instead proceeds to list extensive categories of what constitutes superstitious practices, including the belief in all manner of supernatural beings, from ghosts [幽霊, *yūrei*], fox possession [狐憑き, *kitsunetsuki*], and *tengu* [天狗] demons, to incantation [加持祈祷, *kajikitō*] and auspicious days [日柄, *higara*].

6 See : Yumoto Kōichi [湯本豪一], *Meiji yōkai shimbun* [明治妖怪新聞], 1999.

tually allowed his and other traditionally performance-based works to circulate in the written medium. The first story of the Western gothic genre to appear in this period was Edward Bulwer-Lytton's (1802-1873) The Haunted and the Haunters : or The House and the Brain (1859), translated in 1880 by Inoue Tsutomu (井上勤, 1850-1928) as *Rondon kidan : Kaikan kyoki* (龍動鬼談 : 開巻驚奇, lit. 'London Demon Story : Surprises Inside'). The significance of this translation, besides the fact that it surfaced so early in the Meiji era when translations of political novels were in high demand and supernaturally-themed narratives were mostly restricted to kabuki plays and tabloid-like articles in newspapers, can be found in the foreword :

> I was in Tokyo some years ago. Sometimes I would meet with the Dutchman, Siebold. One time, we got to talking about the mystery of our country's tengu. Siebold laughed and said there was no basis for such a thing. After reading the translation of my son Tsutomu's Rondon kidan recently, I was surprised at how strange and mysterious it was. It would appear that such mysterious occurrences happen even in Europe. And despite this, people are fixated on the view that monsters don't exist. Why is it something that needs to be laughed at so excessively (if at all)? On the contrary, in this vast expanse of a world we live in, people need to know that there are things out there that cannot be explained with human knowledge. People should also be aware that through the study of logic, any doubts that we may harbor about such things may go away completely. That being the case, a small book of enjoyable kaidan tales is not completely without use to young scholars. Confucius never spoke of the mysterious. But he never

said that such things didn't exist, either. Understandably so.[7]

May, Meiji 13 (1880) – Fumei Koji[8] (Inoue 1880, 'Jo' [序, Foreword])

There are two significant aspects to this foreword. The first is that Fumei Koji (Inoue Fumei) evokes the idea of 'read first, ask questions later': that perhaps the things people read or experience in life can be explained with logic through "academic pursuits" [*kōkyu*, 講究] and perhaps they can't [*jinchi no hakaru atawazaru koto aru*, 人智の測る能はざる事有る], but in the meantime that shouldn't stop people, particularly "young scholars" [*kōgakusha*, 後学者], from enjoying supernatural tales [*yūgi kaidan*, 遊戯怪談]. The second significant aspect is that he highlights the fact that mysterious occurrences happen "even in Europe" [*ōshū gen ni kono kai ari*, 欧洲現に此の怪有り] thereby effectively aligning Japan's model of an ideal modern society — the West — to the very thing that threatened to oppose such aspirations (i.e., traditional cultural systems and belief in the supernatural). Despite the scarcity of translations of gothic fiction and foreign supernatural tales from this period, Inoue Tsutomu's translation represents the first vestige in a series of transcultural undertakings that would transpire in the years to follow, beginning most notably with Aeba Kōson's (饗庭篁村, 1855-1922) trans-

7 "往年余東都に在り、愛蘭人西婆兒多に接す。話次我が邦天狗の怪に及ぶ。西氏嘲り笑ふて妄誕と為す。このごろ兒勤が訳するところの龍動鬼談を閲すれば、奇々怪々、愕くべし、畏そるべし。欧洲現に此の怪有り。而してその邦の人、無鬼論を執って移らず。豈笑ふべきの甚だならずや。嗚呼、茫々たる坤輿の際、人智の測る能はざる事有る、固より知るべし。後世その理を講究して疑団を氷釋するも亦た知るべからざるなり。然れば則ち遊戯怪談の小冊子、未だ必ずしも後学者に無益とせざるなり。尼聖怪を語らず。而して必ずこれ無しと言わず。故有る哉。明治十三年五月 不鳴居士撰ぶ" Translations herein are the author's own unless otherwise stated.

8 Pen-name of Inoue Fumei (井上不鳴, 1812-1892), father of Rondon kidan translator, Inoue Tsutomu.

lation of Edgar Allan Poe's "The Black Cat" seven years later, in 1887.

The first translation of "The Black Cat," analyzed in the subsequent sections of this study, provides a reference point for further research into the translations of Western gothic and supernaturally-themed tales carried out in Japan's Meiji period and their sociocultural impact on the development of the kaidan genre. While translation studies theories, such as Even-Zohar's (2000) "polysystem theory," Bassnett and Lefevere's (1990) "cultural turn," Toury's (1995) "norms," Snell-Hornby's (1995) "integrated approach", and Lefevere's (1992) theory of "rewriting" all provide useful tools for the examination of translation practices relevant to this study, particular focus here is given to a transcultural reading of the text and the importance of intertextuality employed in translation as a meaning-generating strategy to draw attention to the transformative nature of translation and the greater societal significance of its ability to shape culture and legitimize multiple readings and purposes of a text. Transculturality understands cultures to be multilayered, interactive and fluid, revoking the idea of domination of one culture over another. A transcultural reading therefore provides that the intersection and intermixing of culture that is encountered through the act of translation occurs with reciprocity — a mutual permeation of culture. Drawing upon cultural studies and historical analysis for insight into the ideological and sociocultural factors surrounding supernatural discourse in Japan leading up to and throughout the Meiji era, as well as literary theory, generic conventions and aspects of translation studies for a theoretical framework of analysis, this study seeks to highlight the development of the concept of the supernatural — a generic device characteristic of gothic fiction and traditional Japanese tales alike — as a shared space in which cultural beliefs and understandings, though not always in agreement, are realized and transformed through the act of translation.

2. Towards a Transcultural Supernatural

Literary theory and genre studies today have come to acknowledge gothic fiction and fantastic fiction as two separate but interrelated entities : separate in the sense that the genres are often identifiable by their individual generic conventions and thematic structures; interrelated in the sense that the boundaries between the two can be fluid and are prone to overlap. The gothic and the fantastic are both prominent genres of the 19th century, and while many modern day researchers in Japan now advocate for a similar classification of the genre,[9] that is, under the label of '*gensō bungaku*' [幻想文学, lit. 'imaginary literature'], supernatural stories in Japan are still categorized in a number of ways that are in most cases interchangeable. The most common signifiers of these genres include the terms '***kaidan***' [怪談], '***kaiki***' [怪奇], and '***kaii***' [怪異], and although these are often understood in English as referring to 'ghost stories,' they can also refer simply to tales of strange or mysterious events that transpire outside the realm of the everyday human experience. And while such a broad definition may suggest similarities akin to Western paradigms, classification of traditional genres like kaidan under the banner of 'fantastic fiction'

9 Such as Sunaga Asahiko [須永朝彦], *Nihon gensō bungakushi* [日本幻想文学史], Tokyo : Hakusuisha [白水社], 1993.

or even 'gensō bungaku' becomes problematic in cross-cultural studies of literature, particularly in periods of early modern or even pre-modern history, as it fails to address issues of cultural heritage and the sociocultural context of that specific point in time. Tzvetan Todorov categorizes fantastic fiction :

> In a world which is indeed our world, the one we know....there occurs an event which cannot be explained by the laws of this same familiar world. The person who experiences the event must opt for one of two possible solutions : either he is the victim of an illusion of the senses, of a product of the imagination— and the laws of the world then remain what they are; or else the event has indeed taken place, it is an integral part of reality—but then this reality is controlled by laws unknown to us.
>
> The fantastic occupies the duration of this uncertainty....The fantastic is that hesitation experienced by a person who knows only the laws of nature, confronting an apparently supernatural event. (Todorov 1975 : 25)

Todorov (1975) distinguishes the fantastic from two other modes : the "uncanny," wherein superficially supernatural phenomena turn out to have a rational explanation, and the "marvelous," in which the supernatural is accepted as real (46). His theory, though, is limited to a concept of "hesitation" of the reader and/or of the character(s) in the story after experiencing a supernatural event, that is, whether one accepts that something supernatural has truly taken place, or whether it can be explained rationally. Alternatively, Eric Rabkin (1976) states that the fantastic posits a reversal of "ground-rules":

> One of the key distinguishing marks of the fantastic is that the perspectives enforced by the ground rules of the narrative world must be diametrically contradicted. (Rabkin 1976 : 8)

Based on Rabkin's theory — a point of view often upheld by modern scholarship — contradictions to these so-called "ground rules" might include the shape-shifting foxes [*kitsune*, 狐] also referred to as wolves *kori* [狐狸], *kappa* [河童] water sprites, or *tasogare* [黄昏, twilight] apparitions that appear so frequently in traditional Japanese tales and kaidan fiction. However, the problem with these definitions of fantastic fiction when applied to literature in the Meiji period and prior — as has been discussed earlier in this paper — is that the supernatural was an inherent element in Japanese culture and its themes and motifs permeated through all forms of literature and art throughout history. In other words, kaidan as a genre in and of itself subverts the question of "hesitation" because it does not expect the native Japanese reader to hesitate — the supernatural world was real and existed in proximity to the everyday world. Interestingly, Todorov places most of Poe's tales in the category of the 'uncanny'[10] ; "The Black Cat," however, he places in the category of 'pure fantastic'[11] as the events of the story at the end remain unresolved. In other words, the reader is unable discern whether the narrator is mad and the events he describes are 'natural,' or the cat in the story really is otherworldly and the

10 Stories in which the supernatural elements have a natural explanation.

11 The reader and character's hesitation is sustained until the end and a conclusion as to whether the events described in the story constitute supernatural occurrences or whether they can be explained logically remains unresolved.

events depicted are in fact 'supernatural.' On the one hand, such an appraisal might suggest is a singular interpretation of the text that aligns with the generic conventions of its origin. Through translation, however, cultural identity can be manipulated to create new readings and meanings, subverting the notion of any one interpretation of a story over another. Aeba Kōson's translation of "The Black Cat" in 1887 presents Poe's tale as a Western-style kaidan — the title itself, "Seiyo kaidan kuroneko" [lit., 'Western Kaidan : The Black Cat'], quite literally reflecting the hybrid nature of the text — and in doing so, generic, cultural, and authorial boundaries become blurred. This study herein aims to elucidate the transcultural dimension of Kōson's text that not only provides an avenue for the creation of meaning and a way to process new foreign cultural forms and knowledge, but also attempts to foster a transcultural mentality in the Meiji reader by highlighting shared experiences and common understandings of traditional cultural concepts (i.e., supernatural phenomena) between Japan and the West.

3. Black Cat as *Bakeneko*

Edgar Allan Poe is regarded as one of the foremost prominent writers of the gothic strain of literary romanticism and his works, introduced in the early Meiji period, would go on to have a profound impact on Japanese literature, particularly on Japanese symbolism in the late Meiji and the subsequent Taisho (1912-1926) periods.[12] His name was first introduced in Japan via an

12 See : Sadoya Shigenobu [佐渡谷重信], "Nihon ni okeru edogā aran pō" [日本におけるエドガー・ア

English studies textbook, the American Authors (1872) edition of Francis H. Underwood's A Hand-book of English Literature in 1873, but it wasn't until 14 years later in 1887 that his work was first made available to the general public in Japanese.[13]

Poe's "The Black Cat" (1843) is a murder-confession tale involving themes of madness, animal cruelty, and psychological guilt. The narrator of the story is an animal lover but is also haunted by his increasing alcoholism and feelings of "perverseness" (Poe 2010 : 532). He adopts a black cat called Pluto which he cares for deeply until one day he decides to gouge out one of its eyes from the socket. His unwarranted anger towards the cat escalates and he hangs the cat in the garden. The home of the narrator then mysteriously burns down leaving nothing behind but one wall displaying "the figure of a gigantic cat" (533). After a while the narrator comes across a second black cat, missing the same eye as his previous cat, Pluto, and almost completely identical except for one white patch of fur on its chest. The narrator comes to see this shape as an "image of a hideous — of a ghastly thing — of the gallows" (535). The narrator eventually tries to kill this cat too, but when his wife intervenes, the narrator accidentally kills her instead. The narrator decides to hide her body inside the wall of the cellar but becomes anxious when the cat doesn't reappear. Police officers come to investigate the wife's disappearance

ラン・ポー], *Studies in English language and literature* 9(2), Seinan Gakuin University, Jan. 1969, 25-76.

13 See : Sadoya Shigenobu, "Pō wa nihon kindai bungaku no onjin" [ポーは日本近代文学の恩人], in Kawato and Sakakibara, (eds.), *Meiji Honyaku Bungaku <Shimbun Zasshi-hen> 19 Pō-Shu* [明治翻訳文学ー新聞雑誌編 19 ポー集], Tokyo : Ōzorasha, 1997, 397-381.

and they discover her body when the sound of a howling voice is heard from within the walls. It is revealed that the narrator unknowingly walled the cat in with the wife's decomposing corpse, ultimately exacting the narrator's own demise (he is charged with the crime and sentenced to death).

The first Meiji era translation of the tale, "Seiyō kaidan : Kuroneko" [西洋怪談 黒猫, Western Kaidan : The Black Cat] by Aeba Kōson, was also the first translation of Poe to appear in Japan, serialized in the Yomiuri shimbun newspaper on November 3 and November 9, 1887. In terms of the modern-style colloquial prose adopted in Kōson's translation, an argument can be made for precedent in Sanyūtei Enchō's (三遊亭円朝, 1839-1900) *Kaidan Botan Dōrō* [怪談牡丹灯籠, The Peony Lantern] (1884), which has been regarded as the first publication to successfully reflect colloquial prose and thus a shift away from the classical *kanbun* [漢文] style that was commonplace in literature up until this period in Japanese history.[14] The use of modern prose and publication in a widely read newspaper suggests Kōson's translation was targeted towards a broad readership. This is further evidenced by liberties taken by Kōson to explain certain words or cultural elements and accommodate for a general (less educated) reader. One such example is the interpolation provided for the cat's name, "Pluto." The source text (herein 'ST'), Poe's original story, reads :

Pluto — this was the cat's name — was my favorite pet and playmate. I alone

14 Author and translator, Futabatei Shimei (二葉亭四迷, 1864-1909), even acknowledging Enchō as the inspiration for his own colloquial style beginning with *Ukigumo* [浮雲] (1887). See : Futabatei Shimei, "Yo ga genbun itchi no yurai" [余が言文一致の由来] in *Bunshō sekai* [文章世界] 1:3, 1906, 11-13.

fed him, and he attended me wherever I went about the house. It was even with difficulty that I could prevent him from following me through the streets. (Poe 2010 : 532)

The corresponding passage in the target text (herein 'TT'), Kōson's translation, reads :

> I called the cat Pluto, but now that I think about it, <u>it was a rather auspicious name as it was also the name of the god of the underworld in Greek mythology,</u> but it was this cat that I adored more than all the other animals.[15] (Aeba 1887a : 1)

Interpolation of the meaning behind the name Pluto here provides the Meiji reader with important contextual information that would otherwise go unnoticed to a reader without knowledge of Greek mythology. Kōson also opts to retain certain words like "perverseness" [translated : *paabaasunesu*, パアバアスネス] and provide explanation of its concept as an "evil thing" [*to iu waruimono*, といふ悪いもの] rather than adopt a Japanese equivalent. However, it is Kōson's use of intertextual references which, when read in the historical and sociocultural context of the Meiji era, reveal the true dynamic nature of his translation as a transcultural narrative. For example, the ST describes the protagonist's encounter with the cat of the title as :

15 "猫の名はプルトウと呼びしが今思へは不詳の名でプルトウとは希臘時代の宗教中にある地獄の神の名であったもの、多くの飼物のうち如何いふ訳か私は一番此猫が可愛くて友達よりも…" Emphasis added by author.

(A) remarkably large and beautiful animal, entirely black, and sagacious to an astonishing degree. In speaking of his intelligence, my wife, who at heart was not a little tinctured with superstition, made frequent allusion to the ancient popular notion, which regarded all black cats as witches in disguise. (Poe 2010 : 532)

The TT reads :

A truly beautiful cat with pitch-black fur like velvet and eyes like golden bells, and also surprisingly smart, to which my wife was a little suspicious. It has long been said that black cats are the transfigured form taken by magic-wielding old women after all.[16] (Aeba 1887a : 1)

To the uninformed reader, a passage like "eyes like golden bells" appears immediately foreignizing,[17] as does the description of the cat's pitch-black fur "like velvet" [*birōdo no gotoku*, 天鵞絨の如く]. And perhaps in the debate of 'faithfulness' and judgement-based studies of translation — of which this investigation is neither — such additional modifiers not present in the ST might beg the question of necessity. However, a transcultural interpretation of the text — and indeed theories explored in translation studies such as Andre Lefevere's (1981/1985) "refracted text" and translation as "rewriting."[18] — subverts the focus on the original as a 'sacred' text

16 「至りて美しい猫で毛は真黒で天鵞絨の如く眼は黄金の鈴に似てかしこきことは驚くほどゆゑ妻は是に付いて少し迷ひが有ツた。夫は昔から黒猫は魔法遣ひの老婆の形を變へたものだといふ事があるので…」Emphasis added by author.

17 A term used in translation studies to denote source-based translation strategies, that is, translations that highlight the cultural strangeness (foreignness) of a text.

18 "Refraction" referring to the adaptation of a work of literature for a different audience, with the intention of influencing the way in which that audience reads the work. "Rewriting" meaning any

to foreground the fluidity of culture and the process of translation as an act of manipulation for the creation of meaning. One form that this manipulation takes is intertextuality and what Stephens (1992) defines as "the production of meaning from the interrelationships between audience, text, other texts, and the socio-cultural determinations of significance" (84). An intertextual reading of Kōson's text, therefore, first necessitates a deeper understanding of the traditional kaidan genre.

Supernatural tales about cats, commonly referred to as *bakeneko* [化け猫, lit., 'shape-shifting cats'],[19] are not uncommon to Japan, while an investigation into the origins and proliferation of cats and their connection with the supernatural in Japan is far too extensive a task to be attempted here, a number of key bakeneko-themed works that have been replicated in various forms throughout history are worthy of mention. These include the kabuki tales of *Nabeshima no bakeneko sōdōmono* [鍋島の化け猫騒動物, lit., 'Bakeneko Chaos at Nabeshima'] by Kawatake Shinshichi the 3rd (河竹新七 (三世), 1842-1901) and Segawa Jokō the 3rd (瀬川如皐 (三世), 1806-1881), Kawatake Mokuami's *Arima no neko sōdōmono* [有馬の猫騒動物, lit., 'Bakeneko Chaos at Arima'][20] and *Okazaki no neko*

text produced on the basis of another with the intention of adapting that other text to a certain ideology, a certain poetics, or both. See : Hermans 2007:127.

19 The term '*bakeneko*' [化け猫] is comprised of two Chinese characters : '*bake*' [化], meaning 'to change form' or 'to transform' — a characteristic often associated with yōkai, ghosts and monsters in general in Japan; and, '*neko*' [猫], which means 'cat.' Bakeneko is often used as a catch-all term for the mysterious and magical cats of Japan; however, other varieties include '*kaibyō*' [怪猫, a broad term literally meaning 'supernatural cat'], '*nekomata*' [猫又 / 猫股, lit. 'forked-tail cat'], and even '*kasha*' [火車, lit., 'flaming chariot,' as it was believed that unattended corpses left sitting idly too long would be taken by a bakeneko that had transformed into a 'kasha' and dragged away].

20 Based on Momokawa Joen's *kōdan* [講談, oral story-telling] tale of the same name. Originally titled,

sōdōmono [岡崎の猫騒動物, lit., 'Bakeneko Chaos at Okazaki'], oral *kōdan* (講談) tales by Momokawa Joen (桃川如燕, 1832-1898), such as his *Hyaku byōden : Haiyū Ichikawa Danjūrō neko no jikki* [百猫伝 俳優市川団十郎猫の実記] (1886), as well as numerous 'real accounts' [jitsurokumono, 実録物] and picture books that depicted stories and illustrations of the fear-inducing felines throughout the Edo and Meiji eras. Of particular interest to this study is Momokawa Joen's *Takayagura rikishi kyūbyōden* [高櫓力士旧猫伝, 'Old Cat Tales – The Sumo Wrestler and the Watchtower'] (1885) (herein referred to as "Kyūbyōden"),[21] the ending of which sees the bakeneko of the story facing off against sumo and samurai in a battle to the death.[22] In the final scenes, sumo wrestler, Onogawa, catches a glimpse of the cat that has been terrorizing the village :

> Looking closely, (I could see that) the creature was entirely black, like it was cloaked in a beautiful velvet, it's tail split in two, it's eyes shone golden, it's very shape was that of a tiger. So this is the form that the aged cat takes.[23] (Momokawa 1885 : 97)

Arimatsu-zome sumō yukata [有松染相撲浴衣, Arimatsu-Dyed Sumō Yukata] (1885).

21 Later published in *Tokyo nichi nichi shimbun* [東京日日新聞], Feb. 13, 1887.

22 For an in-depth analysis on the storyline and differences in bakeneko stories *Arimatsu-zome sumō yukata* [有松染相撲浴衣] and Momokawa Joen's *Takayagura rikishi kyūbyōden* [高櫓力士旧猫伝] and Onogawa shinjitsuroku : *Hyaku byōden no uchi* [小野川真実録 百猫伝内] (1893), see : Miura Masao [三浦雅夫], "Mokuami no kaidan to kaii : Meiji ishin ikō no hensen (zoku) – Nihon kingendai kaidan bungakushi 9" [黙阿弥の怪談と怪異、明治維新以後の変遷 (続) — 日本近現代怪談文学史9], in *Saitama gakuen daigaku kiyō (Ningengakubu-hen) dai 14 gō* [埼玉学園大学紀要(人間学部篇) 第14号], Dec. 2014.

23 「瞳と定めて覗き見れば惣身一体眞黑にして其美麗き事天鵞絨の如く尾は二股に裂廣がり眼は金色に光り輝き其形容宛然畫ける虎の如く是ぞ全く猫の年經し者と見定め」 Emphasis and parentheses added by the author.

Before the final showdown a further description of the bakeneko is provided :

> The large cat looked the size of a dog, it's mouth gaping from ear to ear, tail split in two and fur all black. It once had red patches of a tortoise-shell coat, but with age it had turned a pitch-black that shimmered in the light like velvet. The fur at the nape of its neck stood on end like needles and its eyes shone like golden bells, radiant like the morning star on a moonless night. Its glower was truly a fearsome sight to behold.[24] (Momokawa 1885 : 101)

Through a comparison of Kōson's "Seiyō kaidan : Kuroneko" and Momokawa's Kyūbyōden, it becomes immediately apparent that Kōson's interpretation of the text is influenced by a much larger cultural context, and in drawing allusions to this context, he effectively begins to enact his transcultural retelling. On the one hand, his translation is a manipulation of the source text in which Poe's psychological tormentor becomes Kōson's bakemono, alluding to aspects of a subgenre that is uniquely Japanese in origin. On the other hand, it incites a new understanding of the 'West' as a culture that partakes in the idea of the supernatural.

Subsequent translations of "The Black Cat" ensued throughout the Meiji

24 「大猫は形は犬と見紛ふばかりにて口は 耳の根元まで裂廣がり尾は二股に割毛色は總て黑けれども其中に赤毛の交りしは以前は三毛の斑なりしが今は年經て眞黑に變じ光りを生じて天鵞絨の如く怒れる襟毛は逆立て宛然針を植たる如く金色を帯て閃々と光り眼は黄金の鈴に似て月無空に明星が照輝くが如く人を白眼む其形容は實に怖ろしき有様なり」Emphasis added by the author.

era : Uchida Rōan's (内田魯庵, 1868-1929) "Kuroneko" [黒猫] in *Chōryūkōgo* [鳥留好語] in 1893; Sakurai Ōson's (櫻井鴎村, 1872-1929) "The Black Cat" in the English language study magainze, *Eibun shinshi : The Student* [英文新誌, The Student], in 1904; Kikuzuki's (掬月生, details unknown) "Kuroneko" in the children's literary magazine, *Shōnen* [少年, Young Boys], in 1905; Hata Kakō's (畑荷香, details unknown) "Kuroneko monogatari" [黒猫物語] in the popular literature magazine, *Shinko bunrin* [新古文林, lit. Forest of Old and New Literature], in 1907; Honma Hisashirō's [本間久四郎, details unknown] "Kuroneko monogatari" [黒猫物語, The Tale of the Black Cat] in *Meicho shinyaku* [名著新訳, New Translations of Famous Works], also in 1907; Kita Tōichi's (紀太藤一, 1879-1936) "The Black Cat : Kuroneko" [The Black Cat, 黒猫] in the English language study magazine, *Eigo no Nippon : The Nippon* [英語の日本: The Nippon, lit., English of Japan : The Japan], in 1909; and Hiratsuka Raichō's (平塚らいてう, 1886-1971) "Kuroneko" in the women's literary magazine, Seitō [青鞜, Blue Stockings], in 1911. Each translation adopted different translation strategies and was published in different platforms, suggesting multiple target audiences and potential readings. And, in this boer-crossing of texts and meanings, genre itself may be seen as a product of systems that are susceptible to change. The various translations of "The Black Cat" in the Meiji period reveals an example of a single gothic text that can be read as Japanese kaidan, Western gothic-horror, literary classic, popular literature, children's tale, English study companion, or any or all of the above combinations. Interestingly, Kōson's second translation of Poe, "The Murders in the Rue Morgue" (1841), translated as "Rū morugu no hitogoroshi" [ルーモルグの人殺し, The Murderer of the Rue Morgue] (1887c), reflects a tale that closer resembles the 'modern' Meiji mindset and an understanding of the supernatural of which Inoue Enryō (mentioned in the introduction of this study) was a prolific advocate. In the investigation of a crime scene with what seemed like an impossible series of events detailing a murder and the perpetrator's escape, the detective protagonist of Poe's murder mystery states :

> It is not too much to say that neither of us believe in preternatural events. Madame and Mademoiselle L'Espanaye were not destroyed by spirits. The doers of the deed were material and escaped materially. (Poe 1887 : 20)

Kōson's protagonist, however, states :

> Neither of us are of the belief that there is such a thing in this world as yōkai-henge [shape-shifting monsters]. The criminal must have a tangible form.[25] (Aeba 1887d : 2)

While the parallel here to the Meiji sociocultural climate is obvious, the tale is reinterpreted in 1899 by Osada Shūtō (長田秋濤, 1871-1915) as "Shōjōkai" [猩々怪, lit., 'Supernatural Orangutan'] in the literary magazine, Bungei kurabu [文藝倶楽部, 'Literary Club']; quite literally positioning the tale as a kaidan tale by stating in the foreword of his text that, "This kaidan was told to me during my time in Paris" (「此怪談は予が嘗て巴里に居つた時分、人から聞いた話で」, 118). Osada then employs a similar

25 「妖怪変化といふ者世にあらんとの考えも我も信ずぜぬことなり凶行者は形ある者に相違なし」Emphasis and parentheses added by author.

approach to that of Inoue Tsutomu in Rondon Kidan by subverting the notion of a purely logical West to one that also partakes in the enjoyment of reading supernatural tales : "Perhaps readers will be surprised to learn that such trivial stories exist in Europe — the source of civilization and enlightenment" (「讀者諸君は文明開化の根元たる欧羅巴に恁様な馬鹿げた話があるかと謂はれるかも知れない」). However, Osada builds on this juxtaposition further by drawing a parallel between Poe's story and the works of native author, Izumi Kyōka (泉鏡花, 1873-1939), stating : "Kaidan are Izumi Kyōka's specialty, and were the pen in his capable hands, the story would no doubt be all the more interesting" (「怪談の如きは泉鏡花君の専賈である、鏡花君の健筆を以て書き下したならば一層面白いかも知れない」, 118). The translator here not only invites the reader to reimagine Japan's model of civilization as a society that enjoys supernatural, albeit "trivial," stories, but also uses his translation to introduce Izumi Kyoka and thereby position a Japanese author who specializes in kaidan alongside one of the great's of American literature who writes gothic fiction. These examples clearly demonstrate once more that translation is a process of manipulation for the generation of meaning (not simply a reconstruction of meaning), and in this process cultural and certainly generic boundaries are susceptible to change.

Although this study has primarily focused on only one of the multiple translations of only a single text belonging to the Western gothic genre in circulation in the Meiji period, Aeba Kōson's translation represents the beginning in what would become a long line of reimagined American and

European supernatural tales in the years to follow. Analysis of the subsequent translations of "The Black Cat" can provide further insight into the fluidity of literary genres in translation. Ultimately, what each of these translations demonstrate is the legitimacy of multiple interpretations of a text across national and cultural divides. The Meiji era represents a unique period in Japan's history that adopted translation practices and utilized foreign literature — often with intertextually charged means — to re-interpret ideological discourse surrounding both foreign and domestic society and reposition the supernatural in popular tales as a transcultural space unbound by a single authority, religion, or culture, open to multiple readings and interpretations.

4. Conclusion

As demonstrated in the forewords of works like Inoue Tsutomu's Rondon Kidan and Osada Shūtō's "Shōjōkai", readers are prompted to understand that the supernatural is a homogenous entity, not entirely unambiguous in culture, but made accessible through the transcultural dimension of translation. In this sense, identity and genre are not static, but dynamic and fluid. Aeba Kōson's attempt to bring Poe's gothic tale into the cache of Japanese kaidan is also one of manipulation that employs intertextual references and borrows forms and content from other literary and cultural traditions (such as his embellishment with the description of the black cat that harks back to the kabuki tales of Edo). The title itself, "Seiyō kaidan : Kuroneko," is a cultural hybrid that acknowledges the foreign source ("Seiyō" : the West) and presents an understanding of the cultural Other that aligns with traditional Japanese culture ("kaidan"). Drawing parallels to commonalities and shared beliefs between cultures and generating meaning through intertextuality was a translation strategy adopted by numerous translators throughout the Meiji era and was in no way unique to Aeba Kōson alone.[26] Through such techniques and processes, the concept of the supernatural in Meiji Japan came to function as a transcultural space. Translations and literary narratives that occupied this space were not bound to a single author, translator, or culture, but served as sites of cultural fluidity. The transcultural dimension of these texts lent to the fostering of transcultural mentalities in Meiji readers that identified shared experiences and common understandings between Japan and the West with regard to the supernatural, whilst at the same time, respected the authenticity of difference.

26 Such as Mori Ōgai's (森鴎外, 1862-1922) "Shinsekai no Urashima" [新世界の浦島, lit., 'Urashima of the New World'] (a translation of Washington Irving's "Rip Van Winkle"; 1819) in Shōnenen (少年園, 1889), which draws an immediate parallel to the popular folktale, "Urashima Tarō"; and Shibue Tamotsu's (渋江保, 1857-1930) translation of Grimms' Fairy Tales (Kinder- und Hausmärchen; 1812) as *Seiyō yōkai kidan : Shōgaku kōwa zairyō* [西洋妖怪奇談 : 小学講話材料] (1891). The 38th tale in the collection, "Shichimei no Sūebiajin" [七名のスウェビア人, The Seven Swabians], for example, ends with the characters "falling victim to kappa" [kappa no ejiki to narishika, 河童の餌食となりしか](252), instead of simply jumping into water and drowning as in the original.

Works Cited

Aeba, Kōson [饗庭篁村] (trans.), "Seiyō kaidan : Kuroneko (jō)" [西洋怪談 黒猫 (上)], *Yomiuri shimbun* <furoku> [読売新聞附録], November 3, 1887a.

——————————, "Seiyō kaidan : Kuroneko (ge)" [西洋怪談 黒猫 (下)], *Yomiuri shimbun* <furoku> [読売新聞附録], November 9, 1887b.

——————————, "Rūmorugu no hitogoroshi" [ルーモルグの人殺し], *Yomiuri shimbun* <furoku> [読売新聞附録], December 14-30, 1887c.

——————————, "Rūmorugu no hitogoroshi" [ルーモルグの人殺し], *Yomiuri shimbun* <furoku> [読売新聞附録], December 27, 1887d.

Ascari, Maurizio, *Literature of the Global Age : A Critical Study of Transcultural Narratives*, Jefferson : McFarland and Company Publishers, 2011.

Figal, Gerald A, *Civilization and Monsters : Spirits of Modernity in Meiji Japan*, Durham and London : Duke University Press, 1999.

Futabatei, Shimei [二葉亭四迷], "Yo ga genbun itchi no yūrai" [余が言文一致の由来], *Bunshō sekai* [文章世界] 1:3, 1906.

Hata, Kakō [畑荷香] (trans.), "Kuroneko monogatari" [黒猫物語], *Shinko bunrin* [新古文林], January, 1907.

Hermans, Theo, *Translation in Systems : Descriptive and System-oriented Approaches Explained*, Shanghai : Shanghai Foreign Language Education Press, 2004.

Hiratsuka, Raichō [平塚らいてう] (trans.), "Kuroneko" [黒猫], *Seitō* [青鞜], December, 1911.

Honma, Hisashirō [本間久四郎] (trans.), "Kuroneko monogatari" [黒猫物語] in *Meicho shinyaku* [名著新訳], Tokyo : Bunrokudō [文禄堂], 1907.

Inoue, Enryō [井上円了], *Meishin to shūkyō* [迷信と宗教], Tokyo : Shiseidō shoten [至誠堂書店], 1916.

Inoue, Tsutomu [井上勤] (trans.), *Rondon kidan : Kaikan kyōki* [龍動鬼談 開巻驚奇], Tokushima : Setoya bunkichi [世渡谷文吉], 1880.

Kashiwara, Yūsen [柏原祐泉], *Nihon bukkyōshi : Kindai* [日本仏教史 近代], Tokyo : Yoshikawa Kōbunkan [吉川弘文館], 1990.

Kawato, Michiaki [川戸道昭], and Sakakibara, Takanori [榊原貴教] (eds.), *Meiji Honyaku Bungaku* <Shimbun Zasshi-hen> 19 Pō-Shū [明治翻訳文学ー新聞雑誌編ー19 ポー集], Tokyo : Ōzorasha [大空者], 1997.

Kikuzuki, S. [掬月生] (trans.), "Kuroneko" [黒猫], *Shōnen* [少年], May-June, 1905.

Kita, Tōichi [紀太藤一] (trans.), "The Black Cat : Kuroneko" [The Black Cat : 黒猫], *Eigo no Nippon : The Nippon* [英語の日本, The Nippon], June-December, 1909.

Komatsu, Kazuhiko [小松和彦], and Naitō, *Masatoshi* [内藤正敏], Oni ga tsukutta kuni, nihon, rekishi wo ugokashitekita "kurayami" *no chikara to ha* [鬼 がつくった国・日本・歴史を動かしてきた「暗闇」の力とは], Tokyo : Kōbunsha [光文社], 2002.

Koschmann, Victor J., "Action as Text : Ideology in the Tengu Insurrection." In *Conflict in Modern Japanese History : The Neglected Tradition, Najita, Tetsuo, and Koschmann*, Victor J. (eds.), Princeton : Princeton University Press, 1982.

Miura, Masao [三浦雅夫], "Mokuami no kaidan to kaii : Meiji ishin ikō no hensen (zoku) – Nihon kingendai kaidan bungakushi 9" [黙阿弥の怪談と怪異、明治維新以後の変遷 (続) — 日本近現代怪談文学史9 —], *Saitama gakuen daigaku kiyō (Ningengakubu-hen) dai 14 gō* [埼玉学園大学紀要(人間学部篇) 第14号], December, 2014.

Momokawa, Joen [桃川如燕], *Takayagura rikishi kyūbyōden* [高櫓力士旧猫伝], Tokyo : Kakuseisha [鶴声], 1885.

——————————, *Hyaku byōden : Haiyū Ichikawa Danjūrō neko no jikki* [百猫伝 : 俳優市川団十郎猫の実記], Tokyo : Suzuki Kiemon [鈴木喜右衛門], 1886.

Mori, Ōgai [森鴎外], "Shinsekai no Urashima" [新世界の浦島], *Shōnenen* [少年園], May-August, 1889.

Osada, Shūtō [長田秋濤] (trans.), "Shōjōkai" [猩々怪], *Bungei kurabu* [文藝倶楽部], Volume 5: 13 [第 5 巻第13編] October, 1899.

Poe, Edgar Allan, "The Murders in the Rue Morgue." *The Murders in the Rue Morgue : and other tales*, New York : Worthington Co, 1887.

——————, "The Black Cat." *The Complete Tales and Poems of Edgar Allan Poe*. New York : Barnes and Noble, 2010.

Rabkin, Eric, *The Fantastic in Literature, Princeton*, N.J.: Princeton University Press, 1976.

Sadoya, Shigenobu [佐渡谷重信], "Nihon ni okeru edogā aran pō" [日本におけるエドガー・アラン・ポー], *Studies in English language and literature* 9(2), Seinan Gakuin University, January, 1969.

——————————, "Pō wa nihon kindai bungaku no onjin" [ポーは日本近代文学の恩人], in Kawato and Sakakibara, (eds.), *Meiji Honyaku Bungaku <Shimbun Zasshi-hen> 19 Pō-Shu* [明治翻訳文学〈新聞雑誌編〉19 ポー集], Tokyo : Ōzorasha, 1997.

Sakurai, Ōson [櫻井鴎村] (trans.), "The Black Cat", *Eibun shinshi : The Student* [英文新誌: The Student], July-December, 1904.

Shibue, Tamotsu [渋江保], "Shichimei no Sūebiajin" [七名のスウエビア人], *Seiyō yōkai kidan*

: Shōgaku kōwa zairyō [西洋妖怪奇談 小学講話材料], Tokyo : Hakubunkan, 1891.
Slimbach, Richard, "The Transcultural Journey." *Frontiers : The Interdisciplinary Journal of Study Abroad* 11, 2005.
Stephens, John, *Language and Ideology in Children's Fiction*, London : Longman, 1992.
Sunaga, Asahiko [須永朝彦], *Nihon gensō bungakushi* [日本幻想文学史], Tokyo : Hakusuisha [白水社], 1993.
Todorov, Tzvetan, *The Fantastic : A Structural Approach to a Literary Genre*, Howard, Richard (trans.), Ithaca, N.Y.: Cornell University Press, 1975.
Uchida, Roan [内田魯庵] (trans.), "Kuroneko" [黒猫], *Chōryūkōgō* [鳥留好語], Tokyo : Keisei-sha [警醒社], 1893.
Yumoto, Kōichi [湯本豪一], *Meiji yōkai shimbun* [明治妖怪新聞], Tokyo : Kashiwa Shobō [柏書房], 1999.

"Processing of Knowledge" and Translation in Modern Japan

The case of "*shin-kango*"*

Noriko Matsunaga (Kyushu University)

1. Introduction : Background and Objectives of the Study

When discussing the history of knowledge import and export, it was often said that "Japan has been inclined to importing rather than exporting in terms of culture." (Kato Syuichi 1999 : 10) At present, however, the overseas presence of Japanese soft power, such as animation, comics, and youth fashion, is gaining attention globally. However, there was already a certain movement toward assimilating Japanese knowledge in modern times. This movement was actively promoted by knowledge intermediaries, such as international students, intellectuals, and Japanese-language teachers, instead of the knowledge producers themselves exporting the knowledge. One such ex-

* This paper was translated from the Japanese version as follows, Noriko Matsunaga "Kindai nihon no 'chi no kakō' to honyaku : 'shin-kango' wo jirei to shite" in *'Chi no kakō gaku' koto hajime : juyōshi, kakōshi, hasshinsuru nihon no gihō* [*Introduction to Knowledge Processing Studies : Techniques for Accepting, Processing and Sending Knowledge in Japan.*], eds. Noriko Matsunaga, Teruhisa Se, Hitoshi Yoshioka (Tokyo : Shinjuku Shobō, 2011), 30-54

ample is "*shin-kango*," (Shen Guowei 1998 : 37) which was created in the Meiji period. "*Shin-kango*" represents the Chinese words created mainly through contact and exchange between the Western and Eastern cultures, produced to interpret Western academic cultures (Takano Shigeo 2004 : 5) in China and Japan, and recently added to the Chinese lexicon.

While contemplating the modernization process of Japan, it is widely known that the translation terms of Western science had already been introduced in Japan through Western books in Chinese or Chinese dictionaries in the pre-Meiji period, which paved the way for the rapid modernization of Japan. The significant influence of the *kango* imported from China on the formation of modern vocabularies in Japan has been extensively studied. After the Meiji Restoration, *shin-kango* was created with Chinese characters by translating the Western academic cultures to express many new concepts and terms of the Western world. Some argue that "translating Western terms with Chinese characters is the biggest achievement in the kanji-based cultural sphere that Japan has made since the modern times." (Cf. Gao Yujun 2009) It is also believed that there was a crucial effect on modern Chinese of "the books translated and written by a lot of students and intellectuals dispatched from the Qing dynasty after the Japanese-Sino War." (Makita Eiji [牧田英二] 1971 : 65) In other words, myriad translations or secondhand translations of Japanese books were exported to China from the 1900s to 1930s, and "*shin-kango*," primarily with respect to academic terms such as 哲学 [*tetsugaku*, philosophy] and 自由 [*jiyu*, freedom], were incorporated into the modern Chinese lexicon, eventually contributing to the modernization of China.[1]

1 SanetoKeisyu [さねとうけいしゅう] (1970 : 291-408); Douglas R. Reynolds(1993 : 26); Shen

Intellectuals and students from Korea, China, and Vietnam, who came to learn from Japan, which had accomplished rapid modernization in the Meiji period, learned about Western civilization in Japanese and utilized their learning for the modernization of their own countries. Chinese characters were originally disseminated from China to Japan; in terms of the academic or technical terms of the West, knowledge was exchanged between China and Japan through the medium of Chinese characters.(Cf. Mizuhara Juri 2010; Yamamuro Shinichi 2002) There is a relatively large accumulation of studies on such vocabulary exchange. Further, the study of this "terminology" in conjunction with the standardization of the academic terms has been actively promoted over the years in Japan, China, and Korea.(Cf.*Nihongo-gaku* 2010 : 12)

Based on these accumulated findings, this chapter focuses on "*shin-kango*," which is considered as one of the key intellectual productions in modern Japan, overviews the characteristics of word formation and translation for "*shin-kango*," and ultimately redefines "*shin-kango*" from the viewpoint of "science of knowledge processing." "Science of knowledge processing" refers to a set of conventional processes and methods for Japan to accept advanced knowledge from others, uniquely process it, and then disseminate the processed knowledge in a way that would be applicable both locally and globally. In other words, the perspective of "knowledge processing" involves clarifying the characteristics of individual "secondary processing" and simultaneously providing universal perspectives and expertise for knowledge sharing and exchange. Hence, "science of knowledge processing" has the perspective of overseeing a body of knowledge and, therefore, it can be called "knowledge

Guowei (2008b : 1-2).

science of knowledge" or even "science of meta-knowledge."

The Meiji period is considered a noticeable era, because cultures and institutions were transformed through the epoch-making Meiji Restoration, and the existing Japanese vocabularies were renewed on a large scale in a short period. (Morioka Kenji 2004 : 122) How was such large scale updating of vocabulary possible? There may have been some distinctive factors that made such a large and rapid change possible in Japan and not in China, the homeland of Chinese characters. Word formation in a larger sense, using katakana and hiragana as well as the Chinese characters, is actively pursued even today; however, post the Taisho period, it is said that "fewer basic words are created using Chinese characters" than in the pre-Taisho period." (Nomura Masaaki 1977 : 276; Miyajima Tatsuo 1967 : 11) Therefore, it is reasonable to conclude that the effects of "*shin-kango*" on modern vocabulary formation were quite significant.

For example, the effects of "*shin-kango*" on Chinese are being extensively investigated by Shen Guowei, in his series of studies on Japanese loanwords.[2] Although several lists of Japanese loanwords were identified through his studies, opinions are divided over these lists, and the exact number of Japanese loanwords is yet to be established.[3] It is almost impossible to bring the whole matter to light; "to identify '*shin-kango*' in the strict sense of the word, collating the lists with all the dictionaries before the Edo period is required (Morikoka 1969 : 410, 417), which Japanese researchers find unrealistic." (Chang Wonjae 2003 : 91) Notwithstanding, there are some empirical studies, for example Qin

2 The representative one is Shen Guowei, 2008a (the first edition is 1992).

3 Main lists are 892words of "*Chinese Dictionary of Foreign Words* : 漢語外来詞詞典" (Liu Zhengyan others. Ed., 1984), and 459 words of "Study of Foreign Words in Modern Chinese : 現代漢語外来詞研究"(Gao Mingkai , Liu Zhengyan 1958).

Chunfang (2010), to demonstrate that the "*shin-kango*" created in Japan were incorporated into the Chinese lexicon through "Jitsugakuho," an academic periodical, and then established in Chinese dictionaries and literary works of those days (e.g., Lu Xun). (Qin Chunfang 2010 : 1-13)

By demonstrating the fact that knowledge has been shared and exchanged through Chinese characters, we could explore the possibility that new concepts and technical terms could be shared and exchanged in a similar manner even in this rapidly globalizing society. Along with the study from the perspective of terminology standardization in "technical Japanese" as mentioned earlier, the study in this field is expected to advance further.

2. Creation of "shin-kango" : Angles and methods of the study

This section begins by defining "*shin-kango*," and then discusses the word formation approaches used by Dutch Learning scholars, which provided a foundation for creating "*shin-kango*" to identify its characteristics and the methods of its creation in Japan. Subsequently, the author categorizes and organizes such methods in Meiji Japan by comparing "*shin-kango*" creation approaches used by Western missionaries.

"*Shin-kango*" is also known as "*wasei-kango*," Japanese-made words of Chinese origin, or according to the Chinese, Japanese loanwords in the sense that they are Japanese-made and back-flowed to China through various channels or words that have been borrowed from Japanese words. This chapter focuses on modern times from the perspective of modern vocabulary formation, and therefore, only the term "*shin-kango*" is used here. Given the possibility of vocabulary import/export and sharing in the kanji-based cultural sphere, the author believes it is meaningful to examine only *kango (words of Chinese origin)."* (Arakawa Kiyohide 1988 : 57)

The study of *kango* in Japan was initiated by Yoshio Yamada (1940), and has been developed based on his works. According to his categorization,[4] "*kango* created through translation of the Western learnings" is equivalent to the so-called "*shin-kango*." In his definition, Yamada further divided *shin-kango* into 1) the adaptation of *kango* in Chinese translation books and 2) those selected by the Japanese to import from Western cultures. The latter is further divided into a) those derived from Chinese classic works and b) those newly selected. (Yamada 1940 : 356-452) From the perspective of knowledge processing, as in 1) and 2)-a, those "*shin-kango*" converted or modified from the Chinese language can be considered as the words "processed secondarily" by the Japanese, whereas in 2)-b, those "*shin-kango*" newly selected, can be considered as the words "processed primarily" by the Japanese.

Major creators of "*shin-kango*" include Western missionaries (e.g., Lobscheid), intellectuals from the Qing dynasty (e.g., Yan Fu, Liang Qichao) in China, Dutch Learning scholars (e.g., Genpaku Sugita) in Edo Japan, and intellectuals (e.g., Nishi Amane, Inoue Tetsujiro) in Meiji Japan. In creating the "*shin-kango*," Western missionaries dictated and Chinese writers transcribed, before Yan Fu and other Chinese intellectuals started to learn foreign languages themselves and to translate the "*shin-kango*" or coin words in Chinese. In contrast, in Japan, the Japanese mostly created words themselves. This is a significant difference between the

4 Yamada Yoshio divides the source of Kango into four categories. (Yamada 1940 : 356-452).

Japanese and Chinese approach. The limitations regarding the missionaries' word formation were revealed by Sun Jianjun (2005). (Sun Jianjun 2005 : 331-334)

Why was it that more "*shin-kango*" created in Japan, were not translated by Chinese such as Yan Fu and Liang Qichao, who created many new conceptual terms, helping form a significant proportion of the Chinese lexicon, even prevalent in contemporary Chinese? Answering this question offers a clue to clarify the characteristics of the Japanese way of "processing knowledge."

In the following pages, the author focuses on the methods of creating modern "*shin-kango*," including those of modifying and processing *kango* translation words adopted from the Chinese language, and examines the Japanese way of "processing knowledge" through comparison with cases in China. Preceding studies have already examined this issue from the viewpoints of 1) social factors and 2) linguistic factors. In this paper, the author deems it necessary to pay attention to knowledge intermediaries such as international students and Japanese language teachers, in addition to the above two; therefore, the author has included an intermediary factor to analyze the issue comprehensively from the perspective of "knowledge processing." Subsequently, the author sums up the role of "*shin-kango*" in the course of modernization in Meiji. Although the academic and cultural exchange between Japan and China has a long and ancient history, the discussion here is limited to modern times because the main subject of this chapter is "*shin-kango*." Therefore, focus is placed on the period from approximately the 1860s to the 1930s, when the knowledge exchange between Japan and China was particularly vigorous, while also noting the words translated and created in the Dutch Learning era from the 1770s to 1860s.

2-1. Approach of creating terms and words for translation by Dutch Learning scholars

According to Shen Guowei (2007), the Meiji intellectuals, with their knowledge of Dutch Learning, "succeeded in its complete scholarship," (Shen 2007 : 260) and it in turn enabled them to create enormous new words for translation in the early Meiji period. In studying word formation and translation in Meiji, it is impossible to overlook their attempts during the Dutch Learning era.

Let us now look at specific cases to confirm the implications of full-scale translation works by Dutch Learning scholars, starting with *Kaitai Shinsho* (Anatomische Tabellen)" in 1774. (Shen [沈] 2007 : 220) There are three patterns of translation by the scholars : "(literal) translation", "semantic translation", (Shen 2007 : 240-242) and "phonetic transliteration." "(Literal) translation" is an approach that employs words from Chinese books in all possible ways, corresponding to "conversion," and is mentioned later. "Semantic translation" refers to the use of "direct translation" or "free translation," corresponding to "coinage (word formation)" as also mentioned later. "Direct translation" is the means of creating words by breaking down loanwords into morphemes and applying the Chinese word base (Tobita Yoshifumi Main ed. [飛田良文主編] 2007 : 163) for proper combination. "Phonetic transliteration" is a way of representing speech sounds in katakana, when this is unavoidable. For example, blind-darum＝blind [盲, *mo*] – darum [腸, *cho* (intestine)] → 盲腸 [*mocho,* caecum] is "direct translation"; bier＝麦酒 [*bakushu,* beer] is "free translation"; and tabaco＝タバコ [*tabaco,* tobacco] is "phonetic transliteration." Among these methods, "semantic translation," which requires deep understanding and practical skills relating to foreign languages, helped forge a new approach to knowledge assimilation. To summarize, the acquisition of foreign languages by Dutch Learning scholars and Meiji intellectuals provided a foundation for new knowledge assimilation.

2-2. Western missionaries' attempts to create "*shin-kango*"

To evaluate the cases in Japan, the author first summarizes Western missionaries' approach to create "*shin-kango*," based on Sun (2005). (Sun [孫] 2005 : 328-329) The words created by the missionaries were introduced in the modern Chinese lexicon through Chinese translations of Western books, and subsequently into the modern Japanese lexicon. Their approaches are largely divided into 1) "new word formation" (words newly created where there are no corresponding concepts in Chinese) and 2) "word conversion" (words converted with new meanings added to the existing Chinese synonyms). (Sun 2005 : 328) The former is further categorized into "phonetic transliteration" (e.g., parliament＝巴力門), "direct translation" (e.g., Upper House＝上院), and "contraction" (e.g., 国政公会＝国会、the Diet). In 2), the local words are used to express an English meaning, with one such example being Election＝選択、推択公挙、選挙.

2-3 . Approaches to create "*shin-kango*" in Meiji Japan

Next, the study by Matsunaga Noriko (2010)[5] is utilized to categorize and summarize Japanese approaches to create "*shin-kango.*" In the preceding studies,[6] the author attempted organization based on Morioka (1969), who presented the most detailed categorization, from the standpoint of *kango* creation methods.[7] Morioka categorizes the Chinese translation methods into the following six approaches : 1) replacement, 2) recycling and conversion, 3) transformation, 4) borrowing, 5) phonetic loan, and 6) coinage. Of these, 1) to 4) involve the use of established words for translation; 5) involves the same approach as "free translation" and "phonetic transliteration," but distinguished from "coinage"; while "coinage" in 6) involves new word formation by combining the word bases of *kango,* and facilitates great productivity in creating words, enabling the free production of new words. On the following pages, the author reviews cases for 1) to 6), with examples shown in 【 】 and underlines and asterisks (*) added by the author. Italicized Kanji versions have been provided in the brackets [ ] for readers' understanding. The methods in 2), 3), and 4) can be considered as a kind of "secondary processing" of Chinese.

① Replacement＝Replace imported vocabularies by Edo words.

【drama＝浄瑠璃ノ類 [*joruri no tagui*], war＝合戦 [*kassen*]】

② Recycling and conversion＝Recycle archaic or obsolete words in their original

5 Matsunaga Noriko (2010 : 1279-0-1279-9).

6 Morioka (1969), Tobita (1994), Morioka (2004 : 106-136), Takano (2004), Gao 2009.

7 Morioka (1969 : 268-291), Takano (2004 : 244).

form and convert them into words with new meaning

【演繹 [*en eki*, deduction] ⇔ 帰納 [*kinou*, induction], 相対 [*soutai*, relative] ⇔ 絶対 [*zettai*] (absolute)】

③ Transformation = transform *old kango* = a. omission, b. change of oral reading method, c. replacement of words

【a. 経世済民 [*keisei saimin*] → 経済 [*keizai*, economy], b. 音声 [*onsei*, voice] (*onjo* ⇒ *onsei*), c. 愈快 [*yukai*, pleasant] → 愉快 [*yukai*, pleasant], 理会 [*rikai*, understanding] → 理解 [*rikai*], 精心 [*seishin*, spirit] → 精神 [*seishin*]】

④ Borrowing = borrow Chinese words ⇒ "established word-to-word translation"

【Liberty (自主・自由 [*jishu, jiyu*]), 「人民ニンミン」→「人民ジンミン [*jinmin*, people]」】

⑤ Phonetic loan = write loanwords in *kango* according to their meaning or pronunciation = (* "free translation" and "phonetic transliteration")

【タバコ [煙草, *tabako*]】【coffee = 珈琲 [*kohi*]】

⑥ Coinage = create new words by combining word bases (roots) of *kango* = (* Incl. "direct translation," "free translation," "transformation from *wago* to *kango*, " and "word formation with the use of prefix and suffix)

【火の事 [*hi no koto*] = 火事 [*kaji*, fire], 反面的 [*hanmen teki*, opposite], 電気学 [*denki gaku*, electricity], 解析/幾何・学[*kaiseki/kika gaku*], 平面//解析/幾何・学 [*heimen// kaiseki/kika gaku*, surface//analysis/geometry], 学長 [*gaku cho*, dean]】

Table 1 depicts the comparative table of "*shin-kango*" creation methods based on the above categories. Comparison between the Western missionaries' approach (A) and Japanese approach (B-E) revealed that four basic methods are found in both approaches for creating "*shin-kango*." These four methods are : a) replacement by the native words of the vernacular language, b) replacement by borrowing and conversion, c) replacement by phonetic transliteration, and d) replacement by creating new words. As portrayed clearly in this comparative table, the difference in "*shin-kango*" creation methods is demonstrated clearly by d), replacement by creating new words, or "coinage."

The categories do not seem to correspond properly with each other in terms of "coinage" in Table 1. "Contraction" and "phonetic transliteration," which correspond to the "coinage" of the missionaries, are not considered "coinage" in Morioka (1969); however, they correspond to "transformation" and "phonetic loan" in his categorization. "Direct translation" is present in both approaches, but the approaches in the shaded columns cannot be observed in the missionaries' work, specifically "replacement," "Kana readings beside *kango*,"[8] "direct translation by combining word bases," "revival of classical words," free translation," "transformation from *wago* to *kango*," and "coinage (word formation) by using prefix and suffix." Here, the reason why the "revival of classical words" is considered as something the Japanese originally devised is that Chinese researchers recognize that archaic *kango* recycled for the translation of Western languages were introduced in a form of Japanese into the modern Chinese lexicon. (Gao, Liu (1958 : 82-98) This is, as elaborated subsequently, noteworthy from the perspective of "secondary processing." However, "conversion" was used by missionaries as well, and historically, "replacement," "direct translation by combining word bases," "free translation," and "coinage (word formation) by using prefix and suffix" were all used in the

8 Examples of Kana readings beside kango is 「免職(ヤクゴメン)」, 「許諾(シヤウチ)」スル, 「金属(カネルイ)」 etc. Cf. Yamada 1940 : 356-452, Sato Kiyoji 1979 : 421-422.

Table 1 | Comparative table of "*shin-kango*" creation methods (Compiled by the author based on the preceding studies shown in the table)

Preceding studies	Category of *kango* creation methods					
A : Sun (2005)		"Conversion"	"Coinage" Contraction		"Coinage" Phonetic transliteration	"Coinage" Direct translation
B : Morioka (1969)	Replacement	Recycling and conversion	Transformation	Borrowing	Phonetic loan	Coinage
C : Hida (1994)		Converted words		Borrowed words		New coinage
D : Morioka (2004)	1. Replacement 2. **Kana readings beside *kango***	Revival of classical words (recyle)		Borrowing and modification of Chinese translation		1.Direct translation (base+base) 2.Free translation
E : Gao (2009)			"Borrowing" 1. Originated from Chinese classics 2. Originated from English-Chinese dictionaries			"Coinage" 1. **Wago → Kango** 2.Base + base 3.Use suffix and prefix

***A** : missionaries' approach; **B to E** : Japanese approach. Shaded parts represent the approaches not adopted by the missionaries.

modern Chinese lexicon as well. Therefore, the approaches recognized only in Japan, from the perspective of "primary processing," could be "transformation from *wago* to *kango*"[9] and "Kana readings beside *kango*" (bold letter in Table 1).

9 Yamada 1940 : 510-511. Example :「かえりごと=返事」,「火の事=火事」,「はらをたつ=立腹」etc.

3. Overview of knowledge import and processing : Discussion of social factors

In this section, the author will describe the characteristics of "knowledge processing" in Japan primarily from the perspective of social factors.

Regarding the acceptance of Western modern civilization or the import of "processing of knowledge," Japan and China adopted similar, but not the same, cultural integration approaches, which are known as "Wakon-Yosai (Japanese spirit and Western learning)" and "Chutai-Seiyo (Chinese content and Western practicality)," respectively. This difference ought to be considered while discussing the characteristics of "knowledge processing" patterns in Japan for sharing and delivering knowledge in the kanji-based cultural sphere.

With this notion, Li Tingquan (1998) identified the following six differences from the perspective of science and culture in both China and Japan because it is necessary to discuss the deep structure of their traditional cultures, which shape the attitude of "Wakon-Yosai" and "Chutai-Seiyo." (Li Tingquan 1998 : 356-366) They are : 1) distinguishing features of ethnic cultures, 2) attitudes toward different cultures, 3) translation methods, 4) leading disciplines, 5) major players in modern science, and 6) consequences of Confucian revival. Table 2 summarized these differences.

As portrayed in this comparative table, the basic differences in cultural acceptance between Japan and China mirror the differences in their ethnic cultures.[10] Specifically, modern China was clannish, clinging to its conservative

10 There is also a view that describing the characteristics of ethnic culture will encourage stereotypes. Therefore, these characteristics are not fixed, and they are taken up as modern characteristics here,

and fixed way of thinking, and resistant to imported cultures since it strongly believed in the superiority of its traditional culture,[11] whereas modern Japan rapidly absorbed the imported cultures in a harmonized way and underwent "secondary processing" to facilitate its prosperity and growth. Chinese scholars' condescending attitudes toward learning and translating foreign languages prevented the spread of Western science and culture. Further, as confirmed in the first section, since the Chinese adopted a translation approach that involved Western missionaries dictating and Chinese writers transcribing, their word formation had certain limitations. Contrastingly, in Japan, those who attempted to learn and translate foreign languages were scholars in the private sector; therefore, modern Western science was accepted rapidly with Dutch Learning as a foundation, providing momentum to reform the entire society.

Hence, behind the rapid assimilation of modern Western science in Japan is the awareness among both non-government scholars and citizen leaders that Japan needs to promptly transform itself into a modern nation through national reforms, to prevent incursions from Western countries and withstand the pressure of opening up to Western powers.

In China too, intellectuals, recognizing the urgency of political reforms since the nation's gradual slide into a semi-colonial state after the Sino-Japanese War, attempted to imbibe knowhow regarding the acceptance of Western civilizational values from Japan, which had undergone the Meiji Restoration in a short period.

knowing that there are differences due to eras and regions and individual differences.

11 Whether taking these Chinese attitudes stubbornly or taking pride in tradition is a different point of view depending on the position. Cf. Suzuki Syuji 1981 : 187-188.

Table 2 | Differences in the perspectives of science and culture between Japan and China (Compiled by the author based on Li Tingquan (1998 : 356-366))

	Wakon-Yosai (Japanese spirit and Western learning) = promoter catalyst	Chutai-Seiyo (Chinese content and Western practicality) = restrictive catalyst
Characteristics of the ethnic culture	Passive stance → adaptability, mobility, quickly changeable, vital racial traits	Self-centeredness/stubbornness and conservativeness = strong immobility, conservativeness, and exclusivity
Attitudes toward the different cultures	Non-exclusive. Smooth harmonizer. Harmony between "Chinese spirit," "Japanese spirit," and "Western spirit."	Xun you bu tong qi = the "body" of Chinese traditions is accepted as "national virtues" and the body of foreign cultures is rejected as "stinky grass."
Translatio methods	Translation by Japanese → tradition of translation → Western culture dissemination spread widely and rapidly.	Dictation by Western missionaries + Recording by Chinese writers → Western culture dissemination is limited in scope and proceeded slowly.
Leading disciplines	Medicine → Accept modern Western culture based on the knowledge of Dutch Learning → Facilitate society-wide acceptance of modern science	Study of calendars and medicine → Accept Western astronomy → From political necessity → No penetration among the public ⇔ No room for Western medicine penetration into traditional Chinese medicine
Main player in modern science	Dutch Learning scholars. Scholars from the Institute for the Study of Western Books = Reformist private scholars.	Confucian writers ⇔ Private scientists were suppressed by society.
Consequences of the Confucian revival	Reactionism fits the experimentalism of modern Western science, leading to the development of Dutch Learning.	Blind sense of superiority regarding the Chinese traditional disciplines drives extreme nationalism.

However, several issues were present in the translation by Chinese writers. For example, their translations were too complex to understand and lacked acceptance among the public because the classical style of language was applied to express modern Western science and technical terms in a society that had resisted accepting different cultures. (Qin 2010 : 7-8; Suzuki Syuji 1981)

In comparison with China, the Japanese harmonic attitudes of accepting different cultures are instrumental among the characteristics of knowledge import. This is why "Japanese spirit and Western learning" in the Japanese approach to knowledge import are also called the "promoter catalyst." Social factors, such as the pervasive spread of education among the public in the Edo period and the academic knowledge of Dutch Learning and Chinese classics among private scholars and citizen leaders, could also be considered beneficial in building a foundation for the Japanese themselves to learn and translate foreign languages and to promote the generalization and popularization of modern knowledge.

4. Characteristics of "knowledge processing" in Japan : Linguistic factors

Let us now look at the characteristics of "knowledge processing" in Japan from the perspective of linguistic factors. Identifying the differences in word formation and translation between Japan and China could help in highlighting such characteristics at this point. The differences can be summarized as follows.

① The primary characteristic of word formation in modern Japanese is the combination of word bases (Tobita 2007 : 163) using both On and Kun readings. (Morioka 1969 : 417; Morioka 2004 : 226-229)

② In modern times, the compatibility and connectivity of the Japanese-made *kango* compound words are higher than those in Chinese.

③ When it came to modern Japanese, translation was done through analytical understanding; therefore, the scope of meaning of two-word compounds was narrowed down and specialized earlier than in case of modern Chinese.

④ Modern Japanese, using free translation with semantic understanding, provides a clearer meaning than that provided by Chinese intellectuals who depended on classical Chinese.

4-1. Combination of word bases using both On and Kun readings

Regarding the first point above, in comparison with new Chinese words created only with the pronunciation of Chinese characters, the On and Kun readings of Japanese (i.e., with one Chinese character broken down in terms of meaning by adding katakana or hiragana) may have had a favorable effect on new word formation, since this phonetic duality helps in breaking down the Chinese characters into word bases, followed by connecting these word bases and affixes flexibly.

The primary reason for this may be the fact that the "ideographic aspects of *wago* and the ideographic approach to express meanings by reading Chinese characters in their Japanese pronunciation (Kun reading) worked flexibly in combining the meanings of the word bases for free translation and new combinations of word bases."(Matsunaga 2010 : 1279.7-1279.8) This hypothesis is yet to be verified, but Takano (2004), a scholar in the field of Japanese word formation and translation, has already revealed that On and Kun readings work effectively in new word creation and formulation for translation.(Takano 2004 : 23) For verification of this aspect, it is necessary to consider the other three characteristics collectively.

4-2. Compatibility and connectivity of Japanese-made *kango* word compounds

With regard to this aspect, there is a perspective that a high level of understanding of the meaning of each Chinese character works effectively in translating new concepts and helps the formation of new two-word compounds. (Morioka 1969 : 121) Suzuki Hideo also mentioned, with "跛王 [*hao*, crippled king]" in *Keikoku Bidan* [Commendable Anecdotes] as an example, that the intellectuals of the time clearly understood the meaning of "跛 [*ha*, crippled]," an affix whose independent nature is seen to be gradually weakening today, and such an understanding "made it easier to create *shin-kango* back then." (Suzuki Hideo 1978 : 146)

Takano (2005), while examining the modern word formation of Chinese origin from the perspective of extinct words, indicated that "difficult terms and the words using Chinese characters with no fixed Kun reading as word bases tend to become extinct." (Takano 2005 : 25) In contrast, there exist Chinese characters in a single On reading, like "確 [*kaku*, positive]," that have the ability to help create words.(Matsui Toshihiko 1981b : 52)

Regarding the recognition of the meanings of Chinese characters, "English-Chinese dictionaries" in China, for example, have the noticeable tendency of "literal translation based on the original meanings and instances of the actual use of a word." In other words, the "individual Chinese character exists in a 'word' unit, and therefore, even two-word compounds tend to become a 'phrase-like' translation rather than one single merged compound." (Shen 2008a : 162) In Chinese, each character stands independently and contrarily the compatibility of the two-word compounds weakens, making it more difficult to create three- or four-word compounds based on two-word compounds.

Conversely, taking the translation in "*Meiroku zasshi*" (1874-1875) as an example, out of 1,566 Japanese-made words of Chinese origin (two-word compounds), 528 words still remain, based on which the other three- or four-word compounds have been created. Thus, some argue that the two-word compounds should be considered as a "word base" rather than a mere "word." (Takano 2004 : 172) The Japanese language has a strong ability to blend and connect two words, and its high compatibility may have been a factor in increasing its productivity in creating new words.

4-3. Narrowing and specializing the scope of meaning of two-word compounds

Regarding the third point of "semantic restriction," the scope of meaning of two-word compounds was narrowed and specialized earlier in Japan than in China. That may be because Japanese intellectuals were highly proficient at recomposing words originating in Chinese literature for translation through their analytical understanding (recycling of ancient words). There are too many recycled classical Chinese words to mention all of them here, but some examples are "絶対 [*zettai*, absolute]," "専制 [*sensei*, tyranny]," "形而上 [*keiji jyo*, metahistory]," "形而下 [*keiji ka*, physical]," "認識 [*ninshiki*, cognition]," and "意識 [*ishiki*, consciousness]." In particular, translations based on an analytical understanding can be recognized in the following cases : "necessary" = 必ず要る [*kanarazu iru*, must need] = "必要 [*hitsuyo*]" and "unit" = 単一の位 [*tan itsu no kurai*, single unit] = "単位 [*tan i*]," where "translation was made by arithmetic addition of the meaning of each word."[12]

Let us look at the process of "semantic restriction." Generally, it follows the same flow as the transformation from *wago* (Kun reading) to *kango* (On reading). For example, metal and blood were originally translated as "金 [*kane*]" and "血 [*chi*]," both *wago*, in the early days of foreign document translation. However, this approach failed to identify the meaning of the word. Therefore, metal was translated as "金属 [*kanerui*]," and blood as "血 [*chi*]" as a noun or "血液ノ [*ketsueki no*]" as an adjective. Thus, thoughtful devising for semantic restriction can be recognized here. Thereafter, they became pronounced as "金属 [*kinzoku*]" and "血液 [*ketsueki*]" in Chinese-derived reading to specify the scope of their meaning. (Sato 1979 : 421-422) "Semantic restriction," as shown in these cases, is considered to have been processed through the Japanese unique word formation methods, such as "transformation from *wago* to *kango*," and "Kana reading beside *kango*," mainly with those Chinese characters that could be

12 In terms of China origin, the word that has been re-synthesized in translation in light of the understanding in line with literally in Japan, 相対(relative), 信託(trust), 投機(speculation), 理論(theory), 階級(class), 条件(condition), 時間(time), 生産(production), 衛生(hygiene), 反応(response), 反動(recoil), 経済(economy), 任命(appointmentetc). Shen 2008a : 199.

read in both On and Kun, such as "金" and "血."

Moreover, regarding the analytical understanding required for this "semantic restriction," the presence of "Yakusho Jirui," a dictionary for translation in the late Edo period, should be noted separately. Words of Chinese characters in this dictionary are defined with several synonyms, semantic restriction or supplementation, and meanings of each polysemic word; they are compiled to give the explanation of words and phrases for readers to read the translated books, and not as a kind of contextual explanation usable only for certain disciplines. This is possible only when readers have an analytical understanding of *kango*. This dictionary is highly appreciated as an epoch-making one because "it aimed to help in reading not only the translations of certain genres," "but also those of any genre." (Matsui 1981a : 206-207)

Thus, the fact that the dictionary was compiled with universality and multiplicity of use as early as in the late Edo period is extremely interesting in terms of "knowledge processing." The new translation approach using "direct translation" may also have contributed to the "semantic restriction" of compound words as such "direct translation" could be considered a kind of analytical composition of compound words owing to its morphemic approach, with which loanwords are broken down semantically into a morpheme, and appropriate morphemes are combined into a compound word.

4-4. Semantic clarity

The fourth point is that Japanese translation is clear and accurate because the scope of the meaning is well defined. In contrast, as mentioned earlier in Section 2, the translation of Western material by Chinese intellectuals (e.g., Yan Fu, Liang Qichao) tends to be difficult-to-read due to its heavy dependency on classical Chinese. For example, "母財" as translated by Yan Fu was not used among the general public, and it was later replaced by "資本 (capital)," Japanese-made Chinese words, while "智学," "群学," and "資生学" as translated by Liang Qichao were also replaced by "哲学 (philosophy)," "社会学 (sociology)," and "経済学 (economics)" in Japanese-made Chinese words, and later established in the Chinese lexicon. (Qin 2010 : 8)

It has been argued that Chinese intellectuals' extreme pride in their own traditional culture underlies their conservative and inflexible way of thinking; they were tied to the idea of "*jitsuji kyuze* (practical search for the truth)," or an attitude of determining their approach based on a rule of thumb and through a study of reality.(Suzuki Syuji 1981 : 226-227) Their Japanese counterparts, however, were excellent at dealing with abstract and conceptual ideas, enabling them to translate abstract concepts such as "抽象 [*chusho*, abstraction]," "印象 [*insho*, impression]," and "象徴 [*shocho*, symbol]" effectively. In short, their different ways of thinking are reflected in their respective translation approaches. Given that most of the abstract concepts and academic terms established as modern Chinese are actually Japanese-made words of Chinese origin, the so-called "*shin-kango*,"[13] this argument is reasonable. In addition, the translation

13 Suzuki Syuji (1981 : 227-228). Abstract concepts such as "論理(Logical)", "概論(Introductory)",

of these abstract terms was made possible through "free translation," in which new words are coined based on the meaning of the words or understanding of the indicated objects."(See Note 23. Shen (2007 : 240-242)) This translation method, being a "semantic translation" approach used for Dutch Learning, was used when certain words and terms could not be literally translated.

It may be reasonable to assume that these four characteristics are brought about not only because of linguistic factors, but are also closely related with social factors. Hence, a major factor behind Japanese intellectuals being able to specify the meaning of a new concept, with several translations adopted earlier than their Chinese counterparts, is their deep understanding and practical skills in foreign languages, which allow them to identify the concept of a loanword through analysis. Another factor is that the existence of dictionaries compiled with universality and multiplicity in mind could facilitate semantic restriction and specialization for translation. Whether the words were "converted" or newly "coined," this analytical understanding of loanwords was the very aspect that enabled the "semantic restriction" of two-word compounds. This aspect will be revisited in Section 5 since it is considered that "semantic restriction" has certain elements that facilitate the categorization and structuration of concepts.

"批判(criticism)", "現象(phenomenon)", "要素(element)", "主観(subjective)", "客観(objective)", "主義(principle)", "唯物(materialistic)", "唯心(spiritualistic)" are Japanese-made Chinese words. In addition, such as「哲学」"philosophy",「論理学」"logic",「経済学」"economics",「政治学」"political science",「社会学」"sociology",「文学」"Literature", which take the "~ Studies" is considered to be almost Japanese-made Chinese.

5. Factors behind the intermediary nature of knowledge

In this section, the author confirms that international students and Japanese-language teachers served as intermediaries, processors, and messengers of knowledge. Thus, such international students and Japanese-language teachers, in addition to intellectuals, got involved in translation, secondhand translation, and the publication of technical books, textbooks, and dictionaries, and even wrote themselves, thus playing an important role in assimilating and disseminating modern knowledge. The Meiji period was when the modern education system was introduced from the West, and educational reform and exploration were active in Japan. During this period, many students came to Japan from the Qing dynasty, Korea, and Vietnam, undergoing the first systematic Japanese language education. Further, the knowledge processed in Japan, or the contents of the modern education system or technical education, were taken back by these students to their homelands, contributing to the modernization of the local education. (Shao Yan · Funaki Tshio 2003 : 75)

5-1. Knowledge intermediation by Japanese-language teachers

Let us first look at Japanese-language teachers. These teachers can be divided into two categories — those who taught Japanese to international students in Japan and "*riben jiaoxi* (Japanese instructors),"[14] who taught in China in response to the Qing government's invitation (hereinafter, collectively Japanese teach-

14 Yamamuro 2001, Saneto (1981 : 139-200) etc

ers). A major figure among them was Matsumoto Kamejiro.[15] He taught both in Japan and China for about 40 years, and made a significant contribution toward the education of Chinese students, including Lu Xun and Zhou Enlai, to the extent that he was said to have taught every single Chinese student. From the perspective of Japanese language education, Matsumoto recognized the significance of English early on, and actively introduced teaching methods for foreign languages into the system of Japanese language education. Further, as he was also well-versed in Chinese characters, Matsumoto taught the Japanese language by using Chinese translation, as necessary. When explaining the particle "に [*ni*]" in a class with Chinese characters, Lu Xun, his student at that time, provided a more appropriate explanation. This episode made him personally understand the necessity of both Japanese and Chinese working together to study the usage of Chinese characters. It was reported that translations by Lu Xun, which are known as "Lu-yi," were well accepted within his own circle of friends. (Matsumoto Kamejiro 1939 : 53) Matsumoto's interaction with these students was reflected in his textbook compilation and he even encouraged them to get involved in textbook development.

For example, "*Genbun taisho – Kanyaku Nihon Bunten Eibun*"[16] [hereafter, "*Bunten*"], which was a huge bestseller at that time, in its 40th print, particularly among the textbooks edited by Matsumoto, was compiled with the help of Chinese students in translation and revision, and is being used even in China. Both Matsumoto and Chinese students recognized that the book

15 Regarding Matsumoto (1866-1945), there is a series of research by Futami Takeshi, Hirano Hideo et al. In China, contributions to international student education have also been highly valued and reevaluated in recent years.

16 What I referred to is corrected 23 version, Kokubundo-bookstore, 1908 (first edition 1904).

contained a "guideline to learn Japanese sentences" (Matsumoto 1939 : 55) and it was useful for every Chinese student at that time. (Saneto 1981 : 341, 343; Saneto 1970 : 134) The features of "*Bunten*" include the description of grammar and sample sentences in both oral and written languages, and comparative presentation of the formal (literary) style and translation into classical Chinese. Since textbooks at that time mainly used the formal style and neither colloquial grammar nor writing in a colloquial style were established yet, this presentation of the colloquial form of language was a pioneering attempt by Matsumoto, who made the most of the practical teaching method of Japanese language. Adding the Chinese translation was also an innovative way of facilitating Chinese students' self-learning. Matsumoto himself mentioned that "since reading this book became a must for understanding almost all textbooks at that time and translating Japanese sentences, it was highly appreciated." (Matsumoto 1939 : 54) In short, "*Bunten*" was used not only as a grammar book, but also as a guidebook to understand Japanese textbooks in the formal style, and therefore served as a semantic intermediary between Japanese and Chinese and also between oral and written languages.

In addition, Matsunaga (2010) indicated, based on the analysis of "*Bunten*," that "*shin-kango*" made by the Japanese were imported to China via technical books, dictionaries, or magazines, and also via "*Bunten*," and were even established in the Chinese lexicon. (Matsunaga 2010 : 1279-0-1279-9) In a way, Matsumoto was the person who led the education of international students by accepting new knowledge from the outside in a flexible way, to meet the needs of the students of that time and also the demands of the times. Therefore, tracing back his footprints could help us understand the history of knowledge acceptance, processing, and intermediation through Japan's international student education. Further study is necessary about the acceptance, processing, intermediation, and dissemination of knowledge that Matsumoto embodied.

5-2. Knowledge intermediation by international students

The next aspect to consider is that of international students. Starting with 13 students on a government grant in 1896, Chinese students accounted for a majority of international students studying in Japan and this reportedly increased to between 8,000 and 10,000 at its peak. (Saneto 1939 : 96) Particularly, the period from the end of the Sino-Japanese War (1895) to the time when most students returned home to join the Chinese Revolution (1911) could be called the first wave of studying in Japan, and the number of Chinese students soared. At that time, what they initially needed were Japanese language textbooks, grammar textbooks, reference books, and dictionaries to learn the language and technical disciplines. For this purpose, various educational institutions, teachers, and international students became engaged in translation and secondhand translation, producing necessary publications in both Japanese and Chinese. The year when the first international students established an association for the Chinese translation of the Japanese texts was 1900, five years after their arrival in Japan. They included technical books, textbooks for special field learners, dictionaries, magazines for studying the Japanese language and literature, and guidebooks for overseas students. The scope of translation and publication was expanded until the 1930s.

It is difficult to gain a complete perspective of the role that these international students played, and hence the author would like to focus on the following three points. The first point is that they promoted the export of "*shin-kango*" mainly for academic or technical terms in China. According to Shen (1998), the peak period of Japanese influx into China was the decade that started in1900 when Chinese students began full-scale translation activities. (Shen 1998 : 46) The books published in both Japan and China as listed in *Chuyaku nichibunsho mokuroku* [Catalogue of Japanese documents translated in Chinese] (Saneto, ed.) totaled to 2,602 in various fields, including textbooks, dictionaries, technical books, and magazines. (Saneto 1970 : 291) In the initial period, the main subjects were education, law, and economics, but the coverage of disciplines gradually expanded, shifting toward the humanities, social sciences, and natural sciences. It should be noted that knowledge export via Chinese students covered the entire range of academic fields.

The second point is that the Japanese style of printing played a part in the import to China. Specifically, since Chinese students were actively translating and publishing in China as well, the Japanese style of printing was introduced in China. The old single-side printing and pouch-binding style was transformed into the Japanese style of double-side printing and Western-style binding. (Saneto 1970 : 297-329) Thus, the translation and publication activities of the Chinese students also promoted the modernization of printing technologies in China.

The third point is that their devotion to Japanese literature laid the foundation for Japanese studies in China. Although this point will be revisited later, there were many students, including Lu Xun and Guo Moruo, who came to Japan initially to learn other disciplines like medicine, but later became devoted to studying Japanese literature and language, and even theatre, which also laid the foundation for Japanese studies in China.

As previously stated, Chinese students, as intermediaries of knowledge, made an immense contribution toward accelerating the modernization of China. On the other hand, their translation was the simple rearrangement of Japanese word orders into Chinese ones, and some "*shin-kango*" were used without translation, thereby making many of them incomprehensible. Further, some defects were pointed out, including that their translation and secondhand translation were often rigid and wrong, and the contents were usually at an introductory level. (Saneto (1981 : 432); Shen 2008b : 4) Therefore, it is also necessary to further examine their role as intermediaries from the perspective of "knowledge processing."

6. Characteristics of knowledge import and processing

In the chapter so far, the author has analyzed the formation of "*shin-kango*" in modern Japan from the three major viewpoints of 1) social factors, 2) linguistic factors, and 3) intermediary factors. In this section, the author attempts to examine the formation of "*shin-kango*" comprehensively from the standpoint of "science of knowledge processing." First, it is necessary to confirm the applicable time period and characteristics of "knowledge processing" in Japan. The focus is particularly placed on the significance of the role of the knowledge intermediaries.

6-1 .Period of knowledge import and export in terms of the formation of "*shin-kango*"

Tables 3 and 4 portray the summary of knowledge import and processing in both Japan and China, focusing on the formation of "*shin-kango.*" The author used Shen (1998) as a reference in determining the

applicable period. (Shen 1998 : 38-46) Shen further divides the period of "*shin-kango*" formation in China into the following two periods : the period of missionaries' word formation (coinage) from the early 19th century to the Sino-Japanese War (1895) and that of borrowing from the Japanese language from the end of the Sino-Japanese War to the May Fourth Movement (1919). His periodization is justifiable since the latter period coincided with the peak period of about 10,000 Chinese students from the Qing dynasty studying in Japan, and translating Japanese books. However, from the perspective of knowledge import and export, the period from the Chinese Revolution (1911) to the establishment of Manchukuo (1932) should be separated. This is because most Chinese students returned home to join the Chinese Revolution in this period, and the number of overseas students from China rapidly decreased. This rapid decline of Chinese students as knowledge intermediaries directly influenced the flow of knowledge, discontinuing it. It should also be noted that, during the period until the outbreak of the Sino-Japanese War (1937), with 1935 being the peak year, there was another revival of the phe-

Table 3 | Knowledge import and processing by China (The author compiled this table based of Shen Guowei (1998, 2008b), Keishu Saneto (1939), and other references)

Period	Direction of knowledge import	Processor	Methods and fields	Characteristics of processing : ( ) shows defects
The first period (Opium War to Westernization Movement)	**West** → China → Japan	Western missionaries, Chinese intellectuals	Chinese translation of Western books, English-Chinese dictionaries, religions, **modern science, and technology**	· Coinage by missionaries · Lack of philosophical ideas and political systems
The second term (Sino-Japanese War (1895) to Chinese Revolution (1911) = boom in Japanese translation)	1) **West** → Japan → China 2) **West** → China	Chinese intellectuals (e.g., Yan Fu), overseas students (e.g., Lu Xun)	1) Chinese translation of Japanese books : **education,** law, and economics → **humanities, social sciences**, and natural sciences 2) Translated words, coined words	1) **Secondhand translation** : secondary processing by Chinese (rigid, wrong, introductory level) 2) Translation : primary processing by Chinese : a) loosely connected words, unstable order of words, word-based semantic construction → (broadly defined meaning), b) dependency on classical Chinese → (unintelligible)
The third period (End of Chinese Revolution to Establishment of Manchukuo)	**Japan** → China	Chinese intellectuals, overseas students	Humanities, social sciences, natural sciences	Secondary processing by Chinese
The fourth period (Before the Sino-Japanese War of 1937)	**Japan** → China	Chinese intellectuals, overseas students	Japanese language and literature, theatre	Evolvement into Japanese studies

Table 4 | Knowledge import and processing in Japan (Compiled by the author)

Period	Direction of knowledge import	Processor	Methods and fields	Characteristics of processing
The first period (late Edo to early Meiji)	1)West → China → Japan 2)West → Japan → China	1) Western missionaries (translation) 2) Dutch Learning scholars/Japanese intellectuals + Chinese students in Japan + Japanese teachers	**Fields :** 1) Chinese translation of Western books/English-Chinese dictionaries 2) Medicine/physics/chemistry → Politics/law/economics/philosophy, etc. **Methods :** creation of "*shin-kan-go*" : a) borrowing of Chinese, b) translated and coined words	Secondary processing by Japanese (Recombining/reconstructing classical Chinese for translation through **analytical understanding** → restriction and specialization of semantic scope)
The second period (Taisho to early Showa)	Japan ⇔ Japan → Asia	Japanese intellectuals	Japanese language Chinese literature	Fewer coinages and translations with "*kango*" → Primary processing and disseminating by Japanese (publication of general books and textbooks in or about Japanese)

nomenon of studying in Japan. It is also indicated that a great many Chinese students in this period later became devoted to the study of Japanese language and literature, which provided a huge foundation for Japanese studies. (Saneto 1939 : 310) Although this aspect has not been focused upon, it is important in terms of the history of knowledge import and export.

Regarding Japan, the author further divided the period as follows : the first period from late Edo to early Meiji and the second from Taisho to early Showa (See Table 4). This could be said to be the very period covering the changing times from when Japan incorporated, processed, and assimilated Western ideas for rapid growth until it started to confront the West and expand its imperialist power into Asia. In other words, this is the period from the "secondary processing" through the coinage and translation of Chinese words to "primary processing and disseminating." During this period, books, textbooks, and magazines about the Japanese language were actively published in conjunction with the national policy of promoting the Japanese language in Asia and other parts of the world. It also indicates that the first period saw a flow of knowledge via Chinese students and the second period did so only within the area of the Japanese empire. Under such circumstances, the launch of translation and study of Chinese literature in the 1930s was noteworthy. However, this period could be considered as a stagnant period of knowledge exchange because the flow of knowledge (import and export) was in only one direction.

6-2 . Characteristics of "knowledge processing" in Japan

A review of the characteristics of "*shin-kango*" formation revealed that knowledge processing by Japan and China share four basic patterns, which indicates the presence of universality. In addition, the characteristics of "*shin-kango*" creation in Japan are clearly reflected in "primary processing" or "new word formation," including the "transformation from *wago* to *kango*" using On and Kun readings, which Chinese does not have, as well as "Kun reading beside *kango*," and in the "secondary processing" of recycling classical Chinese. Particularly, the characteristic noticeable in processing into modern Japanese is that loaned concepts were combined to create new compounds through analytical understanding supported by a deep understanding of foreign languages; there was even semantic restriction.

In summarizing the role of "*shin-kango*" in the process of modernization, it can be said that the creation of "*shin-kango*" facilitated the narrowing and specialization of the semantic scope of technical concepts and terms earlier and more rapidly in Japan than in China, which is one of the major factors that accelerated the modernization of Japan. Thus, "*shin-kango*," as mainly found in academic or technical terms, were incorporated in the modern Chinese lexicon and have worked favorably in the modernization of China. It also means that the Japanese are provided with significant benefits while reading Chinese sentences. (Saneto 1970 : 407) As stated above, knowledge has been circulated mainly via Chinese characters in the kanji-based cultural sphere around Japan and China, and this relation has never been only one-way. If so, what determines the direction of knowledge (import and export) in each occasion? Several factors can be pointed out, such as speed of modernization, economical power, and military power. The author puts forth another factor here, namely the attitude of accepting different cultures. In modern times in particular, such an attitude encouraged intellectuals to learn foreign languages and facilitated the generalization and popularization of knowledge, which is vital for modernization.

Speaking of the "semantic restriction" of compound words of Chinese characters from the perspective of the "science of knowledge processing" (science of meta-knowledge), this could be considered to have promoted the categorization and structuration of vocabulary concepts, and ultimately the categorization of academic disciplines. (Suzuki Syuji 1981 : 185-186, 227-228) In one such example, Amane Nishi divided learning into "psychological science" and "physical science" and coined a new word, "哲学 (*tetsugaku*)," for "philosophy." This division was so highly acclaimed that it was even said to have "revolutionized the world of Japanese ideas" (Suzuki Syuji 1981 : 185-186) in the sense that it marked the starting point of dividing mental science and physical science.

Hence, "semantic restriction" could be considered as a major characteristic of "knowledge processing" in Japan.

7. Conclusion

In this chapter, the author took up "*shin-kango*" as a topic for discussion, since it is considered as one of the major factors behind the production of knowledge in modern Japan, and examined what kind of characteristics its word formation and translation have from the perspective of the "science of knowledge processing." It is argued that the Japanese ability to create words has been declining since the Taisho period. In terms of modern Japanese, however, new words have been actively coined by giving new meanings to classical Chinese to express new concepts, transforming *wago* to *kango,* or using the word bases of *kango* with both On and Kun readings, thus contributing significantly to the categorization and structuration of disciplinary concepts. The author also mentioned that the introduction and exchange of new knowledge via *kango* has been vigorously promoted with the help of knowledge intermediaries, which contributed to the modernization of both Japan and China. However, it cannot be denied that this study remains conceptual. Further study is necessary given its implications, particularly regarding the intermediary factor.

In the beginning, the author mentioned that the study of "terminology" has been actively promoted in connection with the standardization of academic terms among Japan, China, and Korea. Regarding Korea, it is pointed out that "despite the promotion of the exclusive use of the Hangul alphabet, more than 60 % of the general terms originated from *kango*,"and the "percentage is even higher for technical terms(Sei Ming Ming 2010 : 46) " in fields like medicine and chemistry. Therefore, the "science of knowledge processing" could continuously provide certain effective perspectives and expertise in pursuing both individuality and universality to share and exchange knowledge in the kanji-based cultural sphere.

What the discipline of humanities, which is now over-segmented, needs most is a perspective of overseeing various studies and theoretically integrating separated disciplines. The "science of knowledge processing" could be effective in overseeing and integrating these disciplines as "knowhow to share knowledge."

Works Cited

Arakawa, Kiyohide [荒川清秀], "Comparison of Japanese Fukugo-kango and Chinese Fukugo-kango : 複合漢語の日中比較", *Nihongo-gaku* [日本語学] Vol.7, No.5, Meiji-syoin [明治書院], 1988.

Chang Wonjae [張元哉], "A Study on the Development of Sino-Japanese/Korean Words in Modern Japanese and Korean and Word Borrowing : 現代日韓両国語における漢語の形成と語彙交流", *Kokugo-gaku* [國語學] Vol54, No3, Nihongo-gakkai [日本語学会], 2003.

Douglas R. Reynolds, "China, 1898-1912 : the Xinzheng Revolution and Japan", Cambridge, Mass. : *Council on East Asian Studies*, Harvard University, 1993.

Gao Mingkai [高明凱], Liu Zhengyan [劉正琰], "Study of Foreign Words in Modern Chinese" [現代漢語外来詞研究], Text Reform Press [文字改革出版社], 1958.

Gao Yujun [高玉軍], "Creation process of the Shin-Kango in modern times" [近代新漢語の造出過程], *Xiashan Association* [霞山同学会], School of Foreign Languages, Shandong Normal University [山東師範大学外国語学院], http://www.kazandogakukai.com/_d269122442.htm, 2009-2-25 update time, cf. 2010-02-02.

Kato Shuichi [加藤周一], "Over "Translation and modern times in Japan"" [『翻訳と日本の近代』をめぐって], *Civilization 21* [文明21], Aichi University International Communication Society Academic General Meeting for the Study [愛知大学国際コミュニケーション学会学術総合研究会], 1999.

Li Tingquan [李廷拳], "Comparison between "Japanese Spirit with Western Learning" and "Chinese-Centered with Western Learning"" [「中体西用」と「和魂洋才」の比較], Ed. YoshidaTadashi [吉田忠], Li Tingquan [李廷拳], *Japan-China Cultural Exchange History Series* Vol. 8 Science and Technology [日中文化交流史叢書第8巻科学技術], Taisyukan-syoten [大修館書店], 1998.

Liu Shuxin [劉叔新], Goto Mineharu [後藤峰晴], Translation : Fukui Mitsuru [福井充], Liu Shu [劉叔], "New-Kango Depiction Lexics : Units of Vocabulary Composition" [新 漢語描写語彙学--語彙構成の単位], *Aichi-Ronso* [愛知論叢], Aichi University Graduate Student Council [愛知大学大学院院生協議会], 2000.

Liu Zhengyan [劉正琰], others. Ed., *Chinese Dictionary of Foreign Words* [漢語外来詞詞典], Shanghai Lexicographical Publishing House [上海辞書出版社], 1984.

Makita Eiji [牧田英二], "Consideration over Chinese, the Japanese Kanji : Japanese as the word of foreign origin put in Chinese" [中国語・日本語の漢字をめぐって—中国語のなかに

移入された外来語としての日本語─], *Koza-NihongoKyoiku* [講座日本語教育] Vol.10, Waseda University Institute for Language Education [早稲田大学語学教育研究所], 1971.

Matsui Toshihiko [松井利彦], "Surroundings of "easy" and "clear"" [「簡単」「明確」の周辺], *Kokugo-Kokubun* [国語国文] Vol.50, No.5, 1981a.

________________________, "Edo period of translation dictionary" [幕末の訳語辞書], *Study of Japanese Language Vocabulary History* 2 [国語語彙史の研究2], Izumi-syoin [和泉書院],1981b.

Matsumoto Kamejiro [松本亀次郎], *Language Contrast Chinese Translation Japan ese Grammar Book* [言文対照漢訳日本文典], Correction 23rd Edition, Kokubundo Bookstore [国文堂書局], 1908/1904.

______________________________, "Retrospective of Foreign Student Education and the Future" [隣邦留学生教育の回顧と将来], *Education* [教育] Vol. 7, No. 4, Iwanami Shoten [岩波書店], 1939.

Matsunaga Noriko [松永典子], "Export and Establishment of "ShinKango" in Modern Japanese Textbook : Focus on Matsumoto Kamejiro "Genbun Taisyo Kanyaku Nihon Bunten" [近代日本語教科書に見る「新漢語」の輸出と定着─松本亀次郎『言文對照 漢譯日本文典』を中心に─], *2010 Proceedings on World Japanese Language Education Symposium* [2010世界日語教育大会予稿集], 2010.

Miyajima Tatsuo [宮島達夫], "Formation of the Modern Vocabulary" [現代語いの形成], *National Language Research Institute Journal : Word of Language Study 3* [国立国語研究所論集ことばの研究3], Syuei-publication [秀英出版], 1967.

Mizuhara Juri [水原寿里], "Intercultural Communication between Japan and China Language Cultural Exchange : Butterfly effect of Kanji" [異文化コミュニケーション 日中言語文化交流におけるカオス理論から見た漢字の変遷 ─ 漢字のバタフライ・エフェクト─], *Kogakuin Common Curriculum Research Journal* [工学院大学共通課程研究論叢] Vol.47, No2, 2010.

Morioka Kenji [森岡健二], *Formation of Modern Japanese : Meiji Period Vocabulary* [近代語の成立─明治期語彙編─], Meiji-syoin [明治書院], 1969.

_____________________, *Japanese and Kanji* [日本語と漢字], Meiji-syoin [明治書院], 2004.

Nomura Masaaki [野村雅昭], "*Coined Word Method* : 造語法," *Japanese Vol.9 Vocabulary and Meanings* [日本語9語彙と意味], Iwanami-syoten [岩波書店], 1977.

Qin Chunfang [秦春芳], "Borrowing Japanese Kanji Words in Modern Chinese in "Practical Journa l" [『実学報』に見える近代中国語の日本漢字語借用], *Japanese Literature* 攷[国文学攷], Hiroshima University Japanese Language and Japanese Literature Society [広島大学

国語国文学会] No.205, 2010.

Saneto Keisyu [實藤惠秀], *History of Chinese Study Abroad in Japan* [中国人日本留学史稿], Japan and China Association [日華学会], 1939.

__________________, *History of Chinese Study Abroad in Japan* [中国人日本留学史], Kuroshio Publishing Company [くろしお出版], 1970.

__________________, *Chinese International Student History* [中国留学生史談], Daiichi-syobo [第一書房], 1981.

Sato Kiyoji [佐藤喜代治], *Japanese Kango : - Its Source and Transition* [日本の漢語—その源流と変遷—], Kadokawa-syoten [角川書店], 1979.

Sei Ming Ming [成明珍], "Comparative Study with Korean Terminology - Focusing on Kanji Used in Chemical Terminology" [韓国の専門用語との比較研究—化学専門用語に用いられる漢字を中心に—], *Nihongo-gaku* [日本語学] Vol.29, No.15, Meiji-syoin [明治書院], 2010.

Shao Yan [邵艶], Funaki Tshio [船寄俊雄], "A Study on the Education Condition of Chinese Normal School Students in Japan in 1890's-1900's" [清朝末期における留日師範生の教育実態に関する研究 : 宏文学院と東京高等師範学校を中心に], *Bulletin of the Department of Developmental Science, Kobe University* [神戸大学発達科学部紀要] Vol.10, No.2, 2003.

Shen Guowei [沈国威], "*Thinking on Studies of Sinkango*" [新漢語研究に関する思考], *Syoin Women's College National Literature laboratory ed., "Bunrin"* (Professor Kikuo Nomoto retirement Commemoration) [松蔭女子学院大学国文学研究室編『文林』(野元菊雄先生退職記念号)], Syoin Women's College Academic Society Study Group [松蔭女子学院大学学術研究会], 1998.

__________________, "*Translation of Ran gaku, and Creation of Shin-kango*" [蘭学の訳語と新漢語の創出], Uchidaa Keiichi·Shen Guowei ED. [内田慶市 · 沈国威編], *Aspects of Various Aspects of Chinese in the 19th Century - Circumference Materials (Europe, America, Japan, Ryukyus, Korea)* [19世紀中国語の諸相—周縁資料 (欧米 · 日本 · 琉球 · 朝鮮) からのアプローチ—], Kansai University Asia Cultural Exchange Research Publication Part 1 [関西大学アジア文化交流研究叢刊第1輯], Yusyodo Publishing [雄松堂出版], 2007.

__________________, Revised edition, *The History of Japanese-Chinese Vocabulary Exchange in Modern Times : Generation and Acceptance of Shinkango* [改訂新版 近代日中語彙交流史-新漢語の生成と受容], Kasama-syoin [笠間書院], 2008a.

__________________, "*Acceptance of Modern Knowledge in China and Japan*" [中国における近代知の受容と日本], *Formation of the modern vocabulary of East Asian cultural sphere var-*

ious language - creation and share [漢字文化圏諸言語の近代語彙の形成—創出と共有—], Kansai University East-West Academic Research Institute International Collaborative Research Series 6 [関西大学東西学術研究所国際共同研究シリーズ6], Kansai University Publishing Department [関西大学出版部], 2008b.

__________________, "*Japan terminology, China terminology*" [日本の術語、中国の術語], *Nihongo-gaku* [日本語学] Vol. 29-15, Meiji-syoin [明治書院], 2010.

Sun Jianjun [孫建軍], "*Limitations of Shin-kango and Coined Words Made by Western Missionaries - Centered on Chinese Translations until the Mid-19th Century*" [西洋人宣教師の造った新漢語と造語の限界—19世紀中頃までの漢訳洋書を中心に], *Japan Studies* [日本研究], International Center for Japanese Culture Research [国際日本文化研究センター], 2005.

Suzuki Hideo [鈴木英夫], "*The Coined Word Method of Shin-kango in the Bakumatsu-Meiji Period - Centered on 'Keikoku-bidan'*" [幕末明治期における新漢語の造語法—「経国美談」を中心として—], *Japanese Language and Japanese Literature* [国語と国文学] Vol.55, No.5, Tokyo University Japanese Language and Japanese Literature Society [東京大学国語国文学会], Shibun-do [至文堂], 1978.

Suzuki Syuji [鈴木修次], *Words of Civilization* [文明のことば], Culture Review Publication [文化評論出版], 1981.

____________________, *Rediscovering Kanji - the Secret of Its Amazing Expression Power, Information Power, Economic Power* [漢字再発見—その驚くべき表現力・情報力・経済力の秘密], PHP laboratory [PHP研究所], 1983.

Takakubo Yutaka [高久保豊], "A Study on the Possibility of 'Kanji Technical Area' - Comparative Analysis of Shin-kango Generation Process as a Case" [『漢字技術圏』の可能性に関する一考察—新漢語生成過程の比較分析を契機として], *The Bulletin of Nihon University Spiritual Culture Research Institute* [日本大学精神文化研究所紀要], Nihon University Spiritual Culture Research Institute [日本大学精神文化研究所], 2001.

Takano Shigeo [高野繁男], *Study of Modern Kango - Japanese Coined Word Method and Translated Word Method* [近代漢語の研究—日本語の造語法・訳語法—], Meiji Shoin, 2004.

Tobita Yoshihumi [飛田良文], *Study of Tokyo Language History* [東京語成立史の研究], Tokyo-dō Publishing Co.Ltd. [東京堂出版], 1994.

________________________, Main ed. *Japanese Language Study Encyclopedia* [日本語学研究事典], Meiji Shoin, [明治書院], 2007.

Yamada Yoshio [山田孝雄], *Study of Kango in the Japanese Language* [国語の中に於ける漢語の研究], Hobun-kan [寶文館], 1940.

Yamamuro Shinichi [山室信一], *Asia as a Thought Issue : Fundamentals, Chains and Projections* [思

想課題としてのアジア―基軸・連鎖・投企―], Iwanami-shoten [岩波書店], 2002.
Zhang Di [張迪], "Translation and introduction of books published in Japan in modern China : the general condition of the early 20th century and the characteristic from the end of 19th century" [近代中国における日本書籍の翻訳と紹介―19世紀末から20世紀初頭の概況とその特徴], *Language and Culture* [言葉と文化] Vol.10, Nagoya University graduate school international language culture graduate course Japan language culture specialty [名古屋大学大学院国際言語文化研究科日本言語文化専攻], 2009.

Reading Reality into the Fantasy of Kafka's *Metamorphosis*

Yeon-soo Kim (Ewha Womans University)

1. Introduction

Since its first publication in 1915, Franz Kafka's *Metamorphosis* (*Die Verwandlung*) has undergone a colorful wave of adaptations and transformations led by a vast number of writers, and one can only imagine the degree to which each varying cultural context has restructured and reimagined the original work. Hartmut Binder first published research on the reception of Kafka's work, first focusing on Germany, the United Kingdom, France, Spain, Italy, and Japan in 1979, moving on to more research on how Kafka's work was adopted and transformed across nations in Eastern Europe and Latin America in 1983, providing a glimpse into the wide range found in the adoption and transformation of Kafka's work (Binder, *Kafka* 624-786; "Metamorphosen" 247-305). Moreover, in the following years, these efforts have continued not only in Europe but also outside of Europe where Kafka's work has been transformed beyond its literary form to encompass performance arts such as theatre. This is a common cultural trend of today that can be found across literary texts, but what is most notable is that Kafka's work, particularly *Metamorphosis*, which is the primary text of this study has been widely discussed in terms of the wide range of possibilities that lie in its interpretation. It has even been said that this text "is interpretable only as the Not-interpretable" (Emrich 127), or even more ambiguously, *Metamorphosis* has been referred to as "fundamentally silent" (Blanchot 73). These views not only make evident the unique quality of Kafka's narrative strategy, but also hints to the various implications that can be reached from age-old literary traditions from its mythological motif, to today's discussion on the human and non-human. Without having to mention previous literary research on this issue, individual readers would easily testify that each act of reading results in a new experience. Then, how can one approach and explain this phenomenon? Is the ventriloquist nature of the text which enables "the multitude of meanings" or "palimpsest upon palimpsest of meaning" (Weninger 281) sufficient in understanding not only the narrative characteristics of Kafka's work, but also the interconnectedness of fantasy and reality?

Looking beyond Kafka's narrative strategies, this paper explores yet another factor that contributes to the wide-ranging interpretations of *Metamorphosis*, which lies in the very moment meaning is created through the act of reading. By examining both the narrative characteristics of the text and what occurs at the moment of reading, I also look into the way communication and interaction takes place between the text and the act of reading to bring light to the elements of realism within fantasy. This is the only approach that allows reflection on the context behind the supernatural event of a human turning into "ungeheure[s] Ungeziefer" (KV 57)[1] and its implications. The interpretive lens for this task will be i) the phenomenon of "narrative Modalität," which is most notable in Kafka's work, and ii) the interaction between the context of Kafka's work and the context of the reader's experienced reality. This approach is necessary due to Kafka's narrative characteristic that denies the clear progression of a supernatural event and continuously encourages the reader to ask questions such as, "Did Gregor Samsa truly become a verminous insect?" and "Why did he become an insect, out of all living things?" That is not the only reason why the interaction between the text and context should be scrutinized. Kafka's work often merges fantasy and reality as one, and the logical and the absurd seem connected upon the same plane, which according to Park Hwan-deok, may have to do with the unique cultural layout of Prague where Germanic and Slavic cultures meet (41). Reiner Stach also noted the overlapping of fantasy and reality and their absorbtion into literature, which is one of the driving forces of Kafka's work (220). As such, the relationship between text and context becomes all the more significant as Kafka's fantasy and reality are closely connected. In what follows, I explore the elements of reality within Kafkaesque fantasy by reading into the historical context, more

1 The primary text used here is *Die Verwandlung*, which is part of the *Erzählungen* of Kafka's complete works. When referenced within the text, it will be marked as KV alongside the specific page number that is being referenced. The translation of "Ungeziefer" also needs to be addressed. Generally, when translated to Korean, the words "beollae" [bug] and "gabchoong" [beetle] were used. Here, it is translated to "haechoong" [a harmful insect] in order to highlight the negativity and unpleasantness associated with "Ungeziefer." When translated to English, H. Lawson had argued that the word "insect" fails to capture the unpleasant connotation of "Ungeziefer." Cf. H. Lawson, Richard. "Ungeheueres Ungeziefer in Kafka's 'Die Verwandlung'." *The German Quarterly* 33.3 (1960) : 216-19, especially 216.

specifically the Jewish cultural history of Europe, and by doing so, demonstrate how the element of reality itself holds the possibility for a variety of interpretations that shift with changes in historical and geographical context.

2. Kafka's Decontextualized Narrative and Varying Interpretations : The "Vermin" Motif as the "Metaphor of Insult"

The main event in *Metamorphosis* is the "transformation" of Gregor Samsa. This transformation does not involve a change in his human features. Instead, he wakes up one day to find himself an animal, and even worse, a "monstrous vermin." This fantastical event is what made *Metamorphosis* a fantasy tale well known throughout the world. The very fact that people can read this simply as fantastic literature is entirely a result of Kafka's narrative strategies. In the words of Adorno, the most striking feature of Kafka's narrative strategy is that the key to unlock his metaphors "has been lost." Adorno explained the characteristics of Kafka's prose as follows :

> Sie (Kafkas Prosa — kys) drückt sich nicht aus durch den Ausdruck sondern durch dessen Verweigerung, durch ein Abbrechen. Es ist eine Parabolik, zu der der Schlüssel entwendet ward. (251)

Adorno characterized Kafka's prose as expressing itself "not through expression, but by evading and interrupting expression." Along the same lines as Adorno's lost key, Walter Benjamin also described the metaphorical nature of Kafka's prose as "a flower bud that blossoms on its own" (420). In short, as a literary text, each metaphor lacks a key to interpretation, and the flower is never shown in full bloom. Metaphors are only mentioned to the point, which allows various different interpretations, but the interpretation of these metaphors only becomes possible when the text comes together with a real reader. The key to the metaphors lie in the context of these readers, and the act of reading is what triggers the flower to truly blossom. In this sense, it becomes clear that the interaction between Kafka's text and the context of the readers plays a significant role in the production of meaning. When this aspect of *Metamorphosis* is considered, it also becomes possible to prove that it cannot simply be read only as fantasy literature, as will be explained in the following.

Adorno's description applies not only to *Metamorphosis*. The evasive elements Adorno writes about have already been identified in other prose such as "Jackals and Arabs" (Schakale und Araber) and "At the Building of the Great Wall of China" (Beim Bau der chinesischen Mauer).[2] Clear representations of China — smoking pipes, braided pigtails, and embroidered silk garments — were erased from the final version of "At the Building of the Great Wall of China," allowing European readers to read the story as one tackling the issue of the Austrian Empire instead of China. There were also cases where his work would be read as Jewish documentaries without a single mention

2 Cf. Kim, Yeon-Soo. "Die Problematik der Diaspora in Kafkas Erzählung Schakale und Araber." *Bertolt Brecht und das moderne Theater* 21 (2009) : 181-205, especially 183-86; and "Kafkas literarisches Spiel mit dem europäischen Orientalismus — Analyse zu China Bildern in der Erzählung Beim Bau der chinesischen Mauer." *Dogilmunhak* 107 (2008) : 103-30, especially 113-25.

of Jews.[3] This enigmatic nature of Kafka's texts can only be deciphered when one observes the interaction of meaning between the text itself and the context of the readers.

Kafka's narrative sensibilities are not built on the assumption that there is a shared frame of thought that enables the symbolism within the text, or a shared belief that this symbolism can be understood by all. For Kafka, the only shared element is language (Anders 40-41). Kafka's decontextualized narrative evades and interrupts expression not by operating at a semantic level that presumes a shared image in the shape of metaphors and symbols, but by making use of "a shared language" of the signifier and the signified. This enables the communication of meaning, but due to the interaction between the literary text and the realism of the context it lies in, it also opens the possibility for multifarious meaning structures to be constructed and deconstructed at the semantic level. Languages generally change over time and the interpretation of literary works can vary dramatically as the differences in time and space increase between the context of production and the context of consumption. For example, the political satire and connotations that were relevant during the time of Jonathan Swift may no longer ring true to today's younger readers who may simply enjoy *Gulliver's Travels* as an adventure story. It is almost expected of Kafka's texts that are rife with word plays "express meaning through the interruption of expression" to result in an abundance of varying interpretations. Therefore, the characteristics in language and narrative that are identified in the interactive procedure of the transmission and

3 Cf. Kim, Yeon-Soo. "Das Treffen von Europäern 'in der Strafkolonie' Kafkas." *Kafka-Forschung* 16 (2006) : 31-50, especially 34-35.

reception of literary texts become crucial sources of understanding.

Then, what is it that is being expressed by *Metamorphosis* through the evasion and interruption of expression? If we were to reverse this question, we would have to begin with the matter of particular types of expressions that were denied and cancelled out in order to effectively express the fantastical nature of the metamorphosis. The image of the insect, or the verminous bug, can be found repeatedly in other works written by Kafka, and were explained by Karlheinz Fingerhut as "the metaphor of insults" (Schimpf-Metapher), which rises from Kafka's relationship with his father, Hermann Kafka (*Die Funktion* 212-15).[4] The metaphor of the vermin is derived from the verbal abuse that came from his own father. In *Brief an den Vater* (*Letter to His Father*), it is described how Kafka's father had objected to his son associating with Yitzchak Löwy who was an actor working for a theatre troupe. He would compare Löwy to vermin, and went as far as to adopt the old saying, "Whoever lies down with dogs, gets up with fleas" to express his disdain for Kafka's friendship with him. In his diary from the 25th of December, 1911, Kafka writes "well deliberated insults roll now and then, and within, the stronger tempers fly" (Literarisch überlegte Schimpfworte rollen hin und wieder, im Umkreis der stärkeren Temperamente fliegen sie) (*Tagebücher* 153). Kafka knew by then that one profane and abusive saying, if packaged in the right way can bring great social and political repercussions. Unsurprisingly, his vermin motif is by far the best example for the "well deliberated insults" Kafka wrote about in his diary.

---

4 Cf. Choi Yun Young also addresses the issue of man and animal found in *Die Verwandlung* and *Ein Bericht für eine Akademie* within the context of Europe's Jewish discourse and its cultural history in *Kafka, the Jew, the Body.* The insult metaphor is also explored in detailed manner. Refer to pages after 164.

The same motif is used in other works such as *Wedding Preparations in the Country* (1912).[5] This incomplete story was planned and written before Kafka started *Metamorphosis*. The metaphor of the vermin is slightly modified to a beetle, and this motif is used when the main character Raban daydreams on his way from his tough life in the city to the countryside where he is to be wed. Raban imagines becoming a beetle to escape from his own wedding and the excruciating pressures of everyday life. This is not so different from Gregor who also lives the exhausting life of a salesman. However, Raban's fantasies have not yet reached the level of vermin. What is different about Gregor is that he becomes a type of insect hazardous to mankind, vermin.

If we look further into the personal context of the author's life, we would find that Kafka's father was not inspired by an image he himself created. The image was drawn from an old saying, a socially shared image of disgust. His son's friendship taunted Hermann Kafka on at least two fronts. According to his worldview and value system, Löwy was an Eastern European Jew, considered the lowest class of all Europeans. Moreover, he was an actor, which meant he brought no practical good in life. Even if Kafka had strongly opposed his father's opinions, there is no doubt that the idea that one should do something practical would have been deeply rooted in his mind. His biographer Stach also noted that everything that could be imagined through the

5 For more on Gregor Samsa's motif of the verminous insect in *Die Verwandlung* and the beetle motif in *Hochzeitsvorbereitungen auf dem Lande*, see : Emrich, Wilhelm.*Peurancheu Kapeuka : Geuui Munhagui Guseong Beopchik, Heomujuuiwa Jeontongeul Neomeoseon Seongsukan Ingan* [Franz Kafka. Das Baugesetz seiner Dichtung. Der mündige Mensch jenseits von Nihilismus und Tradition, 프란츠 카프카 : 그의 문학의 구성 법칙, 허무주의와 전통을 넘어선 성숙한 인간]. 1975. Trans. Pyeon Youngsu [편영수], Seoul : ZMANZ, 2011.

image of vermin was in fact "already operating as an important aspect of Kafka's inner world" (215). Therefore, his father's insults found in the context of the author's personal life can be "interpreted" to have been realized through the fictional world of text. However, in the text-based world of fiction, it is never once said that Gregor became a monstrous insect because he did not go to work early in the morning, just as his father had warned through his insults. The "facts" that can be verified through the author's biographical information is never mentioned within the text itself. This is Kafka's narrative characteristic that functions like a metaphor that has lost its key, and expresses itself by avoiding or interrupting expression. Only when the text itself and the various contexts come together can one reach an interpretation.

It is, of course, possible to read into the transformation as a very unusual supernatural event, without ever taking into consideration the different contexts that may be involved. Nevertheless, Kafka's narrative techniques have a certain magical quality that encourages the reader to actively connect the text with different contextual levels. The text may appear to have a hidden layer disguised under darker shades, much like the work of Maurits Cornelis Escher who tried to capture the third dimension on a flat two dimensional surface and to make the image turn back upon itself in ways that appear reasonable at the local level, but that reveal impossibility at the level of the entire image. The content itself may also be altered depending on the individual act of reading, just as with holograms, where the shape of an object can change depending on the movement of the screen. The same effects of Escher's sketches and holograms within Kafka's text can be found in the narrative. The supernatural event of a human transforming into an insect that occurs in this fictional world does not progress through a clear and definite storyline. Instead, the narrative constantly prompts the reader to ask, "Did Gregor Samsa really become a monstrous bug?"

In order to specifically locate this characteristic and analyze it, we must look into the narrative modality. Briefly put, narrative modality refers to "a part of the speaker's individual contribution (…) to the speech event" (Fowler 78). Modality relates to the real presence of a narrator or the credibility within what is being said. It can also demonstrate a particular point of view on a certain topic, demonstrate a connection with the decisions made by the narrator, and present judgements of various kinds (78). In *Metamorphosis*, the most extraordinary event takes place, where a human turns into an insect, yet the readers are also exposed to a particular "voice" that adds the mystery to the story and expands the scope of interpretations. In the following, such hybrid narrative tendencies within different modalities will be examined in order to discover how Kafka's fantasies lie open to such a wide range of interpretations and how these fantasies also entails elements of realism.

3. Gregor Samsa's Fantasy as Signifier and Reality as Signified : *Wenn-Phantasie*

3-1. Characteristics of the Narrative Modality : Between Man and Animal

To examine what prevents readers from taking as literal this extraordinary event in which the main character transforms into a verminous insect, we must first look into two aspects of the narrative characteristic of *Metamorphosis*, or its narrative modality. Here, what is most notable is Kafka's choice of words and word order that creates the effect of *erlebte Rede* (i.e., free indirect discourse) and renders the events unfamiliar and distant. The narration and the inner thoughts of the characters arrive at various points of disagreement or conflict, which repeatedly prompts the reader to question the narrator's claim that Gregor has indeed become a verminous insect. This is what adds the riddle-like feature to the story and highlights characteristics shared with the work of Escher and the changing shapes of a hologram.

1) *Erlebte Rede* : The Hybridization of Two Voices

Erlebte Rede refers to the narrative technique used when the narrator directly delivers the experiences, inner feelings, and thoughts of the characters. This narrative voice is already a hybrid of two different voices, one of the characters and one of the narrator itself. The narrative technique in *Metamorphosis* is closer to *erlebte Rede* than to stream of consciousness, as Kim Tae Hwan notes, and Kafka's use of *erlebte Rede* also differs from the more traditional forms of *erlebte Rede* and its more modern usage, which can be found in Thomas Mann's writing (17-18). This is in fact very much the case. Kafka's use of *erlebte Rede* will be explored further in the following sections, but it is worth mentioning that the two combined voices in this narrative technique often experience fissures and conflicts that could result in an effect that distances the reader. In the case of *Metamorphosis*, the conflict between the narrative voice and the inner thoughts of the characters shakes the very foundation of the most central event and weakens its factual basis. In short, this is the paradox that is so often hailed as characteristic of Kafka's work (Politzer 273).

Kafka, or the narrator of the story, begins with the first sentence "As Gregor Samsa woke one morning from uneasy dreams, he found himself transformed into some kind of monstrous vermin" (KV 57). In the paragraph that immediately follows the physical description of the transformation, it is stated with clarity that "it was not a dream" (57) and the transformation was real. This extraordinary event which is clearly a stated reality in this fictional world is then ridiculed as "alle Narrheiten (all these idiocies)" in the very next paragraph as Gregor thinks, "What if I went on sleeping for a while and forgot all these idiocies" (57). The transformation had been a confirmed fact and reality just one paragraph earlier, and with this menacing sentence this reality comes under question. This suspicion becomes even more evident in the following paragraph :

> Zunächst wollte er ruhig und ungestört aufstehen, sich anziehen und vor allem frühstücken, und dann erst das Weitere überlegen, denn, das merkte er wohl, im

> Bett würde er mit dem Nachdenken zu keinem vernünftigen Ende kommen. Er erinnerte sich, schon öfters im Bett irgendeinen vielleicht durch ungeschicktes Liegen erzeugten, leichten Schmerz empfunden zu haben, der sich dann beim Aufstehen als reine Einbildung herausstellte, und er war gespannt, wie sich seine heutigen Vorstellungen allmählich auflösen würden. Daß die Veränderung der Stimme nichts anders war als der Vorbote einer tüchtigen Verkühlung, einer Berufskrankheit der Reisenden, daran zweifelte er nicht im geringsten. (60)

The contexts surrounding this particular passage reinforce the suspicion that Gregor's transformation itself may be but a fragment of his imagination, which reveals the foregrounding premise of story. As he woke from uneasy dreams, he found his body to have changed into an insect, and he struggled to get to work on time but missed the train, yet fortunately managed to hide his transformation from his family, thanks to a habit he picked up as a travelling salesman of sleeping with the door locked. His family stands outside calling out to him. It is in this situation that the quoted passage above is written. What is also striking is the three-page-long description of his room, the "kleines Menschenzimmer," where his cherished magazine cut-out — the fruit of his only hobby — hangs from a frame, the difficulties of moving due to the changes to his body, the hellish work that goes into being a salesman, and the fact that he cannot leave his job because of his parents.

While Gregor lies wriggling in his bed, the narrator lays out information about the main character's past and present. In other words, the narrative arrangement for the event at hand comes from the narrative act of a third person. The order in which the event itself progresses as well as the content that is being narrated do not fall under the same neat order. The narrator also marks the act of narrating in each paragraph with words such as "dachte er" (is what he thought) or "Gregor aber dachte" (but Gregor thought). The readers cannot avoid the mounting suspicion regarding his transformation and the thought that this may all be imagined by Gregor, even as they are reading through Gregor's inner thoughts that are being delivered to them through the narrative voice. When the narrator reveals the musings of Gregor and that he was curious to see how his present impressions would gradually fade away, a discrepancy is exposed between the fact of the matter, which is the transformation of the main character, and that all of this is not a dream.

Within the fictional world of the text, the protagonist has clearly become a verminous insect, yet his mental capacities in no way resemble that of an insect. He worries about getting to work, when to take the train, and how to deal with the situation at hand. Even as he struggles to figure out a way to maneuver his own body, his thoughts are focused on what could potentially be done about the situation. His body may have become an insect, as the narrator specified, and this body truly struggles to make sense of itself. On the other hand, the inner thoughts, emotions, and mental processes suggest the abilities of a man who is still lying in "a human being's room." Thus, Gregor is depicted as a hybrid between man and animal (Kwon 53). He may be a vermin in the objective sense, but subjectively, he is a human (Sokel 18).

These human mental processes are mediated through *indirect speech*, and often times his thoughts are expressed in *the subjunctive*. The use of the subjunctive is Gregor's attempt to assess *possible* or *impossible* ways to remedy the situation. For example, Gregor is said to have thought, "What if I went on sleeping for a while and forgot all these idiocies" (Wie wäre es, wenn ich noch ein wenig weiter schliefe und alle Narrheiten vergäße, dachte er) (KV 57). In other musings, it is asked, "But what was he to do now? The next train went at seven; to catch that, he would have to hurry at a frantic speed" (Was aber sollte er jetzt tun? Der nächste Zug ging um sieben Uhr; um den einzuholen, hätte er sich unsinnig beeilen müssen) (59) or "What if Gregor were to tell them he was sick? But that would be extremely embarrassing and suspicious" (Wie nun, wenn er sich krank meldete? Das wäre aber äußerst peinlich und verdächtig) (59). Other than the protagonist's thoughts and musings on different possibilities, his wishes are also expressed in the subjunctive. At one point, Gregor thinks how simple this would all be if his father and the maid came to help : "it occurred to him how simple it would all be if someone came to help him. Two strong people — he thought of his father and the maid — would have been entirely up to it" (fiel ihm ein, wie einfach alles wäre, wenn man ihm zu Hilfe käme. Zwei starke Leute — er dachte an seinen Vater und das Dienstmädchen — hätten vollständig genügt) (62). These thoughts directly clash with *the fact*, provided by the narrator in the very first sentence that the protagonist has become a verminous insect. The protagonist's thoughts that become known through the narration are not actualized as facts in the fictional world. They are mere possibilities conjured up by Gregor. However, this thought-play (Gedankenspiel) involving various possibilities can trigger the reader to reconsider the credibility of the narrator and create a level of unfamiliarity. The reader would distance him or herself from the narration and begin to question whether the protagonist has truly become an insect or not. Moreover, readers would become curious to know what the early morning "impressions" really were.

2) Word Choice and Word Order : Distancing or the Dualization of Meaning

Other than Kafka's use of *erlebte Rede*, another narrative characteristic that prevents readers from taking Gregor's transformation literally is word choice and the order of words, which is essentially a result of a particular style of narrative delivery.[6] Depending on the choice of words and the context, identical content can be delivered with the implication of two to three different meanings, leading to a wide range of varying interpretations. These effects can be commonly found throughout *Metamorphosis*, and they will be explored with detailed examples.

The narrator lays out the transformation as a factual event in the very first sentence; however, when the protagonist "found himself," the verb "fand er sich" already implies the subjective view of the protagonist (Fingerhut, "Die Verwandlung" 45). It was the protagonist himself, not anyone else who discovered his own transformation, and in this sense the narrative is based on his point of view. However, this particular sentence was not written in the subjunctive as is the case with other sentences that feature thought-play. Instead, it is written in the imperative as a way to state a fact. Nevertheless, the words used in the sentence were carefully selected so that the aforementioned subjective viewpoint is not entirely erased. In fact, the word choice helps this subjective point of view come across. Another noteworthy element of the first sentence ([...] fand er sich in seinem Bett zu einem ungeheueren Ungeziefer verwandelt) is the German preposition "zu." By writing "zu einem" instead of "in einem" it becomes

6 When it comes to Kafka's style or word choice, the influence of Prague German may have reinforced the effects of irony or paradox within the story. Cf. Politzer, Heinz.

clear that the protagonist is in the course of gradually becoming an insect rather than implying that the transformation is complete (45). Considering how the transformation begins to settle through Gregor's interaction with his family, one can assume that this word choice was highly deliberate.

So far, it is not only evident that the author used expressions that involve additional connotations, there were also parts that were written specifically to create dual meaning. For instance, on the morning of his transformation, the sentence that depicts the discomfort that rises from the change suddenly shifts direction, and the narrative focuses on the past to discuss Gregor's work conditions. When Kafka writes, "He slid back into his previous position" (Er glitt wieder in seine frühere Lage zurück) (KV 58), he not only expresses the uncomfortable movements of someone who has just turned into an insect; when this is read in conjunction with the following sentence, he could also be signifying the harsh work conditions of the travelling salesman, as well as Gregor's predicament that forces him to continue work in order to support his family. The past and the present are closely interconnected in terms of the textual structure through these words or sentences that have more than one meaning. These sentences require attention and cannot be read through a cursory glance. Readers will often see these types of sentences that cause great discomfort. These are the sentences that can result in entirely different interpretations depending on how the additional connotations are understood.

There are also elements that reinforce the very question that readers have asked themselves from their early moments of reading — did Gregor actually become a monstrous insect? These are the elements that also trick us to think that there may be another painting hidden under the immediate surface as is the case with Escher's work. Towards the end of the story, as Gregor prepares to take his "last breath" (sein letzter Atem) (KV 103) as a monstrous insect, there appear a number of words with double meaning that suggest the *possibility* of Gregor having left home and his family. It is worth noting that his death came almost immediately after his sister announced her final judgement. She declares she can no longer accept the disgusting vermin as part of her family and urges her parents to comply. "And now?" Gregor asks himself as the narrator lets the readers know that "[h]is own opinion that he should vanish was, if possible, even more determined than his sister's" (Seine Meinung darüber, daß er verschwinden müsse, war womöglich noch entschiedener als die seiner Schwester) (103). Here, Gregor feels he "should vanish" (verschwinden müsse), instead of feeling he "should die" (sterben müsse). Upon first glance, the verb "vanish" simply seems to mean "die and become dust," but this is another example of the dual meanings that appear with consistency. As her determination grows, Grete cries, "It has to go" (Weg muß es) (101) before she argues the following, "Wenn es Gregor wäre, er hätte längst eingesehen, daß ein Zusammenleben von Menschen mit einem solchen Tier nicht möglich ist, und wäre freiwillig fortgegangen" (102).

Gregor's death is thus described with expressions such as "elimination," "disappearance," "leaving of his own free will," and the impossibility of living together. Grete's word choice when she persuades her parents that "[I]t has to go" clearly exhibits her determination to no longer see him as family. This also implies the act of "removal" or "handling," which suggests a more aggressive push than to wait for him to "vanish." Here, the connotation is also clear that his death would be the death of the vermin, not the death of Gregor. In addition, the possibility of such connotations is not just mentioned at the end of the story; they can also be found in the very beginning of the story in the way the morning of the transformation is described.

On the morning when Gregor missed work due to his transformation, he locked himself into his room and listened to the different reactions from his family. Each seemed to respond to his predicament differently depending on how close they are to Gregor. When the chief clerk came by and caused a scene, Grete began to weep out of concern that her brother might lose his job, and this weeping was heard from Gregor's room. Upon hearing Grete's weeping, this was the way the protagonist felt according to the narrator : "Surely for the time being these were unnecessary worries. Gregor was still here and didn't have the slightest thought of deserting his family" (Das war doch vorläufig wohl unnötige Sorgen. Noch war Gregor hier und dachte nicht im geringsten daran, seine Familie zu verlassen) (KV 64). Through the modal adverb, "wohl" (surely), the narrator here evidently did not have full confidence in the content of the sentence, which hints at the possibility of Gregor leaving his family. At the same time, there is fair trust in that he would not leave them that very morning. Therefore, written between the lines is the suggestion that not going to work and losing his job would mean that he could no longer live with his family and would have to leave. Considering the entire context of the story alongside Grete's final announcement and the insect's death, it now becomes clear that the death of this verminous insect does not only signify Gregor's death, but also his "vanishment" and the outcome of him being "impossible to live with."

If this scene is read within the context of other scenes, the word "worry"

(Sorgen) and "unnecessary worries" (unnötige Sorgen) signify not only the relationship between the protagonist and his family, but also the psychological aspect of the relationship between the protagonist's economic activity and his death/vanishment. The person who finds Grete's weeping as "unnecessary worries" is none other than the protagonist Gregor himself. On that morning, he was more than motivated to go to work. Nonetheless, when the chief clerk pays a visit, his situation is expressed as an effort to protect himself from his own family, since Gregor is seen to be barricading himself from his own family in the eyes of the chief clerk.[7] To the chief clerk, all of this causes "unnecessary worries" to Gregor's parents (KV 65). To Gregor, when Grete cries because he did not go to work, her weeping is seen as "unnecessary worries," while his absence at work, in the eyes of the chief clerk, causes "unnecessary worries" to his parents that Gregor could easily remedy. He tells the chief clerk the reason why he is to return to work soon is his "concern for his family and sister" (die Sorge um meine Eltern und die Schwester) (69) and tries to make his way to work. The subject of this "worry" and "unnecessary worries" shifts from one end to the other once again when he dies as an insect. Gregor sometimes feels moments of liberation as he becomes accustomed to moving around as an insect (83); however, at the same time, he feels intense "shame and sorrow" (Scham; vor Beschähmung und Trauer) (75, 80) at his situation that has led his younger sister to go out and earn money. This young and delicate sister then grows up to no longer feel the need of her older brother. She is no longer the little girl who cried over her brother's inability to go to work. She no longer relies on her brother and the money he earns, and she has even

7 The chief clerk said, "Sie verbarrikadieren sich da in Ihrem Zimmer"(KV 65).

freed herself from the obligation of feeding a disgusting insect that does not even work. She had realized that this obligation was merely "unnecessary worries." Gregor sees this change sweeping through his family, especially his sister "with affection and love" (mit Rührung und Liebe) (103), and this observation is what led him to think that "his own opinion that he should vanish was, if possible, even more determined than his sister's" (Seine Meinung darüber, daß er verschwinden müsse, war womöglich noch entschiedener als die seiner Schwester) (103). Gregor then dies, or depending on the context, he leaves his family.

In this sense, Kafka's word choice and word ordering were all part of a very deliberately planned structure and this is what allowed the production of "extra meanings" (Fowler 92-109), which then comes into contact with the readers to be realized through their active production of meaning. This narrative characteristic is most like what reminds the reader of an Escher or a hologram.

3-2. If-Fantasy : "If I Were a Verminous Insect"

With a better understanding of the narrative characteristics, the basic structure of the story gains better definition. One morning the protagonist wakes up as a verminous insect, which causes quite a commotion, then dies a verminous insect. At the same time, its structure necessarily implies the possibility of his death being read as a departure or a disappearance. What exactly occurred between the transformation into an insect and the death of the vermin that is discussed in the ending? Within the fictional world inside of the text, how is this supernatural phenomenon of a human becoming a monstrous insect understood and how does the event unravel? How should this event be read and understood outside of the text? Kafka's narrative force, which lies outside the text, eliminates the "verminous insect" as the "metaphor of the insult" which is rooted in his own biographical context. In the most decontextualized form, the story of a man's transformation into a monstrous bug unravels, primarily at the textual level, as a fantastical tale. However, this is a fantastical story that progresses by "jumping from the tiny diving board of reality outside of the text and leaps into the vast yet complex and interwoven horizon" (Anders 49). In other words, Kafka had erased the insignificant insult that was part of this tiny diving board of reality outside the text. However, from this diving board, the story would jump right into the fantastical event and become a tale of "if-fantasy." Why did Kafka or the protagonist take a leap into this horizon of "if-fantasy?" What is it that he is trying to observe through his thought-play or thought- experiment?

In earlier analysis of the clash between the narrator's voice and the inner thoughts of the protagonist, which are mediated by this same voice, the point has already been made that in the fictional world "within the text," the metamorphosis is reality and not a dream, but this can be within the imagination of the protagonist, as explained by the narrator. Here, the narrator informs the reader of the protagonist's thoughts, as Gregor is said to be "curious to see how his present impressions would gradually fade away," but does not go into details about the content of these impressions or his imagination. Before Gregor thinks these things, what is mainly explained is how far the story has progressed. In many ways, this can be understood as the protagonist asking the same question he asked himself earlier, as if the protagonist is watching his family through a one-way glass window, asking them silently "if I became a monstrous vermin, how would you treat me?" The "if-fantasy" supposition carries a story within a story, where the reader becomes aware of "ein Blick von außen" (a view from the outside) (Stach 214), the view of the animal gazing at the human, or the view from the outside the family. While the "if-fantasy" that follows the supposition "if I became a monstrous vermin" will be analyzed in the following, it should also be noted that this idea also gives way to a connotation of a slightly different nature : "if I did not go to work." It is not clear whether there lies a causal relationship in the situation, or whether he became a monstrous bug because he could not go to work although he had to or whether he could not go to work because he had become a monstrous bug. What becomes clear, however, is that the two different ideas, one being the transformation and the other being Gregor's absence from work, almost entirely overlap within the fictional world and are treated as having layers of meaning. The spatial set up can also suggest that the boundary between Gregor and his family was more strictly defined than ever. As the chief clerk put it, Gregor had "barricaded" himself in what could only be seen as a standoff with his family. It is then possible to suggest that the "impressions" that crossed Gregor's mind earlier mean Gregor thought of himself in the shape of a verminous bug, watching his family from a one-way window. These double meanings need to be further explored on two different levels. The first is the triad consisting of "absence from work–transformation–father (warning)," and the second is "absence from work–transformation–sister (his concern and love for her)." Kafka's Escher-like narrative structure and the qualities of a hologram will become more evident by looking into these different levels of meaning.

1) Absence from Work–Transformation–Father

The father, mother, and sister standing outside Gregor's room each responds differently to the "fact" that Gregor has still not left his room and has not left for work. They are not yet aware of Gregor's transformation into a verminous insect. The relationship between Gregor and each member of his family becomes apparent through Gregor's reaction and the way the narrator depicts the situation. When his mother knocks at the door, Gregor reacts with an emotionally charged "[t]hat gentle voice!" (Die sanfte Stimme) (KV 59), while the narrator describes his father's reaction with "he warned again in a deep voice" (mahnte er noch mals mit tiefer Stimme) (60). By contrast, as if she is afraid of their father, his sister "begs him in a whispering tone" asks him to "open the door, I swear" (60) in an attempt to promise him she will keep any secret if necessary, and "his sister began to sob" (begann die Schwester zu schluchzen) (64). From his sister's reaction, it is clear that she is ready to do anything for her brother in situations that go against their father's wishes. From this morning fiasco, it is already clear that the three different elements — "absence from work," "transformation into a verminous insect," and "father's warning" — are already closely interconnected. First of all, the implication is that Gregor, who has kept his job despite harsh work conditions solely for the sake of his parents, will be warned by his father if he ceases to work. In short, readers can easily surmise that if Gregor did not work for the sake of his parents or his family, he would have received the same warning "in a deep voice" on any day other than this particular morning.

The close connection between Gregor's transformation into a verminous insect and his absence from work also has much to do with whether or not

Gregor belongs to the "human realm" (menschliche[r] Kreis) (KV 67). In other words, if he ceases to work, he would no longer be part of the human realm within his relationship with his family, particularly his father. For example, on the morning of his transformation, as Gregor tries to move his newly transformed body, he considered a *possible* scenario where he receives help. He imagines the help of his father and the maid, coming to his aid as he struggles to move. Here, readers can notice the thought-play of the narrator, who is mediating Gregor's thoughts through free indirect speech in the form of the subjunctive :

> (W)ie einfach alles wäre, wenn man ihm zu Hilfe käme. Zwei starke Leute — er dachte an seinen Vater und das Dienstmädchen — hätten vollständig genügt; sie hätten ihre Arme nur unter seinen gewölbten Rücken schieben, [...] Nun, ganz abgesehen davon, daß die Türen versperrt waren, hätte er wirklich um Hilfe rufen sollen? Trotz aller Not konnte er bei diesem Gedanken ein Lächeln nicht unterdrücken. (62)

As he thinks of a situation where his father and the maid arrive to help him, he cannot help but smile to himself, which is sufficient evidence to suggest that this is simply an "unrealistic" thought. Therefore, this possibility stops at the level of thought-play or thought-experiment and never becomes a fact within this fictional world. His transformation alone can be the reason for a warning from his father since he did not obey him and failed to go to work. Considering this, it is only natural that his father would not even entertain the thought of entering Gregor's room to help him. Such an event simply does not occur in the fictional world of the text, because Gregor himself decided this would be impossible from the other side of the one-way window and simply erased the possibility.

From this textual structure, one can assume that the transformation into a verminous insect is a punishment from his father. There are also clear connotations that he has undergone a downgrade from human to animal. When the chief clerk visits, and noises are heard outside to call a doctor and a locksmith, Gregor feels as though he "once again was drawn back into the human world" (KV 67). Here, there is an underlying desire to be considered a family member and a colleague, even if he is an insect that does not work. This is why the thought that crossed Gregor's mind in the morning was in fact a musing in the subjunctive : "[i]f I became a verminous insect as a result of father's warning, how would my family treat me and would I still belong to the world of humans?" Within the structure comprised of Gregor's "absence from work," "transformation," and "relationship with (his) father," he may have tested his own family with the "if-fantasy." Nevertheless, in this fictional world of his subjunctive musings, his transformation into a verminous insect is in the third-person, a *fact*.

2) Absence from Work–Transformation–Sister

Gregor simply refuses to acknowledge the physical mark that is suggestive of a punishment from his father, and the deeply humane quality of his mental processes stand in stark contrast to his transformed body. This quality also comes forward in parts there Gregor thinks of his sister. After the chaotic incident that occurred in the morning, Gregor seems to be at a crossroads between living the life of an insect who has been liberated from the hellish work conditions, and belonging to the world of humans, or at least "human" by his family's standards. He shows signs of hesitation due to his affectionate feelings towards his sister. As mentioned earlier, that very morning, having heard his sister weep, he thinks that she is unnecessarily worried and demonstrates a sincere willingness to go out and work. He even tried to open the door to the chief clerk when he heard the man's voice from the living room. Such was his desire to quietly accept his life as the key life-support for his family. Although Gregor had clearly told the chief clerk that he would soon be dressed and would do his work willingly, the chief clerk leaved. Gregor attempts to grab hold of him but fails and falls to the ground, where "he felt at ease with his body for the first time that morning" (fühlte er zum erstenmal an diesem Morgen ein körperliches Wohlbehagen) (KV 71). In this sense, giving up his job was perhaps the first step to becoming comfortable with his life as a verminous insect. This is not the only moment of hesitation Gregor experiences. His painful dilemma can also be found when his mother starts to turn her back on him and when his sister plays the violin.

As Gregor becomes increasingly familiar with his life as a verminous insect, having given up his job after failing to hold back the chief clerk from leaving, his own words begin to sound like "an animal noises" (eine Tierstimme) (KV 66), or a "hissing" (Zischlaute) (72), rendering communication with others impossible. He begins to "enjoy hanging on the ceiling" and "breath[es] with ease," and sometimes falls into "happy oblivion" (83). The key to his door is now placed in the part of the lock on the outside of his room instead of the inside. This signifies the isolation that resulted from his transformation. It is no coincidence that his name "Samsa" means a lonely person in Czech (Doppler 92). The "if-fantasy" of wanting to observe his family is gradually becoming a fact within the fictional world of text.

However, at times, the urge to be human grows strong. This is when he is struck with "shame" and "grief" (KV 75, 80), when his seventeen-year-old sister is forced to work. He begins to regret not being able to work. His father, by contrast, now throws apples at his son who has "barricaded" himself after having turned into a verminous insect. This violent act is described with the verb "bomb" (bombadieren) (90), in order to signify the rising tension between father and son. Although his father wasted no time on giving up on his son, his mother grieves over the incident. Only when everyone is the family is "exhausted" (92) to the point that they are no longer able to take care of him does she tell his sister to close the door to his room. That causes a fresh wound and Gregor loses many nights of sleep because of this feeling of "renewed pain" akin to when he was hit by his father's apple. Just as the door symbolizes the dynamic between Gregor and his family, his mother's instructions to "[c]lose the door" inflicted a pain as sharp as the pain he felt when he was attacked with apples. During many sleepless nights, Gregor sometimes thought that "when the door was next opened he might take the family's affairs fully in hand again" (Manchmal dachte er daran, beim nächsten Öffnen der Tür die Angelegenheiten der Familie ganz so wie früher wieder in die Hand zu nehmen) (93). These musings first of all show how Gregor had been able to listen in on conversations through the small crack of the door. However, far more significant are the thoughts that follow. He begins to think of the people he had worked with : his boss, the chief clerk, the apprentice, store clerks, and his other colleagues. He begins to think of the possibility of resuming work. However, this was yet another possibility that had become impossible. The narrator reports his thoughts as follows : "but instead of helping him and his family, they were completely unapproachable, and he was glad when they disappeared" (aber statt ihm und seiner Familie zu helfen, waren sie sämtlich unzugänglich, und er war froh, wenn sie verschwanden) (93). He is reminded of his working days when he thinks about crossing the boundary of the door to once again engage with his family, only to realize that this was an option no longer accessible to him. However, faced with the impossible, he is in fact "glad," much as he felt a sense of comfort when he fell trying to grab hold of the chief clerk.

The human characteristics of Gregor's internal self stand in contrast to his vermin exterior. The most powerful example that demonstrates his human quality is when his sister plays the violin. He crosses the boundary of his door and shocks the tenants with his filthy appearance, and yet, "he felt as though the way to the unknown nourishment he longed for was being revealed" (Ihm war, als zeige sich ihm der Weg zu der ersehnten unbekannten Nahrung) (KV 98). Even the narrator adds a comment on the human side that lies within Gregor in the form of a question : "Was he a beast, that music should move him like this?" (War er ein Tier, da ihn Musik so ergriff?) (98). Even as his existence as an insect becomes more and more clear, this comment effectively captures the undying human side of Gregor even as it contradicts the narrator's usual stylistic tone. Gregor's sister was the main reason for his feeling of shame, and even when he had worked, the key motivation other than supporting his family was to save up enough money to send her to music school. To Gregor, music is the "unknown nourishment" that signifies art.[8] After giving up the possibility of working again, Gregor still has the mind and will to think of asking his sister to play the violin for him, which suggests that he may have considered art as a new possibility to explore for a new chapter in his life. This is why music as a proxy to art is called the "unknown nourishment he longed for."

Considering the dynamic between "absence from work," Gregor's "transformation," and "the love that he has for his sister," his transformation into a verminous insect not only involves shame, but also seems to take on a decisively human quality thanks to the "unknown nourishment" provided by the artistic expression of his sister. If Gregor were ever to return to the human world, or return to work, it would be solely for his Grete. Here, music is presented as a third option that he may resort to, even as he decides not to return to work and not to return to the human world.

3) Death as a Verminous Insect, Departure as Human Being

Within the "if-fantasy" frame of thought, Gregor's identity both as a verminous insect and a human being appear in overlapping form. The earlier parts of the story do feature more of Gregor as a human, and towards the end, the fantastical aspects of the transformation are increasingly described as a factual event. In a letter sent to the Georg Heinrich Meyer on the 25th of October, 1915, Kafka writes that he cannot draw the vermin itself.[9] Just as

8 Based on biographical information regarding his relationship with his sister Ottla as well as letters and journals written by Kafka himself, some see *Metamorphosis* as a story that addresses the issues of being an artist. Cf. Politzer, Heinz. *Franz Kafka : Der Künstler.* Frankfurt a. M. : Suhrkamp, 1978.

9 In a letter to Georg Heinrich Meyer on the 25th of October, 1915, Kafka writes : "Das Insekt

the detailed contours of the insect could not be presented by replacing them with subtle shades, Kafka's writing offers the possibility of understanding the transformation and death differently. This falls in line with Fingerhut's view that Gregor continuously traverses the physical realm and the spiritual, emotional, and reflective realms, blurring the boundary between the signified and the signifier ("Die Verwandlung" 69).

The vermin motif as a "motif of insult" functions as a very small diving board that allows the leap into the endless stretch of the "if-fantasy," and the connecting bridge between the exterior and interior of the text. In this sense, the protagonist's transformation into a verminous insect is an identity given by his father whose orders had been disobeyed due to Gregor's absence from work. In other words, it is an identity that is given from the outside, not the protagonist's inner self. His transformation into this verminous creature was hardly a life-shattering, extraordinary, impossible event. It was "a great misfortune" (ein großes Unglück) (KV 66). His family regards him as something they can no longer live with, a "monster" (Untier) (100). Gregor looks back on the relationship with his family and the possibility of remaining a son and a brother when he dies as a verminous insect. Moreover, it was his voluntary choice to die. After traversing the boundaries defined by his father, the boundaries between the animal and human worlds, he fails to return to the

selbst kann nicht gezeichnet werden. Es kann aber nicht einmal von der Ferne aus gezeigt werden. (...) Wenn ich für eine Illustration selbst Vorschläge machen dürfte, würde ich Szenen wählen, wie : die Eltern und der Prokurist vor der geschlossenen Tür oder noch besser die Eltern und die Schwester im beleuchteten Zimmer, während die Tür zum ganz finsteren Nebenzimmer offen steht" (qtd. Engel and Auerochs 166). Cf. Engel, Manfred, Bernd Auerochs eds. *Kafka Handbuch*, Stuttgart and Weimar : J. B. Metzler, 2010.

world of man and dies a verminous insect.

As mentioned earlier in an analysis of word choice with dual meaning, Gregor's death implies double, triple meanings of "elimination," "vanishment," and "leaving of his own free will." The word "animal" (Tier) would have sufficed to describe Gregor, yet "monster" (Untier) was the word of choice selected by Grete in her moment of great anguish. While "Untier" highlights the hate and disdain against Gregor, it also negates the "Tier" with the prefix "Un-" which suggests the opposite of Gregor being an animal (Choi 152). Under this light, Gregor's death can also be read as a form of farewell. Here lie the connotations of Gregor's will to leave, departure, disappearance, and death when faced with the resolute farewell voiced by Grete, who represents the family. The story thus ends as the possibilities of a wide-ranging interpretation extend far beyond Gregor's death as a verminous insect, his departure as a human, and the disintegration of the family unit.

3-3. Between the Fictional World of the Text and the Real World of the Context : The Possible and the Impossible, the Realistic and the Unrealistic

If the various possibilities that lie in the production of meaning are already implicated in the construction of a text, the more precise interpretation of these potential meanings are unveiled through the act of reading, a point noted earlier by Adorno or Benjamin as a characteristic of Kafka's narrative. The relationship and structure of the communication between the text and the reader play an even greater role in fantasy literature.[10] Whether a fantastic, unprecedented event will be read as an unreal, supernatural, and fanciful tale or as a symbolic system or an allegory of a realistic story lies entirely in the relationship of the context of the reader's acceptance. Kafka has already set down a narrative groundwork — the possibility of interaction between the fictional world of the text and the realistic world of the context — *inside the text* of this work :

> Gregor suchte sich vorzustellen, ob nicht auch einmal dem Prokuristen etwas Ähnliches passieren könnte, wie heute ihm; die Möglichkeiten dessen mußte man doch eigentlich zugeben. (63)

The narrator conveys the thoughts of the protagonist that the story of Gregor morphing into a verminous insect is something that can happen to anyone. In other words, once the condition of turning into a verminous insect from *inside the text* is read as a *possibility* in the real world *outside the text*, this fantastic and *unrealistic* occurrence can be read as a realistic story. If the realistic insulting metaphor of a *verminous insect* was a *small diving board of reality* into the what "if-fantasy" from the perspective of *inside the text*, the protagonist's metamorphosis into a verminous insect, which was based on an

10 One can observe an attempt by Hong Jin-ho to review the theory of fantasy literature by Louis Vax, Roger Caillois, and Tzvetan Todorov based on the theory of fantasy and theoretically, persuasively approach the crash of the fantasy and reality in fantasy literature by distinguishing the experience-based reality of the reader, the reality of the fictional world and the supernatural event while contemplating the interactive relationship in his paper. For more details refer to the following paper : "Fantasy and Reality : The Crash between Reality and Supernatural events in Fantasy Literature." *Kafka-Forschung* 21 (2009) : 325-50.

insult from reality, would create a social and political sensation with a single "refined literary insult" from the perspective of *outside the text*. This can be seen as "[t]he thoroughly subversive and marginal nature of the fantastic" (its Grenzcharakter) (Murphy 309).

The extent to which the story impacts the reader or the direction of interpretation may differ according to which group a reader is in — the group who can construe the word Kafka's father used to insult his son Franz's Eastern European Jewish friend, namely "verminous insect," as an insult that carries an image of hatred towards the Jews, having lived in the same era as the author or the group from a very different space and time context and are therefore completely oblivious unless they conduct extra research. There are readers who can deduce the *realistic* meaning from of this fantastic event by capturing the connotation of the metaphorical insult "verminous insect," and there are those who cannot do so. This is mainly due to the fact that the real world that the readers have experienced plays an important role in generating the meaning of the text in the communication structure between the (fantastical) text and the reader. As noted earlier, if the text of Kafka, which did not include a single word related to *Jews*, was read as a Jewish documentary by European readers because they shared the same space and time context with the author, then Kafka's work may be read simply as an unrealistic fantasy novel by the youth of Korea today. Therefore, there exists a difference in understanding and interpretation between readers who speak the same language as the author, and readers who do not. This, in turn, indicates a possibility that there may be contrasting interpretations among readers on whether they can evoke the image of the Jewish people from the signified point of view by looking at the signifier, the "verminous insect." With these conditions in mind, there is a need to analyze how the supernatural event where the protagonist morphs into a verminous insect can be read once it enters into the context of reality of the readers.

For European readers who lived during the same era as Kafka and had either directly or indirectly experienced anti-Semitism, the "verminous insect" referred to Jews — especially Eastern European Jews — and this expression can be read as an anti-Semitic insult. There is an abundance of cultural historical examples to support this connection. For example, although the documentary film directed by Fritz Hippler, *The Eternal Jew* (1940), was produced as an anti-Semitic propaganda in 1940 Nazi Germany, it vigorously employs the "images of hatred depicted in the relics of nineteenth century anti-Semitism" (Benz 48). The Jewish people living in the ghettos of Poland, Lodz, are shown to be equivalent to a hoard of cockroaches and the on-screen juxtaposition of images of cockroaches and rats with Jewish people fuels the hatred for Jews — explicitly showcasing the social prejudices of that particular era (Lorenz 207). Moreover, during the Nazi rule, where anti-Semitism was systematically encouraged and rampant on a social level (which was some years after the publication of Kafka's work), a cartoon printed in *Die Brennessel*, a Nazi magazine of the Third Reich, depicted a drawing of heads of famous Jews attached to the bodies of verminous insects. The same can also be observed in the historical novel *Jahrestage — aus dem Leben Gesine Cresspahls* (*Anniversaries : From the Life*

Figure 1

of Gesine Cresspahls), where the history of a family is narrated during the settlement of the Third Reich in Germany. The protagonist, Gesine Cresspahl writes of his family and the history of Germany in his diary entry on March 5, 1968 while he is living in New York with his ten-year-old daughter Marie. In the particular entry, a "huge vermin" (Ungeziefer), a cockroach, makes an appearance in his New York apartment, which is followed by a detailed, almost academic report of the annihilation of the cockroach with Zyklon B (Johnson 822-27). The same Zyklon B that was used in the gas rooms of the concentration camps (KZ) is utilized to evoke a certain image as well.[11] One can also surmise that the "image of the cockroach" is a popular metaphor of disdain for the Jews, as noted in *Dialektik der Aufklärung* by Adorno and Horkheimer (253). The wealth of material from cultural history confirms the direct connection between the vermin motif of Kafka and the anti-Semitism images of that era. From this perspective, European readers read this fantastic event of the protagonist morphing into a verminous insect as a *realistic* narrative, rather than an *unrealistic fantasy*.

However, there is a higher possibility that the vermin motif will be read as an *impossible* and *unrealistic* fantasy by those who do not speak the "shared language" and do not share the space and time context with the author as opposed to being read as a *realistic* story of the Jews. Nonetheless, readers who can tap into the "extra meanings" by understanding the narrative aspects found in the construction of the text or by layering double, or triple mean-

11 Refer to Norbert Mecklenburg's paper for more on the cultural history research related to the vermin motif and New York Jews in the chapter of Uwe Johnson's novel : "Ungeziefer und selektiertes Volk : Zwei Aspekte von New York in Uwe Johnsons Jahrestagen." *The Germanic Review* 76.3 (2001) : 254-66.

ings will also be able to decipher the theme of the modern isolated peripheral individual inside the relationship dynamics of the family structure. We can easily encounter an interpretation of the work as a life of a *stranger* or a problem of the Other in the multicultural modern society in which we now live (Kwon 53; Ålund 318). These cases can be seen as the result of the reader actively conjuring up the image of the Other, or in this case, "European Jews" from the signifier of the vermin motif within the reader's own context. When read in this context, the fantasy is an *unrealistic tale* but it can be accepted as a *possible story* that can actually occur. Thus only when the interaction between the fictional world of the text and the real world of the context is taken into consideration can Kafka's fantastic quality can be fully understood.

4. Conclusion

This study examines the way in which various interpretations of a text can already be potentially embedded in the composition of the text by analyzing the unique characteristics of Kafka's writings in its narrative strategy and therefore, in this sense, studies the reality and possible generation of realism of the fantasy by examining the supernatural fantasy occurring in a fictional world *inside the text* and how it can be accepted *outside the text*, meaning the contextual aspect of the readers' real world. Not only is one able to read with questioning the transformation of the main character itself through Kafka's experiential phenomenon, a hybridism in the discordance of the narrator and the main character's voice, but also acknowledge the different level of the narrator's narrative act and the narrated through the narrative aspect. Furthermore, by analyzing the possibility in the creation of double and triple connotations entailed by the uniqueness in the choice and arrangement of vocabulary, Kafka's text can be admitted to have a narrative effect much like the art of Escher or a moving hologram.

According to the communicative structure between the text and its reader and in particular in the context of how Kafka's fantasy is accepted by the realistic reader, this type of narrative allows a story to be read rather realistically than in a mere simplistic way of perceiving a supernatural fantasy. The transformation of the main character into a verminous creature is the visualization of the insult from the outside, and the signified symbol of the "vermin" can be read in Kafka's historical and cultural context through the realistic reader's act of reading. This signification that the reader can accept transformation in the context of time and space can explain the foundation of how this book was exceptionally accepted in various different ways in a large number of different countries. This paper is significant in the sense that it is the basis of comparison of how Kafka's fantasy was either accepted equivalently or differently in various language and cultural regions. Further comparative research into Kafka's *Metamorphosis* and its acceptance in Korea will be on the way with the help of the implications gained from this study.

Works Cited

Adorno, Theodor W., "Aufzeichnungen zu Kafka." *Prismen. Kulturkritik und Gesellschaft*, 1955, Frankfurt a. M. : Suhrkamp Verlag, 1992.

Adorno, Theodor W., and Max Horkheimer, *Gyemongui Byeonjeungbeop* [Dialektik der Aufklärung, 계몽의 변증법]. 1969. Trans. Kim Yu Dong [김유동], 1969, Seoul : Moonji Publishing Company [문학과지성사], 2001.

Ålund, Aleksandra, "Alterity in Modernity," *Acta Sociologica* 38.4, 1995.

Anders, Günther, *Kafka Pro und Contra*, 1951, München : C.H. Beck, 1972.

Benjamin, Walter, "Franz Kafka. Zur zehnten Wiederkehr seines Todestages." *Aufsätze, Essays, Vorträge, Gesammelte Schriften,* Vol. 2. Frankfurt a. M. : Suhrkamp taschenbuch wissenschaft, 1977.

Binder, Harmut, *Kafka-Handbuch.* Vol. 2. Stuttgart : Alfred Kröner Verlag, 1979.

———, "Metamorphosen. Kafkas 'Verwandlung' im Werk anderer Schriftsteller." *Probleme der Moderne. Studien zur deutschen Literatur von Nietzsche bis Brecht.* Ed. Benjamin Bennett, Tübingen : Max Niemeyer Verlag, 1983.

Blanchot, Maurice, "Kapeuka Ilgi" [Reading Kafka, 카프카 읽기]. *Kapeukaeseo Kapeukaro* [From Kafka to Kafka, 카프카에서 카프카로], Trans. Lee Dal Seung [이달승], Seoul : Greenbee [그린비], 2013.

Benz, Wolfgang, *Yudaein Imijiui Yeoksa* [Bilder vom Juden, 유대인 이미지의 역사], Trans. Yun Young Seon [윤용선], 2001, Seoul : Pureon Yeoksa [푸른역사], 2005.

Choi, Yun Young [최윤영], *Kapeuka, Yudaein, Mom* [Kafka, the Jew, the Body, 카프카, 유대인, 몸], Seoul : Minumsa [민음사], 2012.

Doppler, Alfred, *Wirklichkeit im Spiegel der Sprache*, Wien : Europaverlag, 1975.

Emrich, Wolfgang, *Franz Kafka*, 1957, Frankfurt a. M. : Athenäum Verlag, 1964.

Fingerhut, Karlheinz, *Die Funktion der Tierfiguren im Werke Franz Kafkas,* Bonn : H. Bouvier u. Co. Verlag, 1969.

———, "Die Verwandlung," *Franz Kafka Romane und Erzählungen*, 1994. Ed. Michale Müller, Stuttgart : Reclam, 2003.

Fowler, Roger, *Linguistic Criticism,* 1986, Oxford and New York : Oxford UP, 1998.

Johnson, Uwe, *Jahrestage*, 1971, Frankfurt a. M. : Suhrkamp, 1983.

Kafka, Franz, "Brief an den Vater," *Hochzeitsvorbereitungen auf dem Lande*, Frankfurt a. M. : Fischer, 1983.

———, “Die Verwandlung,” *Erzählungen*, Frankfurt a. M. : Fischer Verlag, 1983.

———, *Tagebücher 1910-1923*, Frankfurt a. M. : Fischer, 1983.

Kim, Tae Hwan [김태환], *Miroui Gujo* [Structure of the Labyrinth, 미로의 구조], 2008, Seoul : Aleum [알음], 2009.

Kwon, Hyuck-Zoon [권혁준], “Kapeuka Tekseuteueseoui Tajaui Hyeongsanghwa—「Byeonsin」gwa「Haksurwone Deurineun Bogo」reul Jungsimeuro” [Darstellung des Fremden in Kafkas Erzählungen : “Die Verwandlung” und “Ein Bericht für eine Akademie,” 카프카 텍스트에서의 타자의 형상화 –「변신」과「학술원에 드리는 보고」를 중심으로], *Kapeukayeongu* [Kafka-Forschung, 카프카연구] 32, 2014.

Lorenz, Dagmar, “Man and Animal : The Discourse of Exclusion and Discrimination in a Literary Context,” *Woman in German Yearbook* 14, 1998.

Murphy, Richard, “Semiotic Excess, Semantic Vacuity and the Photograph of the Imaginary. The Interplay of Realism and the Fantastic in Kafka's Die Verwandlung,” *Deutsche Vierteljahrsschrift für Literaturwissenschaft und Geistesgeschichte* 65, 1991.

Park, Hwan Deok [박환덕], “Kapeukaui Sasangjeok Baegyeonggwa Yudentum” [Kafka's Ideological Background and Judentum, 카프카의 사상적 배경과 유덴툼]. *Dogilhyeondaejakgawa Munhagiron* [German Modern Authors and Literature Theory, 독일현대작가와 문학이론] Ed. Bakwandeok Gyosu Hoegapginyeomnonmunjip Ganhaengwiwonhoe [Publication Committee for Prof. Park Hwan Deok's Sixty-Year-Old Birthday, 박환덕 교수 회갑기념논문집 간행위원회], Seoul : Beomwusa [범우사], 1993.

Politzer, Heinz, “Problematik und Probleme der Kafka-Forschung,” *Monatshefte* 42.6, 1950.

Sokel, Walter H., “Von Marx zum, Mythos : Das Problem der Selbstentfremdung in Kafkas Verwandlung,” *Monatshefte* 73.1, 1981.

Stach, Reiner, *Kafka. Die Jahre der Entscheidungen*, Frankfurt a. M. : Fischer Verlag, 2004.

Weninger, Robert, “Sounding Out the Silence of Gregor Samsa : Kafka's Rhetoric of Dys-Communication,” *Studies in 20th Century Literature* 17.2, 1993.

Figure 1. “Systemverrätern”, Die Brennessel 9 Sep., 1933.

Chapter 2

Transculturation in East-Asia

Another "Paris in the Orient"

Overlapping Exoticism in Japanese Modernism around 1930*

Tsuyoshi Namigata (Kyushu University)

1. Introduction

How was "Western" modernism received in Japanese literature, and how was it transformed in the 1920s–30s?

This question once referred to the influence of the style or form of Western modernism on Japanese literature, such as stream of consciousness or the camera eye, and it has been a key practice for a long time in the comparative research to approach this topic from the aesthetic perspective. However, post-colonial theory sheds new light on the subject, suggesting a different angle to the reading of modernist canons. Imperialism and modernism are inseparably related, and especially after World War I, Western modernists felt a crisis or instability in the authenticity of their own culture, so they tried to establish a new art and cultural trend through appropriating the exotic "objects" from the non-Western world. If this viewpoint is true of Japanese literature as well,

* This paper was first published in *Trans-Humanities*, Volume 9, Number 3, Ewha Institute for Humanities, October 2016, 191-210, supported by JSPS KAKENHI Grant Number 26370430.

we can arrange the question above like this : How was Western exoticism, exemplified by modernism, received in Japanese literature, and how was it transformed in the historical and cultural context of imperial Japan in the 1920s–30s?

We can say that modernism is, on the one hand, the cultural product of a highly civilized Western metropolis, whilst on the other, it also signifies the practice of exoticism in its representation of a non-Western cultural other. This was how modernism was translated and received in Japan as well. Of course, Japanese modernism was deeply concerned with Americanism and the age of mass consumer culture; however, modernist writers in Japan also shared an interest in African masks and "negro" dancers like Josephine Baker who were admired by the surrealists in Paris (Clifford 197-200), to the point that they even appropriated Western exoticism in their own works. The "savage" that they depicted in their works, though, was not one in opposition of "civilization," but a new type of "savage beauty" that coexisted with civilized culture in a "modern" metropolis. Shanghai at the time was known as the "Paris in the Orient" and was renowned as a place where one could experience the modern culture of the West. Accordingly, there are numerous examples of Japanese writers having visited Shanghai and penning their modernist works, a prime example being Yokomitsu Riichi (横光利一)'s *Shanghai* (上海).[1] Meanwhile, for Japan of the 1930s, Harbin was another such place.

When Harbin became another target of such attention, two "Parises in the Orient" became entwined within the "Shōwa Modan" period, generating a

1 Cf. Lippit 73-116; Peng 99-130; Tierney 19-20; Thornber 274-78.

heightened sensibility towards exoticism. This paper, focusing on the travel writings and novels of the Japanese modernists such as Abe Tomoji (阿部知二, 1903-1973), Nii Itaru (新居格, 1888-1951), and Gunji Jirōmasa (群司次郎正, 1905-1973), aims to elucidate the overlap of exoticism that can be seen regarding themes of Paris, dancers, and the underlying context of eroticism examined through the images of Shanghai and Harbin, to reveal the process of cultural translation in the early Shōwa period in Japan.

2. "Shōwa Modan" and the Representation of Josephine Baker

Of course, the concept of "modern" can be defined in various ways, but, from the translation history in Japan, it first appeared in 1926 by way of the terms "modan gāru" [モダンガール, modern girl] and "modan raifu" [モダンライフ, modern life], and then in 1930, with "modanizumu" [モダニズム, modernism], the concept entered mainstream circulation. While this largely relates to the permeation of Americanism, the reception of Western modernism occurred in tandem with the reception of exoticism in the West. The West's interest in the non-Western world was embraced by Japan, and played an important role in modernist literature. Movies imported from Europe and America, such as hunter/beast movies and adventure films like *Tarzan*, amplified the image of "savage Africa" in the early Shōwa period in Japan. Yet, this image meant not only the uncivilized, degenerated world to the West, but also a source of new value, the origin of cultural energy, and the essence of "primitive" passion. Japanese authors therefore also chose to focus on the "beauty of Africa," quite in contrast to the savageness. In implicating the aesthetic nature of Africa, the one who played an important role was the dancer Josephine Baker. Even in Japan, she was known by the name, "Black Venus." Amongst the avant-garde movements that were occurring one after the other in reaction to euro-centricity following World War I, Japanese authors and intellectuals sought to imitate this non-Western, primitive strength that was being so well received.

Josephine Baker, whose very being represented primordial beauty in Japanese eyes, began to appear in mass culture at around the same time. She made a significant appearance as the queen of "Revue" in the 1931 published *Gendai Ryōuki Sentan Zukan* [現代猟奇尖端図鑑, Illustrated Guide to the Contemporary Hyper-Bizzare], which could also be considered to be a culmination of "ero-guro-nansensu" [エロ・グロ・ナンセンス, erotic, grotesque, nonsense]. However, she also appeared in the "Erotic" section of the same illustrated guide, even being lined up next to naked Japanese and various other nationalities and races of women. Furthermore, the illustrations that appear under the heading "Grotesque" introduce the half-naked lifestyles of "barbaric races," and when allotted with these images, the image of the "savage" becomes more pronounced, and from this perspective, Baker could even be received within a primitive or decadent context.

In light of this situation, critic Ōya Sōichi (大宅壮一) makes the following statement :

> Now erotic-grotesque-nonsense has diverged from the interests of avant-gardists, who were floating between cinema, café, and artistic literature, and has

become a philosophy of daily life for the common people who, through severe economic depression and unemployment (or fear of unemployment), have lost their moral compass along with their economic foundation. This is especially true of the middle class, whose defensive powers are weak.

The thing that the public desires after losing hope for the future, and compounded by the stresses of life is, first and foremost, intense sensory stimulus. What rules the realm of the senses depends not on quality but on intensity. On the one hand, you have the revival of savage beauty — if it's in regard to music, it's jazz; if it's a color, it's a primary color — and on the other hand, you have erotic content being emphasized in bigger and more revealing ways — rather than theater it's cinema, rather than cinema it's revue, rather than revue it's a hostess, or a prostitute, and so on.

今やエロ・グロ・ナンセンスは、シネマとカフェと芸術派文学との間を泳 いでゐる一部尖端人の趣味から離れて、殺人的不景気と、失業ならびに失業 の不安によつて、生活の経済的基礎とともに従来の生活指導精神を失ひつゝ ある一般大衆、殊に抵抗力のもつとも弱い中間層の生活哲学になつて来たのである。

前途は希望を失ひ、生活に緊張を失つた大衆がまづ第一に要求するものは、強烈な感覚的刺激である。ところで、感覚の世界を支配するものは、高度で はなくて強度である。そこで一方では、野蛮美—音ではジヤズ、色では原 色— の復活となり、他方では、演劇よりもシネマ、シネマよりもレヴユー、レヴユーよりも女給または私娼といつた風に、エロチシズムの含有量のより 大なるものに対する要素がますます増大して行くのである。(205-06)

When "the common people" adopted the "interests of avant-gardists" and these interests were transformed into "a philosophy of daily life for [...] the middle class," the varying elements of "ero-guro-nansensu" became unified and began to be enjoyed as "intense sensory stimulus." And this "intensity," which distracts from the "severe economic depression and unemployment," is found in "savage beauty."

The Shinkō Geijutsu-ha [新興芸術派, Rising Art School], which was formed around the same time as the sudden rise in Shōwa *Modanizumu* literature, published twenty-four volumes of its "Shinko Geijutsu-ha Sōsho" [新興芸術派叢書, Rising Art School Library] series under the publisher, Shinchōsha [新潮社]. Of these volumes, four authors contributed two volumes on their own. One of those authors was Abe Tomoji who wrote *Koi to Afurika* [恋とアフリカ, Love and Africa] (1930), and then *Umi no Aibu* [海の愛撫, Caress of the Sea] (1930).

Tomoji, a translator of countless works of English authors such as Edward Foster, Jane Austen, Oscar Wilde, Emily Brontë, Charles Kingsley, Conan Doyle, and American authors including Herman Melville and William Faulkner, wrote the following passage that was published in an anthology of critical essays in 1930 :

> When you focus on the production process, literature becomes a reproduction of order, namely, the order of using intellect to expand our range of emotions and seek out the unknown in the world. However, when commenting on or critiquing in this regard, by being intellectually aware of this realm of emotions, literature becomes the vessel that holds our experiences in orderly abundance.

製作を中心にしていへば、文学とは、知性を方法としてわれわれの感情の前後左右にひろがる未知の世界を探求し、これに秩序をあたへて再現する、といふ やうなことになる。又、このことを、観照、批評の方面からいへば、その感情の世界を知的に認識することによつて、われわれの経験を秩序ある豊富さを持つものとすることになる。(*Shuchiteki Bungakuron* 5-6)

The point I would like to make here concerns the following passage from a novel that was written by the same person and published around the same time as an anthology of critical essays :

If you don't believe it, that's fine, but put simply, love is Africa. All of life's mysteries have gradually disappeared and love, just like Africa — the only dark continent that remains on the map of the world — is the only thing left over that is still relatively "unknown." There's still more to be discovered.

噓と思ふならそれでいい、要するに恋がアフリカなのだ。人生は次第にその神秘を失つて来たが、ただ恋愛だけが、世界地図のうへにのこつたただ一つの暗黒大陸アフリカのやうに、未だ幾分の「未知」をのこしてゐるのだ。探検の余地があるのだ。("Koi to Afurika" 122-23)

What sustains the expression "love is Africa" is the fact that both elements are in their own way "unknowns" in the world and therefore, in principle, contain aspects that are still "to be discovered." Therefore, according to Abe, the relationship between emotion and intellect simply transitions to a relationship of domination : of male/female, and of civilized/savage. Novels of intellectualists manifest desires towards sexuality and ethnicity, and ultimately give birth to the paradox that is depictions of characters dominated by emotions.

In this novel, you can also find the expression "woman is Negro." The setting of the story is always a regional city in Japan and all characters are Japanese, so the abruptness of an expression like "love is Africa," or "woman is Negro" is quite indelible. However, this particular point was not a problem for Japan of the 1930s, the reason being that, a foundation of explicit exoticism in Japanese modernist literature already existed by this point and was dominating culture in the tri-partite form of erotic, grotesque, nonsense. Therefore, it was nothing particularly out of the ordinary (Silverberg 227-30).

In the novel *Koi to Afurika*, "Africa," "savage," and "beauty" all coexist. And the collection of short stories is a succession of exoticisms, as it were, and the connection between "Africa" and "Japan" becomes a less obscure one. This is the result of hunter/beast movies and information about African-American dancers being tied together in the same period. This attention towards "savage beauty" was not a phenomenon seen in avant-garde movements such as Dadaism or Surrealism alone. It was an element that can be found in the *ero-guro-nansensu* that prevailed throughout Japanese *modanizumu* in its entirety. In the period that Abe published *Koi to Afurika*, the latest literary trend of thought in the West concerned non-Western exoticism, and that information was then brought into the realm of Shōwa *Modan*. You could say that Abe was well attuned to these states of affairs, which he reflected in his novels.

3. Overlapping Images of Shanghai and Harbin

Paris was too far to visit for the regular Japanese modernist, so they sought out the cities closer to home. Shanghai was already famous as a modernized metropolis, full of "Western" and erotic, grotesque atmosphere (Driscoll 182-91), but, in the early Shōwa period, much attention was also paid to Harbin in northeast China as another "Paris in the Orient." In February 1930, Shinchōsha organized a roundtable discussion on "Modanizumu Bungaku oyobi Seikatsu Hihan" [モダアニズム文学及び生活批判, Criticism of Modernist Literature and Life], which appeared in the magazine, *Shinchō*.

Such was the extent of topics that the discussion covered. Needless to say, European and American imports, like literary, musical, and filmic works, as well as imports relating to lifestyle, like café culture, bobbed hair, and free love, and all received attention at this discussion. The focus of this paper, however, is the position and relation between Japan and East Asian culture in the Western-inspired modern age. In light of this, attention should be drawn to the following dialogue that transpired towards the end of the discussion :

> Okada : Isn't it good the way the women in China walk around wearing pants.
>
> Yoshiya : In Shanghai they have bobbed hair and wear military caps like officers.
>
> Nakamura : Nii-san, you've been to Harbin, haven't you? In a place like that with no traditions, surely they would have a grasp on *modan* trends?
>
> Nii : At any rate, Shanghai is an absurd place, so it's probably easy to do anything you want there.

岡田。支那の女のパンツを穿いて歩いて居るのはいゝですね。

吉屋。上海なんかでも士官のやうに断髪して軍帽を被つて居るのがありますが……。

中村。新居さんはハルピン位まで行つたんでせう。あゝいふ伝統を持たない所にはモダンのはしりがあるでせう。

新居。兎に角、上海なんかは無茶苦茶にやられるから、やり易いでせうね。(Nakamura, et al. 146)

Nakamura Murao (中村武羅夫), who prompts Nii Itaru, "Nii-san, you've been to Harbin, haven't you?" was not only the editor of the magazine *Shinchō*, but also involved with writing literature, formulating criticism, and forming literary groups as a central figure in the rise of *modanizumu* literature in Japan. All the participants in the discussion, including Nakamura, seemed to broach on the topic of Harbin and Shanghai as places of "*modan* trends" and "no traditions." The conversation was sparked by Yoshiya Nobuko (吉屋信子) stating, "The *modan* that I have come to understand, largely concerns women across America and all of Europe becoming more like men," and the closest example of this tendency that the reference is not of the Japanese women in Ginza or Asakusa, but of the Chinese women in Harbin and Shanghai.

Also of great interest is the subtle divergence in the dialogue between Nakamura Murao and Nii Itaru regarding the modern cities. In the second half of the quote, Nakamura raises Nii's experience of Harbin, prompting his response to the expression, "*modan*." Nii responds instead by referring to Shanghai. Nii Itaru was a critic who is scarcely paid heed today. However, he was a strong supporter of the anarchist movement, as well as being credited for coining the terms "mobo" [モボ, modern boy] and "moga" [モガ, modern girl]. His body of work also includes the Japanese translations of Pearl S. Buck's *The Good Earth* and John Steinbeck's *The Grapes of Wrath*, and his rise to the position of Mayor of Suginami Ward in Tokyo following the end of World War II.

In 1929, he set out for the Chinese mainland, in a sense, in search of the ideal *modan gāru*. Nii Itaru toured China from August to September 1929. Going from Tokyo across the Kanmon Straits, crossing over to Dalian by boat, and after stopping by areas such as Lushuko, Andong and Mukden, arrived in Harbin at the end of August. He also made visits to Beijing and Shanghai. Travelers who joined him along the way changed with each place he visited, and such company included Horiguchi Kumaichi (堀口九萬一), Yamada Kazuo (山田一雄), and Katō Takeo (加藤武雄).

His impressions of the women he met in Shanghai were often clear departures from those of the women he had met elsewhere. The following are two quotes from the article "Chukaminkoku no Onna" [中華民国の女, Women of China], which appeared in *Machi no Hōbutsusen* [街の抛物線, City Parabola].

> Walking the streets of Shanghai, I saw many new women strutting around stocking-less with bobbed hair. They wore their collars high in the fashionable way. They held their posture straight as they walked. The latest Western trends have been appropriately incorporated into Chinese women's fashion. China's modern women are worth keeping an eye on in the future. Moreover, they seem wonderfully practical. That's why I found them so fascinating.

私は上海の街を歩いて、断髪は愚かスタツキングレスで闊歩する幾多の新女性を見た。彼女等の襟はハイカラの如く高くし。垂直の姿勢で歩いてゐた。支那の婦人服に洋服の新流行を適当に合体させてゐる。支那の近代女性はたしかに将来注目すべき存在だ。それに彼女等は素晴らしく実行的である。それだから面白いのだ。(347-48)

Sometimes I give lectures at the Lida Academy in Jiangwan in the outskirts of Shanghai. I have given lectures at the academy in front of Laodong University students and Lida Academy students. They have a free, utterly free, academic style, and it was because of this very environment that I was able to speak whatever I liked without restriction. But that's insignificant. I will never forget the sagacious young female students I saw as I glanced around the room from my rostrum, and seeing their eyes so full of courage. My strongest impression of the women in China that I want to relay is their eyes, or to be more specific, their eyes so forged with intent, emotion, and ideology.

わたしは上海郊外の江湾にある立達学園の講壇に立つことがある。その学園で労働大学の学生と立達学園の学生とを前にして講説したことがある。自由、きわめて自由な学風で、そこでこそ私は何等の拘束なくして喋べることが出来た。が、そんなことはどうでもいい。わたしはそのとき演壇から瞥見した若き女学生達のさかしくも亦勇気のありさうな瞳を忘れることが出来ない。わたしが支那の女の感想として最も印象的でありうるのは全く彼女たちの瞳であること、もつとハツキリ云へば、彼女たちの瞳に含まれた意思・感情・思想から晶形されたそれだと云ひたいのである。(350)

Nii Itaru paid attention to the outfits of the Chinese women walking around Shanghai. The appearance of these women walking the streets without stockings and their collars raised was a fresh sight to a *modan gāru* critic, Nii Itaru. He was also impressed by their skillfulness to "appropriately incorporate" the "latest Western trends" in fashion. Furthermore, he found Shanghai's "female students" to be intellectual and full of confidence, and their "free, utterly free" atmosphere aligned with his ideal *modan gāru* that he searched for. However, Nii simply felt a freshness to their appearance — they did not become the focus of his attention. What Nii felt in Shanghai was the "anarchistic tinge" as evidenced by their "extreme joy in freedom and the independence of their actions" and the women's receptivity to that type of atmosphere.

The local newspaper *Manshū Nippō* [満洲日報, Manchuria Daily Newspaper] was the first to report on the situation in the area at the time, and it was here that Nii revealed his initial impressions of Harbin :

> I walked through Kitajskaya numerous times. I prefer more Occidental places, so I didn't quite grasp just how much I would enjoy walking around the streets here more than in Ginza in Tokyo. I especially loved the hotels and the modern-ness. I also enjoyed all the vestige of a Russian city that Harbin maintained. But these are just common observations. I also came to like the elegance of Majiagou. What was unfortunate, however, was all the Chinese soldiers coming in from Jilin, frequently being violent, so now there are very few beautiful Russian girls walking around outside and playing in the sun. If only I had visited before it got this way, I would have been able to see all the Russian women moving

around so pleasant and carefree.

キタイスカヤ街もわたしは幾度となく散歩した。わたしの好みはオクシデンタルなところにあるが故に、その街での遊歩は東京の銀座よりもどれだけすきになれたか分からなかつた。取分けオテル、モデルンのあたりを愛した。わたしはハルピンのもつロシヤ都市の面影がとにも角にもうれしいものだつたのだ。だがこんな観察はあまりにも月並みであるにちがひなからう。馬家溝あたりの風趣もすきになれた。たゞ残念なことには吉林から入り込んだ支那兵が頻々として乱暴をするとかで、ロシアの綺麗な娘たちが外光を浴びて楽しんで散歩するその姿が著るしく減つてゐると云ふことだつた。さうでないときに訪れられたら、どんなにか、快適に且つ彩麗に動くでもあらうロシア女の情景がスナツプアツプ出来たであらうと云ふことだつた。(2)

The first thing to jump out at Nii during his time in Harbin was the Western-ness of Kitajskaya. He points out that the "Occidental" atmosphere far surpasses that of "Ginza in Tokyo" and you can see evidence that he thoroughly enjoyed his time in this modern city of the Chinese mainland. On the other hand, you can see his lamentation at the absence of "beautiful Russian girls" gracing the streets because of the "violent" behavior of the "Chinese soldiers." Tens of thousands of white Russians who migrated to Harbin in the 1920s following the revolution found themselves caught between conflicting demands of the Chinese and Soviet governments. It was perhaps because of this political instability that Nii did not get to "see all the Russian women moving around so pleasant and carefree".

In his "Harupin" [ハルピン, "Harbin"] that appears in *Kindai Seikatsu* [近代生活, Modern Life, 1929], Kato Takeo describes, "Amongst the dancers there was one that he said resembled Greta Garbo, so Nii-kun must have really taken a liking to her" (46).[2] What is interesting is the fact that the city of Harbin is being discussed symbolically through the relationship between "the city of the day" and "the women of the night." The attention of both is drawn to areas that have an air of the West to them more than the cities in Japan. But at the same time, their interest in the city becomes linked to the women who live there and the flesh of these women. The women who lived in Harbin were more Western than the Western-fashion-wearing *modan gāru* in Japan. And even though it may have fit with the *ero-guro-nansensu* trend at the time, it was still a distant stretch from Nii's ideal *modan gāru.*

4. Politics of the Gaze

Japanese writers who wrote about their experiences in Harbin were greatly attracted by the modern/Westernized women in Harbin, especially the immigrant women from Russia, because of the modernity they represented. Japanese writers admired the bourgeois women of Russia for their highly Westernized lifestyle. Paradoxically, however, they regarded the Russian dancers in cabarets as a symbol of degeneration in Western culture. To take some examples, Kiyozawa Kiyoshi (清沢洌), the author of *Modan Gāru* [モダンガー

2 "踊り子の中の一人を、グレタ・ガルボオに似てゐるといふので、新居君は大変気に入つたらしい" (46).

ル, Modern Girl] (1926), described the Japanese modern/Westernized women, contrasting them with modernized women in Harbin. Gunji Jirōmasa, who gained his reputation with his "modern girl" novels such as *Miss Nippon* [ミスニッポン, Miss Japan] (1930), visited Harbin and published *Harbin Onna* [ハルビン女, Harbin Woman] in 1932.

The romance plot between an Occidental/masculine colonizer and an Oriental/feminine colonized can often be seen in Western colonial texts. In the travelogues of Japanese writers, however, this plot is transformed into a romance between an Oriental/Japanese man and an Occidental/Russian woman. Their romance assigns him "the yellow man's burden" to save the woman from the degenerated world. Was such a trope a medium by which Imperial Japan tried to legitimatize the Japanese colonial occupation of Harbin?

Gunji Jirōmasa is almost forgotten today, but was hugely popular and influential in the 1930s. Focusing on two of his novels, his detective novel, "Ana – Odoriko Oruga Arurowa Jiken" [穴 — 踊子オルガ・アルロワ事件, The Hole – Orga Arlova's Case] (1931), and *Anna Orlova* (1939), I shall argue that these two novels are testimonies to mixed feelings on the part of Japanese writers towards Russian women in Harbin, and, more generally, towards the relationships between modernization/Westernization and colonialism.

It is worth noting that Harbin attracted many Japanese tourists in the early 20th century, especially through ad campaigns run by The South Manchuria Railway Company. Harbin developed into the "Paris in the Orient" through this company backed by Japanese colonial policies, and it was this company that helped to construct the Japanese puppet-state of Manchukuo in northeast China.

The South Manchuria Railway Company increased its capital and tried to expand the railroads into the northeast of China in the 1920s. With the expansion of its railroads, the company began to construct the cities along the railroads and aggressively advertise for Manchuria's development to the industrial companies located in Japan. Japanese people who lived in Harbin were also caught up with the trend. *Harbin Annai* [ハルビン案内, Harbin Guide Book] (1925) is filled with photographs that tried to give the Japanese readers the impression that Harbin was a "modern" city like European cities. In addition, this book gives a lot of information about Harbin, such as its climate, timetable from Japan, hotels, souvenirs, and Russian and Chinese phrases needed for travel. The book was published by Harubin Shōhin Chinretsukan [ハルビン商品陳列館, Harbin Goods Display Center], which issued a lot of booklets in order to attract factories and offices from Japan (Minchiello 56).

The more the Japanese people began to exploit Harbin, the less the power of Russian immigrant bourgeois society became, with some forced to live in poverty, abandoning their honor and wealth. Okuno Tamio described the state of these people in his travelogue *Harbin Yowa* [ハルピン夜話, The Night of Harbin] (1923). His interest, however, was shown in places such as cabarets or striptease parlors. He paid particular attention to the Russian women who worked as striptease performers and prostitutes. Kiyozawa Kiyoshi also compared Russian prostitutes in Harbin with Japanese prostitutes in *Modan Gāru*. At that time, Harbin was represented as one of the most exotic and sexualized cities in the Orient.

It was important for Japanese men to meet Russian modern/Westernized women. Their exoticism had a lot to do with Japanese men's inferiority complex as well as their admiration of the Occident. Because of their inferiority complex, Japanese men wanted to conquer and appropriate the Occident, if not in reality, then at least through narrative. This is part of the reason why Japanese men saw the Russian women in ambivalent ways. On the one hand, Russian women were degenerated, like striptease performers and prostitutes; on the other hand, they were still noble aristocrats before the Russian Revolution. When a Japanese man spent a night with a Russian prostitute, he became a Westernized Oriental gentleman, and he felt superior to the Occident through such an interpretation.

These images aroused Japanese modernists' imagination. Gunji Jirōmasa visited Harbin and wrote a detective novel, "Ana – Odoriko Oruga Arurowa Jiken." In the novel, Orga Arlova was a dancer who moved from Shanghai. Her father, a Chinese man, was killed by the Jewish manager. Though her fiancé knew who the murderer was, he could not speak and was later arrested as the murderer. A Japanese tourist, the protagonist of the novel, meets Orga in this situation. He happens to know the truth when he finds a hole in a wall of her room and a drawing of the murderer. But he does not tell the truth to the police and leaves Harbin with Orga.

Orga Arlova represents the politics of sexuality and ethnicity in Harbin at that time. She is exposed to the gaze of men in the cabaret as well as in her room. The men who are watching her are Chinese, Jewish, Russian, and Japanese. So, if we think about this story from another point of view, we can say that this story is a geopolitical allegory of that time. At first, a Jewish man killed a Chinese man in order to get the hybrid (Russian and Chinese) body. And a Russian, who is arrested, relinquishes his control over the body, leaving a Japanese to take priority in the end.

This reflected the political situation in Harbin. The expansion of the South Manchurian Railway Company accelerated the cultural hybridity in Harbin. A lot of people, Japanese, Chinese, Russian, Jewish, French, German, and so forth, gathered there. They were bureaucrats, tourists, journalists, businessmen, laborers, beggars, prostitutes, and so on. This kind of cultural hybridity is made up of a combination of images such as "savage," "grotesque," and "mysterious." In the novel "Ana – Odoriko Oruga Arurowa Jiken." the politics of the gaze represents the colonial desire of the Japanese Empire. When we see the aesthetics of degeneration in this novel and travelogues with the geopolitical context during the 1920s to 1930s, they show us the politics of Empire.

5. Yellow Man's Burden

Harbin, another "Paris in the Orient," was where the West and the East met, and was also the place where capitalism and communism, in other words, the Western world and the Eastern world, met. In Gunji Jirōmasa's first short novel, "Puroretaria" [プロレタリア, The Proletariat] (1930), the proletarians in the story were not the people of Japan but of the Soviet Union and of China. That is, Gunji Jirōmasa was drawing on the proletarian people from Russia who aimed at class solidarity, overcoming racial differences in "Puroretaria" at almost the same time as he was representing Harbin as an Occidentalized, exotic bourgeois/degenerated culture in "Ana – Odoriko

Oruga Arurowa Jiken." Harbin as a city where the proletariat from all nations gathered against bourgeois, and Harbin as a degenerate city of bourgeois decadence.

The same kind of contradiction can be found in Gunji Jirōmasa's travelogue, *Harbin Onna* (1932), in which he describes his escape from Harbin with a woman named Anna Orlova when the war began on September 18, 1931. He went on to write a novel in English based on this experience, called *Anna Orlova : No Gun and No Soul.* Interestingly, in this case, the author's name is O'hara Juni, and Gunji appears as the publishing agent for the book. What is more, we can find only the third limited edition in Japan, which tells the readers that this book was first printed in Shanghai and since second in Tokyo.

A summary of the plot of *Anna Orlova* is as follows. A British businessman named John Harvard comes to Harbin from Shanghai for an enterprise expansion, where he meets a Russian woman, Anna Orlova, who lives and works in the city as a dancer. Although she was engaged to a Russian migrant named Alexander Ivanovich, she marries John Harvard to gain economic standing. The timeline overlaps with the Soviet army's march towards Manchuria, and John Harvard surrounds his estate with a fence to try and protect the woman from Russia under the British national flag. While Alexander Ivanovich works as a laborer making the fence to earn his daily living, he is getting tired of waiting for the arrival of the Soviet army. Before long, the Soviet army invades the estate of John Harvard and also brings about the whereabouts of the love-triangle between the three (John, Anna, and Alexander) following the death of Alexander Ivanovich. John Harvard and Anna Orlova then decide to leave for Spain.

A love triangle between a British man, a Russian woman, and a Russian proletariat man can be taken as an allegory of the complicated relationship between Capitalism, Harbin, and Communism. Anna Orlova holds contradictory positions because she, while being an Eastern woman, is also highly Westernized, that is, modernized, hence, a "degenerate" woman. The contradictory positions Anna Orlova occupies are equivalent to the paradoxical geo-political meanings of Harbin; Harbin, as the "Paris in the Orient" might look like the Occident, yet even so, from a Euro-centric point of view (which most Japanese writers shared), it was still in the "Far-East." In short, Anna Orlova, as well as Harbin, provokes desire and anxiety precisely because they cannot be defined by any clear-cut binary oppositions, like communism vs. capitalism, or the East vs. the West. Rather, they cross the border between the East and the West, embodying the hybrid nature of modernity.

The element of proletarian literature is inherent also in *Anna Orlova*. Anna Orlova goes back to Alexander Ivanovich in the Soviet Union later in the novel. Her decision is told like this : "If I go to the Soviet, it will be to take Alexander's hand as a friend, and not as a lover" (181). That is, she shows a class consciousness that is stronger than the feeling of love. Possibly, Gunji Jirōmasa needed to advertise the possibility of such class solidarity to the reader, and wrote this novel in English to escape censorship by the Japanese Government.

Alexander Ivanovich died in the battle between the Soviet army and the Chinese army, and the love between Alexander Ivanovich and Anna Orlova, as well as their comrade-friendship, died. John Harvard heard about Ivanovich's death and then concluded the relationship between Alexander Ivanovich, Anna Orlova, and himself as follows :

> But Bill, it's not a good idea to see him as an individual. To my conception he represents modern thought, which trends toward Communism, while I represent Capitalism. Don't you see, Bill? I have no regrets over that loss, in(s)tead I am glad to realize the fact that Capitalism still has some power; and I also possess the power to win her. (244)

Without doubt, John Harvard trusted in the power of capitalism. Then, is the text simply celebrating the victory of capitalism over communism? The writer seems to challenge the power of capitalism. John Harvard's estate was occupied by the Soviet — symbolically, the British supremacy was violated. The inviolability as a British territory did not function, and his enterprise ended with failure. He survived, unlike Alexander Ivanovich who participated in the battle. In this sense, John Harvard won in the eternal triangle involving Anna Orlova, but he lost almost everything. Not wanting to admit his defeat, he says, "I am glad to realize the fact that Capitalism still has some power."

Furthermore, after the conversation, the writer goes on to write, "What pity — yet, this may be the struggle of present mankind" (244). This means that the suffering of the democracy was not the confrontation of capitalism and communism, but the suffering of a person put and required to select the position between both intervals. That is, "modern thought" can be read as the period when the boundary of capitalism and communism becomes vague and confusing.

It is significant that in the love triangle of the novel, Japanese men have no space to occupy. In the case of "Ana – Odoriko Oruga Arurowa Jiken," a novel written in Japanese for Japanese readers, a Japanese narrator in the novel acts as an agency of the writer's, or more generally, a Japanese man's desire and anxiety towards a hybrid, modernized/Westernized woman in Harbin. As I have argued, the plot of the novel in which a Japanese man "occupies" and "conquers" a Russian woman, driving a Jewish, a Chinese, and a Russian man away from her, can be read as an allegory of Japanese colonial desire for Harbin. Yet in the case of *Anna Orlova*, things are much more complicated, for there are no Japanese men playing significant roles in the love triangle story.

You can regard these novels as the case of Japanese appropriation of the classical Orientalist stories. As with most forms of appropriation, it must depend on the basic formula of the original — "good, white, bourgeois man from the West" saves, loves, and is loved by "native" woman. In the case of "Ana – Odoriko Oruga Arurowa Jiken," a Japanese man takes the "white man's burden" and privilege upon his shoulders. In the case of *Anna Orlova*, however, the role of the reliever is given to John Harvard, a British, bourgeois man, following the classical Orientalist romance stories more faithfully. Japanese man cannot be, after all, an Occidental/masculine colonizer who is beloved by an Oriental/feminine colonized, as the novel seems to imply.

The hybrid nature of modernity represented by Anna Orlova and Harbin, and the author's identity as a Japanese, Westernized modernist, complicate the situation further. As a modernized/Westernized woman, she is, while being an embodiment of the "degenerate," terminal condition of capitalism, also the "barbarous" East. If she had been a "pure," "native" woman, uncontaminated by Western influences, love between her and John Harvard would have been a straightforward Orientalist romance between an Occidental/masculine colonizer and an Oriental/feminine colonized. As with Anna, the author, Gunji Jirōmasa, a Japanese modernist, is a monstrous hybrid of modernity/ Westernization — he is, at least on the level of culture and tastes, "colonized" by Western modernity, and he knows all too well that he is not allowed a space to occupy in a romance plot between an Occidental/masculine colonizer and an Oriental/feminine colonized.

The story "Ana – Odoriko Arurowa Jiken" is narrated by a Japanese for a Japanese readership that symbolizes the author's, and the entire Japanese male population's, desire for Western women. The story ends with the Japanese man getting ready to depart on a journey with the mixed Western/Eastern figure, Orga Arlova. However, at the end he verbalizes his doubts of his being with her. The point that the victor imitating a Western viewpoint arrives at is the impossibility to imitate a tale of a Western victor. In *Anna Orlova* this impossibility can be seen in the relationship between the characters and the author. A *Modan* novelist, Gunji Jirōmasa, well understood what Orientalism was. So he realized how comical it would be to novelize a story for Western readership about a Japanese Oriental protagonist caught in a love triangle with a Russian. Accompanying the full-length novel at the end is also the short story, "The Paris of the Orient." Here a Japanese character finally appears. However, this is more about the appearance of an Oriental character to guarantee Orientalism in the full-length novel — there is no expectation on the character to play the protagonist of a romance story.

6. Conclusion

Within the current of *Shōwa Modan* cities like Harbin and Shanghai aroused the imagination of Japanese literature, and the Japanese modernist writers tried to create a new style with their own interpretation and translation of the cultural others. While the Japanese modernist writers absorbed the aesthetics and politics of Orientalism in terms of "modernization," the frameworks, such as the West/non-West, the Occident/Orient, the civilized/savage, capitalism/communism, overlap and cross their borders, amplify and overlap the contradiction or the ambivalent identity of Japanese imperialism through the process of translating Western exoticisms into a Japanese context. From this viewpoint, it can be said that "modan" signifies the encounters of the East and West in the geographical and political sense, and modernist literature represents that struggle that took place on the cultural-political stage in East Asia. This is, I think, modernism in Japan, and could be modernism itself.

Works Cited

Abe, Tomoji [阿部知二], "Koi to Afurika" [Love and Africa : A Tenor's Tale, 恋とアフリカ – 或るテノールの話], *Koi to Afurica* [Love and Africa, 恋とアフリカ], Kōseikakusyoten [厚生閣書店], 1930.

__________________, *Shuchiteki Bungakuron* [Intellectualism in Literature, 主知的文学論], Kōseikakusyoten [厚生閣書店], 1930.

Clifford, James, *The Predicament of Culture : Twentieth-Century Ethnography, Literature, and Art*. Harvard UP, 1988.

Driscoll, Mark, *Absolute Erotic, Absolute Grotesque : The Living, Dead, in Japan's Imperialism, 1895-1945*, Duke UP, 2010.

Gunji, Jirōmasa [群司次郎正], "Ana – Odoriko Oruga Arurowa Jiken" [The Hole : Orga Arlova's Case, 穴 – 踊子オルガ・アルロワ事件], *Shinseinen* [New Young Men, 新青年], vol. 12, no. 16, 1931.

Kato Takeo [加藤武雄], "Harupin" [Harbin, ハルピン], *Kindai Seikatsu* [Modern Life, 近代生活], vol. 1, no. 18, 1929.

Lippit, Seiji M., *Topographies of Japanese Modernism*, Columbia UP, 2002.

Minichiello, Sharon A., editor. *Japan's Competing Modernities : Issues in Culture and Democracy 1900-1930*, U of Hawaii P, 1998.

Nakamura, Murao [中村武羅夫], et al. "Modanizumu Bungaku oyobi Seikatsu Hihan" [Criticism of Modernist Literature and Life, モダアニズム文学及び生活批判], *Shinchō* [New Tide, 新潮], vol. 27, no. 2, 1930.

Nii, Itaru [新居格], "Chūkaminkoku no Onna" [Women of China, 中華民国の女], *Machi no Houbutsusen* [City Parabola, 街の抛物線], Sentansha [尖端社], 1931.

______________, "Harubin nite" [A Letter from Harbin, ハルビンにて], *Manshū Nippō* [Manchuria Daily Newspaper, 満洲日報], 9 Sept. 1929.

O'hara, Juni, *Anna Orlova : No Gun and No Soul*, 3rd limited ed., Curran, Lea & Co., 1939.

Ōya, Sōichi [大宅壮一], "Kindaishakai Shoku" [The Color of Modern Society, 近代社会色], *Mainichi Nenkan* [Mainichi Annual, 毎日年鑑], Mainichi Shinbunsha [毎日新聞社], 1932.

Peng, Hsiao-yen, *Dandyism and Transcultural Modernity : The Dandy, the Flâneur, and the Translator in 1930s Shanghai, Tokyo, and Paris*, Routledge, 2010.

Silverberg, Miriam, *Erotic Grotesque Nonsense : The Mass Culture of Japanese Modern Times*, U of

California P, 2006.

Thorneber, Karen Laura, *Empire of Texts in Motion : Chinese, Korean, and Taiwanese Transculturations of Japanese Literature*, Harvard UP, 2009.

Tierney, Robert Thomas, *Tropics of Savagery : The Culture of Japanese Empire in Comparative Frame*, U of California P, 2010.

Study on Kim Kirim's Surrealism and Modernism

Jin-hee Kim (Ewha Womans University)

1. Issues of Kim Kirim's Modernism and Surrealism

Kim Kirim, an English literature scholar, a literary critic, and a poet of standing in the history of Korean Poetry, established a modernist poetics that responded to the new modern, civil society, and the fact that he simultaneously produced creative works was acknowledged for its significance. Kim Kirim's poetics and works of poetry were discussed through the viewpoints and notions of imagism, intellectualism, avant-gardism, futurism, surrealism, and so on within the framework of modernism, and especially what was at the center of intellectualism in the early 1930s, as compared to English/American-modernism.

This paper focuses on surrealist literary criticism, as it was the basis for Kim Kirim's intellectualism of the early 1930s. Compared to preexisting studies, where surrealist theory has been dealt with one-dimensionally, I plan to expand it into poetics, and discuss it as a foundation for intellectual methodology. Furthermore, I plan to consider the "intellectual methodology centered on English/American modernism in the existing studies and expand it into surrealism. Moreover, in the comparative studies with Japan, and based on the the decision made by Japanese literary historians that the literary tendency of *Shi to Shiron* [詩と詩論], which became the birthplace of intellectualist theory, was surrealism, I would like to understand the circumstances of Japanese Surrealism in the 1920s and further look into the relation with intellectual literary theory. Along with the process of such argument, I would also like to study the correlation between 'perspective' of Kim Kirim's literary theory and surrealism. This demonstrates that Kim Kirim's modernism was created through the Japanese modernist discourse, hence indicating a need to identify the mainstream of Japanese modernism between the end of the 1920s and the end of the 1930s.

According to Kim Kirim's literary theory, surrealism had a significant degree of influence, yet a detailed study has not been done. He deals with surrealism in many of his writings, from those specifically on surrealism, to analyzing works and writings that establish standards for evaluation or the comparative value of decision making, and from a simple mention to a detailed explanation. This in turn shows that surrealism functions as the foundation of his literary theory. Yet, the reason why research on surrealism has not advanced is that Kim Kirim himself repeatedly emphasized that the point to highlight in surrealism is "the description" of poetry. Kim emphasizes the virtue of surrealism in the position of modern poetry, and this made possible the evaluation that Kim understood surrealism as technique of poems on a limited, superficial level. Second, the fact that Kim Kirim is a scholar of English literature and that he developed a modernist poetics are related to the fact that the evaluation of Kim's overall literature work continued with an English/American modernist focus. Therefore, the understanding of such a research situation allows for the possibility of reconsidering the evaluation that claims Kim Kirim only understands the spirit of surrealism or its ideas on the surface level, that he only partially uses its methodology, and that due to his lack of understanding of the traditions and historicity, he does not fully recognize the key to English·American modernism.

Accordingly, in this paper I look into Kim Kirim's surrealism with a broad perspective over poetics in general and with delicacy. Kim Kirim applies his literary theory of surrealism in both poetic theory and poetry, and in this article, I will examine its correlation with surrealism, centered on the intellectual methodology. Moreover, since the term "intellectual" was introduced through Japan, I will discuss the distinct characteristics of the reception English/American modernism as well as the difference between the reception in Japan and in Korea : in other words, I will discuss on the distinctive characteristics of Kim Kirim's modernist theory. In such comparative understandings, a poetics methodology due to Kim Kirim's attitude concerning perspective would be much clearer and have literary historical significance.

2. Surrealism of Japanese Poetic Circles in 1920s

After the mid-1920s, surrealism took over Japanese poetic circles. When Nishiwaki Junzaburo (西脇順三郎) came back after finishing his studies in the United Kingdom in 1925 and started teaching at Keio University (慶應

大學校), European Dadaism and Surrealism became a trend. Moreover, in the same year Horiguchi Daigaku published a translated collection of poems called *Gekka-no-Ichigun* [*Crowd Under the Moon*, 月下の一群]. In this book, he included surrealist works of Philippe Soupault, Guillaume Apollinaire, and Yvan Goll. Since the introduction of Paul Éluard in the magazine *Bungei-tanbi* [文藝耽美, 1927], many writings on surrealist writers such as Louis Aragon, André Breton, Robert Desonos, and so on were written. After going through a partial introductory period, writers created a surrealist poetry magazine on their own, developing Japanese surrealism, and magazines such as *Bara, Majutsu, Gakusetsu* [*Rose, Magic, and Discourse*, 薔薇魔術學說] and *Fukuiku Taru Kafu Yo* [A deep scent of man who lights a fire, 馥郁タル火夫ヨ] and so on were translated into English, and delivered to Louis Aragon and André Breton introducing the synchronism of Japanese surrealist poetry. In 1929 *Bara, Majutsu, Gakusetsu* and *Fukuiku Taru Kafu Yo* [馥郁タル火夫ヨ] were combined and published under the name *Isho No Taiyo* [*Sun of Costume*, 衣裳の太陽], and in 1928, some surrealist writers participated in the publication of *Shi to Shiron*.

If Western surrealism reflected an unstable consciousness after the First World War, it had the color of social resistance, Japanese Dadaism and surrealism could not receive such spirit. There was an affiliation of supernaturalism that centered on Nikiwaki Junzaburo, who accepted surrealism, and an affiliation of Takiguchi Shuzo (瀧口修造) that accommodated the surrealism of Breton, and especially poetics and poetic works centered on Nishiwaki's surrealism, as expanded by his students. They led a more religiously secluded life than André Breton, and they accepted the purity-transcendence viewpoint of the surrealist poet Pierre Reverdy, who broke relations with reality, and understood a pure form of poems that does not carry any realistic meaning as surrealism,(Sawa Masahiro, Wada Hirofumi ed.(1995), 5) and methodologically respected Yvan Goll's theory. In other words, they respected consciously complete thinking, and not expressions of dream or unconsciousness, as artistic activity :

> *Cerebrum ad acerram recidit* [the heart sinks into an incense box]. Reality is nothing more than the brain. The goal of surrealist art is to destroy this brain. All forms of noble art are surrealistic. Therefore, a noble poem is also a surrealist poem. A poem forms a vacuous desert in the brain and in it beats down all sensation, sentiments, and ideas that belong to experiences in reality, to squeeze the brain purely as on method. Here lies pure poetry. The brain becomes a glass-like thing of ultra-pink. Poems destroy the brain in such a way. The destroyed brain is fragrant, like a destroyed perfume bottle. Here is the honor of a perfume store. (Nishiwaki Junzaburo 1927)

In the preface to the poetry magazine *Fukuiku Taru Kafu Yo* [馥郁タル火夫ヨ], Nishiwaki Junzaburo understands the pure state where one cuts all ties with reality as the principle of surrealist poetics. The terms 'vacuous' and 'pure' symbolically reveal such understanding. Ueda Toshio (上田敏雄), who published the surrealist poetry magazine *Bara, Majutsu, Gakusetsu* also says that the surrealism of the time is related to pursuing infinite world of spirits through deliverance in the writing "Watashi-no Chougenjitsu Shugi" [我の超現實主義]. Such a tendency in understanding surrealism in the Japanese poetic world shares context with an understanding in Dadaism, surrealism's predecessor. As a major performer of Japanese Dadaism, Takahashi Shinkichi (高橋新吉) claimed that all denials conducted in Dadaism return to nullity (無) and that the world of nothingness is Dadaism and Zen [禪]. This is to give up on Dadaism's ultimate state with the "self" of reality and see it as a transcendent state(Yoshikawa Nagi 2015 : 75-80). Likewise, the European avant-garde that resisted existing social values and policies was received and understood as a method to break from all values of reality. This could be understood as a specific quality of Japanese culture that accepts Western culture.

Nishiwaki, the surrealist, would use the term "surrealism" without a problem and also use it in the title of the book of criticism, yet it had a strong reason that the term meant a revolutionary literature that rejects emotional romanticisms and goes against realism, and was different from the surrealism that André Breton argued for. Even though it was called surrealism, Nishiwaki did not have the tendency of respect for unconsciousness or dreams that Breton had, but was creating a surrealist world squeezing intellectual thoughts from a combination of images. His works seemed like they were a prose poetry that was automatically written but in fact it was intentionally accessed to discontinuous image. As it is apparent in the "Preface" quoted above, he uses such technique in the sentences like poetics and presented writings that was discontinuous and difficult to understand. Nishiwaki attempted to reveal his way of surrealism through such sentences and constructed his poetic works by confusing nature and supernatural, reality and unreal, and so on. Therefore, he created a surrealist relationship through contradictions, irony, and a combination of heterogeneous things, as the structure of poems. In this sense, Nishiwaki is not exactly a surrealist poet but is a theorist using techniques of modern intellectual poetry. He can be evaluated as a poet, yet in this sense he was positioned as a leader of the Japanese "new poetry movement" with an intellectual attitude in literary history.

By writing works that are intentionally difficult to understand, Nishiwaki led the way to intellectual work in composing poetry. In his theory of poetry he explained, "the major element of a poem is supernaturalness, surrealism, and the surrealism that Goll or Breton argues is not but a mental phenomenon. My 'theory of surrealism' is not Goll's particular theory nor Breton's. Rather it is nothing but a way to describe the principles of a common modern poetry." Nishiwaki emphasized that French surrealist theory was nothing more that an expression of supernatural and surreal minds; and this was the core to Nishiwaki's theory.

It is a meaningful point for Kim Kirim or Japanese literary circles that Nishiwaki pursued "the principle of modern poetry" through surrealism. The reason why Nishiwaki was able to become a major author for *Shi to Shiron* with the goal of "overthrowing the non-poetic rejection of the old poetic circle, and thereby demonstrate justly today's poésie" in 1928, was that first, his poetics, which was based on surrealism, was able to establish a fixed modern methodology of poetry or "poetics" in the contemporary poetic circles, and second, his surrealist poetics demonstrated the point at which the process of creating order and combination of heterogeneous language, as a creative methodology for surrealism, and the intellectual methods in English·American modernism came together. These characteristics showed the difficulties of writing surrealist poems, in other words, the problem of internal structure of limited problems of language.

Mita Bungaku [三田文学], which was republished in year 15 of the Daisho Period, had Seiichirō Katsumoto (勝本清一郎) as the editor and new modernism authors that were called "Shin Mita Ha" (新三田派), such as Kuno Toyohito (久野豊彦), Rryūtanji Yū (龍膽寺雄), and Hara Keiichiro (原奎一郎), made their appearance. Ueda Toshio (上田敏雄) was the only one diligently presenting his poems in the magazine, and Nishiwaki seemed to write many articles that explained (補遺) "Profanus," yet from September of year 3 of the Showa Period he presented his poetics and poetry works in every issue of *Shi to Shiron*. In it, surrealism is categorized under modernism, but at the same time similar magazines were published in different places rejoicing over modernism. The motive that arose centered on the magazine was creating a new poetics and new poetic style, but it was rare to see a start with a dramatic introduction of a new poetics. Thus, Nishiwaki's poetics on *Shi to Shiron* and the discussions of Haruyama Yukio were a rare occasion, but it can be said that it had an overflowing of modernist spirit by year 5 of Showa, in the sense that it rejected existing literature and created revolutionary works. (Sato Saku 1928.12)

We are able to see how meaningful modernism was in the late 1920s and the status of surrealism through the writing that includes surrealism and the above quote that demonstrate the literary circle's situation of the time. "Shin Mita Ha" (新三田派), which was introduced at the beginning of the above quote, refers to the literary circles or a group of new artistic circles that arose arguing for the artistry and the autonomy of literature, responding to the political utilitarianism of Marxists literature. The fact that this literary circle introduces the contemporary Western modernist poetry as an "emerging poetry circle" makes surrealists an emerging arts school as well, and in the viewpoint as stated in the quote "reject existing literature, and create revolutionary works," makes them modernists. In other words, 'modernism' was a term used widely in the process of creating new poetic theories and poetic styles in the contemporary Japanese literary circle.

Furthermore, *Shi to Shiron* was a magazine advocating surrealism in such a mood where it was organized as modernism that pursued new literature in the later years but it did not mean English/American modernism. Particularly, it claimed various poetic theories such as formalism, surrealism, futurism, dadaism, and so on, yet the basic direction was surrealism, and in later years it was organized as a modernist movement. Therefore, the term modernism was not used in their literature at the time.

It further implies that the surrealist literary theories of Abe Tomoji and Haruyama Yukio, which supported perspective and intellectual methodology and centered on *Shi to Shiron* in the mid- to late 1920s, were also in the context of surrealist literary theory.

3. Kim Kirim's Surrealism Theory

Kim Kirim entered his senior year of Meiku Junior High in Tokyo in the spring of 1925. Before he went on to college, he was in Japan, and he was admitted into the Arts College of Nihon University in the spring of 1926 and studied English literature and the arts. According to the memories of the alumni, the atmosphere of the Arts College in Nihon University was quite free. Moreover, due to the restoration after the Great Kanto Earthquake, popular culture grew socially, and it was full of life. Also, cultural movements in emerging arts were at their zenith. There were other universities, such as Meiji (明治), Chuo (中央), and Senshu (專修), around Nihon University and where he lived, creating a unique school district, including an old bookstore on Jimbocho (神保町). Kim Kirim was able to learn freely of movies, arts, as well as the emerging arts(Aoyagi Yuko2010 : 198-201). In this context, rather than claiming that Kim studied Japanese sources on surrealism and literary theories in Korea, we can say that he studied them directly within the changes and reception of the emerging arts while studying in Japan from the mid-1920s.

At the time of Kim's stay in Japan, Abe Jiro (阿部次郎) and Kikuchi Kan (菊池寛), who were both writers and critics as well as major figures in the journalism of a literary circle, were teaching (until 1926) in the Arts College at Nihon University, and professor Matsubara Kan (菊池寛) was teaching philosophy and aesthetics with a socialist background. The information on contemporary culture and literature, and of the literary circle that Abe Jiro and Kikuchi Kan provided, allowed Kim Kirim to actively accept the emerging arts and literature, including surrealism, and the influence of professor Matsubara Kan allowed Kim to question capitalism and the problems of class.

The literary theories that Kim Kirim presented in the early 1930s were based on surrealism in many ways, and he also produced many writings that specifically deal with surrealism. It is believed that he developed a good understanding of psychoanalysis and surrealism while studying abroad in the late 1920s. In the 1929 writing that he composed after he came back, he says that he deals with literary friends, surrealism, Dadaism, cubism, and so on. He then suggests that Seohae Choi's novel demonstrates the world of individual unconsciousness, and he later analyzes and evaluates this work in the viewpoint of stream of consciousness. He emphasizes, "though I do not quote Freud's psychoanalysis, it is the writer's subconsciousness, the words that come out from the world before consciousness; in other words, it is the true human words within the writer." We can see that Kim utilizes surrealism and psychoanalysis in the analysis and evaluation of literary works.

> Futurists today are feeling the glory in the mission as a loyal bandog under Mussolini's fascist nation, and Paul Valéry's pure poetry is so lonely that no one can approach it. The revolution of surrealism that was advocated by Lee Wan-gol, Breton, Soupault, and Aragon is nothing more than a succession of the interaction of self-destruction of Dadaism. (…) I should agree with the efforts that surrealism did not start and end in the destruction of Dadaism and attempted to reach to a new "poésie." As they have said, they have prayed to become a "stillness" of the century.[1]

In the chapter titled "The Tragedy of Surrealism," Kim Kirim acknowledges the methodology of poetry, in other words the significance of surrealism as a poésie, yet he criticizes the general status of the European avant-garde. This is related to a statement made about the same time, "I have never seen poetry

1 Kim Kirim [김기림], "Hyeondaeisiui Jeonmang, Sangatabui Biggeuk — Ssapoeseo Chohyeonilpakkaji" [Outlook of Modern Poetry. Tragedy of Ivory Tower — From Ssapo to surrealism, 현대시의 전망, 상아탑의 비극-싸포에서 초현실파까지], *Donga Ilbo* [동아일보], 1931.7.30-8.9.

standing outside the activities of live sensitivity and criticisms of reality." In other words, Kim understood the European avant-garde to have lost its resistant attitude toward reality, and criticized that they hadadapted to irrational reality and that they were unable to present productive solutions. Furthermore, he presents a writing that delves into surrealism.

> We cannot understand surrealism without an understanding of the perplexity and anxiety of the mental world according to the before and after condition of Europe. However, within surrealism, there is something you cannot gain from Dadaism. That itself distinguishes the two and adds the significance of the former as the developed version of the latter. What I mean by 'that' is nothing more than the motivation in order. This in turn creates surrealism as the revolutionary methodology of modern poetry. Surrealism as a psychological movement has already lost the grounds for its existence of the times and society. Yet, the impression surrealism left as a poetic methodology is very apparent. Though we do not follow it as it is but the direction that it teaches is mostly developed within the new poems of today. What I am stating here today is not the extinct surrealism as as a psychological movement, but surrealism as a methodology that had decisive influence and allusion over the development of the form of poetry. (...) Surrealists do not just seek for beautiful dreams. What is more, they are not buried in dreams, but they seek to explore the reality of dreams by mercilessly analyzing dreams and their essence. For such reasons, surrealism has a side that encounters realism when observed.[2]

2 Kim Kirim [김기림], "Hyeondaesiui Baljeon" [Development of Modern Poetry, 현대시의 발전], *Chosun Ilbo* [조선일보], 1934. 7.12-22.

This writing is divided into short chapters titled "Dream," "Beauty and Hideousness," "Surreal," "Automatic Writing," "Language," "Beauty of Form," "Metaphysics," and so on exploring "Surrealist Methodology" connecting it to poetry. In this writing Kim Kirim asserts that we cannot understand surrealism without understanding the perplexity and anxiety of Western mental world post World War I, yet it has lost its significance of spirituality that connects surrealism with its times since the timely, and social situations where surrealism originates, have changed. However, he emphasizes that internal power as a revolutionary methodology of the arts lies in surrealism. Additionally, the foundation of such power is "the motivation of order," and share similar characteristics with Dadaism on the point that it tries to reject and deconstruct the existing arts and customs, and social value. Kim Kirim takes notice of the language technique, and the mechanism that orders the field of unconsciousness and emotions in surrealism, and this is an important point in the aspect that it expands its understanding in the methodology of modern poetry.

Automatic Writing

Poems that have the surrealist world as their context should be based on entirely different techniques from the poetic techniques of the past. Thus, the famous Automatic Writing was devised as a corresponding method. It is attempting to record our dreams in the dream state in withthe most appropriate method. Therefore, hypnotic questions and answers are examined at times. In other words, surrealists try to capture the dream mechanism in the most precise

> and profound way through automatic writing. Surrealism attempts to analyze and reveal by delving into the world of the unconsciousness, the biggest secret of human beings, which is a very different approach from the previous symbolism, where a mysterious world was imagined incomprehensible, and careful implications and expression were made. (Ibid.)

Surrealism anticipated reaching a new understanding of human beings by exploring the human world of the unconsciousness that is veiled from reason and rationality. Therefore, they regarded the daydream, the state of being half-asleep, the state of hypnosis, and including the state of dreams that are in the middleground of the psyche as something important. This was so that they would not lose the potential possibility of the human psychology. For such goals, as Kim Kirim mentioned, an entirely different method of poetry from existing techniques must be pursued. What surrealists hoped to gain through automatic writing was to have human psychology completely recede from the outer world and listen to a potential voice that expresses the authenticity of the "self" that is to listen to a voice that cannot be heard by someone who uses language just as an exchange means with others. The reason behind seeking for such wonders and mysteries is that they believed that a certain aspect of the world that was ignored or unkown to human beings would be revealed through imagination and that artists should naturally figure out the new aspects of the world and share them with others to reform the world(Hwang Hyeon San 2012). Kim Kirim reads a completely different revolutionary value of surrealism from such attitudes of existing art :

The oscillation that "surrealism" impacted on the post-World War poetry (or all arts areas) was quite serious. Surrealists in fact overly suffered due to the consciousness of modern people, and had to cope with the concerns of modern intellectual hierarchy with their own bodies. When we stand in front of Salvador Dali's paintings our hair would stand on its end with horror due to the ghastly screams gushing out from them. Also, there times when we might just faint from the heavy despair left behind after reading or looking at their works. There are many pathological aspects that explain why their artworks do not acquire many friends, but on the one hand, it is because we do not have any knowledge or try to distinguish their concerns and refined emotions.[3]

In the paper that was presented in the late 1930s, Kim Kirim inquires deeply into the spiritual and artistic significance of surrealism. Kim claims that even though Western surrealism carries pathological aspects socially, what is more significant is that it was conscious of the tragic reality and despair of the times and that it tried to demonstrate this consciousness in the artworks. Yet, he understands that even with such significance, this was not widely known because their refined emotions and methodology were not understood. Through Kim's explanation, we can observe that he is evaluating surrealism on its ideological and spiritual significance as well as placing surrealism within the methodological evolution of art history. From such understanding, we can see that it is different from how the Japanese poetry circle comprehends surrealism. In other words, Kim's attitude of reading the

3 Kim Kirim [김기림], "Hyeondaewa Siui Reunesangseu" [Modernity And the Renaissance of Poetry, 현대와 시의 르네상스], *Chosun Ilbo* [조선일보], 1938.4.10.

"intellectual hierarchy" concerns of "reality" from surrealism is an emphasis of the social and political significance of surrealist arts.

André Breton in his work *Manifesto of Surrealism* explains surrealism as the following :

> Encyclopedic explanation. Surrealism philosophy is based on the faith of self-less effects of the superior reality and the omnipotence of dreams and thinking that is carried by a certain type of association form, which was ignored in the past. There is a tendency to solve important questions of life on behalf of them and definitively destroying and to definitively destroy all psychological tools of others. (André Breton 2012 : 90)

Breton emphasizes association forms and daydreams as new artistic principles on the one hand, and on the other emphasizes the importance of real life related to these things. Kim Kirim's theory of surrealism sufficiently acknowledges and reflects the ideological and philosophical direction that Breton emphasized. As mentioned, after World War I, surrealism, which was born from the overall disbelief and resistance of life and human understanding, with a basis of objective conditions of reality and ideological background, had a tendency to actually reform life conditions on the one hand, and on the other secured freedom of imagination to create new literature. That is to say there was an attempt to unify poetry in the form of literature and poetry in the form of survival. According to C.W.E. Bigsby, the author of *Dada and Surrealism*, "surrealism is not a shocking image, unreasonable passage, or dreamlike structure, for these are just means. Surrealism by essence is art that frees imagination and has interests in inflating justice in reality."

4. Surrealism as Methodology for Modern Poetry

> New poems of Chosun were unable to take the form of a poetry movement based on a unified poetics. What exists are individual experiments scattered about. Moreover, there are rarely any published poetics. (...) The one thing that can be said with confidence is that most poets assume surrealism as their standard point, or they move past it, or are a little shy of it, or are stopped within it. Yet, whether the individual poet is conscious of this or not, I believe that I can say such a thing phenomenologically. (...) There is no way that the young poets of our poetic circle, who grew always influenced by foreign poetic circles, would be entirely deaf to the trend of the most stimulating surrealism, and this is a purgatory of training that an apostle of poetry should pass through at least once.[4]

In the above passage, Kim Kirim states, "as a methodology of poems the footprints that surrealism left are very clear. Even if we do not follow its footsteps, the direction that it teaches are in most of today's new poems as they develop." Kim also emphasizes that the appearance of "new poems" in Chosun of those times are related together. He also explains that the movement of surrealist poetry in Chosun at the time was not collective as in Europe or Japan, but as Chosun's poetry circle was influenced in the trends of

4 Kim Kirim [김기림], "Hyeondaesiui Baljeon" [Development of Modern Poetry, 현대시의 발전]. *Chosun Ilbo* [조선일보]. 1934.7.12-22.

foreign poetry circles, the acceptance of surrealism was a natural thing. Furthermore, he evaluated surrealism as a "purgatory of training" that all apostles of poetry must go through, and this entails that the poets were aware of the importance of methodology and the critical mind that surrealism provided in language and technique, imagination and order. Kim Kirim positioned the contemporary works of Jeong Ji-yong, Jang Seo-un, Yi Sang, and Cho Byeok Am in such a trend, analyzing and evaluating them, and noticed that their works well 'ordered' emotions by using terms such as emotion, intelligence, sculpture, and so on. He applied and theorized the fact that surrealism and the development of modern poetry are closely connected to each other.

> Post World War poetry is actually largely indebted to psychoanalysis (rather than) to Mr. Freud. The belief that influence did not question borders had its hands on poetic circles around the world that were growing in global relation in material and immaterial form but was dominantly afftected. The five letters that spell Freud havas become a mandatory gate to enter the new postwar poetry. First, it provided a new area to the subjects of poems. Second, it brought revolution to technique of poems. Third, it brought a whole new philosophy to poetry. (…) What poetry gained from Freud after the war does not end in such technical implications. Glaring at the terrible causes that led to ugly result named modernity by looking back at the abyss of unconsciousness. In this sense, it was a severe criticism of modern civilization. (…) And so psychoanalysis provided theoretical basis to surrealism, one of the biggest literary movements of the 20th century.[5]

5 Kim Kirim [김기림], "Peuroideeuwa Hyeondae-si" [Freud and Modern Poetry, 프로이드와 현대시], *Inmunpyeongnon* [인문평론], 1939.11.

In the above excerpt that summarizes the influence of Freud and surrealism on modern poetry, Kim Kirim was able to present that, first, psychoanalysis provided a new area of human psychology, that is, the unconscious and dreams, to the subjects of poems, and, second, by introducing a revolutionary method to the technique of poetry in dealing with language, they were able to present new philosophies and principles to modern poetry. However, Kim Kirim takes a step further, exploring the sociocultural significance embedded in surrealism, and through this connects criticism of the arts and modern civilization of surrealism in the aspect that, through psychoanalysis, the causes for the ugly modern civilization can be recognized. In this sense, it suggests the key to understanding Kim Kirim's modern poetics in the early 1930s, the understandings of the techniques of poetry and criticism of civilization, the "revolution of ideas," and so on started from surrealism : [6]

> There were two challenges that the poems that deal with unconsciousness must had to face. One was that it should have universality if it was not simply the technology of a symptom . (…) What then depicts the world of unconsciousness is simply the modest realism of the past days. Yet, the issue is that the only change is the object of depiction. We cannot but help conscious-raising happening in order for the world of the unconsciousness to enter into the poetic enjoyment. In other words, conscious-raising should be delivered as meaning.[7]

6 Kim Kirim [김기림], "Siui Gisul, Inshik, Hyeonsil Deungui Jemunje" [Subjects of Description, Perception, Reality of Poetry, 시의 기술, 인식, 현실 등의 제문제], *Chosun Ilbo* [조선일보], 1931.2.11-14.

7 Kim Kirim [김기림], "Peuroideeuwa Hyeondae-si" [Freud and Modern Poetry, 프로이드와 현대시], *Inmunpyeongnon* [인문평론], 1939.11.

Kim Kirim argued that the zeitgeist, or the idea of the time, requests form as a conception process that is most adapted to it. The position also demonstrates the perception of surrealism being an embedded art form in the instability after World War I. Kim saw that in order for poetry to not be limited as simple techniques, it should hold universal meaning even if it started from individual management. Here, universality means relative universality, the recognition of ideology, zeitgeist or cultural level that applies to historical levels. He also found that attitude that only believes in the state of dreams can be sentimentalism that falls into subjectivity, and leaving poetry up to the emotions is therefore dangerous to do. Thus, we should overcome such apects within the restricted and planned order, and the aspect that raises such consciousness is emphasized as "clear intelligence."[8]

These are things that Kim has focused on as characteristics of surrealism, and this focus is related to the fact that the difference from Dadaism is that surrealism tries to unify unconsciousness and emotion, and that it has the desire to organize. This means that for the unconsciousness to have realistic significance, it must go through the process of organization. Kim was able to lay out, namely, that actively accepting automatic writing and its mechanism into language for intellectual and conscious production is the major principle and direction for modern poetics. As looked into in an earlier section in this paper, the Japanese surrealist poerty circle — as it was with Nishiwaka Junsaburo — demonstrated a difference with Kim Kirim, who accepted surreal-

8 Kim Kirim [김기림], "Siui Gisul, Inshik, Hyeonsil Deungui Jemunje" [Subjects of Description, Perception, Reality of Poetry, 시의 기술, 인식, 현실 등의 제문제], *Chosun Ilbo* [조선일보], 1931.2.11-14.

ism, in that they replaced the abyss of the human psyche with innocence, and by doing so lost the social and realistic significance, and as a result expanded the purification of human psychology. What is more, English·American modernism pursued order and harmony through the intellectual process of poets, who are known for fresh images of objects and the creation of analogy, but what they aimed for was awareness in tradition and the classics, and hoped to find poetic order in the authority of the classics and tradition. Such an aim was also a different point in the acceptance of surrealism in the contemporary Chosun or Japan.

The focus on such characteristics signifies the need to consider comparison with the characteristics of *Shi to Shiron*, which was studied related to Kim Kirim's intellectualism in the existing researches. *Shi to Shiron* which was published in 1928, gathered modern poets, who were influenced by new arts of the West, such as surrealism, formalism, and imagism. These poets led the way in introducing Western literary theory, and they published the translation of André Breton's *Manifesto of Surrealism,* introducing surrealist artists making the introduction of surrealism abundant. They also explained their creative consciousness and their intention to establish a methodology to create artworks. They attempted to have a different creative attitude, and Haruyama Yukio's "The Demise of Modern Japanese Symbolist Poetry", representatively, demonstrates such change. He emphasized that the 20th century poetry must be objective and intellectual, moving away from subjectivity and sentimentality (Haruyama Yukio1928.9) :

> Moving away from logical measure to reject emotions, as simply finding rep-

resentation and sentience, poems can become literature that possesses a single "method." Intellect cannot be employed by a simple society or axiomatically. Moreover, poems do not exclude emotions. Poems believe in the existence of emotion within literature and its expansion. As we are trying to understand the "method" to overcome emotions, we couldn't explore the abyss of emotion that could be thought of as its nature of limitlessness and mysteriousness according to its "intellectual method." Intelligence by essence carries strength to recognize reality. And when we recognize this reality, we should express with the best of our abilities. (…) We should not give up emotionally. In order to precisely release the emotional state, we must do so with strong and diligent effort. (Abe Tomoji 1930)

Abe Tomoji's above pasage presents the grounds to demonstrate why we need "intellect" in modern literature. The "intellectual" method is a method that reveals the reality that the area of human psychology has, which can be named as infinity, mysteriousness that is the abyss of unconsciousness. This explains the need of strong and diligent efforts of poets. Kim Kirim also pointed this out : "(S)urrealists do not only seek for beautiful dreams. What is more they are not buried in dreams but they seek to explore the reality of dream by mercilessly analyzing dreams and their essence. For such reasons surrealism has a side that encounters realism when observed."[9] It is an identical comprehension with the argument, yet Kim mentions that in order to reach such a state, they would need to "train." As such, we can observe that in both Chosun and Japanese poetic circles, an "intellectual attitude," was

9 Kim Kirim [김기림], "Hyeondaesiui Baljeon" [Development of Modern Poetry, 현대시의 발전], *Chosun Ilbo* [조선일보], 1934.7.12-22.

emphasized as an intellectual process of organizing human unconsciousness into language, and that in the basis of this movement, surrealism was at its work.

5. Intellectual Attitude and Modernist Poetics

In relation to Kim Kirim and the Japanese poetic circle, the relationship with Abe Tomoji and Haruyama Yukio was continuously discussed. Kim Kirim's theory on literature was influenced more by the logical and fixed theory of Abe Tomoji, a scholar of English literature, than the declarative and metaphorical theory of Haruyama Yukio.

Abe Tomoji adds the following explanation of intellectual literary theory in his "Preface" :

> If "-ism" cannot be expressed in any other way than the way expressed by the Japanese word "Shugi" [主義], then the word "intellectualism" has to be used. However, "-ism," in our country, if not careful, could mean to follow a particular doctrine in observance, and to tie down all human beings' actions. (…) If it is used with such a definition, we ought not use the word "intellectualism" in this case. Moreover, as I am concerned by this issue, I believe that we should not use this term. More reasonable would be to think of intellectualism as "intellectual tendency" in consideration of the literature. It would mean such if the term "intellectualism" is used hereonafter. (Abe Tomoji 1930)

Abe Tomoji suggests that "intellect" has different tendencies or attitude from "intellectualism" of English/American modernism. The term "intellectual" has a limited use that means the ways or attitude of dealing with language, rather than in the ideological or in the literary thought definition. Abe Tomoji's "intellectual tendency" is expressed as "intellectual attitude" with Kim Kirim. What the restricted use of the term "intellectual" demonstrates is that as Abe Tomoji and Kim Kirim both emphasize as scholars of English literature in English/American modernism, highlighted on the role and effect of intellect, yet "intellectual attitude" was not identical with the principles of English/American modernism. As aforementioned, those who based their thoughts on surrealism emphasized intellect, intellectual attitude, as a conscious process that organizes human unconsciousness. It hence cannot help but have differences with the literary thought and ideological meaning that "intellectualism" implies.

Abe Tomoji and Haruyama Yukio also put forth "intellectutal literary theory" and "intellectual poetics" as the new methodology of modern literature, and the key to Kim Kirim and others' literary theory is that poetry is something "produced," that is it is not something through which the poet's emotions are sung naturally, but the fact is that it is "consciously made." What makes such conscious process possible is the intellectual attitude :

> The reason we say that literature (usually) is used even as it is only delivering the expression of emotions is that we need to think, as a starting point, that we intellectuals are in the thing that handles those emotions. If this is discussed from a production-centered point of view, literature is something that uses intellect as its

ways to explore the unknown world where our emotions are spread all around, and representing by endowing order to this. And if we say this in an intuitive and critical point of view, it becomes something that allows our experiences to have organized richness by basing that world of emotions on something intellectual(Abe Tomoji 1930).

A poet should be conscious of producing poems. A poet is to be active towards the creation of one goal=value. In doing so, consciously intended value should be demonstrated as poetry. This is an entirely different method of creating poetry that is in opposition to the simple expressionism method. People often called this the "intellectual attitude." (…) Poetry, first of all, is something that is composed. There ought to be a conscious methodology that desires and attempts poetice value.[10]

Haruyama Yukio emphasizes, "All literary works are results of action. […] A poet in today's world begins with being aware of his own methods of his poetic actions. The performer of value of artistic actions of poetry, the engineer of professional critical methods, that is what a poet is in today's world." Haruyama suggests that 'critical' methodology is being unconscious of writing poems, and calling the methods of writing poetry as 'spontaneous' method.

Moreover, the key to intellectual poetics is that poetry is a technique as well as methodology, but the background to such a method is emphasized as intellect.

10 Kim Kirim [김기림], "Sijage Isseoseoui Jujijeok Taedo" [Intellectual Attitude in Writing Poems, 詩作에 있어서의 주지적 태도], *Shin Donga* [신동아], Vol.3 Issue4, 1933.4.

On the other side of such an assertion by Haruyama Yukio was Ueda Bin (上田敏), who dominated Japanese poetic circles from the early 20th century, and his strategic overcoming of the effects of symbolism. He stated in the first issue of their literary magazine that the reason behind the publication and the key to intellectual poetics of *Shi to Shiron* was to overcome the "no-poetics" of symbolism, which regarded subjectivity and emotions as important, and to establish modern poetics. Such a situation is similar to that of Korea. After the reception of the symbolism of memory, and considering the view that lyric poems were developed as subjectivity was widely emphasized, Kim Kirim's argument that the development of modern poetry must be achieved through an intellectual attitude moving beyond romantic poetry, which emphasizes emotion and subjectivity, can be sufficiently speculated that it was related to creating a new map of power in the contemporary poetic circles.

On the one hand, Abe Tomoji suggests the phenomenon of contemporary civilization, the subject that intellectual literature must handle. He questioned the contents of literature and what methods would be used on the premise that literature has a similar intellectual characteristic with science. He then suggests the exploration of this society that is being built on scientific development as the contents that literature should deal with. Abe Tomoji claims that with literature consciously taking on a scientific method (such as social science, natural science, psychology), our civilizational phenomenon and its zeitgeist is continuous and that through this, civilizational phenomenon and literature can meet. In other words, Abe Tomoji talks of scientific cultural phenomena as contents of poetry as well as forms of poetry that can use the scientific method. Likewise, if Japanese modernism discussed the acceptance of civilization, the English/American modernism emphasized on the destruction and the restoration of civilization. English·American modernism believed that the value and the creation of order to salvage the devastated modern civilization, was possible from the historical awareness of tradition, but the actuality of that historical awareness did not exist :

> A work of poetry is itself one unified world. (...) That is always a criticism of civilization from a fresh point of view. Therefore, poetry always has deep relations to life. It only needs to have the power to move actively towards life, and not as an ornament of pleasure belonging to a consumerism system. Poetry thus gets the right to request a position as a value formation in the cultural phenomena, and would consciously put forth effort to aim for a position of glory. Therefore, the reality in poetry is not a simple fragment of reality. That is a meaningful reality. Moreover, reality must be an organized thing through language by being identified in the timely and spatial relations of civilization. Here, when I discuss the meaningful reality, I mean the essential aspect of reality. That is a fragment of reality, yet it represents all of reality that it is concerned with.[11]

However, Kim Kirim emphasized criticism of the civilizational phenomena, whilst dealing with them at the same time. He should have taken note of the fact that we reveal criticism in relation with reality, whilst showing a positive attitude towards accepting modern civilization as an East-Asian colony. He argues that poems should demonstrate the poet's unique world of civiliza-

11 Kim Kirim [김기림], "Poesiwa Modeoniti" [Poésie and Modernity, 포에시와 모더니티], *Shin Donga* [신동아], Vol. 3. Issue 7, 1933.7.

tional criticism and that it should not be an ornament of pleasure belonging to a consumerism system, and needs to have the power to move actively towards life. Therefore, the "reality" that is shown in poems is not a simple fragment of reality but should include the essence of reality, a fragment yet should represent reality as a whole.

On the other side of the claim that poems have to deal with the essence of reality is the request for an objective yet unique point of view and consciousness. On this point, Kim Kirim argues, "the real reality is showing the things we come into contact with everyday, and the things we only see mechanically in a new point of view as something that we see for the first time," and that "the poet in today's world should always at anytime prepare himself with those points of view, and should know how to change and move those points of view."

Kim Kirim believed that such changes the angles and points of view would create a meaningful order of reality within the literary pieces. However, such characteristics are where Abe Tomoji and Haruyama Yukio are divided. As aforementioned, Kim Kirim explains that surrealism is an artistic tendency that bases psychological despair and anxiety post World War I, and that Surrealism succeeds Dadaism, except the point that Surrealism is essentially the "desire for order." This is the direction of intellectual literary theory that states, "the most respected thing in art is the power and value of expressing the deepest confusion in the most tightly knitted order."

However, Kim Kirim takes a step further by emphasizing that we can create a new and a meaningful order of "reality." What Kim highlights of intellectual attitude, as the principle of modern poetry is also the fact that language does not fall back as a simple technique, but a critical thinking on reality through a conscious process, and the reason for civilizational criticism is in relation to this. Yet, the Japanese intellectual attitude has been reduced to the issue of technique, and that it lost its initial artistic revolutionary energy of surrealism is the judgment made by Japanese literary history. The researchers of Japanese literary history claimed that the term intellectualism was not be used lightly, but it is said that Abe Tomoji and Haruyama shouted out "intellect"ever so lightly. This demonstrates that they had the motivation to take this as the methodology of modern poetics, yet were indifferent towards the significance and the sociocultural critical power. This is a broader point as to how the writers who put forward surrealism or intellectual poetics are related to "The Newly-Rising Artists Group" who claimed artistry and autonomy of literature in response to the political utilitarianism of Marxist literary theory, after the mid-1920s.

Therefore, "poésie" is something that is is a term used in full consciousness of production methods, and in the case of Haruyama Yukio, who advocated intellectual methodology, rather wrote his poems basing them on the formalist method of pure meaning. Haruyama Yukio explored the possibility of new methods of poetry through experimenting with form in creating his poems. The third piece, "Shiroi Shoujo" [*White Girl,* 白い少女], in his famous work, *Shokubutsu no Danmen* [A side of Plant, 植物の斷面], he repeats "白い少女 白い少女 白い少女 白い少女 白い少女 白い少女 白い少女" in 16 lines. Haruyama Yukio explains that this piece expresses a different reality from the actual depiction. In the piece where "白い少女" is the only thing mechanically arranged in a well-organized manner, there isn't the poet's consciousness, nor the poet's claims to endow a new order to the background of the character. The poem is closer to a shape consisting of symbols of abstract words. Provided that we can feel something from the poem, what we feel is the pure emotion that is created by the encounter between "white" and "girl." Likewise, one could say that he used formalist ornament-like things to eliminate sentimentalism, yet such attempts were criticized by literary history as "insincere intellectualism."(Ōoka makoto 1980 : 64) Ultimately, *Shi to Shiron* ceased within the poetic circle in which undifferentiated notions and reality, a surrealism that aimed for intellect, pursued the extremes of intellect and have been evaluated as reaching "the world without actual sensation," an abstract world that lost all things human.

Kim Kirim also criticized the characterization of Japanese surrealism as created with intellectualist poetics as its foundation. Kim argued that "formalism is the poem's accidental beauty, and not the essence. Formalism biased against physical beauty is much more deformed."[12] Japanese surrealism aimed for purity, and such a situation removed the meaning of poems and developed such poems into pure formalist poems that used language as symbols, and only came to pursue effects such as form of the text, recital, figure, change, and movement. Kim Kirim believed that adhering to physical beauty was not a characteristics of surrealism, and the reason why such criticism was possible was because Kim Kirim's surrealism poetics as intellectual methodology also kept reality in mind. Kim apparently held a critical point of view on the poems and poetics of the Japanese poet Haruyama Yukio, and in "Concert

12 Kim Kirim [김기림], "Hyeondaesiui Gisul" [Description of Modern Poetry, 현대시의 기술], *Siwon* [Poetry Garden, 詩苑], 1935.2.

Without Audience",[13] Kim quotes Haruyama's words on reading surrealist poetics before reading surrealist poems, and criticizes that any poetic works that does not contain the reality of life will isolate the poem from the public. Haruyama and Kim Kirim both tried to realize the logic of surrealist poetics through literary theory and poetic works as is stated : "all perfomers should begin from self-awareness of the objectives and values of the action."(Haruyama Yukio 1930) However, if the intellectual attitude based on Japanese surrealism had strategic objectives and values to realistically overcome a poetic circle's subjectivity, Kim Kirim's literary theory can be evaluated as aiming for objectives and values to recreate an order of reality according to criticism of reality.

6. Conclusion : Surrealism and Korean Modernism

Kim Kirim would have been able to experience the extremity of the pathological elements of surrealism, while encountering Japanese surrealism that demonstrated severity with society and purity, and where criticisms and resistance towards existing society, which surrealist spirits carry, are lost. However, he actively focused on the significance of the societal, and of the times that surrealism came to Japan, and how it accommodated itself into establishing modern Korean poetics. He accommodated the mechanism that organizes the unconscious world into the process of language and the poem's tech-

13 Kim Kirim [김기림], "Cheongjungeomneun Emakeo" [Concert Without Audience, 청중없는 음악회], *Munyewolgan* [문예월간], 1932.1.

nique, and expanded it into an intellectual attitude that overcomes emotions and organizes itself. But at the same time, creating a new order would mean creating a new stance and order for reality, he clearly emphasized that active interest, and civilizational criticism must exist within an intellectual attitude.

In the early 1930s, when Kim Kirim's modernist poetics made its start, the expression "intellectual attitude" was included in modernism and was explained within English/Ameican modernism together. However, when reading the literary theory and the literary works in actuality, there existed a gap that cannot be explained through English·American modernism. This study noted the influence of surrealism on the basis of the intellectual attitude of Kim Kirim's modernist poetics in the 1930s. The existing studies of Kim Kirim's surrealism are not as active, yet this study discusses the fact that surrealism played an important role in establishing Kim Kirim's modern poetics. Therefore, in understanding Korean modernist poetics and texts of the early 1930s, it is possible to reconsider the significance of surrealism beyond English/American modernism in literary history. There is a need for a reconsideration of the relation between surrealism and the poetic works focused on the book of collected poems of the early 1930s called *Customs of the Sun* (태양의 풍속), yet his achievement that is apparent in literary theory is the result of actively accommodating surrealist literary theory and social realist resilience, and this is the definite difference with English·American modernism or the Japanese poetic circle's surrealism or intellectual tendencies. In this sense, Kim Kirim's modernist literary theory of the early 1930s was able to guarantee a certain historicity.

Works Cited

Abe Tomoji [阿部知二], "Shuchiteki Bungakuron no Ryakuzu" [A rough sketch of Intellectualism in Literature, 主知的文学論の略圖], *ShuchitekiBungakuron* [Intellectualism in Literature, 主知的文学論], Tokyo : Kousei Gaku Shoten [東京 : 厚生閣書店], 1930.

Aoyagi Yuko [青柳優子, *chosen bungaku no chisei kin kirin* [The Intellect of Korean Literature Kirim Kim, 朝鮮文学の知性・金起林], Shinkansha [新幹社], 2010.

Haruyama Yukio [春山行夫], "Nihon Kindai Shouchoushugi Shi no Shuuen" [The Demise of Mordern Japanese Symbolist Poetry, 日本 近代象徵主義詩の終焉], *Shi to Shiron* [Poem and Poetics, 詩と詩論], Book 1, 1928.9.

____________________, "Chougenjitsushugi Shiron" [Surrealism Poetics, 超現實主義詩論], *Shi no kenkyuu* [A study of poetry, 詩の研究], Tokyo : Kōseikakusyoten [東京 : 厚生閣書店], 1930.

Hwang Hyeon San [황현산], "Haeseol-sangsangnyeongui Wonchikgwa Marui Him" [Interpretation-Principle of Immagination And Strength of Words, 해설-상상력의 원칙과 말의 힘], Andre Breton [앙드레 브르통], *Choheyonsiljuui Seoneon* [Manifestoes of Surrealism, 초현실주의 선언]. Hwang Hyeon San trans. [황현산 번역 주석 해설], Mimesis [미메시스], 2012.

Nishiwaki Junzaburo [西脇順三郎], "Jyobun" [Preface, 序文], *Fuku iku Taru Kafu Yo* [A deep scent of man who lights a fire, 馥郁タル火夫ヨ], Issue 1, 1927.

Ōoka Makoto [大岡 信], *Showa Shishi* [A poetic history of Showa era, 昭和詩史], Tokyo : Shichosha [東京 : 思潮社], 1980.

Sato Saku [佐藤朔], "Nihon no shururearizumu —Taisho kara Shouwa e" [Japanese Surrealism—from Taisho to Showa, 日本のシコルー レアリスム-大正から昭和へ], *Isho No Taiyo* [Sun of Costume, 衣裳の太陽], 1928.12.

Sawa Masahiro, Wada Hirofumi ed. [沢正宏,和田博文(編)], *Nihon no Shururealisumu* [Japanese Surrealism, 日本のシコールレアリスム], Kyoto : sekai shisōsha [京都 : 世界思想社], 1995.

Yoshikawa Nagi [요시카와 나기], *Gyeongseongui Dada, Donggyeongui Dada-Dadaiseuteu Gohanyonggwa Chinguideul.* [Gyeongsung's Dada, Tokyo's Dada-Dadaist Ko Hanyong and Friends, 경성의 다다, 동경의 다다-다다이스트 고한용과 친구들], Ima [이마], 2015.

The Nude in the Meiji Era

Reception and Representation of the Female Body in Modern Japanese Literature

Tsunehiko Matsumoto (Kyushu University)

1. Introduction

The objective of this paper is to reexamine the introduction of body image and the Japanese perception of the body as reflected in the literature of the Meiji era. Certainly, discourse on the body existed prior to the modern era and the potential issues for discussion vary greatly. Focusing on the dominant issues in the modern era alone provides a near endless source of topics, for example, the order and formation of military group exercises, the introduction and permeation of education based games, exercise, sports and physical education, changes in bodily habits and body techniques associated with aspects of daily life (clothing, food and shelter) in accordance with the modern-

* This paper was translated from the Japanese version as follows, Tsunehiko Matsumoto "Nihon kindai bungaku ni okeru shintai no juyō to hyōgen : meijiki ratai hen" in *'Chi no kakō gaku' koto hajime : juyōshi, kakōshi, hasshinsuru nihon no gihō* [*Introduction to Knowledge Processing Studies : Techniques for Accepting, Processing and Sending Knowledge in Japan.*], eds. Noriko Matsunaga, Teruhisa Se, Hitoshi Yoshioka (Tokyo : Shinjuku Shobō, 2011), 107-125.

ization of living standards, the formation of a generalized view of the body through the popularization of medicinal and anthropologic study, the development of body expression through art, literature and dance, issues of birth control and childbirth promotion in accordance with population problems, body maintenance carried out under the title of health and beauty, and so forth. Each issue requires historical assessment in its own right, and yet, the historical contexts of these matters are all profoundly related. To look at the complex system of issues in its entirety and only analyze the representations of the body that can be found in the relevant novels and literature incites that Japanese saying, "*yoshi no zui kara tenjō wo miru*" [to look up at the ceiling through the pistil of a reed].[1] In saying that, though, there is no convenient made-to-order method for surveying an issue in its entirety when it comes to such big issues requiring historical investigation. Therefore, we must move forward one reed at a time. What can we hope to achieve from a single reed? From a literary studies perspective, first and foremost, there is the potential to take the literary map that the research of authors, literary works and literary history has achieved thus far, and rearrange it to create a new map that highlights the space between individual works. If the countless number of works of literature in the modern period were stars in the sky, then it would be like drawing the old constellations in a new way, or giving meaning to stars that had previously been thought meaningless. One of the defining characteristics of modern literature is the increasing attention provided to depictions of the

1 Like looking up at the ceiling through the tiny hole in the stem of a reed and thinking you are seeing the entire ceiling. This is a Japanese saying to express cynicism at one's narrow-mindedness or shortsighted views.

face and of the body. Representations of the body as depicted in many of works of this era may not appear significant at first, but through careful observation, slightly altered sensitivities towards the body begin to reveal themselves. However, in the time and space within which to write this article, it is not possible to observe the celestial sphere of new representations of the body in its entirety. Here I shall focus primarily on how the Western view of body image and perception of the body was represented and altered in its import into the field of literature in Japan, as well as the various issues that arose as a result of these processes. Depictions of the body are diverse, and so in order to provide a concise sketch of the issues in question, the scope of this study shall focus primarily on depictions of "*ratai*" [the naked body; the nude].

2. The Naked Body as 'Public Form'

Dorinda Outram opens her publication, *The Body and the French Revolution* (1989), with the statement, "The body is at once our most intimate experience and our most inescapable public form. Because it is at once so inalienably private and so ineluctably public, it has also formed, in most western cultures, the most basic political resource."(Dorinda Outram, 1989 : 5) The period of enlightenment that was the Meiji era instances the pursuit of a new 'public form' to replace those that were established under the former feudal system. The 'naked body' was one such form. The simplest example is evidenced in the promulgation of the "*Tokyo ishiki kaii jōrei*" [Ordinance for the breech of etiquette and misdemeanor violations in Tokyo] released as *Tokyo-futachi dai 737-gō* (8 November, 1872 [Meiji 5]). "Breech of etiquette", as stipulated in the ordinance, included "Article 11 : Persons bearing tattoos on their bodies," "Article 12 : Persons operating mixed bath houses," and "Article 22 : Nudity or bodily exposure from the waist up, or exposure of one's thigh or lower leg, or otherwise maintaining an unsightly appearance in public." These ordinances were later incorporated into the list of crimes subject to court action and the "Police Offenses Punishment Order" abrogated by the Minor Offences Act. However, the issuance of this ordinance concerning the 'public form' was not adopted concurrently throughout Japan in its entirety. "*Dajōkan fukoku dai 256-gō*" or "*Kakuchihō Ishiki Kaii Jōrei*" [Ordinance for the breech of etiquette and misdemeanor violations in regional areas] stipulated the abovementioned Article 11 and 12 as misdemeanor offences, whereas Article 22 was not. On the other hand, it reflected "regional state of affairs" not provided in the "Tokyo" ordinance, namely, regulations against certain conduct in "another person's territory" such as "the taking of seaweed without permission" (Article 23), "the setting of fish traps" (Article 24), and "the use of poison in the capturing of fishes and birds" (Article 25). Accordingly, the "Ordinance for the breech of etiquette and misdemeanor violations" as issued in Osaka as "*Ōsaka-futatsu dai 332-gō*" ('Osaka prefectural decree no.332'; issued 7 November, 1887 [Meiji 10]), also prohibited body ink/tattooing, mixed bathing at public bathhouses, and public nudity or bodily exposure in streets and at shopfronts. However, the banning of tattoos was only added in a later decree, "*Ōsaka-futatsu dai 148-gō*" (Osaka prefectural decree no.148; issued 7 November, 1887 [Meiji 10]), defined under Article 36. Thus, we can observe that the Tokyo ordinance wasn't adopted in Osaka in exactly the same manner, but in a process of stages. The introduction of a 'public form' that imposed conformity towards the 'naked body' cultivated a 'gaze' in the public to view the tattooed body, the mixed-bathing body, the naked body as a violation of 'public form' And while it wasn't an officially acknowledged system, this 'gaze' then proceeded to help construct another implicit 'public form' that was the everyday sensitivities and perceptions of the national people.[2]

From the point of view of the laws of a culturally enlightened country this disconnect between laws regarding the naked body in "Tokyo" and "regional" Japan, or the temporal disconnect of laws that saw the introduction of prohibition of tattoos added later in Osaka, signifies a non-uniform "public form." Historically speaking, though, in light of the rather recent transition from the feudal system, these differences in provisions according to locale ("Tokyo," "Osaka," or "regional") is in itself representative of the 'public form' of that era. One could even argue that by establishing different provisions of the law based on territory and not guaranteeing a unified 'public form' to be adopted concurrently throughout Japan like a national law would, also would have worked to cultivate and train the Japanese public's 'gaze' towards 'public form.'

There is one more example that is of interest to this study regarding the issues surrounding the nude as 'public form' in the enlightenment period and that is the image of the bathing woman as represented in the photographs and dolls of the era. For example, C. H. Stratz (1858-1924) visited Japan mid-Meiji, and his report, "Seikatsu to geijutsu ni arawareta nihonjin no

2 However, the characteristic of the "gaze" as a 'public form' is in its visuality molded by society and history, and, as Hal Foster in "Vision and Visuality" (the Japanese version "*Shikakuron*" (Heibonsha, 2006) translated by Kurenuma Norihisa) states, "within that visuality there is also difference."

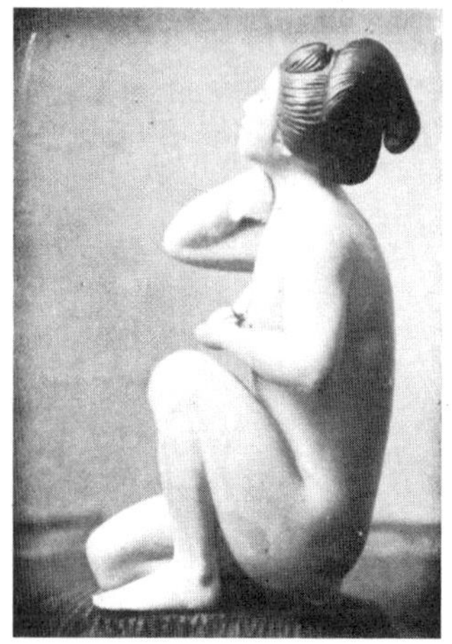

Figure 1

karada" [Die körperformen in kunst und leben der Japaner, The body in the art and life of the Japanese],[3] presents a large number of photos and drawings of the nude. While there are naked bodies in various poses throughout, the female bathing pose is almost without exception configured with the shin of the right leg one flat against the floor and the other shin perpendicular so that the knee of the other leg is raised (see Figure 1).

Mid-Meiji also gave rise to the "nude butterfly controversy" [*rakochō ronsō*], to be discussed later in the paper, as well as the rise in popularity of lithographic prints depicting scenes of women just having taken a bath, or '*yokugo*.' These images too, regardless of publisher, portray Japanese women just as the women in Stratz's photos, with one knee raised. Going back an era, you can find *nishiki-e* woodblock prints of women in the Edo period, such as those in Torii Kiyomitsu's "Gyōzui no zu," depicted in the same pose (Figure 2).

Figure 2

This image of the raised knee and buttocks pressed to the floor is perhaps a display of the 'public form' of a traditional bodily habit that Japanese women exhibit when they wash their bodies. Additionally, the poses of the

3 C.H. Stratz, *Seikatsu to geijutsu ni arawareta nihonjin no karada*, trans. Takayama Yōkichi (Toe Shoin, 1969).

Figure 3

Figure 4

naked women seen in photographs intended as souvenirs for Westerners in the Meiji period, such as the single-standing-knee poses in the bathing photos, and the hair-washing poses of women with their upper bodies exposed and washing their hair in the washbasin (see Figure 3), can also be found in the *nishiki-e* prints of the Edo period (see Figure 4).

That the poses of the women in the photographs and in Edo *nishiki-e* are the same bears evidence that these are portrayals of an actual bodily habit. Perhaps because the Japanese were unaware of nude expression as an art form, when they were being photographed for souvenirs for Westerners, they turned to the only example they had : the *nishiki-e* prints. Thus, the pose for washing the body is passed along as an implicit "public form," and as these poses become the subjects of prints and photographs and commercialized, the nude expression of the 'public form' is passed along also.

However, conformity of the 'naked body' through a 'public form' was not achieved through such readily understandable representations as legal ordinances and body habits alone. Why do people were clothes? We wear them to avoid public scrutiny, i.e., the various 'public forms' that we are subjected to the moment we become naked. There is the punished nude, the unworthy nude, the admired nude, the diagnosed-as-overweight nude, the laughed at nude, the loved nude, the bought nude, the in-shape nude, etc., etc. And yet, it only has to be a single form of nudity to attract all of the 'scrutiny.' Various fields of discourse and systems of interpretation create meaning and carry out specific approaches towards 'the naked body' in their own way. The 'naked body' is an integrated space that accepts all the different approaches and created meanings imparted on it and allows them to coexist.

3. The Naked Body as Integrated Space

The most obvious example of confusion generated by the dynamic and integrated nature of the body transpired in the mid-Meiji period with the "nude drawing controversy" [ratai-ga ronsō].[4]

Comments regarding nude drawings can be found prior to when the controversy took place. Generally speaking, however, explication of the nude drawing controversy in Japan most often begins with Yamada Bimyō's novel,

4 For more research in the field of art and literature on the particulars, specific examples, and problematic issues surrounding the controversy, see : Kanzaki Eishi, *Nihon kindai bijutsu hatasushi* (Tokyo bijutsu : July, 1974); Nakamura Yoshikazu, "Bijutsu ni okeru sei to kenryoku : ratai-ga ronsō" (in *Nihonkindai bijutsu ronsōshi* (Kyūryūdō : April, 1981)); Miyashita Kikuo, "Ratai hyōgen no henyō" (in Tsuji Nobuo, ed., *Bakumatsu Meiji no gakka-tachi* (Pelican : December, 1992)); Kitazawa Noriaki, *Kyōkai no bijutsushi* (Brucke : June, 2000); Nakayama Akihiko, "Ratai-ga, ratai, Nihonjin" (in *Disukūru no teikoku* (Shinyōsha : April, 2000) etc.

"Kochō" [Butterfly],[5] and its nude illustration by Watanabe Seitei (see Figure 5, below), which together incited the "nude butterfly controversy" [*rakochō ronsō*]. Much research has been done on the particulars surrounding the matter and does not require further comment here. The issue I wish to focus on, rather, is the novels that were written using this controversy as a direct catalyst. One of these novels was Kōda Rohan's "Fūryūbutsu" [The Elegant Buddha].[6] The novel also included an illustration by Hirafuku Suian, which created further friction in the debate surrounding the nude body and the "nude butterfly controversy." Another was Ozaki Kōyō's "Rabijin" [The Nude Beauty].[7] Shortly after the release of Bimyō's "Kochō" Ozaki wrote "Kochō-dono,"[8] criticizing the illustration in "Kochō," not so much for its representation of the nude itself, but its composition and taste. In terms of their dates of release, "Fūryūbutsu" predates "Rabijin." However, in considering the nude body as an integrated space, "Rabijin" evinces more of a direct response and thus heeds first consideration here. Ozaki's short story "Rabijin" begins with the following remarks :

Figure 5

Those curves! Those beautiful curves! The naked body of a woman and her

5 In *Kokumin no tomo* (January, 1889).

6 In *Shinchohyakushu* (September, 1889).

7 In *Yomiuri shinbun* (22, 23 November, 1889).

8 In *Garakutabunko* (January, 1889).

magnificent composure of curves – that is the true essence of "beauty"! Yes, yes, that's right. I am an artist and I have long been a believer in the teachings of the "nude beauty faith." One of the valuable teachings of this religion that I wish to share, is that there are a lot of false saints in this world who don't even look at the true form of nude beauty and negate the naked body in a few mere words as a disruption to the morals and customs of the world and that is just absurd. No, I am determined to repel this fog of foolish misunderstanding from the minds of my common man!

As stated in the opening, the protagonist of the story is an "artist." He teaches his beliefs in the "nude beauty faith," and the method he adopts to try and help the general populace — who prohibit "nude beauty" for its "disruption" to the "morals and customs of the world"— see reason, is by having his soon-to-be-wed wife attend their wedding reception in the nude. Under the title of "artistic research," he preaches the necessity of "a sacrifice of one's own interests," and the protagonist (the artist) tries to persuade this of his bewildered wife by stating the following :

It hardly need further explanation. A woman's naked body is the true essence of beauty and you, an artist's wife, should be well aware of this. Sad to say, the people of our country are uncivilized, one only need observe their opposition to my "nude beauty faith" to see just how scant of artistic thought they are. I am a respectable artist, but even the relatives to the high priest of Hōryūji Temple will follow blindly the views of a layman...How pitiful that the only believer of this faith is me. (omission) People who garrulously denounce the nude beauty faith might appear to be lacking in knowledge or refinement, but that is simply not true, and I do not understand why they cannot see my truth. Most likely they have glanced upon the lithographs of women bathing or fishing for abalone that are on display at the print shops and thought to themselves, so *this* is the thing that the nude beauty faith worships, and jovially they confute something which they never understood in the first place, so if they could only see it in its true form they would surely come to appreciate the essence of beauty and become devout followers of nude beauty too.

The "true form" that he speaks of refers to the "magnificent composure of curves" of his wife's naked body. The protagonist states that if after seeing his wife's naked form all were to become followers of the "nude beauty faith," the "honor" is not only theirs as a couple, but "the honor of Japanese art." After hearing her husband's remarks, the wife bursts into tears. But the artist husband only continues to insist her nakedness at the reception, telling her, "Oy, oy, why do you cry? Wait, that's it, your hair, you must wear it down, disheveled. We can't have you stand naked before everyone with your hair pomaded like a regular bride— it would be a disgrace. Oy, oy, enough with the tears." In a predicament, the to-be bride goes to inform her husband's mother what he told her. The mother is shocked by the story and decides to take her daughter-in-law and leave her son. The housemaid too reveals that she was "ordered to attend the wedding naked just like the wife." The novel ends with all three women walking out on the "artist" husband. Yamada Bimyō's novel and genesis of the "nude butterfly controversy" [*rakochō ronsō*] is based on the Japanese classic, "Heike Monogatari," told through tragedy. In contrast, Ozaki Kōyō's endeavor was a completely comical one. The sarcasm directed at Bimyō in this comicalized story is obvious, and undoubtedly there is a hidden element of sarcasm towards Kōda Rohan as well. The protagonist in Ozaki's story attests, "I am a respectable artist, but even the relatives to the high priest of Hōryuji Temple…" which is suggestive of the Buddhist image sculptor and protagonist of Rohan's "Fūryūbutsu" which appeared two months prior to Ozaki's "Rabijin." However, that is not because "Fūryūbutsu" opposed "nude beauty faith." Rather, "Fūryūbutsu" is Rohan's own representation of "nude beauty faith." The point on which we receive the line, "The common people are in opposition to my "nude beauty faith"" and the following context of "the high priest of Hōryūji Temple…" run counter to each other." Nude beauty faith" might be comicalized in Kōyō's novel, but the stance regarding its necessity is the same in both Rohan and Kōyō's works. Kōyō also wrote a piece relating to the "nude butterfly controversy" in which he criticizes Yamada Bimyō, called "Kochō-dono." In his commentary Kōyō states that unlike the "*okina*" [elderly] and "*kyōwaranbe*" [people of the capital] who reproach the "*akahadaka no sugata*" [naked female body], "I am not one to judge on this or that; on the contrary, I support the view that this is the essence of beauty." Accordingly, if he is in fact implicitly criticizing Rohan and "Fūryūbutsu" by mentioning things like the "high priest of Hōryūji Temple," his intent is in the context of the "respectable artist" who "follows blindly the views of the layman" and this notion of "following blindly." The point at which Kōyō criticizes Bimyō in "Kochō-dono" is the depiction of the nude in the novel and in the illustration without regard for the historical or social context of the status of the female protagonist who is a noble of the Heike clan. In other words, it is the representation of the nude and the feeling of strangeness provoked by the context of its representation. Therefore, it is not so unthinkable that Kōyō who made this criticism to deem the developments of "The Elegant Buddha," in which the Buddhist sculptings carried out by the protagonist to liberate him from his earthly desires overlaps with the naked body of former lover to form a double image – of Buddhist statues and the nude – as "following blindly the opinions of laypeople."

A detailed analysis of the storyline of "Fūryūbutsu" will be addressed later. The mockery depicted in Kōyō's novel, "Rabijin," directly pierces through this problem of the naked body as an integrated space, perhaps more so than even the author himself intended. As evidenced earlier, Kōyō agrees with the view of the nude female body being the essence of beauty. In other words, he isn't mocking the character for his conversion (devoutness?) to the "nude beauty faith." To the modern reader, the humor in "Rabijin" is readily identifiable. It's in the actions of the protagonist, who regardless of his position as an "artist," takes the actual 'naked body of a woman' and worships it artistically as the 'main idol of the nude beauty faith.' For the 'nudity' of a real woman to be represented and accepted artistically as "rabi" [nude beauty], the 'public form' of 'art' which appreciates the beauty of the nude body is a requisite. The one who should understand this the most is the "artist" and yet he confuses the generalized 'naked female body' and the 'artistic' nude body, just like a regular person who doesn't understand the 'public form' of 'art' would. So on that point, he himself possesses the "opinions of the common man" that he is so critical of. The humor here arises from this confusion of 'public forms' through a disregard of context. However, it also begs the question of just how established the 'public form' of 'art,' which was necessary to appreciate the 'nude' as 'nude' in Japan during the "nude butterfly controversy" era circa 1890, actually was. Concerning nude pictures in the Meiji period, art historian, Kitazawa Noriaki, states the following :

> (The crux of the matter) is not in the contrastive nature of "art" in Japan and the West, but in the fact that the social framework with which to rightfully position representations of the nude body in "art" were not yet established in Japan vis-à-vis the asymmetric East-West state of affairs.[9]

Society and its social classes, its economy, ideology, religion, character, even its aesthetic sense, are formed by a diversity of people. Accordingly, trying to measure whether a society has an established "social framework" and to what degree a society maintained a mutual understanding of said framework is no easy task. In this instance, however, we can confirm that the "social framework" of 'art,' i.e., the 'public form' of 'art,' at that time, was "not yet established." The evidence of which can be found in the discussions of that era surrounding nude pictures, in which they repeatedly confuse the naked bodies of actual women and pictures of the nude. For example, Futabatei Shimei, the forefather of modern literature in Japan, wrote in his essay "Rakochōzuron" [Commentary on the Nude Butterfly Illustrations] (1889), "If you look upon the naked body with the eyes of a human, the naked body will appear unsightly." It seems only natural, though, that various confusion and disorder would arise during this period of amorphic state, when the Western concept

9 *Kyōkai no bijutsushi* (Brucke 2000).

of 'art' was yet to firmly establish itself in Japanese society as a 'public form.' And so the existing 'public form' was adopted as an easy way of making sense of this contentious field of confusion and disorder. And as a result, comparisons of East-West civilization, modern vs. pre-modern times, morals and ethics, and so forth, were introduced into the controversy surrounding nude pictures as a scale of measure that was easy to understand for the Japanese people of that era. The introduction of which inevitably effected the un-fixed (disoriented?) position of 'art' in society and the provisions for the nude as an integrated space.

Based on this notion of a 'public form' of the human body in the real world and 'public form' of the artistic body and how to differentiate between the two, Kōyō's "Rabijin" makes fun of the 'artist' for his inability to make such distinction. However, his mockery is more than just a mere joke at the wielder of superficial knowledge; it is also an enlightened jibe at the people in social and cultural positions to introduce 'public form' and the fine tuning of that which they import. Through the assertions of the 'artist,' whose belief in 'nude beauty' is pedantic, the novel paradoxically problematizes the importation of 'public form' void of fine tuning. Understanding the confusion over 'public form' as the source of humor in the novel is variable to the anchoring of the 'public form' of 'art' in society. In other words, it becomes more obvious over time. Perhaps it was such enlightenment that Mori Ōgai, too, intended in his message, "Hadaka de yuke ya, Poejī!" [Go naked, poésie!].[10] Accordingly, Kōyō's "Rabijin" connotes such sophistication. On the other hand,

10 Suggesting that poésie (poetry), or more broadly, the arts, should be more accepting of the nude. In *Yomiuri shimbun* (13 January, 1889).

however, "Rabijin" is oriented towards enlightenment of the unlearned and the complete opposite as well. The final scene of the novel brings together the three female characters in the story, the mother, the bride, and the maid servant — all of who represent the 'unlearned' based on their ignorance of 'art' and the "nude beauty faith." The three women all decide to leave the 'artist' and that's where the story ends. As the mother that gave birth to and raised him, the wife that he was to wed, and the maid that served him all leave the house together, the male 'artist' is left behind. How should one interpret such an ending? The finale sees the unlearned ones — the intended receivers of 'public form' — abandoning the 'artist' — the one imposing said 'form' — and thus ironically mocking the rigidity of enlightenment. The criticism of Kōyō, who himself agrees with the teachings of the "nude beauty faith," is rather directed towards a certain stolidity and self-righteousness of 'artists.' In order to extensively propagate the "nude beauty faith" (art), awareness on the part of society to its acceptance, as well as the method and form through which it is to be accepted are of great importance. However, the "artist" in the novel harbors no sensitivities toward the social context of the recipients of his views, only his own obtuseness and self-righteousness, as manifested in his unilateral attempts to force his "nude beauty faith" on those around him. Kitazawa Noriaki likens the artists of the Meiji period to "naked emperors who don't possess the social garments called "art.""[11] What Kōyō indicated in "Rabijin" was that the "artist" is the "naked emperor" and the "naked emperor" is in fact "naked." The humor attempted in the novel is not a sophisticated joke at the ignorance of the culturally superior to the culturally inferior,

11 *Kyōkai no bijutsushi* (Brucke 2000).

but rather directs the laughter towards the ridicule of the 'emperor' that doesn't understand the opinions of the general public. The relative weight and method of representation of this sophistication and ridicule changes diversely as the 'public form' called 'art' transitions through history. And it is in these diverse changes that the nude body as an integrated space manifests its idiosyncrasies.

"Fūryūbutsu" depicts the nude as an integrated space in a different way. The work is Rohan's own unique response to the "naked butterfly controversy" [rakochō ronsō]. The opening chapter, entitled "Beginnings" [Hottan], contains the phrase, "like watching the falling cherry blossom petals and wishing them to transform into butterflies." Sekiya Hiroshi interprets this phrase, "the expression is reminiscent of Arakida Moritake's poem, "The falling petal I saw drift back to the branch was a butterfly" [Rakka eda kaeru to mireba kochō kana].[12] Sekiya also points out the phrase "tenma no bi" [natural beauty given by the heavens] in "Chapter 9 – Nyozeka" and its connection with Bimyō's novel, "Kochō" [Butterfly]. The thing that was made apparent through the "naked butterfly controversy" was the difficulty of representing the nude body as a symbol of beauty in a time and place that had not yet established a 'public form' for 'art.' In regards to that difficulty, "Fūryūbutsu" employed the 'public form' that was most easily understood by the Japanese people at that time. Namely, it borrowed from the beauty of the image of Buddha in Buddhist art and tried to express 'nude beauty' as 'Japanese art' through words instead of trying to directly import it from the West. However, the very idea of 'nude beauty' was the ultimate goal, and beyond its import as Western aesthetic value, the 'nude

12 *Kōda Rohan shū* (Iwanami shoten : 2002).

beauty' constructed by the novel "Fūryūbutsu" would inevitably become an integrated space comprising both 'Japanese art' and 'Western art.' In the opening chapter, "Beginnings", 21-year old Buddhist sculptor and protagonist of the story Shu'un states, "How unfortunate it is to be born into Japan, this country of fine arts, in an age when the great craftsmen of Hida are no more" [Nihon bijutsu kuni ni umarenagara, ima no yo ni Hida no Takumi nashi to iwasengoto zannen], but it is through his own craftsmanship that he determines to dispel his resentment for "the foreigners that look down their long noses at us." The scene isn't a negation of the 'long-nosed foreigners' plaster work' as 'art,' but rather a proclamation of intention to absorb their 'art' and combine it with 'Japanese art.' Such vestiges of cultural appropriation can also be seen in the scene where Shu'un talks about the profession of Buddhist sculptor.

> In the West, poetry that uses color instead of voice is called painting, and a painting that depicts not scenery but gives form to spirit is called sculpture. How then could one such as I, who is accomplished in their respected arts, be inferior to Michelangelo?

The setting of a Buddhist sculptor as the protagonist is a device to adopt and give expression to the nude body as aesthetic body in Japan. Shu'un's carvings of 'Buddha' was the 'public form' adopted by author Rohan in order to establish 'nude beauty' in the Japan of that era. It was an experimental attempt. The true essence of the experiment of "Fūryūbutsu" is not in using 'Buddha' as a pretext to allow the representation of the nude body, though. The true essence of the experiment is in Shu'un's carvings of 'Buddha' also appearing as the 'nude body' of a beautiful woman. Shu'un carves images of 'Buddha' to forget an unhappy love, and as he does so, his carving of 'Buddha' transforms into the 'naked body' of the beautiful "Otatsu," his long-lost 'love.' So there is the sacred body of 'Buddha,' the sexual body of the beautiful woman he was in 'love' with, and the aesthetic body which comprises the duality of both 'Buddha' and 'lover,' and it is in this representation of the nude as one all-encompassing integrated space wherein lies the pioneering experimentalism of "Fūryūbutsu." A concrete portrayal of this can be found in the book's final chapter, "Danen" (finale):

> He raised his head and gazed at the elegant Buddha, its face with all the calm and composure of one who has attained enlightenment (omission) The room grew dark, everything awash with the hues of diluted ink, save for the vibrant figure of Otatsu, the glow of her white skin floating in the darkness. It was just like seeing the real Otatsu on a hazy moonlit night, if he called out to her she would surely answer. (omission) With the volition to sever his love and his lingering affections for Otatsu, Shu'un stood up straight before the elegant Buddha and raising the hatchet in his right hand high into the air cried out, *even iron shall yield!* But the elegant Buddha was noble, pure, and brimming with love. Her naked body looked so soft and supple like a body of water that were he to cut it warm blood would gush forth (omission) The elegant Buddha's arms smooth and warm wrapped gently around Shu'un's neck, her hair as soft as a cloud laced with a scent that words evade brushed against his cheek. In a gasp of astonishment Shu'un quickly turned to the statue to find the figure of his former love, in the flesh. *Otatsu, it's you?* Shuun embraced her and pressed his lips against her fore-

> head. Did the statue come to life or had Otatsu really come back to him? Such questions are foolish and answers to such questions once the moment has passed are irrelevant. It is a mystery among mysteries that cannot be explained.

The elegant Buddha is composed of a "calm and composed face of one who has attained enlightenment" and the "white skin" and "soft and supple naked body" of Shu'un's former love : contradictory elements in the one form. The 'naked body' of the "elegant Buddha," which comprises both inanimate 'statue' and living 'woman,' is fundamentally sublating elements of spirituality and sexuality which both work in mutual defamation of the other. In that sense, "Fūryūbutsu" is a representation of the body as an integrated space. And in another sense, the personality of Otatsu that's contained within the elegant Buddha is another integrated space. When Otatsu met Shu'un she was an unhappy pickled-flower vendor, but she also actually belonged to nobility — the daughter of a viscount. So here within this one girl we can also see an infusion of contradictory elements. In other words, the elegant Buddha in the story is the embodiment of two or three integrated systems. The personality of the body in question (integrated space) is also of relevance to author Rohan in the penning of this work. In "Fūryūbutsu Enki," prefatory note to "Fūryūbutsu", Rohan reveals the difficulty he experienced in the penning of his novel ("Fūryūbutsu") and writes of how he travelled to the alters of various Buddha to pray for its completion. The last deity he visited in his pilgrimage was "Benten of Shinobazu Pond," where his desperate wish was heard by Benten-sama who, "parted her red lips to reveal her pearl-like teeth and laughed, Ho, ho, ho, ho, ho." Rohan explains that it was only with this divine assistance that he was able to complete "Fūryūbutsu." The body of the woman who "parted her red lips to reveal her pearl-like teeth and laughed, Ho, ho, ho, ho, ho" conveys an allure of a sexual nature, but the body in question is also that of "Benten of Shinobazu Pond," whose very existence is a sacred one. Author Rohan thus possessed the experimentality and intentionality to give expression to the body as an integrated space. This stance is further exemplified with the release of "Engai no en" the year following the release "Fūryūbutsu."[13] "Fūryūbutsu" was an epoch-making novel in the modern literature of Japan for its attempts to represent the nude as an aesthetic body and for its active approach to the integration of sexual elements.

How to evaluate sexual elements and how to express them (or not express them) when it comes to representing the nude as an aesthetic body, or put plainly, representing the nude as art, is an important issue for consideration. Even after the "Naked Butterfly Controversy," the question has been raised in both art and literature in various forms. The next chapter looks at the conflict between the aesthetic body and the sexual body in Meiji literature in the years following "Fūryūbutsu."

4. Conflict on the Border Lines

Mori Ōgai, another key player in the "naked butterfly controversy" and the man who famously stated, "Go naked, poésie!" translated a work by Eduard

13 In *Nihon no bunka* (January, February, 1890). Later republished as "Taidokuro."

von Hartmann released as "Shinbiron" [Aesthetics].[14] In the final chapter to this piece, entitled "*Bikajō to jitusjō to no sakugo oyobi konko*" [original title : Verwechselung und Vermengung aesthischer Scheingefuhle mit realen; English translation : The Alteration and Mixing of Aesthetic Emotions with Reality], he states, "An example of an inappropriate way to enjoy art in the natural and habitual sense (…) would be to look upon nude works in a gallery and feel sexual desire." This admonishment of mixing the aesthetic image with real subjects also exemplifies Ōgai's critical stance regarding the "naked butterfly controversy." The "artist" in Ozaki Kōyō's novel "Rabijin" [The Nude Beauty] too, while not portrayed as 'feelings of sexual desire,' does represent an example of this "alteration and mixing of aesthetic emotions with reality." However, the true nature of the instruction here is not in the indication of the "alteration and mixing" of "aesthetic emotions" and "reality," but rather, in the supposition of "alterations and mixing" it is the "reality" itself that serves an indispensable function. In other words, subjects of artistic expression like 'the nude beauty' are 'aesthetic images' not 'reality,' but it is in the inextricable link between 'aesthetic images' or 'aesthetic emotions' and 'reality' wherein lies the true essence of Ōgai's edification. On this point, "Shibiron" posits the following example :

> As previously stated, the alteration and mixing of aesthetic images and reality is a travail to art appreciation. The same applies to the relationship between aesthetic emotions and reality. When we are shown an image, if we accept it as reality

14 In *Shigaramizōshi* (October, 1892; June, 1893). Original publication translated by Ōgai : Eduard von Hartmann : Ausgewdhlte Werhe. Band IV. Aesthetik. Zweiter systematischer Theil : Philosophi edes Schonen. Leipzig : Verlag von Wilhelm Friedrich. 1887.

and not as an aesthetic image, and yet think that we are experiencing something aesthetic, then that is utterly wrong. Let us say that someone is walking through a mountain path at night and they're suddenly caught in a violent storm. And let us also say that there is someone who crossing the ocean in a small boat when they're suddenly hit by a tempestuous typhoon. If these two people think of the storm and the typhoon as fearful and in their hearts feel personal danger, then already these are insufficient circumstances for the situation to be viewed with beauty. If the two men were to try and see beauty in the storm and the typhoon, they would have to boldly feel no fear, have a sensitivity towards perceiving beauty, and not to mention the ability to forget about the danger at stake. However, if the two were able to disregard the frightfulness of such a sight completely, then they fail to see the bigger picture. Of course the bigger picture doesn't solely relate to feelings inspired by awe, but to understand the greater meaning in the face of a phenomenon such as the destructive force of nature, one cannot neglect the feeling of awe. That being the case, the spectator must respond with feelings of fear and awe, but not respond with fear of personal danger due to the threat of the actual situation at hand. How then does the spectator harbor the feelings that should be harbored and not harbor the feelings that shouldn't? The answer is thus. The person traversing the mountain or crossing the ocean that is met with typhoon or storm, can only remove the phenomenon from reality and regard it as an aesthetic image.

The effect and result on the spectator of such a sight saturated in imaginative emotion is a feeling of real and vivid pleasure, that which accompanies every variety of aesthetic experience, even the most tragic. This resultant enjoyment is also projected involuntarily into the object, so that, for the moment at least, subject and object seem absolutely identical. This is the only feature of real illusion in the sphere of beauty.

The phrase I want to focus on here is "to understand the greater meaning, one cannot neglect the feeling of awe." On the one hand there's the need to "separate" oneself from "reality," but on the other, if one is not to "neglect the feeling of awe," then one cannot possible abandon "reality" and submit to "aesthetic emotions" entirely. To be enclosed in 'aesthetic emotion' void of 'reality,' is like the person who "thinks that they are experiencing something aesthetic" (when really they're not), and also like the "artist" in Kōyō's "Rabijin." Although the quoted passage doesn't contain any expressions related to 'nude beauty,' it need scarcely be said that the comments regarding the "travail to art appreciation" and the attitude of the "spectators" is clearly indicative of the situation regarding representation of the nude. The "personal danger" experienced by ones encounter with "natural phenomena" like the "storm or typhoon" that is instead "accepted as beauty," is equivalent to the danger of an encounter with nude beauty. We could even reflect on Bimyō's "Kochō" (Butterfly) and replace the "woman's naked body" regarded as the "essence of art" with the word "nature." Then, if we were to analyze the line "if one is to understand the greater meaning (…) one cannot neglect the feeling of awe," the 'nude beauty' that doesn't incite 'sexual desire' when looking on from a safe zone, then — to use "Fūryūbutsu" as an example — it is just like the 'wooden statue' of Otatsu, that is, not her "soft and supple naked body" but the one drained of the "warm blood." And if one is to look upon her "soft and supple naked body" with 'sexual desire,' the situation changes to one of "personal danger." The person "walking through the mountain path at night" and the one "crossing the ocean in a small boat" should feel obliged to accept their "personal danger"; however, as they remove that "danger" from "reality," they become the artist who must create the flesh-and-blood 'aesthetic image' that's linked to 'personal danger' through the umbilical cord. The gaze and attitude as 'spectators' and the creation of the 'aesthetic image,' if of its original character, can only create conflict on the border line of 'reality' and 'aesthetic emotion.' The experimentality of Rohan's "Fūryūbutsu" is such a conflict of boundaries — attested to by the role of the naked body as an integrated space. Kōyō's "Rabijin" too positions 'reality' and 'aesthetic emotion' together, but there is no conscious awareness of the border line, and as such, there is no conflict, either. On that point, "Rabijin" is a caricature of "Fūryūbutsu."

Returning to the passage from "Shinbiron" [Aesthetics], the reason for such a long quote concerns the example that was used. To explain the "alteration and mixing" of "aesthetic images and reality" and "aesthetic emotions and reality" an example of someone "walking through a mountain path at night when they're suddenly caught in a violent storm" is raised, and to see the "beauty" in the situation, the "spectator" can only seek to "remove the phenomenon from reality and regard it as an aesthetic image." As a literary expression, it calls to mind the most elegant naked body depicted in the literature of Japan's modern era. Indeed, it is Natsume Sōseki's "Kusamakura" [Grass Pillow].[15] The novel starts as follows :

Going up a mountain track, I fell to thinking. Approach everything rationally

15 First published in *Shinshōsetsu* (September, 1906).

and you become harsh. Pole along in the stream of emotions and you will be swept away by the current. Give free reign to your desires and you become uncomfortably confined. It is not a very agreeable place to live, this world of ours. (omission) Strip off from the world all those cares and worries which make it an unpleasant place in which to live, and picture before you instead a world of graciousness. You now have music, painting, or poetry, or sculpture. I would go farther, and say that it is not even necessary to make this vision a reality. Merely conjure up the image before your eyes, and poetry will burst into life and songs pour forth. Before even committing your thoughts to paper, you will feel the crystal tinkling, as of a tiny bell, well up within you : and the whole range of colours will of their own accord, and in all their brilliance, imprint themselves on your mind's eye, though your canvas stands on its easel, as yet untouched by the brush. It is enough that you are able to take this view of life, and see this decadent, sullied and vulgar world purified and beautiful in the camera of your innermost soul. (Natsume Sōseki 1988 : 12-13)

The protagonist of "Kusamakura" is a man "going up a mountain path" and who is also an artist by profession. As evidenced from the citation above, the narrative describes the protagonists' creations and the meaning behind his actions in relation to art and poetry and his role and attitude as an artist. You could say that it is Sōseki's own "Shinbiron" in the pretext of a novel. And while the artist in this story "going up a mountain path" doesn't quite face a 'terrible storm,' he does find himself caught in the rain. Walking through the rain the artist begins thinking about "detachment from feelings and emotions," which is similar to the problem surrounding "aesthetic images and reality" and "aesthetic emotions and reality." 'Picturing' the reality of the world which is an "unpleasant place in which to live," reality is a place concerned with 'knowledge,' 'emotion' and 'thought,' it doesn't depict the "poetry" and "paintings" of the "world of graciousness." A world which is "unpleasant to live" comes with "all those cares and worries which make it unpleasant," and so one is called to "strip off" the un-pleasantries and "picture" a better world. This is the behavior of one who "tries to see beauty," and the 'public form' that is 'art' requires a gaze (a way of looking) that must be fostered (trained) for the institutionalization of oneself. The artist of "Kusamakura" calls this behavior or gaze, "detachment from feelings and emotions" as he continues to climb the mountain path.

> I wonder how it would be if, while I am on this short journey, I were to regard events as though they were part of the action of a Noh play, and the people I meet merely as if they were actors. Since this trip is concerned fundamentally with poetry, I should like to take the opportunity of getting near to the Noh atmosphere, by curbing my emotions as much as possible, even though I know I cannot disregard them entirely. (Ibid., 23)

Here we can confirm that the artists' "detachment from feelings and emotions" is the behavior of "removing the phenomenon from reality and regarding it as an aesthetic image." But while he knows that he "cannot disregard them (his feelings and emotions) entirely," he is also aware that he cannot remain "in the position of an onlooker" safe from the "violent flurry of pros and cons, advantages and disadvantage." (Ibid., 18) In the closing paragraphs of the first chapter, the streaks of rain grow stronger, signaling the difficulties of "wandering through a land which is completely detached from feelings and emotions." (Ibid., 21)

> When I think of it as happening to somebody else, it seems that the idea of me soaked to the skin, surrounded by countless driving streaks of silver, and moving through a vast grey expanse, would make an admirable poem. Only when I completely forget my material existence, and view myself from a purely objective standpoint, can I, as a figure in a painting, blend into the beautiful harmony of my natural surroundings. The moment, however, I feel annoyed because of the rain, or miserable because my legs are weary with walking, then I have already ceased to be a character in a poem, or a figure in a painting, and I revert to the uncomprehending, insensitive man in the street I was before. I am then even blind to the elegance of the fleeting clouds; unable even to feel any bond of sympathy with a falling petal or the cry of a bird, much less appreciate the great beauty in the image of myself, completely alone, walking through the mountains in spring.
>
> At first I had pulled my hat down over one eye and walked briskly. Later I gazed down fixedly at my feet. Finally, very subdued, I hunched my shoulders and took one dejected step after another. On all sides the wind shook the treetops, hurrying a solitary figure on his way. I felt that I had been carried rather too far in the direction of detachment from humanity! (Ibid., 25-26)

The thing to disrupt the "land which is completely detached from feelings and emotions" (21) is not only the rain. The dialogue that transpires when he reaches the tea house in the rain is the perfect opportunity to "regard events as though they were part of the action of a Noh play, and the people… merely as if they were actors" (23), but even the "gossip and chat" (38) with the "Obahsan" (old lady of the tea house) (29) becomes the "dirt" (39) of this "wretched and unsavory world" (39) that makes his body feel "heavy" (39). There are many dangers that threaten to break his state of "detachment of feelings and emotions," but his honor is called into question when he comes across the "naked body" of a "woman" at the onsen (hot spring). The woman begins to descend the stone steps to the bath, unbeknownst to her that it is the same bath currently occupied by the artist. To the artist, in the steam of the onsen the woman looks like a dragon. Of most interest in this scene is the figure of the approaching woman, who in a normal situation and being a real woman, should be received with "real feelings and emotions" (reality), however, through the gaze of the artist and his "detachment from feelings and emotions," he states that upon "sight of her (the woman)" (106), (omission) "(m) y whole being was filled with the realization that I had discovered a beautiful artistic subject" (106). Immediately after this the artist begins a commentary on his negative impression of nude art, stating, "I have no complaint to make against classical Greek sculpture, but whenever I see one of those nude paintings which seem to have become the lifeblood of contemporary French art…" (106). However, his negation is not of nude painting in general, but of the excessiveness of the artists who "go to extremes to express the beauty of uncovered flesh" (106), and "try with all their might to get the nakedness to scream out to you from the canvas" (106). This interval to introduce nude theory serves to strengthen the impression that the movement of the woman descending the stone steps is suspended in midair, like a painting. While he negates "those nude paintings which seem to have become the lifeblood of contemporary French art," the artist acknowledges the figure of the woman through the steam of the bath as having "(s)uch complexity" and yet "unity of structure" (108), and comments that "(i)t would be impossible to find a shape so natural" (108). The passage continues as follows :

> It was not in fact thrust flagrantly into view like the average nude, but being only dimly visible in the midst of a strange aura of enchantment which lent mystery to all within it, gave no more than a subtle hint of its full beauty. (omission) If it is true that a dragon on which every single scale has been carefully painted looks ludicrous, then conversely the naked human body when looked at with deference retains its sublime loveliness. When I first caught sight of this figure I thought it might be some beautiful maiden who had fled down to earth from the kingdom of the moon, and who now stood there hesitating, surrounded by the rainbow which had pursued her. (Ibid., 108)

As is succinctly expressed with the term "beautiful maiden…from the kingdom of the moon," the naked body is looked upon as the culmination of beauty, however, the woman also possesses the "naked human body," and as she draws nearer to him, the "beautiful maiden" falls from the "kingdom of the moon" and the destruction of her "sublime loveliness" cannot be avoided. If the "strange aura of enchantment which lent mystery to all within it" had completely concealed all trace of the "naked human body" from the outset, it would unlikely have given birth to the feeling of "sublime loveliness." The setting of the woman descending the stones steps towards the tub where the artist is bathing creates a site of conflict of ideas of beauty, between "aesthetic emotions" and "reality," and conveys the meticulous authorial intent to point out the close proximity of those boundary lines. The passage above continues as follows :

> The whiteness of the woman's skin came floating towards me, and I feared that with one more step my maiden from the moon would degenerate into a being of this common world. Just then, however, her thick blue-black hair streamed around her with a swish like the tail of some gigantic legendary turtle cleaving through the waves. Next moment her white figure was flying up the steps tearing through the veils of mist. A clear peal of feminine laughter rang out in the corridor and gradually echoed away into the distance, leaving the bathroom quiet again. The water washed over my face, so I stood up. As I did so, startled waves lapped against my chest, and splashed noisily over the sides of the tank. (Ibid., 108-109)

"I feared that with one more step my maiden from the moon would degenerate into a being of this common world" : this represents the very moment that the "beautiful artistic subject" incarnates itself in the "human naked body" and the moment at which the "maiden of the moon kingdom" shines most beautifully. It is the moment as seen in "Fūryūbutsu" when the aesthetic nude appears as an integrated space combining sacred body and sexual body, and only materializes in the form of conflict on the border lines. The depiction of the woman that immediately follows, "her white figure was flying up the steps tearing through the veils of mist" with a "clear peal of feminine laughter" trailing behind her, is clearly to instill the sexual elements of the integrated space (the body). However, her laughter is not that of a woman of flesh-and-blood, degenerated to the "common world." A woman who laughs like that is one who possesses hair like "a legendary turtle cleaving through the waves." Rohan depicted laughter from "Benten-sama" in "Fūryūbutsu," and the laughter of the woman in this scene is quite similar.

Both Rohan with "Fūryūbutsu" and Sōseki with "Kusamakura" portray the nude body as an integrated space. Reflecting on these two novels, in the sense that they both portray protagonists who undertake "art" as a profession and who both embark on a journey as a sort of training for their "art" where they meet a woman, and both represent the woman as a nude (aesthetic) image, their structure is the same. Viewing the two as a single grouping calls for further research, for example, the study of "Fūryūbutsu" as a pretext to Sōseki's "Kusamakura," however, the point I wish to make for the time being is that when these authors portray the nude as an aesthetic body in their works, they don't remove the element of sexuality. The difficulty here is two-fold. To begin with, the criticism surrounding the dispute over the nude was, fundamentally, an attack against the sexuality assumed by nudity in art from an ethical and moral point of view, and it was in the study of Western aesthetics, like "Shinbiron," that advocated against "feelings of sexual desire" when looking at nude paintings. In the space and discourse surrounding the nude, perhaps Rohan and Sōseki, with their grounding of knowledge most relatable to the Western view of "art," that is, with the stance to accept the removal of sexuality from the body (integrated space) as a natural undertaking, in a rather trial-and-error sort of way they portray the nude incarnate. They also portray a Japanese-ness (Eastern-ness) in the sacredness of the body through the "elegant Buddha" and "moon goddess," so one may also observe the nude here as a Japanese appropriation of the Western aesthetic body. Generally, that's not an easy thing to conceive.

Kenneth Clark, author of *The Nude : A Study in Ideal Form* (Pelican Books, 1960; originally published : Bollingen Series, 1956), one of the most fundamental studies on the nude in fine arts today, has been translated into Japanese by Takashina Shūji and Sasaki Hideya as *Za Nūdo : Ratai geijutsu-ron* [The Nude : A Study on the Nude in Fine Art] (Bijutsu Shuppan-sha Co., Ltd., 1971). In the preface to the Japanese edition, author Kenneth Clark writes :

> For me personally, the translation of this book into Japanese is both moving and somewhat confusing. The underlying argument of this book is that the nude in fine arts brought about a transformation to the creation of certain structures based on geometric principles of the human body, and therefore, would be practically incomprehensible to the cultural sphere not influenced by the trends of 5th century BC Greece.

He immediately follows this by stating the error of such a remark, "It can help to adjust the imaginative abilities required for art lovers in Japan to understand the complexity and artificial composition of the classical nudes of Western Europe," and the utterance is certainly not without its tinge of diplomatic lip service. In the same preface he also states, "The triumph of this work is the study on Rubens," and says that "when I recall the name Rubens,

I can't not but feel renewed in my astonishment at the fact that Japanese readers will read my book," the reason being that the "image of the nude" is "not so much a representation of reality as it is a form of art," and while it is "ultimately dependent on a type of joyous experience," "Ruben's nude women will no doubt appear repulsive to a Japanese." In Chapter 1 of the book we can also find the passage, "The idea of offering the naked body for its own sake as a serious subject of contemplation simply did not occur to the Chinese or Japanese mind, and to this day raises a slight barrier of misunderstanding." (7) In other words, with regards to the comprehension of the "nude in fine arts" by a "cultural sphere not influenced by the trends of 5th century BC Greece," you could say that his view is exceedingly skeptical. I wish to now focus on the revered Kenneth Clark's statement regarding sexual elements in "nude fine art."

> "It (the human body) is ourselves, and arouses memories of all the things we wish to do with ourselves; and first of all we wish to perpetuate ourselves.
>
> This is an aspect of the subject so obvious that I need hardly dwell on it; and yet some wise men have tried to close their eyes to it. 'If the nude,' says Professor Alexander, 'is so treated that it raises in the spectator ideas or desires appropriate to the material subject, it is false art, and bad morals.' This high-minded theory is contrary to experience. In the mixture of memories and sensations aroused by the nudes of Rubens or Renoir are many which are 'appropriate to the material subject.' And since these words of a famous philosopher are often quoted, it is necessary to labour the obvious and say that no nude, however abstract, should fail to arouse in the spectator some vestige of erotic feeling, even although it be

only the faintest shadow – and if it does not do so, it is bad art and false morals."
(Kenneth Clark 1960 : 6)

"If the nude is so treated that it raises in the spectator ideas or desires appropriate to the material subject, it is false art, and bad morals" – these are words, the author indicates, "from a famous philosopher" which "are often quoted," and when one recalls the endeavors of Rohan and Sōseki in the Meiji period, this point cannot be stressed enough. If you are going to discuss the matters in the mid-twentieth century in the vein of "cultural spheres" which were "influenced by the trends of 5th century BC Greece," then people like Rohan and Sōseki who intentionally tried to import those many "memories and sensations" "which are 'appropriate to the material subject'," through the medium of art of Western origin and its visual appeal, which they converted to an expression of language, in other words, going through a two-fold process of appropriation (re-shaping), they conducted the very leading initiative that Kenneth Clark speaks of. One cause for not being able to see through to such pioneering experimentalism is the dated literary style of "Fūryūbutsu" and "Kusamakura." However, were it not for that particular style, they would not have been able to establish the nude body as the integrated space that they tried to represent. A big problem lies in the process of re-shaping (appropriation), but I wish to put an end to the indication of problems for now. At any rate, in their representation of the nude body as linguistic expression of the Meiji period, Rohan and Sōseki were authors who were thoroughly aware of the border conflict which was deeply related to the import and appropriation of Western knowledge, as evidenced by their efforts of representation of the nude body as an integrated space.

Works Cited

Clark, Kenneth, *The Nude : A Study of Ideal Art*. Harmondsworth, UK : Penguin Books, 1960.

Foster, Hal, *Shikakuron* [視覚論] (original title : *Vision and Visuality*), Translated by Kurenuma Norihisa [榑沼範久], Heibonsha, 2006.

Futabatei, Shimei [二葉亭四迷], *Rakochō zuron* [裸胡蝶図論] in *Ochiba no hakiyose Futakagome* [落ち葉のはきよせ 二籠め], 1889.

Kanzaki, Eishi [神崎永錫], *Nihon kindai bijutsu hattasushi* [日本近代美術発達史], Tokyo bijutsu, 1974.

Kitazawa, Noriaki [北澤憲昭], *Kyōkai no bijutsushi* [境界の美術史], Brucke, 2000.

Kōda, Rohan [幸田露伴], "Fūryūbutsu" [The Elegant Buddha, 風流仏] in *Sinchohyakushu* [新著百種], 1889.

Kōda, Rohan [幸田露伴], *Kōda Rohan shu* [幸田露伴集], Noborio Yutaka [登尾豊], ed. Iwanami shoten, 2002.

Miyashita, Kikuo [宮下規久朗], "Ratai hyōgen no henyō" [裸体表現の変容] in Tsuji Nobuo [辻惟雄], ed., *Bakumatsu Meiji no gaka-tachi* [幕末・明治の画家たち], Pelican, 1992.

Nakamura, Yoshikazu [中村義一], "Bijutsu ni okeru sei to kenryoku : ratai-ga ronsō" [美術における性と権力—裸体画論争], in *Nihonkindai bijutsu ronsōshi* [日本近代美術論争史], Kyūryūdō, 1981.

Nakayama, Akihiko [中山昭彦], "Ratai-ga, ratai, Nihonjin" [裸体画・裸体・日本人] in *Disukūru no teikoku* [ディスクールの帝国], Shinyōsha, 2000.

Natsume Sōseki [夏目漱石], *The Three Cornered World*, Translated by Alan Turney, Washington, D.C. : Regenery Gateway, 1988.

Ōgai, Mori [森鴎外], "Shinbiron" [新美論], in *Shigaramizōshi*, October, 1892 – June, 1893.

Outram, Dorinda, *The Body and the French Revolution : Sex, Class and Political Culture*, New Haven : Yale University Press, 1989.

Ozaki, Kōyō [尾崎紅葉], "Rabijin" (The Nude Beauty) [裸美人], in *Yomiuri shinbun* [読売新聞], 22, 23 November, 1889.

Ozaki, Kōyō [尾崎紅葉], "Kochō-dono" [胡蝶殿], in *Garakutabunko* [我楽多文庫], 1889.

Stratz, C. H., *Seikatsu to geijutsu ni arawareta nihonjin no karada* [生活と藝術にあらわれた日本人のからだ] (original title : *Die körperformen in kunst und leben der Japaner*), Translated by Takayama Yokichi [高山洋吉], Toei shoin, 1969.

Yamada, Bimyō [山田美妙], "Kochō" [Butterfly, 胡蝶] in *Kokumin no tomo* [国民之友], 1889.

The Modern Publication of Pre-Modern Literature and Its Significance

The Change of Intellectual Accreditation in Korea's Enlightenment Era*

Sun-hee Kim (Ewha Womans University)

1. Facing the Other : Imperial Japan, Lead Types, and Time

The social situation of those days is well-known that it need not be discussed here, yet the categorizing and distributing of our ancient texts among the intellectuals then were just as good as that of today's as good as the categorizing and distributing today. The first reason is that it was part of the ideological groundwork for a probable future independence in a state of independence under the then-current conditions of losing one's country and being oppressed by the Japanese, and second it was done in desperate efforts to maintain our deteriorating culture, reacting against the Japanese assimilation or cultural annihilation policy(Kimchundong 1963 : 223).

* This paper is revised from the article published in *Minjongmunhwa* [the Journal of Korean Classics, 민족문화] vol. 46 (2015.12, 257-283) issued by Hanguk Gojeonbeonyeogwon [the Institute for the Translation of Korean Classics, 한국고전번역원]

According to the memoir of Kim Chundong, who participated in the publication during the 1940's of the works of the 19th-century scholar Yi Gyu-gyeong (李圭景, 1788-1865) under the title *Oju Yeonmun Jangjeon San-go* [Scattered Manuscripts of Glosses and Comments of Oju, 五洲衍文長箋散稿]. This was then transferred to a magazine publisher and a man of letters named Choe Nam-sun (崔南善, 1890-1957) This quote that proves the efforts of Choe Nam-sun and his colleagues, who collected Joseon texts – and published them – demonstrates a scene of Joseon in distress at the start of the Japanese occupation.

During those times, Choe Nam-sun organized and published Joseon texts of various fields, in other words "ancient texts" (고문헌, 古文獻) with those who believed in the mission, to distribute among the public. In 1908, Choe Nam-sum established a research and publication institute of Joseon texts, named "Joseon Gwangmunhoe" [조선 광문회]. However, this article does not aim to observe the situation of the times or the process or results of the modernized publishing. It strives to delve into the fact that early 20th century intellectuals called Joseon texts, "ancient texts" and that they did a befitting work to its name.

In fact, Confucianism in Joseon's scholarship, system, and ideology, was never objectified. Traditionally Confucianists never have captured their own scholarly tradition from an outer view. Confucianists called their own scholarly tradition named "Confucianism" (유학, 儒學) as "this culture" (사문, 斯文), and when they called themselves "We Confucianists" (우리 유가, 吾儒), and what this expression holds is the idea and pride that their scholarship is the only tradition and authority itself. These scholars who never objectified their own scholarship did not feel the need to name it.

Then from when were Joseon's intellectual tradition and scholarly resources called "ancient texts" and "ancient writings"? In Joseon, the text *The Analects of Confucius* (논어, 論語), from 5 B.C.E., was not regarded as an ancient text to the 14th century Goryeo Confucian scholar Mok-eun Yi Saek (목은 이색 (李穡), 1328-1396), nor to the 16th century Neo-Confucian scholar Toegye Yi Hwang (퇴계 이황 (李滉), 1501-1570), nor to Dasan Cheong Yagyong (다산 정약용 (丁若鏞), 1762-1836), who is believed to have lived until the 19th century. Not only that, Toegye's writings that were 300 years old, in Dasan's times, were not considered ancient.

Here, it is difficult to say that "ancient texts" (고서, 古書) was a term that simply means old texts, since we cannot categorize texts that are from only one generation before as "ancient texts." In fact, the list of books to be published from Joseon Gwangmunhoe, which was active in the 1910s, included one by Yi Gyu-gyeong (1788-1856), *Oju Yeonmun Jangjeon San-go*, and one by Cho Han-Gi (최한기 (崔漢綺), 1803-1879), *Injeong* (인정, 仁政) and so on that were from just a generation before. In this context, we can say that Joseon's intellectual paradigm itself had changed whereby Joseon's intellectual traditions become ancient text, classic, and ancient writing in the early 20th century.

Moreover, the fact that Joseon's intellectuals in the early 20th century called texts from the previous generation "ancient texts," published and distributed in new ways, demonstrates a rupture in the intellectual subject or intellectual system at the time. Needless to say, the project of objectifying Joseon's intellectual tradition in "time' perspective had already started at the end of 19th century. Before the loss of national sovereignty, at the end of the 19th century, Joseon's intellectuals commenced to observe their intellectual tradition in terms of "time". A group of intellectuals who were showered with concepts of civilization from the West wanted to implement "Civilization and Elightenment" in Joseon as well. The slogan of "Civilization and Enlightenment," which functioned in the sense of crisis over the Great Powers that flushed in, quickly convinced Joseon's intellectuals through the growing modern newspapers and journals. The demands of the times to implement the New Studies or Western discipline, divided traditional intellects into various branches, and such responses surfaced as the "new/old discipline controversy."

The more important point was that a new concept of time that categorized traditional Confucianism into "old" discipline (구학, 舊學) and Western discipline as "new" discipline (신학, 新學) than to differentiate between the branches or to track down the aspects of the argument. The introduction of a new time categorization method categorizing Confucianism, which was the root of Joseon, and all its branches, into "old discipline," meant that Modern Western scholarship and system have already taken over Joseon's intellectual fields and its distribution structure. However, the dispute of new/old discipline can be seen as a conflict that was aroused by the different viewpoints on "modern" to the traditional intellects that still use Chinese characters (한문, 漢文). In such context, it is difficult to say that this dispute carried a strong inner power that would overturn Joseon's intellectual field in entirety. The reason behind is that Confucian scholars that argued for the new discipline did not give up on the values and ideas, as well as the traditional language "Chinese characters," of the old discipline.

In the early 20th century, the change in the formation and distribution structure of knowledge pushed down the existing intellectual field of Joseon into the "past" and endowed a strong time concept into Joseon's intellectual tradition. The time fault that divided Joseon into past and present, became more apparent in the 20th century Joseon especially through a modern medium called Lead Types (연활자, 鉛活字), and a publishing house that systematically operated this medium. This paper aims at delving into the changes of method and objectives of intellectual accreditation in the enlightenment era through the publications (공간, 公刊) of 18-19th century literature of Seongho, Yeonam, and Dasan that were created in the early 20th century.

2. Publication of *Yeonamjip*[1] and the Modern Summoning of Park Ji-won

The first time that modern printing was introduced was in 1883, year 20 of Emperor Gojong (고종, 高宗), when a new Printing Office named Bangmun-guk (박문국, 博文局) was established and new Japanese Lead Types were brought in to print Joseon's first modern newspaper, *Hansung Sunbo* (한성순보 漢城旬報). Soon after, a full-fledged introduction of printing technique and equipment were made into Joseon, and a rapid increase in the number of printing houses and publishers. Furthermore, commercial publishing houses appeared and were active around 1905, Protectorate Treaty between Korea

1 Collection of Park Ji-won's Works, 燕巖集.

and Japan (Eulsa Treaty) in 1905(Gangmyeonggwan 1999 : 52).[2]

The publishing movement at the time was part of the patriotic enlightenment movement rather than for profit, and with a sense of crisis due to the loss of national sovereignty, it had the strong nature of a social movement with various bodies participating. It is a known fact that the introduction of modern printing machines and technique changed the intellectual field of Joseon even without a detailed study. However, it is too early to say that this establishment of printing medium transported Joseon's intellectual stage straight into modern foundation. We can base our assumptions through the increase of publications of individual collection of works (문집, 文集), which was the core to pre-modern publishing(Sin Haneul 2015 : 7), under the Japanese occupation, in the early 1910s when print media were rapidly supplied.

According to prior studies, among the traditional publication of Joseon era, collection of works were about 40%, which was quite high at the time(Sin Seungun 2001 : 366). Since people attempted to secure the name of the family by registering as part of the intellectual genealogy through these anthologies, it was a natural phenomenon to put an emphasis on collected works. However, an important issue is that the traditional publications of anthologies did not decrease but rather increased during Japanese rule when the transfer into modernity was taking place. Individual anthology publication in Korea was a phenomenon that was consistent well into the 20th century, yet the total number of anthologies published during the Japanese occupation surpassed that of the total amount of anothologies published in Joseon era(Hwang Wiju

2 According to previous researches, there were 67 publishing houses established between 1905 and 1910.

2013 : 203-204).[3]

There may be various reasons for such phenomenon, but the changes in printing technique could be one of the reasons for encouraging the increase of anthology publications. After the 1910s, rather than using wood blocks,[4] a modern printing technique of lithography, *Seoginsul* (석인술, 石印本) that could save time and cost(O Yeongnan 1977 : 12-21)[5] were used most often to publish anthologies.

During Joseon era, lead types were already in popular use, yet when there was a need to print in vast amount people preferred to use woodblocks, and there were many cases where they had to reprint with wood blocks after printing in metal types in a hurry. Unlike lead types where they are taken apart after printing, wooden blocks could be used at any time since they can be preserved. Not only this, but many intellectuals believed wooden blocks that could be preserved were the original block, and that lead types that have many typos are only a temporary means. When mass printing in cheaper price became possible, many started to publish their collected works.

---

3 According to previous research, collection of works of those who died after 1910 is estimated to be 52 in Seoul/Gyeonggi region, 302 in Chungcheong region, 663 in Jeolla region, 391 in Daegu/ North Geyonsang region, and 462 in Busan/ South Gyeongsang region, which totals up to 1800 different kinds.

4 Sin Haneul, 2015, 7. According to this research, the first publication of collection of works printed in wooden blocks in the first half of the 20th century were about 317 kinds, and 95 kinds that took about 30% were published in the 1900s, which gradually decreased where only 9 kinds were published in wooden blocks by 1940s. Ibid., 17.

5 According to previous researches government-run factories, and Government printing office of the department of agriculture, commerce and enginnering (農商工部) were the first to start lithographic printing by placing an order in Germany and by inviting a typographer around 1899. Lithographic printing technique is simple compared to other methods. There is a limit to mass printing, but it is appropriate for sophisticated priting in small amounts.

Such a phenomenon demonstrated that even with the introduction of Western technique and system, and a reformation of system and education of using only Korean Character in official documents, due to Political Reform in 1894 (갑오경장), there was still an unshakeable base of a system of traditional knowledge production. Of course, as a result, Modernism arrived and settled in Joseon, and changed Joseon. Nevertheless, this process of advent, change, settlement should not be considered a soft-landing of Western modernism toward universality.

One way of distancing self-denial that understands the advent of the modern as a process of reaching towards global universlity through overcoming identity/particularity is to view Joseon's transition into the modern as the sum of a complex and heterogeneous state, and to set the degree of interpretation in a sensitive manner. One of the ways of this interpretation degree is the process and mechanism of a temporal transition, where the timeless intellectual tradition of Joseon becomes a collectable classic, and an ancient text of the past.

In 1897, when Japanese and Russian attempts of invading Joseon's national sovereignty became apparent, Emperor Gojong changed his Yeonho [era name, 연호] into Gwangmu (광무, 光武), and changed the name of the country into Great Korean Empire (대한제국) in the hopes of making groundwork for sovereign independence. With the basis of Gubon Shincham [구본신참, 舊本新參] policy that means to use tradition as a base and to use new, Western civilization as a reference, Emperor Gojong attempted "reform from the top down" in order to maintain Joseon's independence. In the midst of this time of change, the intellectual situation could not help but be shaken by what was going on. One of the aspects of such restlessness was the 20th century summoning of the 18th century Joseon intellectuals.

With the publication of *Yeonamjip* by Yeonam Park Ji-won (朴趾源, 1737-1805) in 1900 as a start, Dasan Cheong Yagyong's (1762-1836) book on criminal law, *Heumheum Sinseo* [New Book on Criminal Law, 흠흠신서 (欽欽新書)], and a book of instructions in governing the people (치민, 治民) for officials, *Mongmin Simseo* [Admonitions on Governing the People, 목민심서 (牧民心書)] were published in 1901 and 1902 consecutively. And more books were published : in 1911 Yeonam's journal of the journey as an envoy to Qing titled *Yeolha Ilgi* [Diary of Travels to Jehol, 열하일기 (熱河日記)] and in 1914 Dasan's theory of reformation of systems titled *Gyeongse Yupyo* [Memorial on Statecraft, 경세유표 (經世遺表)].[6] Moreover, a historical text by Yi Geung-ik (이긍익 (李肯翊), 1736-1806) was published under the title *Yeollyeosil Gisul* [Narratives of Yeollyeosil, 연려실기술 (燃藜室記述)] and a book on moral training by Yi Deok Moo (이덕무 (李德懋), 1741-1793) was scheduled to be published under the title *Sasojeol* [Paragraphs for a Learned Gentleman, 사소절 (士小節)]. Most of the works written by those who are categorized as "scholars of *shilhak*" [Practical Learning, 실학 (實學)] in Korean scholarship today were mostly published officially through modern publication process for the first time between the early 1900s and the Japanese rule.

---

6 The modern publication of Joseon texts recommences in the 1930s. In 1929 Sŏngho Yi-ik's (이익 (李瀷), 1681-1763) *Seonghosaseol Yuseon* [Sŏngho's Selected Essays, 성호사설유선(星湖僿說類選)] was published in Mungwang seorim [문광서림, 文光書林] with Jeong In-bo (정인보)'s editing, and between 1934-38, *Yeoyudang Jeonseo* [Complete collection of Jeong Yagyong's works, 여유당전서(與猶堂全書)], and in 1939 Damheun Hong Dae-yong's (홍대용 (洪大容), 1731-1783) *Damheonjip* [Collection of Damheun's works, 담헌집(湛軒集)] was published in Shinjoseonsa [新朝鮮社].

Yeonamjip (1900) opened the doors to the 20th century. Though it had already been edited by his descendants,[7] it was not published officially due to Yeonam's writing, and the uniqueness and the disparateness of his ideas. As it is generally known, Yeonam showed a disparate writing through various writing styles that cannot be categorized in one group and aversion as much as the breadth and the complexity of his writing continued from the time he was active and well into his postmortem times. Yeonam was a clear target for "*munche banjeong*" [문체반정, 文體反正], a literary style reform movement that called for changing any perverse literary style to old and innocent sentences. The nationwide criticism and regulation on Yeonam's free and original style continued its influence well after he died, and consequently stopping his works from being officially published. The power of his followers and defenders were able to defeat the power of criticism and prohibition 100 years after his death.

In order for an anthology to be published in Joseon, it had to undergo a social approval process that recognized its literary authority. In Joseon society, an anthology reveals the academic historical relationship that is its scholarly genealogical trace, such that its publication goes beyond a private meaning of publishing a personal work. Traditionally, publishing an anthology was done mostly by descendents or students after the author had died. Sometimes, more than a hundred years passed before publishing a book since publication was expensive and thus only possible when the descendants were financially

7 According to 'Gwajeongnok Chugi'[A addition to Gwajeongnok, 과정록추기(過庭錄追記)] written by Park Jong chae (박종채), the son of Park Jiwon in 1831, the collection and organization of literary works were completed before 1829.

secured. However, the most important aspect of publishing a book was the scholarly evaluation of the author and of the publication. Even if one had the financial ability to publish one's work in the early Joseon period, it couldn't be published if the work was not socially recognized, and even if it was published it couldn't be distributed(Jangwonyeon 2009 : 63).

As Yeonam's works couldn't be published without a determined evaluation, publishing anthologies in pre-modern Joseon was not just a personal decision, it was an act of registering into network of intellectuals and the genealogy and the hierarchy of scholarship. In this sense, the publication of *Yeonamjip* by Changang Kim Taek-young (金澤榮, 1850-1927), though it was only of selected works (선집, 選集), can be seen as a case that showed a change in the intellectual field in Joseon. Kim Taek-young, one of the top three poets of the late Joseon period and a patriotic enlightenment activist, sought asylum in China, and settled in Tongzhou [통주, 通州], a region in the lower reaches of the Yangtze River. He then worked in a publishing house called Hanmungrim Publishing Company [한묵임인서국, 翰墨林印書局] and interacted with Yan Fu (嚴復, 1853-1921), a Chinese liberal intellectual(Kimdonghun(2005), p.113). He used a copper type called Jeonsaja (전사자, 全史字), created and used since 1816, the year 16 of King Sunjo, to publish *Yeonamjip* in 1900, in a full 6 volumes of 2 books, and in 1901 its serial in 3 volumes of 1 book.

In fact, the 1900 publication of *Yeonamjip* by Kim Taek-young was done in an extension to the pre-modern intellectual field, in a strict sense. The reason why *Yeonamjip* was and was not published was all in Yeonam himself. The reason why *Yeonamjip* could be published was because of his brilliant sentences. Kim Taek-young said, "(compared to other Joseon literary men) only

Yeonam's spirit is particularly great and has all the strengths of the others. It is grand and deep, and changes but is remote as if the Creator bestowed a great diversity in form and figure along water,"(Kim Taegyeong(1917)) finding the value of *Yeonamjip* in Yeonam's sentences. Yeonam is summoned in the 20th century, remaining in pre-modern scholarly assessment.

However, there is one particular point to pay attention to. It is the place where Kim Taek-young published 7 volumes and 3 books of *Jungpyeon Yeonamjip* [Re-edition of Collection of Park Ji-won's Works, 중편연암집 (重編燕巖集)] with new lead types in 1917(Kim Yeongjin 2005 : 49). *Yeonamjip* was born into the world in an unfamiliar Chinese land, crossing the borders of Joseon's intellectual field. Kim Taek-young, who sought asylum in China, republished *Yeonamjip* in China, and not Joseon. The time and spatial movement of *Yeonamjip's* publication (公刊) signify that Yeonam's writing lay in a different route from formation and distribution of regular books. The fact that *Yeonamjip* came into the world, especially that it was published in China and not in Joseon, shows the subject that approves and distributed knowledge, and the traditional intellectual field below it have become weak or that it is moving. In Joseon, approving the transition of knowledge, validity, and cause was due to the fact that it was a country that operated various systems and policies, including national official examinations.

Yet, the changes of the intellectual field that the *Collection of Park Ji-won's Works* demonstrates does not simply limit itself to the weakening of national sovereignty or the idea of "righteous scholarship" (正學). Yeonam was already read from various angles during this time.[8] Yeonam is already not limited to

8 Regardless the publication of *Yeonamji*p, Yeonam was evaluated as 'a pioneer that opened his eyes

the traditional writers in the eyes of Unyang Kim Yunsik (운양 김윤식 (雲養 金允植) 1835-1922), a disciple of (門人) Park Kyu-soo (박규수 (朴珪壽) 1807-1877) and as a man who interacted with Kim Taek-young (金澤榮) and Yi Gun-chang (李建昌). Kim Yoon-sik, who was a member of Moderate Reformer (온건개화파), who was knighted by the Japanese Government-General of Korea after the Annexation, but lost his knighthood after 3.1 Independent Movement, and went through various hardships, evaluated the *Collection of Park Ji-won's Works* as follows :

> Looking through the contents of this anthology, it naturally combined the most needed and important issues of the day. In general, the 10 articles of the theory was a result of pursuing with all the efforts possible and concentrated thinking in the case of Westerners, only one or two things were accomplished with a powerful country implementing them in one or two hundred years. The master sits quietly reaching to that point and about the time he converses, he discloses and demonstrates in between compiling his writing.[9]

In this writing Kim Yoon-sik compares Yeonam to Rousseau and Montesquieu, and evaluates him as a person who takes a first step over the intentions of the modern meaning of impartiality (평등겸애, 平等兼愛) and sociology, and a person who forsees railways (철도, 鐵道) or studying abroad (유학, 遊學). They do not summon Yeonam into 20th century Joseon through his writ-

---

to relative world view, moving away from China-centrism, and a person who promoted equality through 'writings that attacked aristocrats' by Reformist intellects already in 1860.

9 Kim, Yunsik [김윤식], 'A Foreword to Yeonamjip', *Unyangjip*[The Collection of Unyang, 운양집] vol.10.

ing, but with his ideas. To them Yeonam is not a subject of succession but a subject of discovery, calling, and summoning. What they hoped to read from Yeonam was not a brilliant penship but the fact that it was a indicator of modernity, demonstrates that the grounds for this calling and summoning was the advancing of "Western Modernity" through imperial Japan.

Yeonam was not the only one who was called and summoned to the modern level. Dasan was also called and summoned in a similar manner. In fact, "resentment" (한, 恨) due to the writings would have been bigger with Dasan than Yeonam. Not only did Dasan earnestly want the publication of his writings in his life, but he also did not have any descendants with wealth and reputation like Park Kyu-soo. However, 20th century was in fact the time of Dasan rather than Yeonam.

The reason for the 20th century being Dasan's time was that the publishing house Gwangmunsa (광문사, 廣文社) established in 1901 by Hyeon Chae (玄采, 1856-1925), who was an interpreter during Korean Empire (1897-1910), later an activist of enlightenment, and an educator, published Cheong Yagyong's *Mongmin Simseo* and *Heumheum Sinseo* [New Book on Criminal Law, 흠흠신서 (欽欽新書)] in 1902. Also, Hwangseong Newspaper Company (황성신문사) published a newly edited version of Dasan's *Abang Gangyeokgo* [Essay on Geography of Our Country, 아방강역고 (我邦疆域考)] named *Daehan Gangyeokgo* (대한강역고, 大韓疆域考) by Jang Ji-yeon (장지연) in 1904. Originally, *Abang Gangyeokgo* was written when Dasan was in exhile in Gangjin in 1811. It was passed on in manuscript, until Jang Ji-yeon edited it in 1903 and Hwangseong Newspaper Company published a printed book with the name *Daehan Gangyeokgo*. Later, Dasan's writings were also published through Joseon Gwangmunhoe, which was established by Choe Nam-seon in 1908. Yi Geon-bang (李建芳, 1861-1939), who wrote the preface for *Gyeongse Yupyo* of Joseon Gwangmun-hoe, calls Dasan's way different from the traditional method.

> The Westerner Montesquieu wrote the book *Esprit des Lois* (*The Spirit of the Laws*) and Rousseau wrote *Du Contrat Social* (*On the Social Contract*), there weren't any governments that did not buy or did not follow as the book says. (…) Many countries in Europe are becoming stronger by the day thanks to scholarship. If I compare the master's writings to Montesquieu, Rousseau, and so on, it is truly difficult to differentiate its importance, yet since they have nothing to hide after criticizing or to be reluctant about something, they were able to present everything in their deepest heart. However, (…) (the master) could not dare to finish his words, sighing often, it is due to the times he met. If for these reasons, the master lacks something compared to those people, then that is not reasonable. (Yi Geon-bang 1908)

Yi Geon-bang also tried to read Dasan through Rousseau and Montesquieu. Such reading was unfamiliar to Joseon's traditional intellectual field.[10] The appearance of Rousseau and Montesquieu demonstrates that Yeonam and Dasan broke away from the pre-modern intellectual field and started to be read in different ways and contexts, with different meanings. They had an epochal quest to make intellectual resources of the previous times into the

10 It was through Liang Qichao's writings that Kim Yunsik or Yi Gun-bang got their information on Montesquieu or Rousseau. Liang Qichao called Confucianist of the late Ming period Huang Zongxi (黃宗羲, 1610-1695) as the Chinese Rousseau

present. This was the response of Seongho, Damheon, Yeonam, and Dasan to the quests they received.[11] The intellectuals of the Japanese occupation that could not possess the newly acquired Western knowledge and directly transplant it into Joseon, and into the language and system, obviously hoped to understand and absorb the Western modern knowledge within the discourses and knowledge they inherited. They reflected Joseon's scholarly inheritance through modern Western ideas.

The process of this overlapping view, takes the form of "discovery", and "selection". It is because they had to inherit the resources that could only respond to Western modernity and not Joseon's entire intellectual heritage. In this context, Yeonam, Dasan, Seongho, and Damheon were "discovered" and "planned" according to specific goals of Japanese occupied Joseon. In other words, they were "a qualified acceptance" (限定承認) of ideological inheritance by the next generation. In fact, such evaluations were a common recognition of the researchers. Yet, there is an issue we must not overlook in the process.

The issue that we shouldn't overlook is the method of accrediting the pre-modern intellectual resources that the intellectuals of the Japanese rule

11 The editorial on the publication of *Admonitions on Governing the People* of the 1902, May 19th issue of Hwangseong Newspaper, complimented that 'even if the the contents of the book were to be practiced in today's world, it wouldn't create much problem,' and that 'it is the latest (新書) in the politics of the Great Korean Empire'. Joseon people of the time hoped to find the grounds of the publication of these books in 'timelessness'. However, it would be difficult to take their words saying that it was their goal to apply it to reality. The reason being is that the morals in the books would have been valid in the past as well. In the times where information on theology and Western modern system poured in, and in the situation where social conflict is revealed due to such information, it would hard to believe that they have all of a sudden recognized the "practicality" of the reformation theory and legistlation theory of the past century. In this sense, there is a big possibility that their publication (公刊) is actually to hold on to the past rather than investing in the future.

inherit, in other words, the method in which the pre-modern Confucianists' works are officialy published. Different from the traditional publication, Dasan, Seongho, and Damheon's works are published not by their descendants or students, and not even by "Confucianists" but by new intellectuals in a modern publication. Later, their works, which are categorized as works of "scholars of *shilhak*", are accredited within the modern intellectual field with intellectual validity through being published by modern publishing houses different from the regular publishing periods or methods.

3. Dasan of the Modern, Seongho of the Pre-Modern

Dasan's works were first published in 1902 by by the modern publishing house Gwangmunsa (廣文社). Those who registered Dasan in Joseon's intellectual field through an unfamiliar method were the founder of Gwangmunsa Hyeon Chae and his colleague Jang Ji-yeon (張志淵, 1864-1921). Hyeon Chae was born in 1856 as a son of an interpreter, and started the life of an official at the age of 18, after passing the interpretation examination (역과, 譯科). He worked as a fourth grade document clerk, and an interpreter under Emperor Gojong's rule, but commenced work in translating and writing in the Ministry of Education (학부, 學部) editorial office around 1896.[12]

With the knowledge he acquired of printing and publishing modern books while working in a college editorial office, he privately created a modern

12 The editorial office of the Ministry of education was the institution that printed and translated, edited and issued textbooks, and verified and managed the books.

publishing house, Gwangmunsa(Jeong Eungyeong 1995 : 10). Hyeon Chae interacted with Unyang Kim Yoon-sik, Wi-am Jang Ji-yeon, and Changgang Kim Taek-young(Tanaka Ryuji 1989 : 12-16), and especially with Jang Ji-yeon and Yang Jae-geon, he published Cheong Yagyong's *Mongmin Simseo* and *Heumheum Sinseo* through the modern publishing house Gwangmunsa. Jang Ji-yeon records this as follows :

> (Year 4 of Gwangmu, age 37) We established Gwangmunsa in Winter October. Hyeon Chae and Yang Jae-geon and more discussed with me (Jang Ji-yeon) in asking Min Chiseol to inform the King to change the previous Simuchong Bosa (시무총보사) (Sin Yongha 2003 : 9)[13] to Gwangmunsa and by using its machines and types to engage in publishing. Therefore, I became an editor and published Cheong Dasan's *Mongmin Simseo* and *Heumheum Sinseo*. (Jang Jiyeon 1979 : 1119)

Gwangmunsa can be described as a modern publishing house that printed and published books, and commercially sold them. Publishing Dasan's books as the first was probably due to the influence of Jang Ji-yeon, who played a major role in establishing Gwangmunsa. Jang Ji-yeon published an article titled, "Summarizing a Major Scholar : Cheong Yagyong's Writings on Our Country's (我國) Administration of Social Welfare (경국제세, 經國濟世)" on April 17-18th,, 1899, in *Hwangsung Newspaper* (황성신문), where he was the editor-in-chief (Sin Yongha 2003 : 3).

13 Sisa chong-bo-sa (시사총보사) was a newspaper company that published *Sisa chong-bo* (시사총보), newspaper of the royal party (皇黨派), which was funded by emperor Gojong himself. Jang Jiyeon was the editor in chief but it was discontinued on July, 1899.

Jang Ji-yeon later edited *Abang Gangyeokgo* (아방강역고) and published it as a modern print in *Hwangsung Newspaper*.[14] Additionally, in the editorial of *Hwangsung Newspaper* on May 19th, 1902, titled "Gwangmunsa's newly-published book, *Mongmin Simseo* [廣文社新刊 牧民心書]," Jang Ji-yeon newly organizes the genealogy of Joseon Confucianism with mid Joseon's Confucianist Kim Yuk (金堉, 1580-1658), Yu Hyeongwon (柳馨遠, 1622-1673), Seongho Yi-ik (李瀷, 1681-1763), Yeonam Park Ji-won, and Dasan Cheong Yagyong. Among them Jang Ji-yeon believed that Dasan was the most outstanding of them all and placing him the center of the genealogy.[15]

The reason for Gwangmunsa publishing Dasan's works in new lead types was that Joseon was still functioning as a nation. Hyeon Chae's Gwangmunsa also received support from Emperor Gojong.[16] Dasan's was a befitting being of Emperor Gojong's policy called "Gubon Shincham" [구본신참] and was planned and published in newspaper and modern publication, and registered in the 20th-century intellectual field.

Dasan's writing appeared in Joseon's intellectual field in full scale through publications of Joseon Gwangmunhoe that was led by Choe Nam-sun in 1908. Those who led the publications were not the descendents or students, or the local Confucianists, but a couple of intellectuals who wanted to re-

14 *Hwangsung Newspaper* 1904.04.06.

15 *Hwangsung Newspaper* 1902.05.19.

16 Min Chi-heon [민치헌], an official during Emperor Gojong's reign, recorded on the conditions of publication, "many intellects grieved over the fact that this book (New Book on Criminal Law). Fortunately, we established Gwangmunsa and published the books owing to our emperor's encouragement of the power of literature, and this book came out first'., Min Chi-heon 'Heumheum Sinseo Bal' [A Postscript of Heumheum Sinseo, 흠흠신서 발(欽欽新書 跋)] in *Heumheum Sinseo*, Gwangmunsa [광문사], 1901.

pond to the request of the time. The individuals who were involved in the publication of Dasan's works in Joseon Gwanmunhoe included many from Choe Nam-sun, the creator of Gwangmunhoe, to Yi Geon-bang, a traditional Confucianist who thinks and writes in Chinese characters, and to Ahn Jaehong who led "the Joseon Studies Movement" by publishing *Yeoyudang Jeonseo* in the mid-1930s, and to Moon Il-pyeong. Unlike Gwangmunsa they did not receive national funding, and published Dasan's work through a modern publishing company as a civilian research group. This is when Dasan was registered in the modern intellectual field through a new method different from the publication method, and the subjects publishing the books, which were far from traditional contexts.

Were Dasan's official publications a natural result of the changes of the times? If we compare the anthology publications of Seongho Yi-ik, a scholar of a generation ahead of Dasan, who can be regarded as Dasan's intellectual master, it is difficult to agree. Seongho's anthology, *Seongho Seonsaeng Munjip* [The Complete Works of Master Seongho, 성호선생문집 (星湖先生文集)], was first published in 1917, in Mylyang [密陽] in Gyeongsang [慶尙] province.[17] Seongho's anthology was edited into 70 volumes by Seongho's nephew Yi Byeong-hyu (이병휴 (李秉休), 1710-1776) 11 years after the death of Seongho, but they weren't able to publish it until it was published by the right wing of the Seongho School (星湖右派), who were active in the Southeastern part of the country. The subjects of publications followed the traditional ways by

17 When *Seongho Seonsaeng Munjip* was published with deleting a part of the book, there was a debate among the scholars, and as a result different scholars re-edited The complete works of Master Sŏngho and published it again. (Sin Hangsu 2002).

distributing letters to the local Confucianists and gathered those who were interested, and then published the book after proper procedures. *Seongho Seonsaeng Munjip* is different from the other publications in that they were published using the most traditional methods.

Of course, there was some modern stimulation with this publication. In fact, the first time that Seongho's writing were published by Joseon Goseo Ganhaenghoe (조선고서간행회) in 1915. Joseon Goseo Ganhaenghoe was established by a Japanese publisher, and Seongho's student Ahn Jeong-bok published *Seongho Saseol Yuseon*, which was edited from *Seongho Saseol* as one of the books in the *Joseon Gunseo Daegye* (조선군서대계, 朝鮮群書大系) series. The publication of *Seongho Saseol* done by a Japanese commercial publisher would have made Seongho's descendants or literary men nervous. Yet, on the one hand, the direct occasion for the publication of *Seongho Seonsaeng Munjip* was when the Yeoju Yi family of Seongho in Mylyang bought a lithographic printing machine. However, *Seongho Seonsaeng Munjip* was printed with a wooden block and not the lithograph. The personnel who were involved in publishing the whole series chose the preservable wooden blocks over the temporary lead type, and by doing so wanted express their feelings of honoring their teacher Seongho. The subjects of publication as well as publication method was done traditionally. The ideology and direction of those who published *Seongho Seonsaeng Munjip* were still remaining in the 19th century.

If the publication of *Yeonamjip,* which was difficult to have officially published in Joseon due to its disparate writing style, was an event that showed the fissure in traditional authority that started to move the situation of Joseon's intellectual field, the publication of Dasan's writings reveals the changes of the social authorization and distribution system of knowledge and the changes of its subject. On the other hand, the fact that Seongho's anthology was published in a traditional method in 1917 demonstrates that Joseon's intellectual tradition still hadn't lost its sense of time and continued to function. There is one thing that can be confirmed, even with the differences in publishing subjects or methods, among Yeonam, Dasan, and Seongho. To the subjects of anthology publication that called and held them to an official medium, Joseon's intellectual tradition was not something that could be tied down by the 'past' or 'traditional' but were intellectual resources that were the present and had the sense of presense.

> Recently, Mister Hyeon Chae has planned to establish Gwangmunsa with a will to let the world know of books by accumulating funds, and to publish the anthology of the dead, or scattered books that may be of help in governing or newly invented books by foreign scholars in an orderly fashion to privilege present days.[18]

This editorial demonstrated that the publication of *Mongmin Simseo* and *Heumheum Sinseo* are only part of the requests of the time, and that they are dealt on the same level as new foreign books that carries modern knowledge. Though they were printed with new lead types and were sold as a product through publishing companies, the leading parts of the 20th century publications placed the 18th century Joseon intellectuals in the "present" and side

18 *Hwangsung Newspaper* 1902.5.19.

by side with the West received expectation that "if the book was distributed, it would help the penal administration (형정, 刑政)," (Jeong Daemu (1901)) and *Gyeongse Yupyo* received expectations that "if the master's book gains the application to politics and lights various systems and foundations, it would not stop in becoming a model for just one country but will become a model for future generations." (Yi Geonbang 1908)

In the early 20th century, the subjects that published Yeonam, Dasan, and Seongho still "read and internalize" these books and believed that they could find an alternative thought to solve Joseon's crisis within the books. The books of Seongho, Yeonam, and Dasan were not old books to be stored on shelves. Then, the summoning of Yeonam and Dasan, and the appearance of Seongho in the early Japanese Occupation that occurred in the 20th century, would have been the last possibility and a sign of mobility before Joseon was to be stuffed in the past, and before pre-modern and modern texts were categorized as "ancient texts".

4. Conclusion

Publishing Joseon books from the start of the Japanese occupation was a modern publishing act that was made up from private to commercial, based on the funding of Joseon dynasty and the Japanese Government-general of Korea. They were taken over by the government-general, which made it comparatively easier to access texts that were categorized and managed by the Joseon dynasty.[19] Through their publishing act, Joseon's texts were able to make their appearance in the modern intellectual field. This commercialized publishing act was created when the justification of studying and understanding Joseon was for efficient colonialization, and Hosaga's interest in collecting and enjoying past Joseon intellectual resources came together with that, and this demonstrates that Joseon's intellectual resources were managed and controlled by the Other and that it became a subject of commercial profit in the modern publishing market.

The biggest influence of this management and control and fabrication is that Joseon's intellectual tradition began to be controlled by a sense of time. Through Joseon's texts, Joseon became the 'past' for the first time and in a new manner. For these people, books from the previous era that were written in Chinese characters still were considered as intellectual resources of the time, but they were not books of the present but 'ancient texts' from the past times or 'extraordinary books' that gains value over time. Different from this, books written by Yeonam, Dasan, and Seongho that became part of modern media in the 20th century, were publications that had no audience in the agenda. Books by Yeonam and Seongho were distributed in traditional methods without being priced. Compared to those books, *Mongmin Simseo* and *Heumheum Sinseo* were sold commercially, but consumers of these books

19 Hosoi Hajime states 20 or so books of ancient texts, collection of poems, and books on novels that they published were selected according to the bibliographical introduction of ancient texts (古書解題) of the Japanese Government-general of Korea. They assert that they have reviewed the contexts of the texts kept in the Japanese Government-general of Korea's Councillor branch office (參事官分室) and have found that the list was lacking, thus, changed the list of books. [鮮滿叢書第一卷の卷頭に, 鮮滿叢書 vol.1, 自由討究社, 1922.1] They selected books that are commercial based on the collected Joseon texts by the Japanese Government-general of Korea.

were not those who just sought for modern reading materials but were readers who grew up in similar intellectual tradition.

However, attempts made to publish through modern media by governmental Japanese and Joseon Gwanmunhoe not only changed the production method but also divides the producer and the consumer. Different from pre-modern knowledge production that published books only after persuasion of intellectual validity was made, modern publication, magazine, and newspaper did not have an official system to evaluate the significance and the validity of the publication, and their promotion itself plays a role of a system accrediting intellectual value. When this system started to operate, pre-modern Joseon texts break free from its original context and were distributed in a new intellectual field.

Needless to say there is no need to evaluate this separation as something negative or limited. Intellectual resources of the previous era can break away from their context and genealogy, and are able to gain new reputation and value by being separated from the subject of knowledge production. Yet, how is this new reputation and value determined? The problem here is that the evidence to endow new stature and value to the texts of the past era did not exist within the text itself. These texts were suggested with unfamiliar questions and responses that were never experienced before.

In the early 20th century Joseon was given an unfamiliar question that came from the outer world. How will it break free from the Japanese rule and recover national sovereignty? How is it going to stand shoulder to shoulder with Western countries? When the country was lost, Joseon's intellectuals formed detailed clauses of questions with unfamiliar ideas such as civilization, enlightenment, new scholarship, the people, science, and so on, and had to suggest the contents of the responses. In this process the intellectuals who were involved with modern publication divided traditional intellectual system into "past" (舊) and "old" (古), and sought to transfer into modern intellectual field selectively. The standard for this selection was 'modernity' and to find the qualities required by ths modernity in the traditional intellectual system created the word "silhak" [practical science, 實學].

Later, during the span of the Japanese occupation, partial knowledge of modern and natural, in midst of Joseon's intellectual tradition, the name "silhak" was given to take part of the modern intellectual field, and neo-Confucianism, Confucian ritual studies (예학, 禮學), Confucian Canon Studies (경학, 經學), and other traditional scholarship were excluded in the name of "old scholarship" (구학, 舊學). Moreover, such structure still remains the same even after recoverying national sovereignty, and standing shoulder to shoulder with the West. The image of Confucianism and neo-Confucianism being outdated was created in this era, and the image of excessive modernism given to *silhak* still exhibits its influence in our society today. Even now where the question has changed, "modernity" still functions as a controlling idea in our academic world. That is to say, the effects of limited approval and dynamic are still in operation.

Works Cited

Gang, Myeonggwan [강명관], "Geundaegyemonggi Chulpanundong'gwa geu yeoksajeokui-ui"[Korean Enlightment Literature; The Publication Movement in the Enlightment Era and its Signfi cance, 근대 계몽기 출판운동과 그 역사적 의의], *Minjong Munhaksa Yeongu* [Research on the history of Korean literature,민족문학사연구] vol.14., Minjong Munhaksa Hakhoe [민족문학사학회], 1999.

Hwang, Wiju [황위주], "Iljegangjeomgi Jeontongjisiginui Munjip Ganhaeng Yangsang'gwageu Teukseong"[The reality and characteristics of publication of traditional intellectuals collections of works in the Colonial era, 일제강점기 전통지식인의 문집 간행 양상과 그 특성], *Minjongmunhwa* [the Journal of Korean Classics, 민족문화] Vol.41, Hanguk Gojeonbeon-yeogwon [the Institute for the Translation of Korean Classics, 한국고전번역원], 2013.

Jang, Jiyeon [장지연], *Jang Jiyeon Jeonjip* [The Collection of Jang Jiyeon, 장지연전집] Vol.10, Danguk University, Dongyanghag Yeonguso[단국대학교 동양학연구소], 1979.

Jang, Wonyeon [장원연], "Joseonsidae Gaeinmunjibui Ganhaeng'gwa Gyojeong"[Publication and Proofreading of Individual Collection in Joseon Dynasty, 조선시대 개인문집의 간행과 교정], *Seojihakbo* [서지학보] vol.34, Hangukseojihakhoe [한국서지학회], 2009.

Jeong, Daemu [정대무], "Heumheum Sinseo Seo"[A Foreword of Heumheum Sinseo, 흠흠신서 서(欽欽新書 序)], *Heumheum Sinseo*, Gwangmunsa [광문사], 1901.

Jeong, Eungyeong [정은경], "Gaehwagi Hyeonchaegaui Jeo, Yeoksul mit Balhaengseoe gwanhan Yeongu"[Bibliographic Study on Hyunchea Family(玄采家)'s Books in the Opening, 개화기 현채가의 저·역술 및 발행서에 관한 연구], Ewha Womans University [이화여자대학교], Master's thesis, 1995.

Kim, Chundong [김춘동], "Nodusaengae – Oju Yeonmun Jangjeon San-go-e chwihayeo"[A Life of an Old Man, 五洲衍文長箋散稿에 취하여], *Minjongmunhwayeongu* [Korean Classics Studies, 민족문화연구] vol.1, Goryeodaehakgyo Minjongmunhwayeonguwon[Research Institute pf Korean Studies, Korea University, 고려대학교 민족문화연구소], 1964.

Kim, Donghun [김동훈], "Kimtaegyeong, Geundaejeok Gakseonggwa Junggungmunindeurui Yeonghyang"[Taek-yung Kim, modern awakening and the infl uence of Chinese, 김택영, 근대적 각성과 중국문인들의 영향], *Hangungmunhag Yeongu* [한중문학연구] vol.28, 2005.

Kim, Yeongjin [김영진], "Park jiwonui Pilsabon Sojipdeulgwa Jakpum Changjangnyeon Go-jeung[Transcribed Version of Park Ji Won's Short Pieces of Collection and Historical Investigation of Writing Period, 박지원의 필사본 소집들과 작품 창작년 고증], *Daedonghan-munhak* [대동한문학] vol. 23, Dae-donghanmunhakhoe [대동한문학회], 2005.

Kim, Yunsik [김윤식], 'A Foreword to Yeonamjip', Unyangjip [The Collection of Unyang, 운양집] vol.10.

O, Yeongnan [오영란],"Hanguk Seokpaninswaesur'e gwanhan Yeongu"[A study on lithography of Korea, 한국 석판인쇄술에 관한 연구], Ewha Womans University [이화여자대학교], Master's thesis [석사논문], 1977.

Sin, Haneul [신하늘], "20segi Chogi Ganhaeng Mokpanbon Munjip Yeongu"[A study on the collections of literary woks by wood-block printing published in the early 20th century, 20세기 초기 간행 목판본 문집 연구], Sungkyunkwan University [성균관대학교], Master's thesis, 2015, 7.

Sin, Hangsu [신항수], 'Yi ik Munjip Ganhaeng'gwa geu Seonggyeok' [Th e Pubulication of Seongho Seonsaeng Munjip and its character, 성호의 문집 간행과 그 성격], *Hansin Inmunhag Yeongu* [Hanshin Journal of Humanities, 한신인문학연구], Hanshin Institute of Humanities, Hanshin University [한신대학교 한신인문학연구소], vol.3, 2002.

Sin, Seungun [신승운], "Yugyo Sahoeui Chulpan Munhwa" [The Publication Culture of Confucian Society : Emphasized the Compilation and Publication of the Anthology in the Chosun Dynasty, 유교 사회의 출판 문화—특히 조선시대의 문집 편찬과 간행을 중심으로], *Daedong Munhwa Yeongu [Journal of Eastern Studies*, 대동문화연구] vol.39., Daedong Munhwa Yeonguwon, Sungkyunkwan University [성균관대학교 대동문화연구원], 2001.

Sin, Yongha[신용하], "19segimal Jang Jiyeonui Dasan Jeong Yagyongui Balgul" [Jang Jiyeon's discovery of Dasan Jeong Yagyong in the end of 19th Century, 19세기 말 장지연의 다산 정약용의 발굴], *Hangukhakbo* [한국학보] vol.29 no.1., Iljisa [일지사], 2003.

Tanaka, Ryuji, "Baekdang Hyeonchaeui Saengae'wa Sasang, [Baekdang Hyeoncha's life and thought, 백당현채의 생애와사상], Yonsei University [연세대학교], Dissertation, 1989.

Yi, Geon-bang [이건방], "Bangnyechobonseo"[A Foreword to Bangnyechobon, 방례초본서(邦禮草本書)], *Gyeongse Yupyo* [경세유표], Joseon Gwangmunhoe [조선광문회], 1908.

The Afterlives of An Chunggŭn in Republican-Era China

From Sinocentric Appropriation to a Rupture in Nationalism

Inhye Han (Ewha Womans University)

On October 26, 1909, when Korea was a protectorate state of Japan, Korean anticolonial activist An Chunggŭn (1879-1910) assassinated Itō Hirobumi (1841-1909), the former Japanese prime minister and first resident-general of Korea, at the Harbin train station in northeast China. Itō had traveled to Harbin for a meeting with Vladimir Kokovtsov, the Russian secretary of the treasury in Manchuria; after An shot Itō to death, An was immediately arrested by the Russian police guarding Kokovtsov and later handed over to the Japanese police. An was incarcerated in the Lüshun prison in the Kwantung Leased Territory, sentenced to death on February 14, 1910, and executed on March 26, 1910.[1] Despite An's nationality and the context of this incident,

1 Upon the outbreak of the Russo-Japanese War (1904-1905), the Japanese emperor proclaimed that Japan was waging war "to protect peace in the East and the independence of Korea [from Russia's invasion]" (Ichikawa 1979 : 143). However, following the Empire of Japan's victory, Japan forced Korea to sign the Japan-Korea Protectorate Treaty (1905) and dissolve its existing political parties. To revoke this unequal treaty, Korea's King Kochong secretly dispatched envoys to the Hague Conference on World Peace (1907), yet the attending countries refused to talk to them. That "underhanded" attempt led to the 1907 Japan-Korea treaty that provided Resident-General Itō Hirobumi with the authority to govern Korea's internal affairs. King Kochong was dethroned

his story was repeatedly recounted, dramatized, and memorialized by the Chinese in literature, criticism, biographies, and journalism throughout the Republican period (1912-1949).[2] In 1928, *Patriotic Spirit* [C : *Aiguohun*] — a film directed in Shanghai by Korean filmmaker Chŏng Kitak — injected for the first time a Korean perspective into existing Chinese nationalist narratives about An. In 1931, the Wanbaoshan Incident, a violent conflict between Korean and Chinese civilians in Manchuria and Korea, led to yet another shift in An's legacy in China. This article examines how An Chunggŭn served as a symbol communicating different meanings in Chinese discourse at these two junctures in terms of Sino-Korean relations and Chinese nationalism.

as a result, and Korea's military sovereignty was annulled, a dramatic political change that prompted the Korean masses, including An Chunggŭn, to mobilize anti-Japanese militia movements. For a historical-political background of the 1909 event and An's trial process, see Nakano (1984, 1996). For a detailed study of the historical Japan-Korea relations, Itō's political career, and An Chunggŭn's activism, see Ichikawa (1979). For an analysis of the complex religious, political, and philosophical bases of An's anticolonial activism, see Hwang (2009) and Rausch (2012). For the responses of Chinese, Russian, and other Western journalists to An's assassination of Itō, see Ichikawa (1979, 186-208) and Bang (2010). Bang's article introduces a few Chinese and Russian articles that critiqued An Chunggŭn and lamented Itō's death, a stance that most previous Korean-language studies of An overlooked. For studies that focus on Korea-Russia relations, see Pak (2009), Sumbirtseva (Сумбирцева) (2010), and Sin (2010). For studies that compare An's view of Russia to others', see Tikhonov (2009) and Finch (2012).

2 Ye Tianni's *Biography of An Chunggŭn* [C : *An Chonggen chuan*] and Zheng Yuan's *An Chunggŭn* are Chinese-language biographies of An by Chinese authors. The exact years of publication are unknown, as the copyright pages of both books have been lost. However, scholars conjecture that Ye's biography was published in 1914 or 1915 and Zheng's was published in the 1920s. A Chinese-language biography of An by Pak Ŭnsik, a Korean scholar living in Shanghai, appeared in the first issue of *Republican Report* [C : *Minguo huibao*] in 1913 and was later published as an independent volume, the publication year of which is also unknown. Chang notes that a number of Chinese poems also dramatized the 1909 assassination. In 1915, the magazine *Virtue-Esteem Bulletin* [C : *Chongde gongbao*] serialized a novel dramatizing An; in 1921, *Historical Novel/Drama in Qing* [C : *Qing shi yanyi*] by Lu Shi'e also dramatized An's true story. Among all genres, plays were the most frequent and drew much attention from mass audiences (Chang 2010).

From 1909 to 1939, sixty-eight articles in Chinese-language periodicals, excluding newspapers, discussed An Chunggŭn. Except for 1909 and 1910, when the actual event and execution took place, there were only two years in which six or more articles about An were published : 1913 and 1931.[3] Daily papers, by comparison, reported more steadily on An and his family, including stories about the financial situation of An's bereaved family, who moved to Shanghai following his death; the death of An's mother; the college education of An's daughter; and the careers of An's brothers. However, newspapers showed a similar pattern — more articles were published in 1909, 1910, and 1931 — with one exception : there were heated discussions in newspapers in 1928 about the film *Patriotic Spirit*, which was an immense hit in Shanghai.[4]

3 The periodicals include *East Magazine* [C : *Dongfang zazhi*], *China* [C : *Zhonghua*, Shanghai-based], *Benefitting All Round* [C : *Guangyi congbao*], *New Century* [C : *Xin shiji*], *Daxia Collection* [C : *Daxia congkan*], *People* [C : *Guomin*, Shanghai-based], *Foreign Affairs* [C : *Waijiao bao*], and *South* [C : *Nan Bao*], among many others.

4 The 1842 Treaty of Nanjing made Shanghai a semicolonial treaty port, a special zone whereby imperialists reached the interior of China only indirectly. Since the semicolonial state delimited imperialist power within treaty ports, assistance from local elites and merchants was indispensible for European and Japanese empires to attain commercial-financial interest. For studies probing interdependency between imperialists and Chinese merchants and elites, see Walker (1999) and Goodman (2000). Goodman's article on the 1893 Shanghai Silver Jubilee offers excellent insight on Shanghainese capacities of reconfiguring the European-led festival as a Chinese event, a novel appropriation that recognizes the presence of foreign powers yet simultaneously celebrates the Empress Dowager's birthday and native-place identities. Although Goodman focused on one specific moment prior to the first Sino-Japanese war (1894-1895), the ingenious Chinese culture of appropriating semicolonial, modern practices continued through the 1920s and 1930s. Chinese did not persistently resist Western culture, yet "advanced" European influences failed to replace or marginalize "backward" Chinese culture, unlike other Asian countries. Instead, both modern Western and traditional Chinese culture thrived side by side. Japanese condemned this resilient quality of Chinese culture, calling Shanghai a "demon city" (Liu [Ryū] 2000). For studies examining the fragmented, multiple, and multilayered forms of semicolonial domination that lacks institutionalized colonialism in most parts of China, showing the partial and limited power of imperialists in

Since the 1910s, then, the most attention was given to An, through reporting and dramatizations, in 1928 and 1931. By connecting these junctures and comparing the use of An as a symbol in Chinese discourse, this study shows how Chŏng's historical-political drama film (1928) and the violent Sino-Korean conflict (1931) unwittingly reinforced nationalism yet caused a rupture in Chinese nationalism, a finding that casts light on the new aspects of the colonial-to-colonial cultural interactions in the 1920s and 1930s.

Tracking Chinese print media's recollections of An, I found striking contrasts in Chinese responses to the 1909 historical incident and to the 1928 film dramatization of that event. Immediately after the incident, Chinese audiences praised An as a "patriotic Korean martyr," whereas later, Chinese discourse obscured An's Korean nationality, privileging either the story of an individual's sacrifice for the nation or formalistic aspects of Chŏng's film. In the 1930s, Chinese discourse about An changed again and expressed even greater admiration of An, despite heightened anti-Korean sentiment in China due to the 1931 Wanbaoshan Incident. This article investigates critical implications of these contradictions in the Sino-Korean cultural interaction during the Japanese colonial era. More specifically, my analysis shows what diasporic Koreans were able to do, other than collaborate or resist, in semicolonized China, where ethnonationalism powerfully appropriated transnational voices.

Later in the article, I elaborate on the complicated relations between nationalism and transnationalism in Republican China, the context in which

China, see Cohen (1984), Duara (1995 : 224), and Shih (2001). For Shanghai's cosmopolitanism as a consequence of semicolonial cultural conditions that go beyond the dictates of nationalism, see Bergère (1981) and Shih (2001). For a literature review of Shanghai studies from the 1990s to 2010, see Fogel (2010).

Patriotic Spirit was situated. Put briefly, in China both nationalism and transnationalism emerged at the turn of the twentieth century, feeding and competing with each other. As previous studies have demonstrated, Chinese transnationalism of this period ranged from state transnationalism — as seen in Sun Yat-sen's Pan-Asianism and his rhetorical slogan of the Republic of the Five Races — to the popular transnationalism of religious orientation, exemplified in Kang Youwei's Great Unity [C : *Datong*] philosophy. Although Chinese nationalism was never self-sufficient and hinged on transnationalism, Sinocentric nationalism co-opted and contained transnational ethics and movements at crucial political junctures (Duara 1998). Whereas previous studies have illuminated two sides of nationalist appropriation of transnationalism — nationalism that dominates transnationalism yet lacks self-sufficiency — this article reveals a self-rupturing aspect of that appropriating process.

Among existing narratives about An, *Patriotic Spirit* offers an excellent opportunity to examine the ways in which Chinese nationalism, embodied in the responses of Chinese audiences and critics to the film, powerfully yet incompletely eclipsed An's transnationalist intentions and vision. Based on the true story of An's assassination of Itō Hirobumi, *Patriotic Spirit* was the first Chinese film directed by a Korean filmmaker and also Chŏng Kitak (1905-1937)'s directorial debut. The success of *Patriotic Spirit* brought Chŏng significant fame in China. *Patriotic Spirit* recast An's true story as a narrative about a Sino-Korean alliance against Japanese colonialism. I show that *Patriotic Spirit*'s transnational voice, which echoes An Chunggŭn's vision of Asian solidarity, initially generated an unintended nationalist response from its audience, yet ultimately brought about a rupture in ethnonationalism at a most unlikely moment — following the 1931 Wanbaoshan Incident, when more than a hundred Chinese and Koreans were killed.

To demonstrate that process, the article is divided into four parts. The first part of this article lays out the political-historical context of An's activism and examines Chinese nationalist responses to An's story prior to *Patriotic Spirit*. The second part discusses *Patriotic Spirit* and its transnationalism. The third part analyzes the unintended nationalist responses of Chinese audiences to the film's depiction of the story. Finally, the last part looks at later responses of the Chinese to An's story in light of anti-Korean sentiments following the Wanbaoshan Incident, showing how the seemingly coherent and cohesive mechanism of Chinese nationalism ruptured. This study argues that 1930s Chinese media inadvertently echoed the transnationalism of An and *Patriotic Spirit*, despite the predominant anti-Korean sentiment following the Wanbaoshan Incident. By attending to Sino-Korean cultural relation in film and print media, I reveal a deconstructive, decentered element within 1920s and 1930s nationalist discourses. Rather than tracking how East Asian nationalisms emerged, developed, and crystallized in the wake of Western and Japanese colonialism, I uncover the incoherent and noncohesive aspects of East Asian nationalism at the time. Hence, this study sheds light on two aspects of ethnonationalism : (1) its exclusionary attribute, which subjugates other nations within and beyond its territory; and (2) the self-rupturing moment of Han-centric nationalism in which it simultaneously excludes and includes another nation.

1. *A Treatise on Peace in the East* (1910) and Chinese Responses to An's Story Prior to 1928

Although An's assassination of a prominent Japanese politician has typically been viewed as an expression of Korean nationalism, his act was based on a vision of Asian unity that challenged ethnonationalism. At his trial, An Chunggŭn stated that in 1905 he encountered the Japanese emperor's statement that Japan was waging a war against Russia "to protect peace in the East [J : *Tōyō no heiwa*, 東洋の平和] and the independence of Korea (from Russian invasion)" (Ichikawa 1979 : 143). As the only Asian country among the world empires, Japan claimed the role of defending Asia from invasion by Western empires, propagating the slogan "peace in the East" that the Japanese emperor and politicians had conveniently employed, since the 1895 Sino-Japanese war, to legitimate colonial invasion. An took literally the emperor's rhetorical call for peace in the East, concluding that it was Itō Hirobumi who rescinded the military sovereignty of Korea, schemed to occupy Manchuria, and therefore interfered with the emperor's political vision. Hence, An argued that killing Itō was a means of maintaining the regional peace, inadvertently appropriating the imperialist rhetoric of Eastern peace for a theoretical ground of anticolonial practices.

The Japanese imperialist version of Eastern peace was a concept familiar to people across East Asia in the early twentieth century. However, it is difficult to assess how widely An's own idea of Eastern peace was known in China at the time of his death. A couple of Chinese-language articles touched on An's political philosophy. In a short piece in *National News Weekly* [C : *Guowen zhou-*

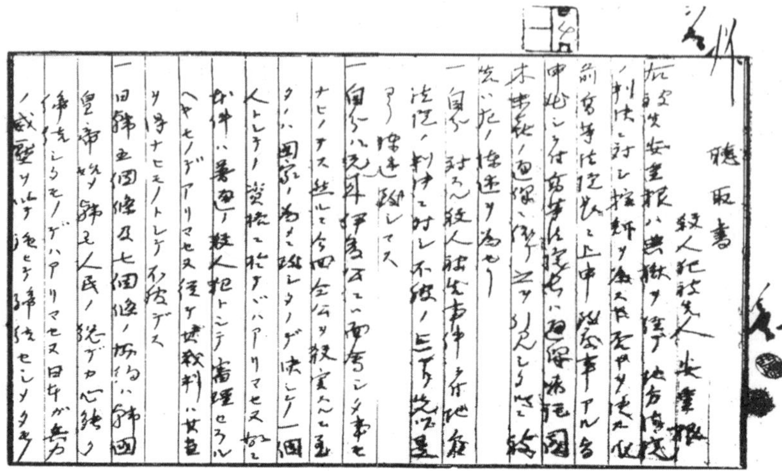
聴取書

Figure 1 | Hearing record. *Source* : Kukka Pohunch'ŏ (1995 : 621). Originally a thirteen-page classified document of Japan's Ministry of Foreign Affairs.

bao], for example, Lü Bo noted, "A person who observed the execution of An quotes (An's last words) : 'I'm leaving (this world). I plead all of you to strive for peace in East Asia'" (1925 : 17), thus informing his Chinese readers of An's call for the communal East Asian pursuit of peace.

In An's unfinished book, *A Treatise on Peace in the East* [K : *Dong'yang p'yunghwa lon*], which he wrote in prison and which was published posthumously, An condemned the schism within the East, especially Japan's war against China, stressing the necessity of racial solidarity among Asian nations in order to resist Western empires. Although that book is too short to adequately present An's specific political vision, the "hearing record" [K : *ch'ŏngch'uisŏ*] from his one-on-one talk with District Judge Hiraishi Ujihito soon after his 1910 trial (see figure 1) reveals his idea of an ideal regional community and a more detailed picture of regional peace. An called on Korea, China, and Japan to establish a Peace Council of the East [K: *Dong'yang Pyŏnghwa Ŭihoe*, 東洋平和會議], a joint "peace army" in which soldiers should speak at least two languages, and also joint banks in Lüshun and other major cities in the three countries. In addition, An argued that China, Korea, and Japan should share a single currency, and that Japan ought to guide Korea's and China's economic development. Finally, An urged Japan to make an official apology to Korea and China for its military invasions (Kukka Pohunch'ŏ 1995 : 621-633).[5]

Chinese cultural responses to An's assassination of Itō trace back to 1911, when the Evolution Group [C: *Jinhuatuan*], a troupe dedicated to modernizing Chinese drama, staged the play *An Chunggŭn Assassinates Itō* [C: *An Chonggen ci Yiteng*]. Deng Yingchao — the wife of Zhou Enlai (1898-1976) who was one of the core members of the Chinese Communist Party — played a role in the production. Without a surviving script, it is impossible to analyze how the play actually presented An's actions, but newspaper sources nonetheless indicate that between 1911 and 1928, Chinese playwrights and actors dra-

5 Sino-Japanese relations during this period also provide an important context for Chinese discourse and narratives about An Chunggŭn. Since the late 1910s, Japan-China relations had become multifaceted, as large-scale anticolonial movements in Japan's (semi-)colonies broke out, and the United States arose as a world power (Yonetani 2006). From the late 1910s to 1930s, Chinese and Japanese intellectuals exchanged ideas and endeavored to mobilize international mass movements against the Japanese Empire and Chinese warlords, linking the momentum of the Chinese May Fourth Movement and that of the Taisho democracy movement (Yonetani 2006; Tanaka 1993 : 276-277). Japanese thinkers — such as Yoshino Sakuzō (1878-1933) and Yanaihara Tadao (1893-1961) in the interwar years and Miki Kiyoshi (1897-1945) and Ozaki Hotsumi (1901-1944) during World War II — viewed China, Taiwan, and Korea not as backward colonies to be dominated, but as potential allies for Japan. Previous studies have shown that China affected policy making in the metropole, and therefore the colony-metropole relationship was not unidirectional. However, by the early 1930s, international and transnational movements within Asia became distinctively militarist and imperialist (Conrad and Duara 2013 : 22). As multifaceted as Sino-Japanese relations were, China's antagonism toward Japan prevailed throughout the Republican era.

matized and revived An's story as a means of bolstering Chinese nationalism. In the 1920s, *An Chunggŭn Assassinates Itō* continued to be performed not only in Shanghai but in other cities across China, a nationwide staging that demonstrates the popular circulation of An's story in China. As Chang's study notes, plays dramatizing An's act were performed in Zhenhai (Zhejiang Province), Haifeng, Tianjin, Wuhan, Changsha, and Guangzhou, among others. Prominent figures of the time, such as Peng Pai, Zhou Enlai, Deng Yingchao, and Tian Han, participated in these plays as directors or actors. The literary group Southern Society [C : *Nanshe*] enthusiastically put on plays about An from the 1910s to 1923 (Chang 2010). On April 21, 1924, a *Shanghai News* [C : *Shenbao*] article reported, "The play *An Chunggŭn* became a hot issue among people. When An Chunggŭn gets arrested after killing Itō, he shouts out one phrase. The audience's heart will ache upon hearing it," suggesting that viewers would sympathize with An's political intention. On May 8, 1925, the newspaper reported that the Youth Propaganda Group [C : *shaonian xuanjiang tuan*] would perform *An Assassinates Itō* the following evening. An's story apparently attracted Chinese authors and audiences not only because the event had taken place in Harbin and had been widely reported on by the Chinese media, but also because the semicolonized Chinese partially shared Koreans' enmity toward the Japanese empire.

On the other hand, a *Shanghai News* article on March 6, 1924, "Lecture Report" [C : *yanjiang xinji*], suggests that Chinese interest in An's anticolonial story reflected Sinocentrism and a nostalgia for the Chinese empire. From the tenth century until China's defeat in the 1895 Sino-Japanese War, Korea had been a tributary state of the Chinese empire, and Chinese intellectuals, both conservative and progressive, viewed Korea as territory that the Japanese empire had usurped from China. The *Shanghai News* article reported on a speech that An Xiansheng, the daughter of An Chunggŭn, had been invited to give at a school to commemorate An Chunggŭn as a "national martyr " (C : *lieshi*). "After her talk," according to the reporter, "the principal Zhao said that the (national) culture of Korea belongs to the Chinese culture" and that the nationalist idea of sacrificing oneself for national salvation actually originated in Chinese culture :

> The principal said that Chinese culture inspired the martyr An with the sense of political justice and loyalty to the nation. "I consider that everywhere in Southeast Asia and also all over the world, there is no place on which Chinese culture failed to have influence. The development of the entire Western civilization, for example, depended on Chinese sailing techniques. A compass that people use for sailing was the invention of one of the Chinese emperors. Japanese culture is also Chinese culture that Japan directly obtained through Korea.... I want to assure all of you that developing Chinese culture is the only way to save (China)."

Zhao's speech here echoes the Sinocentric stance of Sun Yat-sen, the founding father of the Republic of China, on the relationship between China and other Asian countries. In assessing the significance of the incident, Zhao not only privileges devotion to the nation, thereby obscuring An's anticolonial achievement, but also, in order to claim Chinese influence on An, conflates modern nationalism with the premodern virtue of loyalty to a monarch. Rather than perceiving other Asian nations as allies of equal status, both

Sun Yat-sen and the principal evoked a past in which the Chinese empire subjugated other Asian nations. This example epitomizes how the Chinese hailed An, a foreigner activist, yet also employed his achievement to celebrate the Chinese cultural legacy, refuting the assumption of previous studies that linked fervent Chinese praise of An with China's appreciation of Korea as a political partner (Yi 1995; An 2001; Sin 2009; Yun 2011a). As Harrison (2001) has shown, whereas the Han nation sought independence from Western and Japanese empires in the Republican era, it maintained its own imperial relationship to other Asian nations (Harrison 2001).

Transnationalism was also present in both state and popular sectors, despite the hegemony of Sinocentric nationalism (Han-nationalism) in the 1920s. As much as Sun Yat-sen endorsed the "Sino-Barbarian dichotomy" [C : *huayizhibian*, 華夷之辨], he also strategically employed the transnational ideology of "all-embracing unity" [C : *dayitong*, 大一統], emphasizing Pan-Asianism internationally and the Republic of the Five Races domestically. Sun Yat-sen's Pan-Asianism foregrounded the same race — the "yellow" race as opposed to the white — common culture, and cultural resistance against Western empires in order to appeal to people across Asia, including Japan. The Nationalist government strategically appropriated a "dualistic, redemptive modernity" by licensing certain transnational elements from religious groups built on Buddhist and/or Confucian universalism to endorse the Chinese version of the modern world, different from that of Western imperialists (Duara 1998 : 653). Ultimately, however, Sinocentrism and imperialism vis-à-vis other Asian nations overshadowed transnational thoughts and practices at critical political junctures in 1920s and 1930s China (Yokoyama 2009).

In 1927, the KMT and other civilian nationalist groups also employed the Chinese play based on An's story in order to promote projects for building a unified, independent modern nation, which required ending the Warlord Era (1916-1928) and reclaiming economic sovereignty from the Japanese empire. These Chinese dramatizations framed An's story within a nationalist context, obscuring An's original transnational pursuit, as seen in three articles in the *Shanghai News*. The first article, appearing on July 12, 1927, indicated that the Nanjing municipal government had organized a large-scale entertainment program for North Expedition soldiers, including a performance of *An Assassinated Itō*. The second piece, on July 31, reported that the Union for Severance of Economic Relations with Japan had organized various demonstrations, including a performance of the play by the Youth Propaganda Group. Finally, the *Shanghai News* noted that on August 5, the southern city district of Shanghai also staged a production of *An Chunggŭn Assassinated Itō* to inspire patriotism among viewers. A number of Chinese dramatizations of the 1909 incident therefore reduced that incident's transnational implications, appropriating the true story to promote the Chinese nationalist project. Despite the popular Chinese depiction of An's story prior to the release of *Patriotic Spirit*, in other words, strong nationalist drives undergirded Chinese dramatizations of the story.

2. Chŏng Kitak's *Patriotic Spirit* in China and Transnationalism

Because the prints of almost all the films produced in Korea in the 1920s and 1930s were lost in the Korean War, Chŏng's films produced in China provide invaluable access to the achievements of Korean film artists during the Japanese colonial period.[6] *Patriotic Spirit* attained both commercial success and critical acclaim in China. Despite these accomplishments, little scholarly work in either Korean or Chinese film studies has examined the aesthetic and political implications of *Patriotic Spirit* in depth or drawn on both Korean- and Chinese-language sources, a gap that this article aims to fill.[7]

6 From 1928 until the Second Sino-Japanese War (1937), six Korean film artists were active in Shanghai, as Yi (1995) and An (2001) note. Kim Ilsong (known as Zheng Yisong in China) played a lead character in *Patriotic Spirit* (1928), *Flaming Cave and Sword* [C : *Huo ku gangdao* 1928], *Three Heroes Compete for a Beauty* [C : *Sanxiong duo mei* 1928], and *Woman Pirate* [C : *Nü haidao* 1929]. Li Kyŏngson directed *Yangtze River* (1930), in which Korean Chŏn Ch'anggŭn played a lead character, and Han Ch'angsŏp was its cameraman. Literary critic Kim Kwangchu's film reviews appeared in *Film Art Theories* [C : *Dianying yishi lun*] and Chinese-language newspapers. Finally, Chŏng Kitak had the most successful career in Shanghai among Korean film artists. See note 7 below.

7 In Korean film studies, Yi Yŏng-il's 1995 article is the first study to identify such work, which has more recently been examined in an MA thesis by An T'aegŭn (2001). Notwithstanding their important contributions, neither work analyzes the films in depth or examines the responses of Chinese media. Also, the existing scholarship on Republican-era Chinese film has not addressed Chinese-language films made by foreigners. Pioneering studies by Yingjin Zhang (1999) and Paul Pickowicz (2012) have illuminated highly dynamic, multifarious, and polyvalent characteristics of early Chinese films in terms of aesthetic qualities and sociopolitical themes. More recent works by Zhen Zhang (2005) and Chris Berry and Mary Farquhar (2006) problematize the nationalist assumption underlying previous studies and stress the overall transnational character of film media. Zhen Zhang redefines the Republican Shanghai film culture as a mediator of the global cinematic "language" of Hollywood film and Chinese experiences and sensibilities. Similarly, Berry and Farquhar focus on the constituted nature of nationalism by foregrounding Sinophone films produced outside the mainland (e.g., in Hong Kong, Singapore, Taiwan, and other areas of Chinese diaspora). These works reveal the varied themes and forms of Republican Chinese films, spanning feminist, socialist, nationalist, anticolonial, and anticapitalist works. However, even when extant

Chŏng Kitak [C : *Zheng Jiduo*](1905-1937; figure 2) had a successful career as a filmmaker and actor in Shanghai from 1928 to 1934, the golden age of Chinese silent film.[8] During this period, he directed eight films and starred in ten, including co-starring in five with Ruan Lingyu (1910-1935), one of the most celebrated actresses in Chinese film history. His works ranged from lowbrow martial arts films to classical melodrama and historical drama.

According to a 1934 article in *United China Pictorial* [C : *Lianhua huabao*], Chŏng's political activism had begun well before his work on *Patriotic Spirit,* as he had been arrested by Japanese police for participating in the March First Independence Movement in Korea when he was sixteen years old. Although

studies challenge the idea of Chineseness through the notion of transnationalism, namely China's relations with the West and the Chinese diaspora, they rarely analyze Asian filmmakers' works made and shown in Shanghai.

8 Chinese cinema in the 1920s and 1930s emerged out of tensions between the influence of American film and that of Chinese traditions, as Zhen Zhang (2005) has shown. Miriam Hansen (2000) has cogently argued that 1920s and 1930s Shanghai cinema falls into her critical category, "a sensory-reflexive horizon" for the contradictory experience of modernity, an aesthetic quality through which a film conveys different meanings to different people. Film offered the Chinese public a vernacular whereby mass audiences found expression and recognition by others in public. Shanghai cinema of the 1920s and 1930s as an instance of vernacular modernism provides us with an analytical tool to examine film's unique role in articulating and disseminating a distinctive historical experience of the time. Yingjin Zhang (2003) notes that although the success of *Orphan Rescues Grandfather* (1923) caused a rapid rise in Chinese film production, increased prices of film stock and overproduction of low-quality films resulted in the bankruptcy of small companies. "From 179 companies in 1927, the number nose-dived to 20 in 1928, and fewer than a dozen were in business by 1930" (Zhang 2003 : 9). Upon Chiang Kai-shek's takeover of Shanghai in 1927, the Nationalist Party strove to regulate influence of Hollywood movies and Western theater and to establish a new civic culture for the Chinese-administered portions of Shanghai, an attempt that included repression of leftist films. Zhang (2003) also notes that the establishment of the Nationalist central government in Nanjing in 1927 interfered with the market-driven characteristic of Chinese film production, an enforced cultural shift that promoted nationalist ideology. The Nationalists' top-down endeavor to police private leisure ended up as an unsuccessful project due to little support from masses and immense corruption (Wakeman 1995).

Figure 2. Chŏng Kitak (right) and Mrs. Chŏng Yilsong. *Source : Xin yingxing* [New Movie Star] (1928 : 34)

he was quickly released due to his age, soon thereafter he was expelled from his high school, which had banned political activism by students. After graduating from another school, he traveled to Japan and entered the Tokyo Music Institute. Despite his anticolonial activism, support from his wealthy family allowed him to benefit from an imperial education. The absence of records about Chŏng's Tokyo years makes it difficult to assess the Japanese influence on his filmmaking. Upon graduation, he moved to Shanghai for a year, where he was exposed to the city's flourishing film culture. After returning to Korea, he started working as a film producer and actor, and his father helped him establish a film production company, Chŏng Kitak Productions. Although Chŏng enjoyed some fame as an actor in Korea, none of the movies released by his company achieved commercial success.

In July 1926, the Japanese colonial government implemented a film censorship law that prohibited artists from creating movies with any anticolonial implications (Kimu 2011), an exacerbated colonial rule that prompted Chŏng to leave for Shanghai in 1928. Upon arriving in China, he was introduced to one of the major Shanghai film companies, Great China & Lily [C : *Dazhonghua baihe*], by the renowned Korean-Chinese anticolonial activist Yŏ Unhyong [C : *Lü Yunheng*, 1886-1947]. Later that year, Chŏng made his directorial debut with *Patriotic Spirit*, which he also wrote and starred in. According to *United China Pictorial*, the film "opened up a nouvelle path for Chinese film of the time" (1934 : 1), although historical or political dramas such as *Patriotic Spirit* were generally unpopular in the 1920s Chinese film market.[9]

When *Patriotic Spirit* premiered in Shanghai in August 1928, most Chinese films fell into the martial arts genre. Until the KMT government's ban on martial arts pictures in the early 1930s, the martial arts genre was extremely popular among Chinese filmmakers. From 1928 to 1931, around forty film companies were operating in China, and approximately four hundred movies were made, 60 percent of which belonged to the martial arts genre

9 In 1926, Chŏng unsuccessfully tried to export Li Kyŏngson's film *Crown of Phoenix* [K : *Ponghwang ŭi myŏllyukwan*], produced by Chŏng Kitak Studio, to Shanghai. Since moving to Shanghai, Chŏng had made films exclusively with Great China & Lily from 1928 to 1930. In 1928 Chŏng directed, in addition to *Patriotic Spirit*, two more films in which he also played a lead character : *Three Heroes Compete for the Beauty* [C : *Sanxiong duo mei*] and *Flaming Cave and Steel Sword* [C : *Huo ku gangdao*]. In 1929, Chŏng directed two films : *Woman Pirate* [C : *Nü haidao*] and *Flower of Screen* [C : *Yinmu zhi hua*]. The latter is also known as *Romance of Liyuan* [C : *Liyuan Yanshi*], which was written by Zhu Shouju. That same year Chŏng played a lead character in four other films : *Pearl Crown* [C : *Zhenzhu guan*], *Great Destruction of Nine Dragon Mountain* [C : *Dapo jiulongshan*], *Burning Down Nine Dragon Mountain* [C : *Huashao jiulongshan*], and *Precious Mirror of Desire* [C : *Qingyu baojian*]. In 1929, all the six films that Chŏng either directed or starred in fell into the martial arts genre. In 1930, Chŏng directed, starred in, and wrote the screenplay of *Knight in Black* [C : *Heiyi qishi*]. When Great China & Lily restructured in 1931, Chŏng left for Tokyo, where he directed *March Song of Shanghai* [C : *Shanghai jinxing qu*] for Imperial Cinema Company [C : *Diguo yinghua gongsi*]. Chŏng had completed approximately half of the film when the company forbade him from continuing to shoot due to perceived sympathy with China's boycott of "enemy goods," including those produced by the Japanese. Chŏng returned to Shanghai, as Imperial Cinema Company forced him to stop filming. Although Chŏng wanted to make new-style films, he was unable to proceed for several months due to a lack of funds. In 1932, United China Cooperation [C : *Lianhua yingye gongsi*] embarked on a new project to revitalize domestic films, and it invited Chŏng to participate as a director. Two months after joining United China, he completed the film *A Way Out* [C : *Chulu*, 1933]. In 1933 and 1934, Chŏng directed *A Way Out* [C : *Guangming zhi lu*] and *Goodbye Shanghai* [C : *Zaihuiba Shanghai*] — his last film — respectively.

(Cheng 1963, 133). Despite the rapid growth of the Chinese film industry, however, American movies still dominated the Chinese film market in the 1920s and 1930s (Lee 1999; Zhang 1999). As of April 1925, British American Tobacco, which owned five major movie theaters in Shanghai, refused to screen Chinese domestic films. These circumstances made the success of *Patriotic Spirit* especially unusual and noteworthy.

The final title of Chŏng's film, *Patriotic Spirit*, resonated with core concepts of Chinese political-social discourse of the period. Unlike in the West and Japan, where central governments systematically implemented policies to produce modern national subjects, in China groups of intellectuals, artists, and activists took on the mission of mobilizing a sense of a united, strong nation due to the lack of a central political power. During this period, as Yoshizawa Seichiro has demonstrated, China's discursive movements from below embodied and propagated the emergent concepts of the nation and national spirit (2003, 18-19, 183). Nor was this limited within the region to China; as Andre Schmid points out, "Like so much of the new conceptual vocabulary of the nation, this [the national soul [K : *kukhon*] or the national essence [K : *kuksu*] was a language shared by nationalists throughout East Asia" (2002, 15). From the late nineteenth to the early twentieth century, intellectuals and statesmen in both China and Korea dedicated themselves to instilling in citizens the idea and sense of a national soul.

The film also appealed to the discourse and practice of political death — of sacrificing one's life for the nation — which Yoshizawa's study of Chinese nationalism argues played a crucial role in imbuing Chinese citizens with a national consciousness (2003 : ch. 5). The film ends with a scene in which An is put to death by Japanese prison officers, depicting An as unafraid of death and proud of his actions. Although the Confucian notion of loyalty to one's monarch [C : *zhong*, 忠] led many medieval and pre-modern scholar-officials and soldiers to sacrifice their lives for their monarchs or dynasties, it was not until the late Qing era (1898-1911) that death in honor of the abstract entity of the nation emerged as a cultural value. Cultural practices, such as memorial services, creation of literature, and various rituals honoring "national martyrs" further inspired the Chinese to abandon their lives for the sake of the nation. The theme of political death in *Patriotic Spirit*, therefore, would have resonated with the political death that Chinese nationalists idealized, although the contexts of those two deaths were not identical.

Although the actual film of *Patriotic Spirit* has been lost, numerous magazines and newspaper articles discussing the film, including a detailed summary by Bi Wu in *Film Monthly* [C : *dianying yuebao*] (Zheng and Liu 1996 : 1561-1565), provide ample resources for imagining the actors' performances, the director's intentions, and the cinematic techniques used in *Patriotic Spirit*. The political tension that this film generated between Japanese authorities in Shanghai and the Chinese censorship bureau led to changes in the film's title, which indicates that Chŏng was forced to compromise his explicit, direct evocation of An Chunggŭn. Chŏng originally titled the film 安重根 [K : *An Chunggŭn*; C : *An Chonggen*]. When Japanese authorities in Shanghai learned from newspaper accounts that Chŏng had finished making *An Chonggen* and that it would be released shortly, they demanded that the Chinese government forbid its screening. Consequently, Chŏng changed the protagonist's name from An Chonggen (安重根) to Yan Zhongquan (晏仲權); although the two names are pronounced differently in Chinese, their pronunciations in Korean are the same. When this accommodation still failed to resolve the censorship issue, Chŏng revised the title again, this time to *Patriotic Spirit.* When the Nationalist government authorities censored the film, they also excised many scenes that explicitly condemned Japanese colonialism to avoid provoking Japanese authorities in China (Beijing Daxue Chaoxian Wenhua Yanjiusuo 1994 : 763-768).

Chŏng's intended transnational message can be seen in *Patriotic Spirit*'s focus on a series of events that took place prior to An's assassination of Itō rather than on the assassination itself. There are three major changes that *Patriotic Spirit* makes to An's story to convey transnational anticolonial messages. First, whereas in reality An traveled to China in 1905 to seek assistance from Korean expatriates in Shanghai but failed to find any, in the film An's Chinese comrades play indispensable roles in his anticolonial plan to kill a powerful politician of the Japanese empire. Second, in reality An Chunggŭn mobilized an anticolonial militia, yet the militia consisted only of Koreans and was formed in the Primorsky region of Russia bordering China and North Korea. In June and July 1909, An's militia crossed the Tu River, attacked the Japanese army, and waged a battle in Kyŏnghŭng and Hoeryŏng of North Korea (Hanguk Kŭndaesa Yŏn'guhoe 1998 : 202-203; Yun 2011b : 78-79). In the film, however, thousands of Chinese civilians and a handful of Koreans formed the militia. Finally, Chŏng's dramatization moves the setting of An's activism from Russia to China, spanning Guangdong, Hong Kong, Shanghai, Hebei, and Manchuria.

To make a successful anticolonial film in a semicolonial state, where anticolonial issues were less urgent and less consistently challenged than in a colonial state (Shih 2001 : 30-40), Chŏng provided his Chinese audience what they wanted to see : other small, powerless nations seeking assistance from China, and Chinese offering them indispensible help. This "granting assistance to subjugated nations" narrative would have satisfied the sense of Han superiority, compensating for the shame and frustration that the presence of multiple imperial forces, particularly Japan's, caused for China.

The film presents two main characters, one Korean (An) and one Chinese (Zhu), who fall in love with each other's sisters. The Chinese characters and romantic plotline are fictional elements that Chŏng introduced to An's story to represent Sino-Korean solidarity. In *Patriotic Spirit*, when An goes to Shanghai to meet the fictional Chinese revolutionary Zhu Hanlong, Zhu immediately agrees to join the anti-Japanese plan. As the film progresses, their comradeship, based on their passion for anticolonial revolution, grows stronger and is reinforced by each one's love for the other's sister. Although another of An's close Chinese comrades, Zhang Yicheng, is also fictional, the other, Liu Dongxia, is modeled on An's real Korean friend from the Seven People's League [K : *Ch'il inhoe*], Yu Dongha. Chŏng strategically adapts Yu Dongha's character into a Chinese national so that all the major characters in the film, except for An and his sister, are Chinese. Chŏng's filmic reconstruction of An's story also depicts his Chinese comrades making many sacrifices for the cause, including Zhang Yicheng's death in northeast China, Zhu's loss of his eyesight during a battle with the Japanese colonial army, and Zhu's sister's death from lovesickness for An. By introducing new Chinese characters and altering the nationality of the historical characters, Chŏng dramatized an important moment in Korean history as a story of Sino-Korean comradeship in the struggle against Japanese colonialism, catering to his audience's political-aesthetic sensibility. While indulging the ethnocentrism of Chinese viewers, Chŏng simultaneously embedded his transnational message in *Patriotic Spirit.*

An, Zhu, and Pak — a Korean comrade of An's — visit An's mother and sister, and An's sister decides to join their effort. The four arrive at the River Tu near the Sino-Korean border, where they stay at the home of their comrade Zhang, who provides indispensible assistance to An's group. However, the Korean army, under Japan's control, follows them to the Sino-Korean border and wages a battle against An and his comrades, during which Zhang is significantly injured. With no hope of recovery, Zhang pleads with his son and An to leave him behind and save themselves. An's group, including Zhang's son, escapes to Hong Kong, where Zhu and An's sister fall in love and, without a common language to speak, communicate by writing. While An's group stays at Liu Dongxia's home in Hong Kong, Zhu's sister remains in Shanghai, longing for An's return. Ill with lovesickness, she sees An in a dream, which gives her momentary comfort, but, a few days later, she dies.

Toward the climax, the film shows that An and his comrades travel to the Haigang area of northeast China and organize a militia of thousands of Chinese to fight the Japanese colonial army in Korea, thereby reconfiguring what had been a Russia-based Korean militia of a few hundred into an army of thousands of Chinese and Korean civilians prepared to wage an anticolonial war. After a period of training, the militia travels to the River Tu on the Sino-Korean border to battle the Japanese colonial army, a scene that represents the ideal Sino-Korean relations envisioned by Chŏng : two countries' trans-national tie at the level of the masses rather than the individual. Although the militia plans to cross the river to attack the Japanese colonial army, Liu Dongxia informs An that Itō Hirobumi is to arrive at the Harbin railway station. Upon hearing this, An asks Zhu to take care of his sister and leaves for Harbin. After An shoots Itō, the Japanese police arrest him and sentence him to death. An is shown facing his death with a sense of calm dignity and of the rightness of his actions, a final scene that inspires the political consciousness of its audience as semicolonized people.

Figure 3. Advertisement for *Patriotic Spirit*. *Source* : *News*, November 7, 1928.

Patriotic Spirit ends with a depiction of the historical assassination, not with a fictional Sino-Korean militia fighting a war against colonialism. However, Chŏng's cinematic rewriting of An Chunggŭn's life to include China in the anticolonial war in Korea reflects what Koreans constantly demanded of China at the time — namely, inter-colonial cooperation, a demand of which some Chinese were also aware, as seen in the *Huazi* newspaper [C : *Huazi ribao*] article discussing An Chunggŭn on November 23, 1909. It is fitting, therefore, that the gathering of the Sino-Korean militia, whose members are eager to battle against the colonial army in Korea, marks the climax of the story, epitomizing the film's transnational anticolonialism.

Patriotic Spirit therefore subtly reveals An Chunggŭn's political beliefs in intra-East Asian solidarity by transforming the true story of a Korean activist into a Sino-Korean narrative in which the Chinese characters play indispensible roles in the plot. By making a film in Shanghai, Chŏng was able to dramatize the transnational and anticolonial implications of An's actions in a way that would not have been possible in Korea at the time. How Chinese moviegoers and reviewers perceived and responded to the film is, of course, another matter, as addressed in the next section.

3. Nationalist Appropriation in 1928

The spectatorship of Chinese audiences in the 1920s and 1930s was multifarious; further, film viewers and critics creatively co-opted films' messages beyond directorial intentions. Republican-era films provided the Chinese mass public with a reflexive horizon for diverse and often conflicting experiences and desires rather than imposing specific ideas and sensations on their audiences (Hansen 2000). This interpretation contrasts with the simplistic and largely unsupported claim of the few previous studies of Korean filmmakers in 1920s and 1930s Shanghai that *Patriotic Spirit* evoked sympathy for Korea among the Chinese in 1928 as director Chŏng intended (Yi 1995; An 2001). My analysis of media reports, advertisements, and reviews of *Patriotic Spirit* that follow demonstrates, first, that the film occasioned unintended readings by its audience and, second, that it nonetheless managed to convey daring, radical ideas of transnationalism. The effect of conveying these ideas would manifest at a most unexpected moment in Sino-Korean relations.

Articles and advertisements about *Patriotic Spirit* appearing in the *News* [C : *Xinwenbao*], which focused on business and economic news, paid attention to the political aspects of the film in contrast to the exclusive attention paid by the *Shanghai News* and the magazine *Movie Star* to the film's formalistic aspects. An advertisement for *Patriotic Spirit* that appeared in the *News* on November 7, 1928 (figure 3) states that the purpose of the film is diametrically opposed to that of typical martial arts films : "(*Patriotic Spirit*) makes an outcry (C : *yi ku*) on behalf of the people who were oppressed by (colonial) powers all over the world.… The film serves to develop insights of the oppressed.… Larger, philosophical implications underlie this film." The advertisement compares the politically provocative and aesthetically stimulating elements of *Patriotic Spirit* to those of films by D. W. Griffith and Rex Ingram, commenting that "the film can awaken the au-

Figures 4a and 4b. Advertisements for *Patriotic Spirit* in the *News* on November 7, 1928 (left) on November 8, 1928 (right).

dience's (political) consciousness."[10] As Shu-mei Shih has pointed out, due to its semicolonized status, pre-1937 Republican China was marked by a lack of consistency, coherence, and comprehensiveness in political consciousness vis-à-vis colonial powers compared to countries, such as Korea and Taiwan, which were directly colonized at the time (2001 : 30-45; Duara 1995 : 224). Under these circumstances, *Patriotic Spirit* could operate as a reminder of China's subjugation by multiple empires.

As a *News* advertisement on the same day demonstrates, Chinese newspaper articles and advertisements conflated Korean activists' anticolonialism with Chinese nationalism. Although the second Great China & Lily advertisement of the film in that issue notes that the director is a Korean with superb artistic acumen, it discusses the film's political implications as an appeal to nationalist sentiment, noting that *Patriotic Spirit* is "an unprecedented movie that concerns nationalism as well as romance. The film politically alerts the entire world [C : *jingshi*]." This advertisement, too, compares *Patriotic Spirit* to Griffith's and Ingram's films, arguing that Chŏng's movie is even better at awakening political consciousness and therefore having a critical impact on Chinese people. The advertisement also presents the film's noble intent to awaken, alert, and edify the Chinese masses as an antidote to the decadent

10 Chinese audiences in the 1920s enthusiastically responded to Griffith's films. *The Birth of a Nation* (1915) was especially well received, "arous[ing] considerable patriotism among Chinese audiences" (Chen 2013 : 27) despite U.S. controversies due to the film's racism. Chen (2013) argues that D.W. Griffith was the single most influential Hollywood director in China during the silent film era. Given Griffith's fame and popularity in 1920s Chinese culture, the reviews acclaiming Chŏng more than Griffith show Chinese enthusiasm toward *Patriotic Spirit*. For more details on the Chinese reception of Griffith's works and Griffith's influence on Chinese perception of film, see Chen (2013).

atmosphere of Chinese society : "The social circumstances (of China)] worsen day by day, and people's minds also tilt toward dangerous things" (see figures 4a and 4b). Hence, these advertisements for *Patriotic Spirit* foregrounded Chinese nationalism, eclipsing the transnational anticolonialism underlying the film.

That the Chinese media hardly articulated or even recognized the transnationalism of *Patriotic Spirit* may have been due in part to Great China & Lily's decision to screen the film along with its documentary news film [C : *xinwen pian*] showing Chiang Kai-shek's inauguration ceremony, making the transnational anticolonialism of *Patriotic Spirit* less relevant than its appeal to Chinese nationalism. The *News*'s November 11 review of *Patriotic Spirit* also conflates the film's message with nationalism, claiming that *Patriotic Spirit* had the power to incite vigorous political, nationalist action on the part of its audience. In the *Shanghai News,* a November 29 article describes it as "an excellent art piece that can stimulate national characteristics [C : *guominxing*]," and another remarks that *Patriotic Spirit* is a rare success story in Chinese film history in that it attained both commercial success and critical acclaim. Whereas Chinese audiences appeared to entirely appropriate *Patriotic Spirit,* suppressing its transnational dimensions for the sake of nationalism, that appropriation and integration of An's story into Chinese culture over two decades, I argue, led unexpectedly to a rupture in Chinese nationalism that the next section will analyze.

Figure 5 | Still photo from *Patriotic Spirit* with caption noting the true story behind the film. *Source* : *New Movie Star* (1928 : 33).

4. An Chunggŭn and a Rupture in Nationalism

One Chinese source in 1928 explicitly, albeit briefly, mentioned the Korean nationality of the protagonist in *Patriotic Spirit*. This example shows that Chinese discourse and narratives about that transnational artwork were not entirely obscured by hegemonic Chinese nationalism. In 1928, the magazine *New Movie Star* [C : *Xin yingxing*] declared that *Patriotic Spirit* dramatized the true story of a Korean anticolonial activist : "*Patriotic Spirit* is a drama based on the real story of a Korean, An Chunggŭn, who assassinated Itō Hirobumi, the prime minister of Japan" (see figure 5). According to the magazine, "Chŏng's *Patriotic Spirit* has different (artistic) colors in comparison to other domestic (Chinese) films." Although *New Movie Star* failed to further explain how the film reconstructed Korean history within the Chinese context, unlike other print media, it did clearly point to An Chunggŭn's story as the film's basis. Whereas numerous newspaper articles and other magazine reviews either reduced *Patriotic Spirit* to a Chinese nationalist film or highlighted the film's formalistic aspects only — such as the actors' performances, the use of light and props, camera techniques, and editing and directing skills — *New Movie Star* clarified that the 1909 anticolonial struggle of Korea against the Japanese empire was the actual model of *Patriotic Spirit*.

It was not until the 1931 Wanbaoshan Incident that newspaper coverage of the film located An's actions primarily in their own political context. That year represented a crucial moment in which tensions in Sino-Korean relations were exacerbated due to this violent conflict, whose death toll exceeded one hundred. In April 1931, Chinese official Hao Yongde granted a contract to eight Korean farmers to lease land in Wanbaoshan without approval from the local government. One of those eight farmers, Li Sŭnghun, and roughly 180 other Korean farmers moved to the Wanbaoshan area, initiating an irrigation project to cultivate their lands, which caused problems in nearby land held by Chinese farmers. The Chinese farmers petitioned the local government to stop the Korean farmers' construction, a demand that ultimately forced the Koreans to discontinue the project. The Japanese consulate in Manchuria had its police suppress the Chinese farmers' opposition, pushing ahead the irrigation construction, which was completed in June 1931. On July 1, some four hundred Chinese farmers, provoked by the completion of the irrigation project, broke out in protest and buried about one kilometer of the irrigated path, which led to a clash between the two groups : the Chinese police and farmers versus the Japanese police and Korean farmers (Zhongguo guomindang xuanchuanbu 1931; Kim 2010). A number of participants in that initial conflict were injured, but there was no loss of life.

Taking advantage of this tension between the Chinese and the Koreans in Manchuria, the Japanese, as part of their unofficial "Discord-Provoking Policy" [J : *rikan seisaku*, 離間政策], manipulated a Korean journalist — Kim Yisam from the *Chosŏn Daily* [K : *Chosŏn ilbo*] — into writing a misleading and provocative article about the Sino-Korean schism in Manchuria on July 2, 1931, in which he claimed that the conflict on July 1 had resulted in tragic death of a number of Korean farmers. As Yi's study (2012) has demonstrated, in the colonial era the significant economic power that overseas Chinese exerted in Korea generated discontent and ethnonational feeling against Chinese among Koreans. The Sino-Korean tension in Wanbaoshan and the false, sensational reportage about it catalyzed and intensified anti-Chinese sentiment in Korea. More crucially, when the Chinese consulate requested that the Government-General protect overseas Chinese upon the outbreak of the incident, the Government-General failed to dispatch a sufficient number of police to control the violence. As a result, 127 Chinese living in Korea were killed and 195 injured; three Koreans were killed and 33 injured (Yi 2012 : 417-477). In retaliation, Chinese killed scores of Koreans (the exact number is unclear) near the Korean-Chinese border. Although intellectuals and activists in both countries urged the masses not to be swayed by Japan's colonial scheme, the hostility between the two countries reached a climax in 1931 (Kikuchi 2007).

Despite a wide range of Chinese nationalisms, from exclusive to inclusive strands, previous scholarship has argued that the Han/non-Han divide was at the heart of Republican-era Chinese nationalism (Yokoyama 2009). Yet some examples of Chinese responses to the Wanbaoshan Incident, discussed below, show that An Chunggŭn's true story escaped the Han/non-Han binary underlying the hegemonic Chinese nationalism. As my analysis of three reactions to the Wanbaoshan Incident demonstrates, the Chinese placed An Chunggŭn in the Korean-yet-non-Korean category, thereby failing to delimit his nationality. I argue that these three cases, among many similar others, thus show that the symbol of An Chunggŭn within Chinese discourses and narratives over time came to deconstruct the dichotomy that the Chinese imposed between Han and non-Han at the height of anti-Koreanism in China. The Chinese critics examined here simultaneously recognized An's Korean nationality and refused to impose national characteristics on An. Hence, I argue, An became a symbolic aporia within the Republican-era discursive paradigm.

The following examples of Chinese use of An's assassination of Itō reveal that Chinese discourses situated An in an ambiguous category, distinguishing him from other "blameworthy" Koreans who were cast as "culturally inferior" non-Hans. The distinction between Han and non-Han is based on Hans' supposed cultural superiority, through which Hans are supposed to civilize or edify "barbaric" non-Hans. When condemning other ethnicities for their savage minds and low culture, Han-Chinese intellectuals offered Han culture and knowledge as a model that other ethnicities should embrace and emulate. What underlay Han nationalism was the idea that non-Hans could not improve themselves without adopting the Hans' high culture. Upon the outbreak of the Wanbaoshan Incident, however, Han-Chinese critics suggested that An Chunggŭn's legacy offered the solution to Korean "barbarity." As a corrective to Korean propensities, therefore, An's activism became part of Han culture. Hence, the nationalist logic was ruptured, because although An was non-Han, he belonged to a Han culture that could rectify and discipline non-Hans. Due to this liminal quality, An Chunggŭn as a symbol unsettled the Han/non-Han divide, deconstructing Republican-era nationalism.

The first example of 1930s appropriation of An Chunggŭn's story underscores the opposition between individuals and the government in the midst of a national crisis. On December 11, 1932, the *Shanghai News* reported that a ninety-three-year-old man, Ma Xiangbo, had urged the Chinese to support the militia that fought the Japanese puppet regime in Manchuria. Strikingly, Ma quotes An, using the words that best represent An's transnational vision of Eastern solidarity, although Ma employs these words to support his own anti-institutionalism by highlighting An's individual and direct action. Arguing that it is urgent that every household in China support the militia of the Northern Expedition and not be subjugated by Japanese colonial power, Ma quotes from An's essay, which promoted a Sino-Korean alliance that challenges ethnonationalism :

> My country's enemy is also China's enemy. I killed Itō for the relationship of our two nations and also for the great mission [C : *dashi*, 大事] of the East. The Chinese people ought to understand what lies at the heart of my political path and realize that the two nations share the same communal fate. In so doing, (we) ought to save twenty million people of my country and four hundred million of China, who are amidst dire suffering [C : *shuihuo zhi zhong*].... Until Korea achieves independence, the Chinese will not have high-pillowed (i.e., carefree) days.

It is not political leaders or institutions, Ma argues, but pioneering small groups and individuals like An Chunggŭn who have built and shaped Chinese history. Ma further contends that the Heaven, the Boxers [C : *Yihetuan*], and the Master of Eight Countries [C : *Baguo zhi chi*] had determined world history at crucial junctures. In Ma's account, An Chunggŭn represents the core of Han-Chinese history and also what has made that history move forward. Ma not only puts An Chunggŭn in the same category as the Boxers and the Master of Eight Countries that embody the Han-Chinese cultural legacy, but also relies on An's political philosophy, even more than Han examples, to endorse Daoism and anti-institutionalism in the modern context. Ma argues that An epitomizes the collective Han-Chinese experience, especially its radical, subversive aspects. Hence, in this piece, An symbolizes a

Han-Chinese characteristic that defies any institutional constraints, including ethnonationalist ones. While acknowledging An's Korean nationality, Ma still argues that An exemplifies one of the most crucial parts of Han-Chinese history, culture, and lived experience. This example therefore shows that by 1932 An had become a sign that disrupted the ethnonational boundary between the Korean and the Chinese.

The second example, a *Shanghai News* article dated September 4, 1931, introduced to its readers the fifth volume of *China Magazine* [C : *Zhonghua zazhi*], the contents of which included articles about the infamous 1931 Wanbaoshan Incident, other forms of Sino-Korean tension, and Jing Wan's biography of An Chunggŭn. Referencing *Patriotic Spirit*, an unidentified author draws on the film and other sources to criticize Koreans for killing innocent Chinese out of anger and not being able to emulate An Chunggŭn. The author stresses that if Koreans acted as An Chunggŭn had (either in reality or in the film) — though not explaining precisely what that way is — then the tragic Wanbaoshan event would not have occurred. Rather than suggesting Han-Chinese examples that Koreans ought to follow, the author endorses the Korean case of An as an ideal to cultivate the "uncivilized" Korean mind. As discussed earlier, however, An neither lived in China nor became acquainted with any Chinese in his life. Even during a short visit to Shanghai in 1905, he contacted only Korean expatriates, rather than Chinese activists, to seek assistance for anti-Japanese movements. Furthermore, a range of political, religious, and philosophical ideas — Catholicism, Confucianism, Asianism, and nationalism — constituted An's highly syncretic thoughts (Rausch 2012). An's autobiography, of which Chinese renditions were published in Shanghai in the 1910s and 1920s and circulated in China afterwards, shows a strong Catholic influence on An throughout his political career. Chinese newspapers also often mentioned An's close ties with Catholic priests during and following An's trial. As much as An appeared to be proximate to Han-Chinese culture, teachings and thoughts of non-Chinese origin formed a central part of An's philosophy. Yet the author of the *Shanghai News* article nonetheless contends that An, rather than other Han-Chinese national martyrs, should serve as a political model to "enlighten" non-Han Koreans. If the article's intended audience had been Koreans, admonishing them would have been a reason for mentioning An Chunggŭn, because Korean readers would be more familiar with political figures of the same nationality. However, its target audience was Chinese who felt outraged about Koreans' killing of innocent overseas Chinese. Most importantly, the article's overall tone is not only ethnonationalist but also Sinocentric imperialist, a stance that attributes the problem of the Wanbaoshan Incident not to a political situation between China and Korea but to a lack of Koreans' cultural cultivation. Acclaiming An Chunggŭn in this context thus indicates that An was deemed to embody Han culture to fix "barbaric minds," beyond simply implying that An was exceptional and better than other Koreans. Within this logic, An comes to represent Han culture despite being a non-Han Korean who neither had contact with living Han culture nor sought an anticolonial ideal in Han-centered tradition, a contradiction that reveals a rupture in Chinese nationalism.

The final example of a Chinese response to the Wanbaoshan Incident also situates An Chunggŭn ambiguously — as Korean yet non-Korean — showing that the Chinese nationalist demarcation of cultural and ethnic belong-ings failed to be held. On October 21, 1931, the *Shanghai News* published an article by Xu Jie titled "Outdated Method of Annexing Korea," which stated that "Korea has been my country's tributary state," suggesting that even four decades after the official end of Korea's tributary relation to China, some Chinese still viewed Korea from an imperialist perspective. Xu Jie delineates how Korea was colonized by Japan to caution Chinese readers that Korea's tragic history might foreshadow their own country's political future. He describes how Koreans resisted Japanese oppression (e.g., by forming myriad anticolonial groups, both public and underground; destroying railroads; and cutting electrical power to public facilities of the colonial government). Xu Jie underlines that although all of these efforts turned out to be futile, "only An Chunggŭn's assassination of Itō in Harbin was an acknowledgeable resistance [C: *chaqiang renyi*].... Although I have described the fall of the Korean nation-state, I have no time to lament for them." Xu's determined apathy and dismissive stance toward colonized Koreans reflect the prevailed anti-Korean sentiment in China following the Wanbaoshan Incident, rather than a reasonable critique of Korean anticolonialism. First, when asserting that An made an exceptional case for anti-Japanese resistance, Xu fails to provide his readers with any evidence. Second, Xu's reason for not sympathizing with the plight of colonized Koreans — the lack of time — has nothing to do with political, cultural, or historical elements, indicating an irrational aspect of nationalism. Third, the death of Itō actually prompted Japan to accelerate a colonizing process in Korea with more coercive measures, a historical-political fact that several Chinese journalists and critics have pinpointed, but that Xu's account obscures. Finally, the political impact of Korean anticolonial movements in the 1910s and 1920s on

East Asia, which ranged from the 1919 March First Uprising to the 1929 Kwangju Student Protest, far surpassed that of An Chunggŭn's action. The contrast between Xu's assessment of An Chunggŭn and the actual limits of An's activism thus shows that the Chinese discursive practice of commemoration and revival turned An's true story into a myth immune to Han-nationalist condemnation of Koreans. Xu's refusal to criticize An Chunggŭn with no reasonable grounds betrays the unarticulated Chinese consciousness or will to categorize An as not-Korean. That is to say, what makes Xu's discussion of An Chunggŭn a discursive aporia is not because Xu contends that An is an exceptional case, but because Xu does so with no explicable reasons. By attributing both Korean and non-Korean qualities to An Chunggŭn, therefore, Xu's article symptomizes a rupture in Republican-era Chinese nationalism.

As these examples illustrate, Chinese discourse about the Korean figure An Chunggŭn confounded the structure of Chinese nationalism — the opposition between us and them, or Han and non-Han — thereby revealing the limitations of nationalist appropriation. That is to say, even when Chinese appropriated Korean culture, that appropriation unwittingly caused a rupture within Chinese nationalism. Although reactions to the 1931 Wanbaoshan Incident manifested that latent change, the constellation of existing political events, social discourses, and literary and cinematic narratives overdetermined that rupture within Chinese nationalism.

5. Conclusion

By tracking changes in Chinese audiences' responses to An Chunggŭn's story before and after the release of *Patriotic Spirit* and the tragic Wanbaoshan Incident, this article has highlighted a twofold aspect of Chinese nationalist power that excluded other nations and minor ethnicities yet inadvertently included what the Chinese themselves excluded. An Chunggŭn as a symbol came to escape the nationalist distinction between Koreans and Chinese, or the opposition between Han and non-Han, as Sino-Korean cultural relations evolved in the late 1920s and 1930s. As Derrida's deconstructionism has illuminated, the collapse of an opposition is part of the system rather than an exception in humanistic discourses (1978). Whereas Derrida identified examples that preceded an opposition, my analysis has uncovered how the sign of An Chunggŭn shifted from a specific referent embodying Korean nationality to a signifier that disrupted the Han/non-Han divide over two decades.

Chŏng Kitak's *Patriotic Spirit* in Shanghai and the Chinese responses to the story also reveal which aesthetic strategies colonized artists in this foreign, semicolonial state were able to take when deprived of means to reject Chinese nationalism. Unable to challenge ethnonationalism openly, the diasporic artist Chŏng subtly insinuated transnationalism while catering to the political and artistic demands of his Chinese audience, as evidenced in his rewriting of An's life into a Sino-Korean narrative in which the Chinese played indispensible roles in realizing An's anticolonial ideals. However, that compromise failed to bring the story to a conclusion. Although *Patriotic Spirit* was appropriated and transformed by Chinese contexts and demands, it also helped make An's story part of Chinese culture as An Chunggŭn replaced and usurped the authority of Chinese anticolonial activists. Like Lydia Liu's (1995) and Michel de Certeau's (1984) analyses of how literary and everyday practices of the powerless become politically productive without rejecting or challenging any superior force, this article demonstrates how a Korean artist's aesthetic practice in Shanghai gradually brought about a rupture in Chinese ethnonationalism without explicitly resisting that nationalism. The strategy of escaping nationalism without leaving it, an example of what de Certeau calls the "consumption" by the powerless of products of the powerful, concerns ways of using and adapting what belongs to the powerful to meet the interests and ends of the powerless. The diasporic artist and colonized Korean Chŏng in semicolonial Shanghai did not resist but rather employed Chinese nationalism to his own anticolonial end. Hence, my analysis has shown how the colonized film artist deflected colonial and nationalist power in China in a way that involved political compromise, yet that compromise ultimately generated a rupture in Chinese nationalist ideology.

Works Cited

An, Chunggŭn, *Tongyang p'yŏnghwaron Oe* [*A Treatise on Peace in the East* and other writing], Seoul : Ch'aeryun, 2010.

An, T'aegŭn, "Ilje Kangjŏmki ŭi Sanghai pa Han'guk Yŏnghwa'yin Yŏn'gu"[Korean film artists in Shanghai during the Japanese colonial era], Master thesis, Hankuk University of Foreign Studies, 2001.

Bang, Kwangsuk [Pang Kwangsŏk], "'Itō Hirobumi chŏkyŏk sakŏn'e daehan kakkuk ŏllon ŭi panŭng kwa ilbon ch'ŏngpu ŭi insik"[Responses of Japan and other countries to the Itō Hirobumi incident], *Dongbuga Yeoksa Nonchong* 30, 2010.

Beijing Daxue Chaoxian Wenhua Yanjiusuo, *Yesulsa* [History of art], Beijing : Minzu, 1994.

Bergère, Marie-Claire, "'The Other China' : Shanghai from 1919 to 1949," In *Shanghai : Revolution and Development in an Asian Metropolis*, edited by Christopher Howe, 1-34, Cambridge : Cambridge University Press, 1981.

Berry, Chris, and Mary Farquhar, *China on Screen : Cinema and Nation,* New York : Columbia University Press, 2006.

Braester, Yomi, *Witness against History : Literature, Film, and Public Discourse in Twentieth-Century China*, Stanford : Stanford University Press, 2003.

Chang Hoepang, "Min'guk Siki Chungguk Munye Chakp'um kwa An Chunggŭn ŭi Hyŏngsang"[Image of An Chunggŭn in Chinese literature during the Republican era], *An Chunggŭn kwa Dongyang P'yŏnghwaron* [An Chungŭn and *A Treatise on Peace in the East*], edited by An Chunggŭn Ŭisa Kinyŏm Saŏphoe, Seoul : Ch'aeryun, 2010.

Chen, Jianhua, "D.W. Griffith and the Rise of Chinese Cinema in Early 1920s Shanghai," In *The Oxford Handbook of Chinese Cinemas*, edited by Carlos Rojas and Eileen Chow, New York : Oxford University Press, 2013.

Cheng Jihua, *Zhongguo Dianying Fazhanshi* [History of Chinese film development], Beijing : Zhongguo Dianying, 1963.

Cohen, Paul, *Discovering History in China : American Historical Writing on the Recent Chinese Past*, New York : Columbia University Press, 1984.

Conrad, Sebastian, and Prasenjit Duara, *Viewing Regionalisms from East Asia : Regions and Regionalisms in the Modern World*, Washington : American Historical Association, 2013.

De Certeau, Michel, *The Practice of Everyday Life*, Berkeley : University of California Press, 1984.

Derrida, Jacques, *Writing and Difference*, Chicago : University of Chicago Press, 1978.

Duara, Prasenjit, *Rescuing History from the Nation : Questioning Narratives of Modern China*, Chicago : University of Chicago Press, 1995.

———, "Transnationalism in the Era of Nation-States : China, 1900-1945," *Development and Change* 29 (4), 1998.

Finch, Michael, "Suicide to Assassination : A Comparative Study of the Views of Min Yŏnghwan and An Chunggŭn on Peace in East Asia and Their Responses to the Japanese Protectorate over Korea," *Acta Koreana* 15-2, 2012.

Fogel, Joshua, "The Recent Boom in Shanghai Studies," *Journal of the History of Ideas* 71-2, 2010.

Goodman, Bryna, "Improvisations on a Semicolonial Theme, or, How to Read a Celebration of Transnational Urban Community," *The Journal of Asian Studies* 59-4, 2000.

Han'guk Kŭndaesa Yŏn'guhoe, *Han'guk Tongnip Undongsa Kang'ŭi* [History of the Korean independence movement], Seoul : Han'ul, 1998.

Hansen, Miriam, "Fallen Women, Rising Stars, New Horizons : Shanghai Silent Film as Vernacular Modernism," *Film Quarterly* 54-1, 2000.

Harrison, Henrietta, *China,* London : Arnold, 2001.

Hirano, Satoshi, *Shin Teikoku to Chibetto mondai* [The Qing empire and the Tibet issue], Nagoya : Nagoya Daigaku Shuppankai, 2004.

Hwang, Chaemun, *An Chunggŭn Pyŏngchŏn* [Biography of An Chunggŭn], Seoul : Hangyŏre, 2011.

Hwang, Chongnyŏl, "'An Chunggŭn p'yŏn Kyorisŏ e nat'anan Ch'ŏn, In, Sekye yihae" [Heaven, benevolence, and world in religious texts edited by An Chunggŭn], In *An Chunggŭn kwa kŭ Sidae* [An Chunggŭn and his times], edited by Sin Unyong, Seoul : Kyŏng'in Munhwasa, 2009.

Ichikawa, Masaaki, *An Jūkon to Nikkan kankeishi* [An Chunggŭn and the history of Japan-Korea relations], Tokyo : Hara Shobō, 1979.

Jiang Hanyang, "Shangchang sheying : kan pai *Chulu*" [On-stage photography : Visiting a studio shooting of *Way Out*], *Lianhua Huabao* 2-5, 1933.

Kikuchi Kazutaka, "Manpōzan—Chōsen jiken no jittai to kōzō" [Wanbaoshan—reality and structure behind the incident in Korea], *Ningen Bunka* 22, 2007.

Kim, Chae-yong, *Manbosan Sakŏn Kwa Han'guk Kŭndae Munhak* [The Wanbaoshan Incident and modern Korean literature], Seoul : Yŏngnak, 2010.

Kimu, Chonmin, "Shokuminchi Chōsen ni okeru katsudo shashin firumu ken'etsu kisoku ni kansuru ichi kōsatsu"[Motion picture/film censorship law in colonial Korea], *Media Shi*

Kenkyū 30, 2011.

Kukka Pohunch'ŏ, *Aju Che'il Ŭhyŏp An Chunggŭn* [The most righteous hero in Asia, An Chunggŭn] Vol. 3, Seoul : Kukka Pohunch'ŏ, 1995.

Lee, Leo Ou-fan, *Shanghai Modern : The Flowering of a New Urban Culture in China, 1930-1945*, Cambridge, MA : Harvard University Press, 1999.

Liu Jianhui [Ryū Kenki], *Mato Shanhai : Nihon chishikijin no kindai taiken* [Demon city, Shanghai : Japanese intellectuals' experience of modernity], Tokyo : Kōdansha, 2000.

Liu jiaxun and Xu Diaoxi, *Wanbaoshan Shijian ji Chaoxian Can'an* [The Wanbaoshan Incident and massacre in Korea], Shanghai : Riben Yanjiuhui, 1931.

Liu, Lydia, *Translingual Practice : Literature, National Culture, and Translated Modernity, 1900-1937,* Stanford, CA : Stanford University Press, 1995.

Lü Bo, "An Chonggen yishi" [Anecdote of An Chunggŭn], *Guowen Zhoubao* 2-40, 1925.

Matsumoto Masumi, *Chūgoku Minzoku Seisaku no Kenkyū : Shinmatsu kara 1945-nen made no "minzokuron" o chūshin ni* [Chinese policies vis-à-vis ethnic groups : From the late Qing to 1945], Tokyo : Taga Shuppan, 1999.

McGrath, Jason, "Acting Real : Cinema, Stage, and the Modernity of Performance in Chinese Silent Film." In The *Oxford Handbook of Chinese Cinemas*, edited by Carlos Rojas and Eileen Chow, New York : Oxford University Press, 2013.

Mōri Kazuko, *Shūen kara no Chūgoku : minzoku mondai to kokka* [A yiew of China from the margins : The ethnic group issue and the nation], Tokyo : Tokyo Daigaku Shuppankai, 1998.

Nakano Yasuo, *An Jūkon : Nikkan kankei no genzō* [An Chunggŭn : Primary figure of Japan-Korea relations], Tokyo : Aki Shobō, 1984.

———, *An Jūkon to Itō Hirobumi* [An Chunggŭn and Itō Hirobumi], Tokyo : Kōbunsha, 1996.

Pak, Boris, *Haŏlbin yŏk ŭi pobok* [Revenge at Harbin Station], Translated by Sin Unyong and Yi Pyŏngjo, Seoul : Ch'aeryun, 2009.

Pickowicz, Paul, *China on Film : A Century of Exploration, Confrontation, and Controversy*, Lanham : Rowman and Littlefield, 2012.

Rausch, Franklin, "Visions of Violence, Dreams of Peace : Religious, Race, and Nation in An Chunggŭn's *A Treatise on Peace in the East*," *Acta Koreana* 15-2, 2012.

Rojas, Carlos, and Eileen Chow, ed, *The Oxford Handbook of Chinese Cinemas*, New York : Oxford University Press, 2013.

Schmid, Andre, *Korea between Empires, 1895-1919*, New York : Columbia University Press, 2002.

Shih, Shu-mei, *The Lure of the Modern : Writing Modernism in Semicolonial China, 1917-1937.* Berkeley : University of California Press, 2001.

Sin Unyong, ed, *An Chunggŭn kwa kŭ ŭi Sidae* [An Chunggŭn and his times], Seoul : Kyŏng'in Munhwasa, 2009.

———, "An Chunggŭn ŭikŏ kwallyŏn 'nokuk kwanhŏn ch'uicho pŏn'yŏkmun' ŭi naeyong kwa ŭimi"[Analysis of the Russian interrogation record of An Chunggŭn], In *An Chung-gŭn kwa Tongyang p'yŏnghwaron* [An Chunggŭn and *A Treatise on Peace in the East*], edited by An Chunggŭn Ŭisa Kinyŏm Saŏphoe, Seoul : Ch'aeryun, 2010.

Sin, Unyong, ed. and trans, *An Chunggŭn sinmun kirok* [Interrogation record of An Chunggŭn], Vols. 1-11, Seoul : Ch'aeryun, 2014.

Sin, Yongha, ed, *An Chung-gŭn Yukochip* [Posthumous work of An Chunggŭn], Seoul : Yŏkminsa, 1995.

Sumbirtseva (Симбирцева), T. M, "Russia ŭi An Chunggŭn Insik" [Russian perception of An Chunggŭn], In *An Chung-gŭn kwa Tongyang p'yŏnghwaron* [An Chunggŭn and A Trea*tise on Peace in the East*], edited by An Chunggŭn Ŭisa Kinyŏm Saŏphoe, Seoul : Ch'aeryun, 2010.

Tanaka, Stefan, *Japan's Orient : Rendering Pasts into History*, Berkeley : University of California Press, 1993.

Tikhonov, Vladimir, "Images of Russia and the Soviet Union in Modern Korea, 1880s–1930s : An Overview," *Seoul Journal of Korean Studies* 22-2, 2009.

Wakeman, Frederic, Jr., "Licensing Leisure : The Chinese Nationalists' Attempts to Regulate Shanghai, 1927-1949," *The Journal of Asian Studies* 54-1, 1995.

Walker, Kathy, *Chinese Modernity and the Peasant Path : Semicolonialism in the Northern Yangzi Delta*, Stanford : Stanford University Press, 1999.

Wang Chunxia, *"Pai Man" yu minzu zhuyi* ["Anti-Manchu" and nationalism], Beijing : Shehui kexue wenxian, 2005.

Yi, Chŏng-hŭi, *Chōsen Kakyō to kindai Higashi Ajia* [Overseas Chinese in Korea and modern East Asia], Kyoto : Kyoto Daigaku Shuppankai, 2012.

Yi, Ŭnsang, trans, *An Chunggŭn Ŭisa Chasŏchŏn* [Autobiography of An Chunggŭn], Seoul : An Chunggŭn Ŭisa Sungmohoe, 1979.

Yi, Yŏng-il, "1930 nyŏndae chŏnhu sanghae mangmyŏngpa yŏnghwa'yin dŭl ŭi chakpum hwaldong"[Korean film artists' work in Shanghai around 1930] *Yŏnghwa Yesul* March : 50-55; April and May : 50-58; June : 50-59, 1995.

Yokoyama Hiroaki, *Chūgoku no Iminzoku Shihai* [China's domination of other ethnic groups], Tokyo : Shūeisha, 2009.

Yonetani Masafumi, *Ajia/ Nihon* [Asia/Japan], Tokyo : Iwanami Shoten, 2006.

Yoshizawa Seiichiro, *Aikoku Shugi No Sōsei : Nashonarizumu kara kindai Chūgoku o miru* [Formation of patriotism : Examining modern China from the issue of nationalism], Tokyo : Iwanami Shoten, 2003.

Yun Byŏngsŏk, *An Chunggŭn Yŏn'gu* [Analysis of An Chunggŭn], Seoul : Kukhak Charyowŏn, 2011a.

———, *An Chunggŭn Chŏn'gi* [Biography of An Chunggŭn], Seoul : Kukhak Charyowŏn, 2011b.

Zhang, Yingjin, ed, *Cinema and Urban Culture in Shanghai, 1922-1943*, Stanford, CA : Stanford University Press, 1999.

———, "Industry and Ideology : A Centennial Review of Chinese cinema," *World Literature Today* 77-3, 2003.

Zhang, Zhen, *An Amorous History of the Silver Screen : Shanghai Cinema, 1896-1937*, Chicago, IL : University of Chicago, 2005.

Zheng Peiwei and Guiqing Liu, eds, *Zhongguo Wusheng Dianying Juben* [Script collection of Chinese silent film], Vol. 2. Beijing : Zhongguo Dianying Chubanshe, 1996.

Zhongguo guomindang xuanchuanbu, *Wanbaoshan shijian ji Chaoxian paihua can'an* [The Wanbaoshan Incident and anti-Chinese massacre in Korea], Nanjing : Zhongguo guomin dang xuanchuanbu, 1931.

Chapter 3

Transformation of knowledge

The Functional Role of *One Thousand and One Nights* As Amplified in the Discourse Of *Some Prefer Nettles*

Elnoby Mohamed (Kyushu University)

Tanizaki Junichiro (1886-1965) is neither a philosopher nor a scholar; he is rather a fiction writer whose treatment of the relation between East and West is serious, sophisticated, and above all imaginative. Given that a mere philosophical understanding of how this relation lacks a conceptual coherence or factual basis, Tanizaki's works constitute one such alternative body of discourse in which the problematic of East and West is not logically explained but figuratively treated through the power of literary imagination.

Tanizaki began his serialization of the novel entitled *Some Prefer Nettles* (蓼喰ふ蟲) in 1928, a work that would mark the inauguration, in Tanizaki's career, of a phenomenon known in Japanese literary criticism as "Return to Japan" (日本回帰). This shift constitutes, at least on the surface, an astonishing break from what had been a long and studied embrace of Western images, of modernity, and of the technology and forms of a newly engendered urban mass culture.

The "Return to Japan" that characterizes much of the fiction produced during the early Showa period has given rise to two major lines of interpretations. Broadly speaking, scholars view this trend either as a result of internal causes — as a spontaneous impulse originating from the personalities of individual authors[1] or as the inevitable literary manifestation of a brutally reactionary and irresistible state of ideology that, as Irokawa Daikichi puts it : "framed people's lives, obstructed their vision like a 'weight upon the eye' and pressed in on them like air that surrounds all things" (310). This latter ideological view, in positing a state-centered, mechanistic, Althusserian form of domination, leaves little hope for individual emancipation, while the former fails to address the objective social structures altogether.

What both of these opposing views fail to address, however, is the particular logic that is at work in what Pierre Bourdieu calls the literary "field of production," a logic that neither completely ignores the external conditions, nor merely reflects them, but rather refracts these forces. Through this very process of refraction, the field of production maintains a kind of autonomy within the larger field of power. The maintenance of this autonomy, the fundamental principle behind literary authenticity in its modern form, underwrites the legitimacy of artistic expression by guaranteeing the freedom of "disinterestedness." But this principle, which frees art from political and economic interests, functions, paradoxically, to marginalize art and to limit its political effect. The very formation of the term "artistic," then, becomes the structural pivot-point of art's social and political indeterminacy.

Some prefer Nettles is both a story concerning a timeless theme as well as the

1 Donald Keene asserts, for example, that Tanizaki's return to Japan may have been an effect, simply, of reaching middle age, a transformation "not very different from that which many other Japanese men have experienced in their forties." See "Dawn to the West," New York : Holt, Rinehart and Winston, 1984, 752.

author's autobiography. Tanizaki, the author, started *Some Prefer Nettles* when he was forty-two years old, following his move in 1923 to Osaka after the great Kanto earthquake, which leveled much of Tokyo. The work's themes presage its author's increasingly complicated life; marked by a divorce in 1930 following an unhappy marriage with his first wife Chiyoko, then his encouragement of a relationship between Chiyoko and his friend and fellow writer Haruo Sato. Yet, Tanizaki was able to assimilate his personal experience with his wife into a larger portrayal of Japan's cultural clashes with the West.

In *Some Prefer Nettles*, Tanizaki attempts to address a number of critical issues of his time, from Japan's relationship with the West and modernity, to the emerging figure of the "modern girl" (*moga*), as well as the combination of the national changes and the characters' sexual orientations. *One Thousand and One Nights* is a pervasive motif in this novel, where some characters share "The Nights" amidst uncertainty and anxiety, while searching for their identity. This article attempts to examine the functional role of *One Thousand and One Nights* in the inaugural fictional piece of Tanizaki's novel. Since *One Thousand and One Nights* represents that fertile zone where the East meets the West, this relationship is featured with antagonism and integration at the same time. Therefore, Tanizaki's usage of it was not for arbitrary purposes but rather for a distinctive goal. This article reveals the motives behind this goal, and how "The Nights" is embedded in the discourse of the novel, giving it other dimensions that could not be acquired without the existence of *One Thousand and One Nights*. Additionally, it touches on analyzing the relation between *One Thousand and One Nights* and Tanazaki's text, revealing the position of "The Nights" within the literary field of the late Taisho and early Showa periods as well as artistic authenticity within social and literary engagements.

1. *Some Prefer Nettles* as Taisho Creative Work

Some Prefer Nettles was written in the early Showa (1926-1989), but still bore literary elements of the Taisho Era (1912-26), sandwiched between the boldly modernizing Meiji Era (1867-1912) and the militarist tide of early Showa. Literary Taisho is Japan's Jazz era, but can it be summed up by a single phrase? It often is : eroticism, grotesquerie, nonsense (エロ・グロ・ナンセンス). Note this sequence : World War I; the 1918 Rice Riots; Taisho Democracy; the founding in 1922 of the Japanese Communist Party; the Great Kanto Earthquake of 1923; the granting of universal manhood suffrage in 1925; and the repressive Peace Preservation Law passed barely two months later.

The Taisho Era transformed the Japanese character in many unforeseen ways. Meet Mobo and his lover Moga — modern boy and modern girl respectively — Mobo in bell-bottom trousers, floppy tie, colored shirt and round-rimmed roido spectacles (named for American silent film star Harold Lloyd), Moga having shed her "shapeless, unbecoming kimono in favor of "Western clothes" that accentuate every curve and hollow, give her body a brilliant surface and lively flowing lines" (Tanizaki 1955 : 29) Mobo's hair was long when Moga's short, sometimes boyishly short; sexuality was out in the open now and not to be hemmed in by simplistic old categories like "male" and "female."

"The white cloth cover, fresh from the bookstore, was clean and sharp as a sheet of metal, and her fingers, against the binding, were clothed in sapphire-colored silk net gloves, the pointed fingernails glowing softly through the tiny holes" (Tanizaki 1955 : 29).

Thus, Tanizaki described Misako in an early scene in the novel, as she and her husband Kaname travel to meet Misako's father at the Bunraku Theater, Kaname, sitting opposite to his wife on the train, he studies her as she reads a volume of translations. Misako, who resembles Taisho's Moga, is the embodiment, in terms of both image and role, of the modern, mass urban lifestyle. Misako dresses in Western clothes, applies her make-up in public "she's inelegant, ungraceful — a woman's charm disappears", reads popular magazines and "translations," listens to jazz, and, most significantly, has begun to assert her own sexual autonomy by taking a lover whom she sees several times a week. Misako's image is full of the metallic sheen of newness and the sharpness of bright, foreign-sounding colors and materials.[2] Her image "glitters"—. Misako, we soon discover, is a woman who complains about sitting on the floor in the puppet theater, who would rather go to the cinema or "go to Suma" — code for meeting her lover – than participate in the revival of a pre-modern dramatic art. It is precisely here, at the level of "taste," that Kaname and Misako most Emphatically differ.

Misako and her husband, Kaname, got married during the period of matrimonial transition from arranged marriages through family connections or brokers to ones based on romantic love. They are in their mid-thirties and

2 Both "sapphire" and "cloth," in the original Japanese, are written in katakana, the syllabary reserved for the transliteration of imported words.

have a son, Hiroshi, who is about twelve years old. They do not hate each other, plot against each other, or even have horrible fights. The husband, simply, feels no sexual attraction for his wife, although he visits a Eurasian prostitute once in a while (the Madonna/Harlot Complex). Both of them can and do have civil conversations, but they describe them as being like two strangers in the inn sharing a bed when the inn is full. The husband even encourages his wife to have an affair with one of her male friends, Aso, to ease her into another marriage.

Kaname's struggle for a culturally authentic experience begins at the level of sexuality, with the complete extinction of his desire for his wife. The deadening of Kaname's attraction to Misako is punctuated by the parallel kindling of an attraction to the old-fashioned culture of the Kansai region – an attraction engendered with the help of Misako's father, who has adopted the subject of traditional tastes as his all-consuming hobby. The crystallization of Kaname's own aesthetic transformation occurs unexpectedly, with the force and unpredictability of a divine revelation, when he falls into a reverie upon entering the Bunraku Theater, a revelry that mixes images of a national cultural memory with his personal memories of his mother.

For Tanizaki, memory is invariably something that begins in music and ends in the notion of motherhood. Thus, when in *Some Prefer Nettles*, Kaname enters a puppet theater for the first time since he was a child, the old familiar sound of the samisens immediately conjures up an inevitable flood of powerful memories. Exactly the same associations are stirred after O-Hisa, the young mistress of Kaname's father-in-law, sings the old Osaka song "Snow" (雪), accompanying herself on the samisen (Pollack 70).

This intensely personal, but also meticulously sensual remembrance of childhood kabuki visits illustrates the "philosophy of history" that would come to characterize much of Tanizaki's fiction during the next decade. In this philosophy, cultural heritage takes on a meaning through a sense of longing for a lost maternal presence and expresses itself through the careful linkage of physical sensation with individual memories and culturally over-determined images. Certain elements that signify a pre-modern native culture — straw mats, wooden floors, kimonos, and plum blossoms — are called upon and combined with maternal remembrances for the purpose of conflating personal memory with national memory.

In *Some Prefer Nettles*, readers can glimpse a state of anxiety and instability. A marriage is not fully-fledged, and relations, emotions, and desires always seem suspended or deferred. This phase of instability is always represented through the symbols of the sexual activities of the characters or through their aesthetic tendencies. These symbols work on two levels. First, the writer himself was going through a period of confusion at that time, after he fled from Yokohama, where he was influenced by Western civilization, and the stage of migration to Kyoto, the core of Japanese tradition. Second, at the other level, is nationhood, since a wide range of intelligentsia recognized the danger of abandoning Japanese culture. The readers not only experience anxiety because of the unanswered questions the author evokes, but also because questions just gave rise to more questions. It is somehow a kind of vital dialectic between the concerns of the intelligentsia over the future of modern Japan and the public culture at the end of the Taisho period, which was deeply affected by Western culture, but without result. Perhaps the result will appear in the following works of Tanizaki.

Kaname, as a consumer of "high culture," is contrasted and separated emotionally from Misako, a consumer of popular culture. Kaname, after years of pursuing Westernized mass-cultural tastes, finds himself on the threshold of discovering his own identity, an identity rooted in a spiritualized aesthetic, which, in turn, is dependent upon the condition of his relationship with women and female objectification, as will be described later in this article.

Kaname is unable to decide anything regarding his life, especially in terms of his relationship with his wife; he sometimes appears as if he is experiencing, practicing Freudian sublimation,[3] and at other times, he is drenched in imaginary pleasures more than actual ones. In this uncertain phase, the functional roles of *One Thousand and One Nights* are reflected. Since most of the criticism or interpretation of *Some Prefer Nettles* tend to find a turning point in Tanizaki's works, where he seems to enjoy restoring the Japanese traditions while stepping away from the admiration of Western culture, a main characteristic of his early works,[4] we find that the literary system used in this text shows that the matter is complex.

3 Sigmund Freud believed that sublimation was a sign of maturity (indeed, of civilization), allowing people to function normally in culturally acceptable ways. He defined sublimation as the process of deflecting sexual instincts into acts of higher social valuation, being "an especially conspicuous feature of cultural development; it is what makes it possible for higher psychical activities, scientific, artistic or ideological, to play such an important part in civilized life."

4 As a result, Tanizaki's strategy of combat between the tradition and modernity has remained hidden for many critics. Although many readings of Tanizaki's work recognize an element of radicalism in the scandal of its sexual frankness, most readings describe the nostalgic moments of his work as simply reactionary. David Pollack, for example, tells us that the passages in *Some Prefer Nettles* that celebrate native tradition capture "the particular appeal of what it might have meant to think like a fascist in the Japan of the 1920's and 1930's" (82). Such readings, however, overlook the complexities and constraints of all "literary" expression.

By the late 1920s and 1930s, the Japanese intelligentsia would increasingly see in culture – and especially in the restorative powers of a nativist vision of Japanese culture – a means of breaking with the Western ideological formations that expressed themselves hegemonically through paradigms of progress, as exemplified by the notion of the pursuit of civilization and enlightenment. The dream of modernization contained in this slogan came under increasing suspicion, and was seen, increasingly and frequently, as a self-defeating illusion that merely served to euphemize a narrative of Western domination. The rejection of modernity, then, and of the ideology of civilization and enlightenment served, on one level, as an attempt to undermine an insidious view of Western superiority.

Two years before this novel, Tanizaki had predicted that a "Return to Japan" would soon become impossible because there would no longer be any old traditions that one could return to. However, he abandoned this idea in this novel, a sign he had reconsidered the power of Japanese traditions. At a later stage, Tanizaki's own "Return to Japan" resonated quite obviously with the then contemporary anti-Western discourse. Generally, for Tanizaki, the "Return to Japan" was probably not a monolithic phenomenon, as is often argued, but rather an issue worthy of careful examination in order to grasp the historical specificity of Tanizaki's career and individual work (See Golley, 1995 : 365-404).

Mitsuhiro Yoshimoto explained that one of the leading literary critics who warn us not to encase Tanizaki in the cliché of the "Return to Japan" discourse is Nakamura Mitsuo. The central point of Nakamura's argument is that the concrete specificity of Tanizaki's individual experience makes it impossible to reduce his change in the 1920s to another example of the conversation of modern Japan intellectuals, many of whom became infatuated with Western culture in their youth and then returned to Japan as they got older. Tanizaki's return to "old Japan" through his move to the Kansai area of Kyoto, Osaka, and Kobe was not a manifestation of the pattern of circular movement from the East to the West, and then back to the East again, but rather a "radical transformation of self, which was carefully planned and accomplished on the level of both art and personal life" (59). Nakamura also claims that when Tanizaki moved to Kansai, he shook off the influences of Western thought and returned to his true self of being a child nurtured in an old merchant milieu of Tokyo's downtown (Shitamachi), which he was reminded of by the old districts and customs of Kyoto and Osaka. As he emerged from Western influences, Tanizaki abandoned the fundamental tenets of civil society and embarked, instead, on the ethos of traditional townspeople. According to Nakamura, what encouraged Tanizaki to turn his face away from the West was the superficiality he experienced of Western influences. Despite his infatuation with the West, Nakamura asserts, Tanizaki never deeply understood Western thought, literature, and art (57).

On the other hand, Gayatri Spivak warns repeatedly against accepting the idea of cultures of pre-colonialism for they cannot easily be restored, and the nostalgia for lost assets could hinder exploring social realities within the critique of imperialism. Spivak suggests that pre-colonial history is always renewed by colonialism and that any original image that could be isolated carefully from the history of colonialism is not available for the public audience. It is possible that Tanizaki/Kaname did realize this problem as an unsolved problem. We feel this tension coming to a head when Misako writes to the old man about the situation between her and Kaname, and the uncle Takanatsu then takes it on himself to intervene. A trip to the old man's home by Kaname and Misako, and a late night visit by O-Hisa to Kaname's room marks the final scene of the novel, to end it in total ambiguity as lingering issues are unresolved.

2. *One Thousand and One Nights* and Uncertain Identity

The first reference to *One Thousand and One Nights* in the novel occurs in the fourth chapter, specifically in the letter sent by Takanatsu, Kaname's cousin, to Hiroshi, informing him about his arrival in Kobe from Shanghai. In this letter, Takanatsu wrote that he found for Hiroshi's father a version of the legendary stories *One Thousand and One Nights,* which he had requested, though it wasn't the version Hiroshi himself would favor. In the sixth chapter of this story, Kaname received a complete set of Burton's edition as a gift from his relative Takanatsu, who tells Kanami how hard it was for him to get it there at the booksellers Kelly and Walsh.[5]

The stories of *One Thousand and One Nights* is counted as the famous Arabic and oriental literary work is well known in Western , Arab literature has often been reduced to a *One Thousand and One Nights*, allowing it sometimes

5 Kelly & Walsh Ltd. was formed in 1876 through the amalgamation and partnership of two local Shanghai booksellers : Kelly and Co. and F. & C. Walsh. Kelly & Walsh was incorporated on 1st July 1885, and was located at No. 11 the Bund, before moving to 66 Nanking Road in 1918, with offices also at 12 Nanking Road.

to be the only representative for this rich literature. The notable metaphor here is that; Arabic critics and historians in the tenth century the time when "The Nights" was written, such as Ibn al-Nadim, and al-Mas'udi, believed *One Thousand and One Nights* to have no literary merit, although they conceded rather disdainfully that they were popular among the illiterate. While the French scholar Antoine Galland who did the first translation for "The Nights" (1714) to European language and his successors look at this work as the best Arabic book ever written and, from "encountering these mercurial stories, decided to 'translate' them and produce a carefully composed and set text, with all the precious mannerisms of courtly" Europe, such that "The Nights" became the concrete creation of Western, rather than Arabic, literature and fantasy (See Rana Kabba- ni 2004 : 26)."[6]

Edward Said, in *Orientalism*, has commented on this, saying : "The basic distinction between East and West as the starting point for elaborate theories, epics, novels, social descriptions, and political accounts concerning the Orient, its people, customs, 'mind,' destiny and so on" (3). According to Said, Orientalism dates from the period of European Enlightenment and colonization of the Arab World. Orientalism provided a rationalization for European colonialism based on a self-serving history, in which "the West" constructed "the East" as extremely different and inferior, and therefore in need of Western intervention or "rescue." That can explain how the ignorance of the rich tradition of classical and contemporary Arabic writing is a reflection of the

6 Actually this variable and incomplete construction, which always accompanied "The Nights" makes it opens to adding and dropping. That created a number of copies of "The Nights" that vary among themselves and this anxiety or uncertainty increases the mysterious identity of "The Nights," that analogy with the state of anxiety gripping in *Some Prefer Nettles*.

West's political and cultural contempt for the Arab world, and for the Muslim world in general.[7]

Sir Richard Burton (1821-1890) was a Victorian explorer, writer, and translator known for his travels in Asia and Africa. Burton was a prolific author, mainly on travel and ethnography. He also translated classical and Renaissance literature, with a particular interest in eastern erotica. He translated and printed the *Kama Sutra* (1883) and *The Perfumed Garden* (1886). He also published a complete edition of the *One Thousand and One Nights* (1885-1888) over the course of seventeen volumes of roughly 800 pages or so each. Burton not only offered an English reading public the first frank and unexpurgated translation of the tales themselves; he also peppered the text with footnotes about esoteric aspects of Islamic culture, especially sexual customs, and closed the tenth volume with a "Terminal Essay" that included a lengthy discourse on pederasty. His translation of "The Nights," he says, presents to his countrymen Muslim manners and customs, laws and religion, but Burton could not resist adding to his translation many sexual scenes or descriptions of sexual intercourse in meticulous detail that did not exist in the original text. Hideaki Sugita explained "It is well known today that Burton often tampered with the text itself in this manner, either to satisfy his own curiosity or to make it suit the special purposes of his anthropological notes" (2006, 142).

Dane Kennedy argues, "This quixotic enterprise thrust Burton into the

7 Many critics criticized Said because he did not differentiate between Orientalists who has been used by imperialism, and those who introduced the real image of Arab and Muslims generally to West, especially German Orientalists.

middle of an intersecting network of debates about sexuality and purity, state regulation and personal freedom, the Occident and the Orient. To examine the intentions that motivated Burton's translation of "The Nights" and the reception it received is to explore some of the crucial elements of the late Victorian crisis of identity" (318). Burton's "Nights" appeared at a critical moment in the cultural crisis of Victorianism. British society in the mid-1880s was in the throes of what Judith Walkowitz has termed a "moral panic" (87).[8]

Burton was trying to reveal the hypocrisy embedded in Victorian society, by providing the habits of East, which he thought were more open than the conservative Victorian community. This goal, which seems noble, controlled his whole translation and anthropological comments. That is what Tarek Shama insisted on :

> Apparently, Burton was trying to obtain the broadest readership by evoking all the different ways in which the *Arabian Nights*, especially his own version of

8 The 1840s ushered in an era of luridly illustrated gothic tales which were marketed to a working-class Victorian audience. These stories, told in installments and printed on inexpensive pulp paper, were originally only eight pages long and sold for just a penny – giving rise to the term "penny bloods" or "penny dreadfuls."

These types of publications were wildly popular, especially with young male readers, and it was not long before the Victorian public began to make a connection between various juvenile crimes and misde.The public outcry it provoked led to the passage of the Criminal Amendment Act (1885), which raised the age of sexual consent for females, while the attached Labouchere amendment codified new penalties for sex between males. Another repercussion was the establishment of the National Vigilance Association (also in 1885), which began to organize an aggressive campaign to suppress erotic literature and enforce a public morality based on strictly defined standards of purity.

Basically it was the rich and powerful worrying about the morals of the poor. After these laws were passed, the poor were expected to be imprisoned for violating them. The rich were expected to be discreet.

> it, could be appreciated. What is clear, however, is that this approach seriously watered down the force of any social commentary he tried to deliver through the translation. What is more, Burton did not become comfortable about delivering his criticism until all the volumes of his colossal translation had been published and delivered to the paying customers. His uncompromising attacks on Victorian morality had to wait for the tenth volume of the Arabian Nights, and, principally, the last, sixth volume of his Supplemental Nights (57).

This Victorian identity problem supported the project or adventure of Burton's translation of "The Nights," encouraging him to go forward with his erotic translation.

The colonialist desire to establish knowledge about the East is in tandem with the imperialist climate that prevailed in Victorian England and offered an invaluable opportunity for personal advancement for Burton, whose itinerant childhood produced a strained identification with England, where he intermittently stayed for brief spells. According to Elleke Boehmer, Burton's colonial gaze is an admixture of "both … conquest and … a form of research" (69). The decision to write a personal comment and notes is a very conscious one, which suggests an attempt to carve out a subjective space of experience beyond the pale of colonialist compulsions.

On the other hand, the anthropological notes in "The Nights" and the parts that Burton added to "The Nights," are not enough to judge the concept of Burton towards Arabs and Islam. Likewise in the *Jew, the Gypsy and El Islam*, Burton defends Islam against many pernicious European prejudices, even as he asserts its relevance purely within Eastern confines, "El Islam prospered amongst kindred races it fell flat elsewhere" (343). In effect Burton's assumption was that religions are determined by geographical and racial conflations. He appreciates all religions as belonging to a temporal continuum, differentiated by cultural markers.

Actually, Japan in the Taisho period had almost the same "moral panic," and suffered from an uncertain identity. Japan's traditional morals and culture struggled with Western morals and culture to restore its own space again after the Westernization of the Meiji Period. The so-called new imperialism at the end of nineteenth century looks like the ambition of Japan to build its own empire in Asia.

Thus, the social factors that created the success of Burton's translation in England seem to be the same factors that gave the success of his translation of "The Nights" in Japan.

In Japan, the first Japanese translation of "The Nights" was done by Nagamine Hideki, in 1875. Several Japanese versions of "The Nights" followed. They were indirect translations made from the English or French versions. As such, "The Nights" has been regarded as English or French literature. While *The World-Famous Classic on Love*, the subtitle of an abridged one-volume Japanese translation of Burton's version, was published by Sakai Kiyoshi (1895-1952) in 1927, it was immediately banned by the censor. This subtitle reveals how Japanese translators were thinking about Burton's version of "The Nights."

The journalist Oya Soichi (1900-70) translated the complete version of Burton in 12 volumes from 1929 to 1930. Sugita criticized this translation saying “its value was impaired by the fact that not only had it eliminated all of Burton’s numerous notes, but it was also filled with mistranslations, omissions and suppressed or censored passages” (2006 : 142).

One Thousand and One Nights took its place as erotic literature in Japan after the translations by Burton and Madras were introduced in the Taisho and the early Showa. Since both Burton and Mardrus’ translations expanded on sexual elements, it was natural for *One Thousand and One Nights* to become popular as erotic literature.

The Japanese translation was also full of mistranslations, which often occurred when the Japanese translators changed the story into a very Japanese style; a major example of this is the scene where a Muslim man prays to the Sun, which is totally forbidden in Islam. Most translators tried to make the story easy for Japanese people to understand. Also, the European erotic-expression, which had been added to the translations, made its Japanese, translated version more sexual (See Sugita 2012 : 117).

The translation of Burton is a zone of cultural multiplicity, where the original narrator’s voice is not the only one that comes to us. The translator’s discursive presence in the translated text becomes discernible too. Lawrence Venuti explained that the voice of the translators is recognized as the author’s, and there is no hybrid between the voices of the original narrator and the translator (See 238). Thus, he calls for the use of nonfluent, nonstandard, and heterogeneous language by producing what he called ‘foreignized’ rather than domesticated texts so that translators could make themselves visible and their voice detectable. But actually in folk texts particularly, as well as other texts, the hybrid voices could be recognized. Thomas Hermans points out that “the translated narrative discourse always contains more than one voice … as an index of the Translator's discursive presence" (27). He refers the "second voice" (27) to the "Translator's voice," which may remain entirely hidden, unable to be detected, and may be directly or forcefully present in paratexts, like prefaces, footnotes, translator's notes, and so on.

Although the voice of Burton attempts to suppress the original voice of "The Nights" and to represent it not only across the text but also through the extensive comments, still this translation retains a voice of the original text, which gives the text an uncertain identity.

This uncertain identity works on two levels : the level of the meeting of West and East in this culture product.

The second level is the translation itself, where the translations either in Europe or in Japan usually have a hidden agenda that exceeds the target of introducing cultural products of others. Those generate difficulties for separating the voice of translator from the original voice. Both voices here are left in peace together without confronting each other to create what is called *One Thousand and One Nights*, which makes for a situation that is only confusing, annoying, and uncomfortable.

Tanizaki added in his novel another level, which is the bifurcation of "The Nights" into two spheres, juvenile literature and pornography literature, which had already begun at that time in Japan.

Takanatsu wrote to Hiroshi, stating : "Tell your father I found his Arabian Nights at Kelly and Walsh – not the sort of Arabian Nights you yourself are supposed to read" (Tanizaki 40).

Later, while Takanatsu was delivering the set to Kaname, Kaname's son, Hiroshi, asks him out of curiosity about the difference between the children's edition and Burton's edition. He tried to get a glimpse of the illustration under his father's hand.

Iwaya Sazanami's (1870-1933) effort that "The Nights" began to be recognized as children's literature in the Taisho period. As a prolific writer and storyteller for children, he published both the World Fairy Tales Series, 1899-1908(世界お伽話)in 100 volumes and the World Fairy Tales Library, 1908-1915(世界お伽文庫)in 50 volumes, in which he included many tales from *One Thousand and One Nights.*

With the gradual increase of public interest in juvenile literature in general and the subsequent flood of children's books and magazines in the Taisho period, various excellent juvenile editions of the *One Thousand and One Nights*, boasting plentiful illustrations, were published one after another. Among them, deserving of special mention is the two-volume "Newly-Translated Arabian Nights" (新訳アラビアンナイト) by Sugitani Daisui (1874-1915), in 1915-1916. It is no wonder that Sugitani's deluxe edition, with its numerous illustrations and plain, sophisticated prose text, had an enormous impact on children from the middle and the upper classes in the Taisho period.

In the last year of the Taisho period, two translations of Edward Lane's edition were published independently and almost at the same time : one by the novelist Morita Sohei (1881-1949) in four volumes, and the other by the poet and scholar Hinatsu Konosuke (1890-1971) in three volumes. Both seem to have been intended not only for the younger generation, but also for folklorists and students of narrative literature (Sugita 2008 : 143).

Therefore, in the Taisho period *One Thousand and One Nights* had two different contradictory aspects that existed together. "The Nights" was a zone where contradictions could meet and stay together neither in harmony nor in hostility, and it is not only West and East, but also translation voice and original voice, moreover adult and children materials.

As shown in the novel, the adult seeks the erotic parts of the "Nights," while the kids are looking for the adventure and fantasy parts of the "Nights."

Perhaps the main reason for the simultaneous appearance of *One Thousand and One Nights* as children's and erotic literature in Japan at that time is due to the fact that the Japanese translators depended on different European translations, and the Taisho democracy also helped in this regard.

In the novel, *One Thousand and One Nights* was brought from Shanghai, the city that in the 1920s was divided between its more European western half and its more traditional Chinese eastern half. Westerners helped to transform Shanghai into a metropolis. British and American businessmen made a great deal of money through trade and finance, and the Germans used Shanghai as a base for investing in China. Shanghai accounted for half of China's imports and exports. The Western part of Shanghai grew to become four times larger than the Chinese part had been in the early 20th century. This cultural fission was apparently more extreme than the situation in Japan. Tsuyoshi Namigata said, "The Japanese modernist sought a nearer city like Paris in East Asia. Shanghai was already famous as a city of modernized metropolis, full of Western atmosphere" (196). Shanghai represented Western culture located in the East during the Taisho period.

If we move to the national scale, Japan itself, where "The Nights" has been brought by Takanatsu the cousin of Kaname, Japan is a country that has double faces regarding Orientalism especially at the first half of the twentieth century, the questions that usually appear here are : Is Japan colonizer or colonized? Is Japan the Orient or the Occident? The West had regarded Japan as an Oriental country. Japan is said to be situated in the Far East as the West call it. Far East is very Eurocentric word. The word reveals that Japan is geographically a part of the Orient.

Various writings on Japan by the West also show that Japan is inevitably a part of the Orient. The French writer Pierre Loti, for example, visited Japan in 1885 and 1900 and published exotic travel essays. Loti was mainly interested in exoticism and tried to represent the country as a land of beauty and mystery. There is no doubt that the French writer treated Japan as a part of the Orient.

On the other hand, a new trend emerged in the Taisho period after Meiji Restoration gave Japan many chances to acquire new colonies, and allowed the nation to behave more like Western colonizers. Taiwan was occupied as a result of the Sino-Japanese war in 1895. A part of Manchuria and southern Sakhalin became Japanese colonies in 1905; and in 1910 Japan occupied Korea. Japan gradually came to behave like the powerful Western colonizers rather than like the weaker, colonized Orient.

"In (In the) modern era, it was frequently the case that when Western ideas were imported into Japan, an attempt was made to invent a corresponding idea in Japanese history…when (When) Edward Said's *Orientalism*….was translated and published in Japanese in 1986, a similar phenomenon [phenomenon] was seen. *Orientalism* was accepted as an authoritative academic paradigm of the west, and as a new, universal discourse. A number of scholars in Japan started to search for and identify Japanese versions of Orientalism in the words used by modern Japanese intellectuals when referring to Chinese and Koreans. On the other hand, however, there was very little research on how Japan was portrayed by the West as part of the orient .... Ironically, however, the more researchers emphasis the fact that an Orientalism existed in modern Japan, just as it did in the West, the more they prove that Japan had accomplished a modernization that could be compared to that experienced by Western nations (Oguma : 352-353).

Acquisition of suzerainty influenced literature. Partial colonization of China and occupation of Korea gradually added imperialistic elements to Japanese culture, consequently to Japanese writers. Tanizaki is one among those writers, for he made three trips to Korea and China in 1918. Tanizaki then started to create exotic stories about China and Korea, such as *Gourmet Club* (1918), *Travel to Suzhou* (1918), *A Night at Qinhuai* (1918), The *Moon of Xihu Lake* (1919), *Dreams of Velvet* (1919), and *An Essay on Korea.*

Through his series of fictional works and travelogues, Tanizaki repeatedly stresses the stagnancy, antiquity, and un-changeability of an old country such as China. He also denies the possibility of development for the nation. On the other hand, Tanizaki was an enthusiastic admirer of beauty, not only of Chinese landscape but also of Chinese women. In these creative works many Orientalist features appeared, such as exoticism, Romanticism, and eroticism. In this sense, Japan's Orientalism is exceedingly similar to Western Orientalism.

For Tanizaki and other Japanese writers at that time, China was a land of exotic beauty. They often compared China to the world of the *One Thousand and One Nights*, where both were thought to be full of strange events and mystery. For example, Akutagawa Ryunosuke mentions *One Thousand and One Nights* in his travel account *Shina Yuki*, and Tanizaki mentions it again in *Lahore Yori* and *Birodo no Yume* (see Daisuke Nishihara 1997 : 23).

However, Tanizaki's Orientalist approach to China could not last long. When he landed on China for the second time in 1926, the novelist encountered anti-Orientalist discourse by Chinese intellectuals. In Shanghai, Tanizaki became acquainted with Guo Moruo (writer, 1892-1978) and Tian Han (dramatist, 1898-1968), both well known Chinese men of letters who highly esteemed Tanizaki, but they readily opposed his opinion. They told the famous Japanese author that China was suffering from exploitation by foreigners. Tanizaki was astonished and realized that his limited understanding of the country was wrong. He consequently revised his Orientalist discourse. After 1926, he never again created exotic stories about China.

This manifests the significant role that this conversation played. Tanizaki's previous monologue displayed in his exotic stories on China was replaced by information presented in the form of a dialogue; one-way discourse was changed into two-way communication. Tanizaki's experience in Shanghai suggests how an Orientalist approach can, and should, be overcome.

It seems that Tanizaki was aware of the position of *One Thousand and One Nights* in the West, and was familiar with the translation of Burton. Tanazaki himself had a complete set of Burton's edition, bought in Shanghai by his friend Tsuchiya Keizo ["土屋 圭造"] (1888-1973) and had it brought to Japan in

1925 by a certain Uemura Kiyotoshi, an employee of the publishing company Kaizosha.

Moreover, in making use of this Shanghai connection, Tanizaki seems to have taken the advice of his fellow writer, Akutagawa Ryunosuke ["芥川龍之介"], who travelled to Shanghai in 1921 to find a complete set, which he bought in 1923. The next year, "Akutagawa contributed to the magazine 『書物往来』 (*Bibliophilism*) an article entitled 'リチャード・フランシス・バートン一千一夜物語について' (On Richard Burton's Translation of *One Thousand and One Nights*), in which he showed how literal and excellent it was, accepting Burton's own words at face value" (Sugita 2006 : 142).

In a letter written to a friend in Shanghai, Tanizaki gave directions about how to send One Thousand and One Nights to Japan. "Although the book is in fact pornographic, there are probably no illustrations, and the name Arabian Nights suggested that it is a book that even children might read, so I believe that there will be no trouble with customs. Please verify whether or not there are illustrations" (Keene : 144).

This situation actually is similar to what Takanatsu described in the novel about bringing *One Thousand and One Nights* To Japan "And those seventeen volumes were a problem too. It's classed as obscene , and it's full of illustrations that give it away. I thought customs might be embarrassing if I got caught with seventeen obscene volumes, so I put all seventeen in my trunk. Which was all right, except then my trunk was practically immovable (Tanizaki : 103)." This can explain how this novel's kind of author autobiography.

At the late of Taisho the government became increasingly heavy-handed in its attempts to control the spread of new political philosophies deemed dangerous to the government. After the end of World War I, the Peace Preservation Law of 1925 increased police powers to prosecute promoters of socialism and of the Korean independence movement. Censorship restrictions were also expanded to cover religious groups. In 1924, the Publications Monitoring Department of the Home Ministry was created with separate sections for censorship, investigation and general affairs. With the outbreak of the Second Sino-Japanese War, the Home Ministry, Army Ministry, Navy Ministry and Ministry of Foreign Affairs all held regular meetings with publishers to provide advice on how to follow the ever-stringent regulations. Penalties for violations increased in severity, and voice recordings (including radio broadcasts) also came under official purview.

The *One Thousand and One Nights* were not far from the Japanese censor scissors in that period, it were banned for a while when Publications Monitoring Department categorized as adults literature .

On the level of revealing the nature of the characters *One Thousand and One Nights* playing an important role in Tanizaki's novel, for example Takanatsu, who brought *One Thousand and One Nights* is neither Kanami nor Misako, although he could be another face of Misako. He is merely a businessman from Osaka, caring about business and how to gain more and more profit regardless of the cultural effect of his goods. When purchasing the book his only concern was how to hide the illustrations from Customs service, and he devoted effort and money on his commodity. He bought *One Thousand and One Nights* for his cousin, at his request, but he never recognized its cultural and literary value. His way of looking at life was very strict. He divorced his wife when he discovered that she was having an affair with another man, which could explain why he is not very comfortable about Kaname and Misako's relationship. His repeated questions to Kaname and Misako could also reveal the inner monologue of the protagonist and heroine that plays an important role in the narration.

Depending on the former demonstration : the first functional role of *One Thousand and One Nights* in *Some Prefer Nettles* could be an indicator of the contradictory world located in the novel.

"The Nights" could be categorized as Western cultural elements. It came from a Western library located in Shanghai, as an English version, and enjoyed a high reputation at that time in Europe. On the other hand, it represents an Eastern traditional culture element beside the Bunraku Theater, Old man and O-hisa. It is something different and disordered. It is a cultural product, talking about the habits and life of Arabs and Muslims in English and is read in Japan. Paradoxically, Kanami reads *One Thousand and One Nights* in English, while he admires the traditional Japanese puppet theater, which reveals the uncertain direction of Kaname or the possibility of a dialogue between cultures, which allows the co-existence of two cultures without displacing each other.

One Thousand and One Nights is working not only to emphasize the transitional situation of the discourse of the novel but also it is the cord that holds all the motifs that confirm this transitional situation.

Without *One Thousand and One Nights* there is no connection between these motifs. Moreover, each motif represents one aspect in both worlds, but *One Thousand and One Nights* represents most of these aspects of both worlds, so it could provide the ideal motifs to enhance the discourse of the novel. It connected the following pairs : West/East, old/new, Shanghai/Kansai, child/adult, original voice/translation voice, and Kaname/Takanatsu.

Additionally, it reflects writer/Kaname's troubled personal life and explained about the state of limbo of the protagonist Kaname not only in his marriage but also in terms of his cultural identity. It represents his uncertain identity.

3. "One Thousand and One Nights" and eroticism illusion

In the eighth chapter of the novel, Kaname takes secret pleasure in poring over Burton's translation. Kaname read "Burton Club Edition, the first complete translation," first volume, which covered only from the first to the thirty-fourth night over three hundred and sixty octavo pages. Kaname read the stories and the notes that Burton wrote. He shows no interest in the notes on linguistic problems, but is concerned about the notes describing Arab customs and those about Arab women containing sexual hints. His romanticized version of it is manifested in the Western wing of his house – particularly the veranda on which he likes to sit–, American movie stars fascinate him, and very potently in an English translation of *One Thousand and One Nights* that he is wont to skim through in order to find the more lewd passages for which Burton's version is famous.

The table of contents shows us that this volume contains the *Tales of Wazir and the Sage Duban*, *Tale of the Three Apples*, *The Nazarene Broker's Story*, and the *Tale of the Ensorcelled Prince*. The most prominent aspect is Kaname's way of reading, as he seems to be searching for fantasy and eccentric parts in the book to enrich his illusory world. Kaname does not completely read a note but moves from one to another. This suggests why Kaname has an overactive fantasy life that he appears to prefer to interact with more than with reality. In the same manner, his interest in the West is rooted more in its fantastical elements, such as *One Thousand and One Nights* and American cinema; the same can be said of his interest in the traditional East, especially the traditional Japanese puppet theater.

The first note he read is about the Arabs' aesthetic standards regarding women, and how Arabs consider a slight gap between the two front teeth a sign of beauty. That seems true in some aspect but also incorrect in other ways. With the region's rich history of cross-cultural integration, the Arabic appearance encompasses a broad spectrum of skin tones and diverse heritage, which means that the same standard of beauty will not apply across all Arab regions. Perhaps what Burton mentioned is acceptable even today in Bedouin and other parts of the Arab world but not everywhere. In Burton's Notes on "The Nights," he applied any phenomena he recognized upon all other regions.

The second note described the personal attributes of the king's barber.

Kaname also read a passage about the position of Muslim women in Muslim society and how they cannot walk alone in the street or they will be arrested. Actually the question of gender roles and the attitude toward women in *One Thousand and One Nights* is a highly sensitive one. The relevant debate is fueled chiefly by opinions on the status of women in Islam, a status that is usually not appreciated in the West. One of the main incentives for discussing gender roles in *One Thousand and One Nights* is the apparent contrast between the position of women in the Islamic tradition and culture and Scheherazade's prominent role as the savior of her gender.

The association of the frame story with the question of gender roles is obvious. Shahriyar is disappointed in his relationship with his spouse and responds to the new situation by terrorizing the marriageable female population of his empire. Then, Scheherazade enters the stage, determined to cure him of his obsession. She succeeds by using her female cunning and eloquence, as opposed to his male fixation on sex and violence. This outcome appears to suggest that storytelling produces a worldview in which feminine and masculine elements are balanced and supplement each other.

"As much as Scheherazade triumphs over masculine violence and saves the women of the empire, it has been suggested that the feminist opening of 'The Nights' should be understood as a guideline for the interpretation of the stories that follow" (2004 : 565). In many of these stories, the refined feminine element vanquishes masculine brutality, or feminine cleverness reveals the weakness of men. In fact, those stories that form the collection's oldest core and are closely linked to the frame story show a remarkable preference for strong, dominant women and ridiculously weak men. It is the women who are in control, particularly in the domain of sexuality, and it is the men who are either humiliated or exploited. It is the women who are clever, while men are stupid and thoughtless. The message appears to be clear : women teach men how the world functions and how social relations are regulated. The best example of this is the stories of first volume that Kaname started to browse, particularly the story of *The Porter and the Three Ladies of Baghdad* which Kaname started to read before being interrupted by his cousin Takanatsu to talk about his problem with Misako.

According to the modernity, there are some similarities between Scheherazade and Misako regarding overcoming the domination of men. Scheherazade's target is infinity. Her stories challenge death itself, and even the name of the stories can reveal this, as many scholars mentioned the addition of an extra "one" in *One Thousand and One Nights* suggests a way to mathematical infinity, Scheherazade perhaps struggled basically against her death but she could save all of her gender to give them eternity through mixing the realms of all the elements (magic, genii, animals, plants, etc.) of nature together that have their own separate domain in reality. On the other hand, the stories are full of eroticism that means not only pleasure or enjoyment but also the perpetuation of the human race.

Misako also challenges her death as a woman by having sex with her lover from Kobe, who is called Aso and who never promised to marry her, and she accepted that, which means the relation between Misako and Aso is basically sexual, although it seems based on a genuine love. The sexual relation between Aso and Misako gives her an ability to continue her life and feel herself to be a complete woman, while Aso looks like a fertility god. Although Kaname has his own sexual relation with a prostitute who is half Russian and half Korean, additionally he is attracted sexually to O-Hisa's traditional beauty that identifies with the image of Muslim women transmitted through the notes of Burton more than the real image of women within the stories themselves. The notes of Burton about women evoke the illusion of Kaname about the ideal women for him, the obedient and traditional one who can satisfy his illusion only with illusion or confidential sexual pleasure. "The Nights" is working as an inspiration of the sexual imagination of Kaname that linked to some elements in reality, such as O-Hisa, and all these pleasure enclose in the imagination of Kaname more than reality.

From the other side, "The Nights" and Bunraku both are traditional popular culture to authenticate the century's long tradition of the Japanese and the Middle East. Tanizaki's purpose is in fact the opposite : "He valorizes popular culture precisely because it problematizes the dyadic scheme of cultural interpretation that perspective, the possibility of popular culture, lies in the ability to cross national, geographical, and geo-cultural boundaries. Popular culture is an active site of interaction, hybridization, and contestation, where Japaneseness and Westernness finally lose any fixed meaning (Mitsushiro Yoshimoto, 72).

Misako's relation is more reproductive and capable of challenging death than Kaname's. In comparing Misako's attitude toward her lover with Kaname's, Misako makes the choice however unwillingly to continue seeing Aso and makes plans however unsure for her future. Misako is willing to stay with him without the promise of marriage, which means without legal or traditional validity; the status of such relationships continues to be scrutinized to this day. Takanatsu's response to her letter refers to her "final decision" and having "no course open to her but to leave Kaname." It implies that her original words to him were equally strong. In addition, her attempted refusals to

Figure 1

see her father are an effort to keep him from changing her mind. She recognizes her own vacillation and tries to fight it.

The chaos of sex which is glimpsed in this novel threatens the patriarchal world that is mainly represented by an old man. Sex becomes a way of resisting male dominance. Evelyne Sullerot wrote "any reversal of roles or sexual characteristics of social conventional or customary surely will create the impression that the world has been turned upside down" (132). The social customs are violated by Misako when she takes a lover outside the framework of matrimony. What is most shocking to society is the realization that Misako seeks sexual satisfaction as a target in itself, and she would not rein in her instinctive impulse by admitting the social and cultural constraints or the social pressure imposed on women to confine their sexual activity to the function of reproduction.

Adolphe Lalauze and Albert Letchford were equally well known as illustrators of Richard Francis Burton's private edition. Lalauze first designed 21 etchings for an edition of Galland's translation in 1881. Subsequently, his illustrations were repeatedly adopted for other editions, for example J. Scott's 1883 edition and John Payne's 1889 edition. In the background of the works by Lalauze, as is the case with Orientalist oil paintings, Spanish and Moorish architecture was repeatedly depicted. At the same time, several illustrations show a taste for Japanese objects.

Letchford, on the other hand, was discovered by Burton, who asked him to create illustrations for him in Italy. Letchford followed Burton's suggestion and studied the manners and customs of the Middle East in museums and libraries. Burton's own collection, amassed while in Cairo, afforded many specimens of arms, lamps, stools, and so on, which greatly helped his work. Letchford's work was all done in Naples, and some of the landscapes were based on the surrounding countryside.

The illustration shown by Albert Letchford (1897) accompanies the story of *The Porter and the Three Ladies from Baghdad*, which Kaname began to read after browsing the notes of Burton and table of contents of the first volume. The illustration represents three ladies in an Arab-style house in the old city of Baghdad, offering wine to men. Two of them displayed fully naked while the third has exposed shoulders. The drawing portrays a large amount of sensuality, as if filming a scene before the start of an erotic party.

Kaname devoted himself to searching for the passages that gave the Arabian Nights its dubious reputation. Sometimes, he stopped at an engaging illustration, but the text beside it generally turned out to be quite ordinary. Although Tanizaki himself did not say what kind of dubious reputation, it is understandable from the context that it is an erotic reputation. Perhaps that is why Kaname does not stop at the previous stories, which occupy about 82 pages of the book, before stopping at *The Porter and the Three Ladies from Baghdad* and starting to read. Actually, the story of the porter seems archetypal of erotic stories.

The lustful illustration of Letchford serves to draw Kaname's attention to the story of "the Portal" while browsing the book, especially as there are many erotic stories before the story of the portal such as the story of King Shahryar and his Brother with Jinni's wife that do not contain the same kind of illustration.

Kaname is not idle sexually as appeared from his relationship with his wife, but he actually prefers a kind of woman who is different from his wife, which is confirmed by his admiration of O-Hisa, who looks like a model for Eastern women according to the Western concept about the East.

In speaking with his cousin, Takanatsu, Kaname reveals that he is only interested in two types of women : the motherly-type and the whore-type (*bofugata* and *shoufugata*, respectively). What he looks for in a woman oscillates between the two, and the fact that his wife is neither one nor the other, but a mix of both, is largely the impetus behind his waning, if not dead, interest in her. Kaname prefers extremes, especially with regard to women.

Noguchi Takehiko discusses the same contrastive images of women in two chapters of his Tanizaki Junichiro book, "The Ontology of Woman" and "The Theme of Longing for the Mother." In the former in particular, he explores the contrasts between Baudelaire's use of the sacred-profane opposition and Tanizaki's, relying in part upon the French poet-critic Pierre Emmanuel's theory of Baudelairean Satanism.

Applied to Tanizaki's works, this Madonna/Harlot contrast can be illuminating, as we shall see; but the analogy between Tanizaki and Baudelaire in this respect cannot be pressed very far. The analogy breaks down when we examine the specific characteristics of the Western concept of the Madonna/Harlot and attempt to apply it comparatively to the two writers. Additionally, Howard S. Hibbett wrote :

> Roughly categorized, Tanizaki's heroines fall into two types : the exquisite, somewhat ghostly woman of classical features and old-fashioned reticence, increasingly rare in modern Japan, and the tainted, sensual beauty who adorns herself in exotic garb and who likes Western amenities, if not Western men. Among the former is the quasi-religious idealized dream figure of Mother in *Diary of a Mad Old Man*; the archetype of the latter is the harlot – not restricted to professionals such as Louise in *Some Prefer Nettles* – who may even go so far as to accept that ultimate degradation, a foreign clientele. (652-653)

It seems for Kaname the question of the moment, while he is standing before the identity door, is not only a sophisticated question but also a daily life question, attempting to answer the question not only for knowledge, but for a more comprehensive and deep cohesion with one's self-heart, although the interpretation of the novel describes the characters as if they are located in a realm where they have only two choices : either Western or Japanese culture. He looks to "The Nights" as containing both spheres inside.

In the rites of passage, a ritual performed in a person's life is indicative of a transition from one social identity to another, including celebrations of crises in the life cycle, and it always consists of three stages : an initial stage of separation, in which the individual is divorced from his familiar environment; a transitional stage, in which his old identity is destroyed and a new one created; and a final stage of incorporation, in which he is reintegrated into society in his new role. The second stage in a rite of passage, entitled a "Transition" (often called the liminal stage), which is an "in-between" time in which the participant has lost his/her old identity, but has not yet been fully re-incorporated into the community with a new identity. It is frequently a period of confusion, testing, education, and "a period of indeterminate identity, full of ambiguity and paradox." In this stage, the ritual dislocation of the self may be ambiguous sex orientation and behavior. Kaname looks like someone who is passing through the second phase where nothing has yet been decided.

4. Conclusion

One Thousand and One Nights plays an important role in the discourse of *Some Prefer Nettles*. On one hand, it reveals about the two contradictory worlds that intersect each other in the novel, and at the same time, these two worlds (East/West, old/new, etc.) are located together in the situation with neither hostility nor amity, they are forced to be together in companionship and that is the irony of that time in Japan and *One Thousand and One Nights*, too. But it seems obligatory to both worlds to leave each oth- er at next stage, this situation cannot continue forever. On the other hand, *One Thousand and One Nights* plays an important role not only in revealing the social contradictions within Japan at the end of Taisho period, but also in revealing about the internal contradiction of some characters, especially Kaname.

This is revealed through the relationship of each character with "The

Nights," as example for Kaname the readers could understand how he has a complex erotic nature, and he is struggling to identify his cultural orientation until the end of the novel, while his cousin is a merchant carrying goods not aware of their cultural value. Although Misako does not have any kind of relation with "The Nights" and seems a model of those who have been impacted by Western culture, but there is a kind of similarity that has combined her with the main character of "The Nights," Scheherazade.

At the same time, through Tanizaki's novel, we could recognize how Japanese society received "The Nights" during the time of novel, it represents the concept of "Other" in Taisho Japanese Literature.

"The Nights" is identical to Taisho and early Showa period and expose its contradictions.

Works Cited

Boehmer, Elleke, *Colonial and Postcolonial Literature : Migrant Metaphors. 2nd ed.* Oxford University Press, Oxford, 1995, 2005.

Burton, Richard, *The Jew, the Gypsy and El Islam*, Chicago, New York : Herbert S. Stone, 1898.

Daikichi, Irokawa, *The Culture of the Meiji Period*, Translated by Marius B. Jansen. Princeton, New Jersey : Princeton University Press, 1985.

Golley, L. Gregory, "The Art of Subversion and the Subversion of Art," *Journal of Japanese Studies* Vol. 21 No. 2 Summer, 1995.

Hermans, Thomas, "The Translator's Voice in Translated Narrative," *Target : International Journal of Translation Studies* 8.1, 1996.

Hibbette, Howard, *Tanizaki and the Femme Fatal*, Tokyo : Yagi Shoten, 1972.

Junichiro, Tanizaki, *Some Prefer Nettles*, Trans. Edward G. Seidensticker, New York : Alfred A. Knopf, 1955.

Kabbani, Rana, *The Arabian Nights as an Orientalist Text*, The Arabian Nights Encyclopedia, Ed. Ulrich Marzolph and Richard Van Leeuwen, California : ABC-CLIO, Inc., 2004.

Keene, Donald, *Dawn to the West*, New York : Holt, Rinehart and Winston, 1984.

Kennedy, Dane, "Captain Burton's Oriental Muck Heap : The Book of the Thousand Nights and the Uses of Orientalism," *Journal of British Studies* 39. 3. July, 2000.

Namigata, Tsuyoshi, "Paris in the Orient : Overlapping Exoticism in Japanese Modernism Around 1930," *Trans-Humanities* 9.3, 2016.

Nishihara, Daisuke, "China as Japan's Orient : 'Shinashumi' Writing and Painting in the Taisho Period," *Colonizer and Colonized* 2. Ed., Theo D. Haen and Patricia Krus. Leiden, 1997.

_______________, "Said, Orientalism, and Japan," *Alif : Journal of Comparative Poetics* 25, 2016.

Oguma, Eiji, *A Genealogy of Japanese Self Image*, Trans. David Askew, Melbourne : Trans Pacific press, 2002.

Pollack, David, *Reading Against Culture : Ideology and Narrative in the Japanese Novel*, London : Coronel U Press, 1992.

Said, Edward W., *Orientalism*, New York : Pantheon, 1978.

Shamma, Tarek, "The Exotic Dimension of Foreignizing Strategies : Burton's Translation of the Arabian Nights," *The Translator*, 1st Ser. 11, 2005.

Sullorot, Evelyne, *Woman, Society and Change*, London : Littlehampton Book Services Ltd, 1971.

Sugita, Hideaki, "The Arabian Nights in Modern Japan : A Brief Historical Sketch," *The Arabian*

Nights and Orientalism, Ed. Yuriko Mamanak and Tetsuo Nishio, London and New York : I. B. TAURIS, 2006.

Sugita, Hideaki[杉田英明], *Arabian Naito to Nihonnjin* [Japanese and Arabian Nights, アラビアンナイトと日本人], Tokyo[東京], Iwanami Shoten[岩波書店], 2012.

Venuti, Lawrence, *The Translator's Invisibility : A History of Translation*, London and New York : Routledge, 1995.

Walkowitz, Judith R., *City of Dreadful Delight : Narratives of Sexual Danger in Late-Victorian London*, 1st ed., Chicago : U of Chicago Press, 2013.

Yoshimoto, Mitsuhiro, "Reexamining the East and the West : Tanizaki Junichiro 'Orientalism' and Popular Culture, Ed. Jenny Kwok Wah Lau, *Multiple Modernities : Cinemas and Popular Media in Transcultural East Asia*, Philadelphia : Temple U Press, 2002.

Acceptance of Socialism in Colonial Joseon and Sakae Ōsugi

Byeong-jin Kim (Ewha University)

1. Introduction

This paper aims to explore aspects of colonial Joseon's intellectual acceptance of socialism in the early 1920s through the filter of Sakae Ōsugi (大杉栄).[1] There have been several previous studies on the effects of anarchism and syndicalism on colonial Joseon's early socialism.[2] However, they have tended to just validate the influential relationship in which the names of Western thinkers, including Peter Kropotkin and Max Stirner,

1 Sakae Ōsugi(1885-1923), who is known as a representative Japanese anarchist, was a figure who made the first full connection between socialist theory and the real labor movement during the height of the popular movement in the Taisho era. (Akiyama Kiyoshi 1960 : 76). Although his name and his influence on Yeol Park (朴烈) have been known in academia in Korea since early on, the specific figure is not known. Although *Jijoden* [Autobiography, 自叙伝], which describes his childhood, adolescence, and prison life, was published in Korean (Kim 2005), it is difficult to identify his conceptualization of the labor movement in his autobiography. It is necessary to introduce his discourse in order to grasp the truth of the people's movement in the Taisho era.

2 These prior studies can be summarized as follows : Cho, Se-hyun (2005), Kim, Min-hwan (2005), Cheon, Myung-hyuk (2006), Park, Yong-kyu (1994), and Lee, Ho-ryong (2001).

and their books were mentioned.[3] Of course, some have described Ōsugi as playing the role of messenger in the process of acceptance.

However, Ōsugi's role was not limited to simple transmitter of the trends of the Western world. The fact that Ōsugi's unique contribution had an effect on the socialists of Joseon through Taishō Life-centrism has not been mentioned so far in the literature.

This paper focuses on the early 1920s, a time known as the transition period of the socialist movement in colonial Joseon. When the March 1 Movement took place in 1919, socialists who were active overseas returned to Joseon, and socialism there experienced a big turning point. When the cultural policy, which was the appeal policy of the governor-general, was implemented, the socialists actively disseminated the ideology they had picked up in Japan and China through mass media such as newspapers and magazines. Among these newspapers and magazines were Joseon Rodong Gongjaehoe's [The Joseon Labor Mutual Aid Association, 朝鮮勞動共濟會] voice *Gongjae* [Cooperative, 共濟] and a general newsmagazine that was founded by socialists called *Sin Saenghwal* [New Life, 新生活]; these were used as data for this analysis.

Joseon Rodong Gongjaehoe, a nationwide organization that studies labor issues and fosters the labor movement, was established in 1920 in Joseon. *Gongjae* was the voice of the association. Kwon (1993) claimed that although the comments that appeared in *Gongjae* varied from author to author, they gave a new meaning to labor and thus constituted a big stimulus to other

3 There is a paper by Park (2008) on the influence of Ōsugi Sakae. However, instead of paying attention to the 'originality' of Ōsugi, it is just a simple argument that he was a propagandist of Western anarchism.

social groups of the time. In the case of *Sin Saenghwal*, editor-in-chief Mae Kang (1922.3) stated that it was published to "express our feelings and at the same time, reflect the needs and desires of people by promoting new life, introducing new ideology with the emphasis on instillation of free thought and the construction of common culture, studying the people's literature and criticizing the general social phenomenon." *Sin Saenghwal*, which was created on March 11, 1922, was published every 10 days from issues 1 to 5, then monthly from the 6th. It aimed to enlighten and promote the new life movement as the first magazine of Joseon. In terms of content, it covered various aspects such as family life, woman's issues, etiquette matters, politics, and ideology (Kim 1996). However, after an article published as a memorial for the fifth anniversary of the Russian Revolution became a problem, it was banned on November 22, 1923 (Kim and Kim 1989).

However, after this incident, socialists began to publish more diverse magazines. In addition to *Joseonjigwang* [The Light of Joseon, 朝鮮之光], *Singyedan* [*New Steps*, 新階段], *Pipan* [Criticism, 批判], *Sasangundong* [Ideological Movement, 思想運動], *Iront'ujaeng* [Theoretical Struggle, 理論鬪爭], and *Nodongundong* [Labor Movement, 勞動運動] are representative. These magazines, published by socialists at the time, were a source of socialist ideas for intellectuals in those days. In this paper, I will focus on *Gongjae* and *Sin Saenghwal*, which are the origins of these magazines, with particular attention to Sakae Ōsugi.

2. Aspects of the acceptance of Japanese socialism in Joseon before and after 1920

First, this study explores the acceptance of socialist ideology that flowed from Japan to colonial Joseon around 1920 from an organizational point of view. In addition, it validates the process of this flow leading to the publication of *Gongjae* and *Sin Saenghwal*.

In the spring of 1915, seven international students, including Cheolsu Kim (金綴株), Duksoo Jang (張德株), and Hyunjin Yoon (尹顯振), went to Japan and decided to engage in the independence movement by establishing a Yeoljidongmaeng [cut finger alliance, 裂指同盟]. Then, they contacted some Chinese students and organized Sinadongmaengdang [the New Asian Alliance Party, 新亜同盟党] in the spring of the following year. Sinadongmaengdang was a secret association that promoted an anti-imperialist national liberation movement, which mainly consisted of international students from colonial or semi-colonial minorities including Koreans, Chinese, and Taiwanese. The Joseon students who participated had a variety of ideological tendencies. Among them, Cheolsu Kim and Duk-soo Jang, the so-called Cheolsu Kim Group, had already established socialism as their ideological base.

The Cheolsu Kim Group had accepted socialism through Shusui Kōtoku's (幸徳秋水) *Shakaisyugishinzui* [The Essence of Socialism, 社会主義神髄]. Kōtoku's writing not only affected contemporary Japanese readers but also influenced them. *Shakaisyugishinzui* was a collaborative work with contributions from various socialist traditions, including *The Communist Manifesto* and *Socialism : Utopian and Scientific* by Karl Marx and Friedrich Engels and works by

Christian socialist William D. Bliss, historian of socialism Thomas Kirkup, and institutionalist economist Richard T. Ely. In addition, it stated that the ultimate victory of socialism would be achieved gradually by using and explaining the laws of nature [天理, Tenri] from Confucianism. The views of the Cheolsu Kim Group at that time also seemed to have this kind of character.

Cheolsu Kim became interested in labor issues through Yuaikai's (友愛会) organ *Rōdō Oyobi Sangyō* [Labor and Industry, 労働及産業], which was a mutual aid association of laborers. At the time, *Rōdō Oyobi Sangyō* approached labor issues to promote mutual aid among laborers and labor-management cooperation. Cheolsu Kim would have been affected as well. However, he was different from other Japanese international students of the time, who were indifferent to the labor problem itself, as he recognized the labor problem not as an individual laborer's problem but a social structural problem, and developed an interest in the reality of workers in colonial Joseon. Duksoo Jang saw that the modern capitalist society was based on individual supremacism and laissez-faire, and thought that modern social organizations and economic systems needed to be overcome because they were illogical. Based on this logic, Jang accepted socialism.

The socialist ideology embraced by the Cheolsu Kim Group was characterized by various socialist ideologies. It was an idea that fostered gradual changes such as institutional reform rather than radical methods as a way of realizing socialism. However, they defined themselves as socialists and criticized capitalist society and labor issues. This is a characteristic of the socialist ideology that the Cheolsu Kim Group embraced in Japan in the mid-1910s.

The basis for the rule of the Joseon governor-general changed from the existing military rule to cultural rule in the wake of Taishō Democracy, which was spreading in Japan, along with the deterioration of international opinion due to the violent suppression of the March 1 Movement. In addition, there was a great change in the socialist movement in Joseon. Although expression was limited due to strong censorship, when newspapers and magazines were allowed to be published, socialist knowledge began to be introduced in earnest. In such a conciliatory atmosphere, a series of intellectuals who embraced socialism in China and Japan in the 1910s moved their base of activity to Joseon. They came to lead the socialist movement in the early 1920s as when legitimate labor and youth organizations were formed, secret organizations were formed within them. There were five secret organizations in Joseon at this time. They included the Seoul Communist Organization in Kyeongseong (established in October 1919), the Joseon Communist Party[4] (a neutral party, established on March 15, 1920), the Social Revolutionary Party (renamed in June 1920), the small group of Yaksoo Kim (金若水) inside the Joeson Rodong Gongjaehoe (May 1920), and Young Lee's (李英) small group, which created the Youth Association Founding Society in June 1920 (Lim 2003).

First, the small group of Kim Yaksoo was formed within the Joeson Rodong Gongjaehoe under the leadership of Yaksoo Kim, Taeshin Cheong (鄭泰信), and Unhae Cheong (鄭雲海). Yaksoo Kim and Taeshin Cheong were editors of *Gongjae*, and Unhae Cheong was a councilor of the Labor Mutual Aid Association. Although their specific activities are not known, their

4 This is a separate organization from the 'Joseon Communist Party', which was established in April 1925 as the Communist International Branch. It was also considered a neutral party as it attempted to maintain balance between the Shanghai group, which continued confrontations overseas, and the Irkutsk group of the Goryo Communist Party at the time.

leading role in publishing the first (September 1920) and second issues (October 1920) of *Gongjae* as members of the editorial department is stated in the magazine. Taeshin Cheong then crossed to Ōsaka in mid-July 1914 and became a companion of anarchists such as Sakae Ōsugi and Sōjirō Yokota (横田宗次郎). From October 3 of that year, he stayed with Yokota, reading newspapers and magazines about anarchism, and then returned to Joseon. Although Yaksoo Kim also stayed in Nanjing, China, in 1918, he returned home via Japan and Manchuria after the March 1 Movement. He got to know Taeshin Cheong when he participated in the Joeson Rodong Gongjaehoe. Socialists who contributed to *Gongjae* and closely interacted with Yaksoo Kim, although they were not part of this group, included Huiyong Byeon (卞熙瑢) and Myungsik Kim (金明植). Huiyong Byeon became an executive of the Joseon International Students Association while studying at Keiō University. He also joined Reimeikai (黎明会), led by Sakuzō Yoshino (吉野作造) and Kyōji Hukuda (福田狂二). Myungshik Kim also became an executive of the Students Association after entering Waseda University in 1915 and participated in the Sinadongmaengdang in the spring of 1916 while contributing to *Hakjigwang* [*Lux Scientiae*, 學之光] (Lee 2001). At this time, the Sinadongmaengdang also interacted with Sakae Ōsugi and Sakuzō Yoshino and was influenced by their ideologies (Choi 2013).[5]

Myungshik Kim, Duksoo Jang, and Cheolsu Kim took on the name the Social Revolutionary Party after moving the activity base of the Sinadongmaengdang to Kyeongseong. Then, they sent eight delegates to the Goryo

5 The contents of the exchange between Yoshino Sakuzō and the Joseon international students are detailed in Lee Kyung-hoon (2004).

Communist Party foundation meeting, which was held in Shanghai in May 1921. In particular, as Myeongsik Kim had focused on *Aseong* [*Our Voice*, 我聲] and *Sin Saenghwal* since 1921, he formed a domestic organization base with the Youth Association or *Dong-A Ilbo* and some members of the Sinsaenghwalsa (新生活社) and Shanghai groups of the Goryo Communist Party.

Meanwhile, Taeshin Cheong and Yaksoo Kim, who were working for the Joseon Rodong Gongjaehoe, returned to Japan around May of 1921. They planned to build an ideological group together with Toshihiko Sakai (堺利彦) and Sakae Ōsugi in Japan. Thus, on November 29, 1921, the Black Current Society (黑濤會), the first ideological group of Koreans in Japan, was formed. Many members of the Association of Working Students (established in Tokyo in 1920), including Yeol Park (朴烈), were members of the Black Current Society. San Kim (1984) recalled that about 800 working students in Tokyo led all of the Joseon international students at the time, and a radical wing of them were anarchists. Bongahm Cho (曺奉岩, 1991), who was also an international student, claimed that 1921 was the era of anarchism, centering around Sakae Ōsugi, and it was a theory that he was very interested in. "Chōsenjin Kinkyō Gaiyō" [Overview of the Korean people, 朝鮮人近況概要], which was issued by the Ministry of Home Affairs in 1922, stated that the ideology of international students and workers was moving to the left. Further, the Ministry of Home Affairs explained the situation at that time as conducive to the rise of the extreme left's adventurous form of socialism (which approached so-called anarchism) or explained the influence of Shanghai's resistance groups(Iwamura Toshio 1965). In the meantime, the Black Current Society was divided into an anarchist group centered on Yeol Park and a Marxist group centered on

Yaksoo Kim, based on the confrontation between anarchism and Bolshevism in Japan in 1922. At the end of September 1922, the Black Current Society was completely divided. Later, the Yeol Park group carried out a propaganda campaign by launching *Hutoi Senjin* [Thick Korean, 太い鮮人][6] and *Hyeonsahoe* [Current Society, 現社會]. However, they became inactive due to the high treason incident[7] during the Kantō Earthquake. Meanwhile, Yaksoo Kim's group also strove for public relations after launching *Daejungsibo* [Mass current bulletin, 大衆時報].

Meanwhile, the Seoul Communist Organization also participated in the publication of *Gongjae* through the Joseon Rodong Gongjaehoe's editorial department. They then operated a domestic secretariat of the Goryo Communist Party's Irkutsk group, which was in rivalry with the Goryo Communist Party's Shanghai group.

The Joseon Communist Party mainly focused on promoting new ideas through publishing activities. It actively posted opinions in the legitimate media, including *Gongjae* and *Aseong*, and secretly issued and published brochures and pamphlets. Notably, it was the Joseon Communist Party that translated and secretly issued *the Communist Manifesto* domestically for the first time in September 1921.

This section provided an overview of the socialists who were active in Jo-

6 This was a name given by Yeol Park as he ridiculed the expression "Hutei Senjin," which the Japanese used to call the Joseon people, thus inviting some trouble.

7 Park and his wife Fhmiko Kaneko were arrested without charge after the Great Kantō earthquake. Based on thin evidence they were eventually charged with high treason for plotting a bomb attack upon the wedding of Crown Prince Hirohito. Both were convicted and sentenced to death on March 25, 1926, but their sentences were commuted to life imprisonment by the Emperor Shōwa. Kaneko died in prison on July 23, 1926, reportedly by suicide.

seon from the second half of 1919 to the early 1920s from an organizational point of view. To briefly describe the characteristics of the people in each group, first there were those who formed their social identities through the March 1 Movement. There were many people who participated in the protest movement or experienced imprisonment. Furthermore, they were the new intellectual class that had completed their secondary school education outside of Joseon. Among the people whose schooling is known, about two-thirds studied at universities in Japan. Those who belonged to several socialist organizations in the early period tried to expand their influence through mass organization, which was legal under the cultural policy of the governor-general(Lim 2003). Participation in the Joseon Rodong Gongjaehoe or Sinsaenghwalsa were part of that effort.

3. Joseon's first labor and socialist magazine and Ōsugi Sakae

After the March 1 Movement, Joseon's governor attempted to shift the dominant policy from military rule through coercive force to pacificatory cultural rule. Using the slogan 'Improvement of Culture and enrichment of civil power', this conversion was deceptive as it was carried out for the purposes of suppressing the uprising of the anti-Japanese national movement by conciliating some of the upper class of Joseon and pushing the assimilation policy more strongly. However, although there were restrictions including censorship and prohibition of publishing, some freedom of speech and publishing was allowed, and it was also possible to establish a group. The labor organizations Joseon Rodong Gongjaehoe and Sinsaenghwalsa, which were ideological groups aimed at promoting socialism, took advantage of this and were established at this time.

Although there was also some consciousness of international public opinion, which became more negative after the governor-general's suppression of the March 1 Movement, the situation in Japan also spurred this policy shift. Japan, which had participated as a member of the Allied Powers in defending democracy against German militarism during World War I, was forced domestically to make improvements to general democracy. As it joined the International Labor Organization, which was organized in conjunction with the launch of the League of Nations in 1919, it approved the activities of trade unions, which had been virtually prohibited. Moreover, the success of the revolution in Russia in October 1917 gave a powerful stimulus to the Japanese labor movement. After Japan dispatched troops to Siberia for a military intervention in response to the Russian Revolution in the summer of 1918, a people's riot [Kome Sōdō, 米騒動] spread nationwide when rice prices surged. This phase of social movement enabled expressions such as "capitalism and socialism," "class and exploitation," and "revolution" to be generally used in journalism. However, the mainstream Japanese labor movement, which had been reciprocal and cooperative until the late 1910s, started to notice changes. Certainly during the war, the rapid adjustment of the economic structure to a large-scale plant system centered on the heavy chemical industry and the news of the Russian revolution had a great impact on the upswing of the labor movement. However, propaganda activities by Ōsugi's group played a major role in the transformation of the labor movement. Through the opening of labor movement research group, the publication of *Rōdōundō* [労働運動], and promotion through various speeches, Ōsugi's activities gradually had an effect.

Of course, not only Ōsugi envisioned radical social transformation based upon labor unions. Socialists who had maintained a revolutionary socialist stance since the Meiji era adopted the tradition of revolution from the direct action of workers, even though there was an ideological difference from parliamentary socialism to anarchism. This similar direction served as a mechanism for raising the spirit of cooperative struggle to overcome each ideological difference.

However, there was also a flaw in this evaluation occasioned by the evolution of the Russian Revolution, and the difference in their positions became apparent over disagreements about a national federation of labor unions. A dispute between anarchists and Bolshevists occurred. Although a collision of organizational theories — one from the anarcho-syndicalism side called "free alliance theory" and one from the Bolshevik's side called "coalition theory" — was the apparent reason for the dispute in terms of the composition of a national federation of labor unions, their difference in understanding of the principles that made up the world was based on that. If the latter was based on 'materialism', the former was based on the principle of 'life'.

Joseon intellectuals who grasped the trend in the Japanese labor movement, and the socialist movement, spread the knowledge of socialism and the labor movement to colonial Joseon through *Gongjae* and *Sin Saenghwal*. However, it did not show the same development pattern as seen in Japan due to the historical and periodical contextual differences between the two regions.

3-1. *Gongjae*

The Joseon Labor Issues Association, which was established in February 1920, heralded the start of labor organization in Joseon. As all those who joined this association were intellectuals — laborers did not participate. They tried to understand the new ideas for labor unions, but thought the time was too early to establish such a union. This was partly because Joseon still had an agriculture-centered industrial structure, and also because the changes in the governor-general's policies were not yet concrete. However, as the spirit of social reconstruction began to spread through Joseon in March, the atmosphere changed. The organization of the labor movement was marked. In this way, the Joseon Rodong Gongjaehoe was founded. Although it was a laborers' mutual aid group in the modern sense, it had the specificity of a labor movement that was organized in the absence of a labor movement or union. Furthermore, there was a disagreement among the members about the direction of the activity, and this was reflected in its organ *Gongjae*. Although the Joseon Rodong Gongjaehoe's executives and *Gongjae*'s editors were mainly in favor of labor-management cooperation, among the authors of the articles, there were many who advocated class struggle. Although both parties were in a confrontational position, their emphasis on the sacredness of labor was shared. Although an analysis on the discourses that appeared in *Gongjae* could be carried out from various angles, this paper focuses on the influential role of Ōsugi. First, let us look at Taeshin Cheong's "Hwal-an" [A living eye, 活眼] (February 1920) :

> As impulsive, or instinctive, acts are of great value, they mean great creative instincts. I think like this. Impulsive and instinctive acts will become a form of antidote to the indecisive youths, instead of being wise today. As this becomes the driving force behind Bergson's so-called creative evolution, it will become an important factor in the settlement of stagnation in modern society and the decadent ethos of a corrupted body.

Did Taeshin Cheong consider the actions of the Joseon people following the March 1 Movement as instinctive? It is not easy to imagine that indecisive and decadent tendencies were a stumbling block for the Joseon youth movement at the time. Further, how was the structure that connects this with Bergson's *Creative Evolution* formed? Although Ōsugi Sakae was not mentioned at all, this article referred to a part of Ōsugi's "Honnō To Sōzō"[Instinct and creation, 本能と創造] (October 1912). Ōsugi's original article was a form of criticism of "Iwayuru Atarashii Onna" [So-called new woman, 所謂新しい女], which was written by Shōyō Tsubouchi (坪内逍遙) regarding Henrik Ibsen's *A Doll House.* It contains criticism of Japanese literary naturalism, which was becoming immersed in the inner part of the individual and in young people's attitudes at the time. Taeshin Cheong expressed a strong desire for "freedom of speech, publication, and assembly" by adding praise of "instinctive acts" to Ōsugi's article. Although some parts were permitted, it still contained criticism on the limited cultural policy of colonial Joseon.

Taeshin Cheong, who is classified as a so-called Marxist in Korean academic circles, described culture as the "external expression" required by the "inner impulse" of "life." He also claimed that as the culture of the present society was distorted by the hollow beliefs of the ruling class, it ignored "the free impulse of human life." To overcome this, he called for the promotion of popular culture, and held the philosophy of evolution as the basis of his own claims(June 1921). He repeatedly studied and discussed this matter as he interacted with anarchists from Japan from 1914. It seems that he shared some reasoning with Ōsugi, which was based on Darwinism, neo-Lamarckism, and Bergson's evolutionary philosophy of life.

Baekwoo Shin (申伯雨) described Marx's historical materialism by citing part of *Grundrisse* in "Yumulsakwan Gaeyo"[Historical Overview of Relics, 유물사관개요] (April 1921), found in issue 7. However, while "Kyegŭpsahoe e Satchŏkgochal" [Historical Study of Class Society, 계급사회의 사적고찰] (June 1921) from issue 8 discussed the class system, it stated that although the present class system was only a transitory phenomenon in history, it had the consistency of an internal "conquest." At this time, the explanation of Baekwoo Shin was based on Ōsugi's "Seihuku no Jijitsu"[The fact of conquest, 征服の事実] (June 1913) rather than a framework of historical materialism. First, he explained that the history of mankind can be divided into two classes : a conquering nation (class) and a conquered nation (class). The method of conquest has also changed according to the historical flow from "force" to "intelligence." As time went by, the development of the ruling technique changed into a form of economic law and institutional regulation, rather than force. As the upper reaches of the conquered peoples grow, they form a middle class and solidify the structure of conquest (domination). An explanation like Ōsugi's can be read as a reaction to ethnic elites who expressed a compromising attitude toward the conciliatory policy of the Joseon governor-general after the March 1 Movement. It may have been a more convincing explanation of the situation of colonial Joseon than Marxism, which describes history's flow as the accumulation of capital by labor marginalization and the emergence of class together with a guard against the toxin hidden in cultural politics.

Jinhee Yoo (俞鎭熙) published Peter Kropotkin's "An Appeal to the Young" in issues 7-8. The original text was a translation by Ōsugi (March 1907). "An Appeal to the Young" was widely read among Japanese intellectuals, whether anarchist or Marxist, in the 1920s (Umeda Toshihide : 1998). The one translated by Jinhee Yoo, who was a domestic organizer of the Shanghai group of the Goryo Communist Party, resembled the phenomenon in Japan. Ōsugi republished Kropotkin's work in *Rōdō Undo* (2nd 1-13, January–June 1921). Moreover, "C.G.T. and the End of the Labor Movement" from issue 7 introduced France's General Confederation of Labour (C.G.T.), which excluded parliamentarian political movements and affirmed the direct action of workers. This reminds one of Ōsugi's appreciation of the value of syndicalism, which was led by politicians through *Rōdō Undo*, "C.G.T. No Kinkyō" [Recent status of C.G.T, C.G.T.の近況], and "Kakumeiteki Syndicalism No Kenkyū" [Research on revolutionary syndicalism, 革命的サンジカリズムの研究].

3-2. *Sin Saenghwal*

Sin Saenghwal was one of the few magazines that was allowed to comment on politics and society under the governor-general's new media policy. However, it made an unsteady departure as the first publication was destroyed by the governor-general's inspector. Though it continued publishing against the tide of censorship, it was eventually banned due to the special issue commemorating the fifth anniversary of the Russian Revolution on November 22, 1922. On January 8, 1923, it was banned from publishing as *Sin Saenghwal* after an indictment in which the president, Heedo Park (朴熙道), and the chief editor, Myungsik Kim (金明植), were persecuted. This is said to have been the first "socialist writing indictment event" in Joseon (Jun 2006). *Sin Saenghwal* is an important medium for identifying the process by which socialist ideology was accepted in Joseon in the early 1920s. Let us now take a look at the characteristics of socialism that are thought to be relevant to Ōsugi.

Sungtae Lee (李星泰) focused on introducing Kropotkin. Hitoshi Yamakaya (山川均) wrote "Sahoe Saenghwal e Chinwha" [Evolution of Social Life, 사회생활의 진화] (March 1922) and "Chŏktcha e Saengjon" [Survival of the Fittest, 適子의 생존] (March 1922) based on "Dōbutsukai no Dōtoku" [Morality in the Animal Kingdom, 動物界の道德(1908), which was a translated version of Kropotkin's work in Japanese. He translated "An Appeal to the Young," which had been translated into Japanese by Ōsugi from Korean. Additionally, he introduced as "Kropotkin Haksŏl Yyŏn'gu"[Kropotkin's Theory Study, 크로포트킨 학설 연구] (July 1922) an extraction from Ōsugi's "Kropotkin Sōjo" [Entire introduction about Kropotkin, クロポトキン総序] (May–July 1920).

Kiahn(飢雁) denied that intellectuals were leading the labor movement or the revolutionary movement by citing a quote from "Chisikin e Silpae"[Failure of the Intellectual, 지식인의 실패] (July 1922). This was based on an interview that was conducted when Alexander Berkman visited Kropotkin, who lived near Moscow after the Russian Revolution. Kropotkin believed the revolution had failed because the Russian Communist Party did not believe in the power of the people. Kiahn seems to have been exposed to the above interview through Ōsugi's "Kropotkin O Omou"[I think of Kropotkin, クロポトキンを想う](1922).

Baek Cheong (鄭栢) cited Ōsugi's "Seihuku no Jijitsu" at the beginning of the eighth issue in a paper entitled "Ingan Soyu wa Banyŏk" [Human Possession and Rebellion, 인간소유와 叛逆] (August 1922), where he wrote the following :

> History is complex. However, it is merely conquest and conquest to be consistent with such complexity. Through the ancient and modern ages, the histories of all societies are indeed the content of conquest, and nothing but a transformation of its color . . . . Life is a sprout of rebellion.

Today's culture, which developed from the "truth of conquest," naturally came to have a structure that alienates a large number of people. However, the human desire to reclaim oneself among the many will develop as long as humans have life. In addition, such a desire goes beyond individual awareness through unity and will lead to social awareness. Although he was known as a Marxist, Ōsugi found the factors that drove change not from historical materialism but the fundamental principle of life. As described above, Ōsugi's statement gave an appropriate answer on why colonial policy was transforming into a soft-line state. In addition, it provided a basis for responding to the logic of the national elites who called for improving the capability of the inner side of colonial Joseon first, since internal contradiction would lead to a socialist society after the industrial structure had matured. At the time of the discussion, in which only the economic field (which is a substructure) was mentioned and social development was discussed, a proper logical response could not have been established by popular Marxism.

From this perspective, the publication of "Chain Factory" in the ninth issue under the pseudonym of RST was reasonable. It was a translation of Ōsugi's fable novel "Kusari Kōjō" [Chain factory, 鎖工場]. The original author's name was not specified, and only the source *S ēno Tōsō* [Struggle of Life, 生の闘争] was revealed. While it criticized modern capitalist society through a story about a factory in which workers made choking chains, it questioned "scientific socialism," which reflects the putative inevitability of history. It claimed that there was no inevitable future, but only a constant effort to expand the self by realizing self-power and authority.

Moreover, "Chisangsŏn ŭl Wihaya" [For the Best Virtue, 至上善을 위하야] (July 1922), which was published in the seventh issue, by Sangsup Yeom (廉尚燮), a writer who lived in Japan from 1912 to the 1920s, was also reminiscent of the discussion by Ōsugi :

> It was Nora who tested a leap toward a naked human world by cutting off the chain of old ideas in a solid greenhouse of self-effacing slavery, mechanical con-

ventions, and morals. Nora was the rebel of justice who strived on the battlefield of liberation.

> The soul that is constantly growing, the life of lively spirit that is full of resilience and vitality, is in "rebellion." There is a new baptism of eternity in life, with the splendor of the soul shining in rebellion against all old, pursuing all newness.
>
> Self-revolt is completed by rebelling against the old self, and expanding a new self. In this sense, rebellion is the best virtue.

Sangsup Yeom positioned Nora, who was a weak and conquered slave in *A Doll's House,* as the "warrior of rebellion" against all of the conventions and morals that were the result of "conquest." The logic of the "just rebel" matches Ōsugi's life-centric idea, as he found the "best beauty in rebellion." By referring to Bergson's, Ōsugi formed the social revolutionary idea that had the fundamental principle of the "expansion of life." He explained that "hate" and "rebellion" toward "conquest" are the "best beauty" that can break the "truth of conquest"; that is, a structured contradiction of class society and the "expansion of life" (July 1913). Sangsup Yeom limited "rebellion" to a moral issue called "virtue" by replacing the "best beauty" mentioned by Ōsugi with the "best virtue." Although he asked people to have uncompromising courage to complete self-revolution, the arrow only points to the family system of conventions and customs. Furthermore, he argued that the pursuit of "desire for the soul's growth and expansion" is "virtue." Unlike the flowery words of Sangsup Yeom, this ultimately lacks a relation with society, and has also been described as the hymn of individualist anarchism, such as by Max Stirner (Choi 2011).

4. Conclusion

This paper examined the traces of Ōsugi Sakae that appear in *Gongjae* and *Sin Saenghwal*. Below is a summary of the situation of the Japanese labor and socialist movements.

In May 1920, when *Gongjae* was published, the fever of the popular election campaign had reached the workers after Takashi Hara's (原敬) resignation from cabinet. However, as Rikken Seiyūkai [立憲政友会], the ruling party in the House of Representatives, had a sweeping victory, the popular election campaign rapidly declined. Instead, anarcho-syndicalism grew rapidly among the laborers. In January 1921, as "Rōdōkumiai e Kaere!" [Return to labor union!, 労働組合へ帰れ!]" by Kotora Takahashi (棚橋小虎), a secretary of Yuaikai, triggered opposition by militant workers, the "Intellectual Leader Disarmament Campaign" took place. The reason why revolutionary syndicalism's tendencies and intellectual rejection are mentioned in "Gongjae" can be guessed here. However, in Joseon, labor unions, which are the basis of syndicalism, were set aside, as industrial development was insufficient and there was no gap between the labor movement and the intellectuals. In other words, it may be read regardless of the situation of Joseon at the time. However, contributors to *Gongjae* or *Sin Saenghwal* did not limit this reason to Joseon, but noted that it affected the entire Japanese Empire.

In the Japanese labor movement from May 1920 to June of the following year, the energy of the cooperative struggle was high. In Kantō, the Rōdōkumiai Dōmeikai [Labor Union Alliance, 労働組合同盟会] was established, whereas in Kansai, the Kansai Rōdōkumiai Rengōkai [Kansai Federation of Labor Unions,

関西労働組合連合] was formed. The Shakaisyugi Dōmei [Socialist Alliance, 社会主義同盟] was launched in December 1920. Anarchism and Bolshevism were regarded as having been consolidated. I think it was because of his attitude to join forces beyond the factions that Ōsugi was often quoted in *Gongjae* and *Sin Saenghwal*.

Ōsugi›s influence, which appears in these magazines, was not limited to his simple introduction of Western anarchism. His repeated recognition of history called "fact of conquest," like historical materialism, gave an interpretation of a reality in which Joseon was present, including its colonization by the Japanese Empire and the governor-general's policy change. The life-centric idea that Ōsugi formed by himself through the theory of evolution, philosophy, and literary theory, was widely accepted beyond his faction in the sense that it complemented contemporary Marxism, which only emphasized the economic substructure.

Works Cited

Akiyama Kiyoshi [秋山清], *Nihon No Hangyakushisō* [日本の反逆思想], Gendaishichōsya [現代思潮社], 1960.

Cheon, Myung-hyuk, *1920s Korean socialist movement research*, Seon-in, 2006.

Cheon, Sang-sook, "Park Yeol's anarchism and national consciousness," *Dongyang jeongchisasang-sa*, 2007.

Cheong, Baek, "Human possession and rebellion," *Sin Saenghwal* No. 8, 1922.

Cheong, Tae-shin, "Hwal-an," *Gongje* No.2, 1920.

———, "Promotion of Popular Culture," *Gongje* No.8, 1921.

Cho, Bong-am, "The way I walked," *Cho Bongam and Jinbodang*, Han Gilsa, 1991.

Cho, Sae-hyun, "Acceptance of Kropotkin's thought in three East Asian countries," *Research of Chinese History*, Chinese History Society, 2005.

Choi, Byung-goo, *Study on the process of the formation of professional literature in the 1920s and aesthetic commonality*, Sungkyunkwan University Graduate School doctoral thesis, 2013.

Choi, In-sook, "Nora in the literature of Sangsup Yeom and its meaning," *Korean Studies Book* 25, Korean Studies Institute, Inha University, 2011.

Iwamura Toshiō [岩村登志雄], "Zainichi Chosenjin To Nihon Rōdōkaikyu" [在日朝鮮人と日本労働者階級], *Asia·Africa Kōza* [アジア·アフリカ講座] Vol.3, Keisōshobō [勁草書房], 1965.

Kang, Mae, "Completing edit," *Sin Saenghwal* No.1, 1922.3.

Kim, Jeong-kwon, "Review of 'Sin Saenghwal'," *Korea Christian History Institute News* No.25, Korean Christian History Institute, 1996.

Kim, Jun-Yeop and Kim, Chang-Soon, *Korean communist movement*, Cheonggye Yonguso, 1989.

Kim, Min-hwan, "Analyzing the content of socialist articles in left-wing magazines under Japanese rule," *Korean Journal of Public Relations* Vol. 49, No.1, 2005.

Kwon, Hee-young, "Joseon Labor Mutual Aid Association and *Gongje*," *Mental Culture Research* Vol. 16, No. 2 (Serial Number 51), Institute for Mental Culture, 1993.

Lee, Hoon-ryong, *Anarchism in Korea*, Knowledge Industry Press, 2001.

Lee, Kyung-hoon, "Medium characteristics of *Hakjigwang* and Japan's effect," *Daedong Culture Research,* 2004.

Lee, Seong-tae, "Evolution of social life," *Sin Saenghwal* No.2, 1922.3.

———, "Survival of the fittest," *Sin Saenghwal* No.3, 1922.4.

———, "Kropotkin's theory study," *Sin Saenghwal* No.7, 1922.7.

Lim, Kyung-seok, *Origin of Korean socialism*, History Critic, 2003.

Ōsugi, Sakae [大杉栄], "Honnō To Sōzō" [本能と創造], *Kindaishisō* [近代思想] Vol.1 No.2, 1912.

———, "Sei No Gakujū" [生の拡充], *Kindaishisō* Vol.1 No.10, 1913.7.

———, "Kusari Kōzō" [鎖工場], *Kindaishisō* Vol.1 No.12, 1913.9.

———, "Seihuku No Jijitsu" [征服の事実], *Rōdōundō* [労働運動], Vol.1 No. 412, 1920.2.

———, "Kropotkin Sōjo," [クロポトキン総序], *Kaizō* (改造), 1920.5-7.

———, "Seinen Ni Uttau" [青年に訴ふ], *Rōdōundō* (労働運動), Vol. No. 1-13, 1921.

———, Kropotkin O Omou (クロポトキンを想う), *Kaizō* (改造), 1922.7.

———, *Osugi Sakae autobiography*, Translated by Kim Eung-kyo, Silcheonmunhagsa, 2005.

Park, Yong-gyu, "A study on leftist journalists under Japanese imperialism," *Journal of Korean Association of Journalists*, paper for Autumn Periodical Conference, 1994.

Park, Jong-lin, *A study on the acceptance of socialist thought under Japanese rule*, Yonsei University Doctoral Thesis, 2006.

Shin, Woo-baek, "Historical overview of relics," *Gongje* No.7, 1921.4.

———, "Historical study of class society," *Gongje* No.8, 1921.6.

Umeda Toshihide [梅田俊英], "Syakaisisōsya No Ichisokumen" [社会思想社の一側面], *The Ohara Institute for Social Research* No.479, 1998.

Wales, Nym, *Arirang*, Translated by Song, Yong-in, Dongnyeok, 1984.

Yeom, Sangsup, "For supreme good," *Sin Saenghwal* No.7, 1922.

Joseonjigwang and the Development of KAPF Literature

Youn-ho Oh (Ewha Institute for the Humanities)

1. *Joseonjigwang* As Modern Field of Knowledge

Joseonjigwang [The Light of Joseon, 조선지광] obtained its permit of the Newspaper Publication law on September 12, 1922 along with *Gaebyeok* [The Genesis, 개벽], *Shinsaenghwal* (New Life, 신생활), and *Shinchunji* (New Universe, 신천지). This permit meant that the manuscripts did not get censored and were only censored after the magazines were published, and were able to deal with current issues and politics. (Jang Sin, 441)

This was a privilege of culture and politics shown by the Japanese after the 3.1 Movement. The first issue was published on November 1, 1922, and it was promoted that it was "confident of becoming the center of Joseon's world of ideas."[1] The first issue had a clearer objective of "survival and development of Joseon's people," and in order to "contribute to world culture," they would "promote all justice, knowledge, and civilization," and "raise awareness of

1 "*Joseonjigwang* Chang-gan" [*Joseonjigwang* magazine launched, 조선지광 창간], *Donga-ilbo* [Dong-A Daily, 동아일보], 5 Nov 1922.

Joseon people's education, industry, and cooperation," and they claimed to "advocate the rights and happiness of Joseon's people." As it was with modern magazines of Japan occupied Joseon, *Joseonjigwang* was published in order to contribute to the social demands of "the formation of the people and its enlightenment, communication of knowledge and contribution to world culture."

For this characteristic, *JoseonJiGwang* was positioned as the successor of *Gaebyeok*[2] among the socialist related magazines. Im Hwa, who was a socialist liberal arts theorist, commented, "The influence and contribution the two magazines that are noteworthy of Joseon's cultural thoughts, *Gaebyeok* and *Joseonjigwang*, had over Joseon's world of thought and the arts until recent years were bigger than the newspapers,"(Im Hwa 1938 : 115) and he explained the historical status and the closeness of relationships between the two magazines. (Han Ki-hyeong(2006 a), 174) Both magazines were published at the same time, and when *Gaebyeok* was discontinued *Joseonjigwang* succeeded *Gabyeok*'s political line. *Joseonjigwang* was issued monthly when it was first published, but it was changed as a weekly issue on its fourth, and when *Gabyeok* was discontinued three months later, it was again published as a monthly issue starting on its 61st issue in November, 1926. "The change of *Joseonjigwang* into a monthly issue was the result of a conscious decision to replace the media void created by the discontinuance of *Gaebyeok*," and it allowed "the pursuit of

2 The magazine *Gaebyeok* integrated various forms of religious movement of Cheondo religion, socialist movement as well as anti-Japanese movements and enlightenment movement, and was the central medium that acquired the "gained" hegemony of the times while mediating various forms of modern knowledge. (Han Ki-young 2006a)

character change as an integrated magazine that represents Joseon's reality as a whole."(Han Ki-hyeong 2006a : 177)

Along with the publication of *Joseonjigwang* it repeatedly experiences seizure and suspension of publication by the Japanese colonial government, and the decisive reason for such oppression was "communist propaganda." When *Joseonjigwang* was decided to be continued on May 3, 1924, Kim Donghyuk was reported as the new publisher. "According to a piece of intelligence for the Jongno police station in June 12, 1924, on the hidden side of *Joseon Ji Gwang* were key communists Ju Jong-gun (주종건, 朱鐘建), Yoo Jinhee (유진희, 兪鎭熙), Shin Il-yong (신일용, 辛日鎔), Byun Hee-yong (변희용, 卞熙瑢) and so on active as journalists."(Jang Sin : 446) In such past history (전력, 前歷), the Joseon Communist Party officially appoints *Joeonjigwang* as a Communist paper in the third convention on February 27, 1928.

In a time of "magazine pursuing socialism = discontinuance" in Japanese colonialism of the 1920s, *Joseonjigwang* continued until 1932. The Public Peace Maintenance Law that pressured socialist movements was enforced starting May 1925, and an advanced censorship system centered in the book department was established in the police department in 1926, when it started operating. Moreover, even with much effort to break up the Joseon Communist "Party," *Joseonjigwang* was still the communist paper for the party and continued its public activities of socialist movement without discontinuing. Han Gi-hyeong evaluates such phenomenon as "accomplishing the goal that the censorship system and the socialist camp each needed." *Joseonjigwang* being a monthly issue, its continuous publication was a big advantage to the socialist group in the aspects of proliferation of the socialist movement and the securing of unique media, and as a censorship agency, it had the opportunity to separate and isolate nationalism, various anti-Japan groups, and socialist groups within the space of media.(Han Ki-young 2006a : 181)

As *Joseonjigwang* rose to an essential medium within the socialist camp, the legal activities of the socialists could not help but be exposed through the magazine.[3] Such a point demonstrates the strategic controlling aspect of an ambivalent and terrifying leadership that the Japanese censorship system had, and brings a spotlight to the refracted role of modern media.

When we observe that the changing process of *Joseonjigwang*, a 1920s magazine that is a modern medium, was closely linked to the social demands (national enlightenment movement, Japanese censorship, socialist movement), and that it was formed from enlightenment and desire for communication of enlightening knowledge, and gradually specialized.

Between 1926 and 1927, *Joseonjigwang* changed the initial nationalistic sense of purpose to the class consciousness of the socialist movement, and attempted to expand socialism theory and movement, and proletarian literature :

> *Joseonjigwang*'s political papers can be seen as concentrated expression of the praxis of the new trend of the times (…) as it became a monthly issue, such a state seems to have improved rapidly and naturally. The literary section's color became

3 "The censorship system demonstrated the pain and scars made by the censorship system that *Joseonjigwang* experienced, and by doing so wanted to check the socialism 'myth.' With the realistic pains of socialist movement surfacing through media 'isolated mobility's' post was created. (…) The scars of *Joseonjigwang*'s texts that were dominated by deletion and symbols, contributed in systemizing fear against socialism." (Han Ki-young 2006a : 183)

heavier, and prominent new artists of the New Tendency Group such as Cho Myunghee, Lee Gi-yeong, Kim Ki-jin, Park Young-hee, Kim Young-pal, Choi Seung-il, Lee Ryang, Hand Seol-ya, Song Young, and so on became the creative and theoretical center of the Literary section of *Joseonjigwang*. (Im Hwa 1939)

According to Im Hwa, during the colonial times *Joseonjigwang*'s proletariat literature was in an important position in theorizing and practicing socialism of the time and within it active discussion was placed on the socialist movement and media, theorization and role of literature.[4] Different from the times where the theory of social evolution required political actions of enlightenment and the construction of a modern nation under the name of science, early 1920s socialism was "introduced as scientific scholarship that attempted to explain social phenomenon once more," and was received as something that provides an important cognitive frame of modern knowledge and that it is a system of thought with scientific color, where we can look into the social aspects.[5] *Joseonjigwang* published 38 pieces on socialist philosophy but at the

4 "Proletariat literature during the colonial times is one of the new cultural politics created by socialism. Socialism understood by Proletariat writers was a practical opportunity to urge changes as well as intellectual source that would allow humans to realize their environment as something structured. Socialist activists yearned to create a new intellectual network through socialist media such as *Shinsaenghwal*, *Joseonjigwang*, *Bipan*, and through *Munye Undong*, *Yesul Undong*, *Joseon Munye*, *and Bipan*, they thought of the role of socialist arts. Of course the two groups are closely related." (Choi Byeong-goo 2013 : 12)

5 "There was a more dominant tendency to explain the fact that labor class society is drawing near through class struggles in the social evolutionary point of view, and such are asserted by the early Japanese Marxists Sakai Toshihiko or Yamakawa Hitoshi. Their claims that the society changes its evolutionary direction from a time of survival competition, to a time of mutual aid, and to a time where labor society arrives through class struggles, reminds us of the process of where previous theory of social evolution, moves on to the theory of mutual and finally reach Marxism." (Song Min-

same time provided non-socialist activists' materialistic views(Choi Byeong-goo 2013 : 23), and by doing so contributed in forming 1920s socialist discourse.

Moreover, the creativity and theorizing of KAPF literature, which unfolded in the early 1920s, were focused on *Joseonjigwang* due to the discontinuation of other socialist affiliated magazines, such that it becomes the representative magazine of the KAPF literature. It is significant in the aspect that it searched for possibilities of scientific theorization of a? the? proletariat literature movement and contemporary interest of Joseon on socialist literature even from a global viewpoint.(Park Sang-joon 1998 : 178)

ho 2012 : 149-150)

2. Turnover Theory and Cho Myunghee's[6] *Nakdonggang*[7]

A full-fledged debate and discussion on KAPF literature led to reorganization of KAPF as a detailed result and the Turnover Theory that took place within KAPF around 1927, and in the center of all this was *Joseonjigwang*. The dispute that began in December 1926 between Kim Ki-jin and Park Young-hee soon developed into a controversy between an anarchist and a Bolshevik. The specifics of KAPF Turnover Theory were "the establishment of partisanship in literary art and the problem of particularity of literary art," and through this occasion anarchists including Kim Hwa San, who argued for the autonomy of literary art, were expelled.

It began with Kim Ki-jin criticizing Park Young-hee's novels *Cheorya* [All Night, 철야] and *Jiogsunlye* [Hell Pilgrimage, 지옥순례], and questioning the "novel's idea and depiction" in *Munye Wolpyeong – Sanmunjeok Wolpyeong* [Literary Monthly Review - Novel Monthly Review, 문예월평 – 산문적 월평], and point out

6 Cho Myung-hee (1894-1938) was active in his writing in many genres such as poetry, novels, drama, literary reviews, and children's literature, starting from 1920 and for the next 8years during her time studying in Japan, and in the mid 1920s he showed prominence as a writer of the New Tendency Group and was active as a proletariat writer with the creation of KAPF. In 1928 when he sought asylum in the Soviet Union, he had a position in the Soviet Writer's Union. he stayed in Maritime Province of Siberia before she moved to Khabarovsk, and became a middle school teacher. He was arrested by the Stalin government on a day in fall in 1937, and was shot to death on May 11, 1938.

7 It is a short novel by Cho Myunghee published in *Joseonjigwang* in July 1927. The story's plot is as follows : a socialist activist, Park Sung Un participates in the independence movement, until he goes back to his hometown *Nakdonggang* [Nakdong River, 낙동강], and in the process of developing night school and union movement, he meets Rosa, daughter of a butcher and educated in the new education system. They fight together with the farmers afterwards to keep the rights for the field of reeds, but Park Sung Un gets arrested, does his time, and released by bail, yet dies soon after. Rosa leaves for Yan-bian area with the nomads full of new hope.

that it is the limitation of "propaganda literature." Kim Ki-jin commented that "the idea in *Cheorya* was most logical," but the details that needed to be seriously represented (what is life, what is lifestyle, is discrimination between the rich and the poor) were handled too easily, and that it only focuses on class consciousness and class struggles. Furthermore, he saw that in *Jiogsunlye*, the depiction of characters was so appalling that it brought an "unfortunate result" to the novel.(*Joseonjigwang*, Dec 1926.) "Accordingly, Park Young-hee asked, "What is Proletarian Literature?" in "The Attitude of a Literary Critic – Reading Comrade Kim Ki-jin's Review" (투쟁기에 있는 문예비평가의 태도 – 동무 김기진군의 평론을 읽고), and asserted that "a true proletarian literature is mobile within the lifestyle of a proletarian class, and it should be ×× that comes out of the cries of class consciousness and ××× that instructs it,"(Park Young-hee, Jan 1927) and he criticizes Kim Ki-jin as a bourgeois critic.

Regarding the "novel's idea and depiction" that Kim Ki-jin argued, he cites Michael Gold's observation, "It required great achievements."(큰 행적을 요구하였었다.) as well as Japanese proletariat literature critic Aono Suekichi (青野李吉), Soviet literary critic Leon Trotsky, and American scholar William James. Soon after, Kim Ki-jin presupposed that Park Young-hee's argument is not different from what he based his argument on, and asserts the completion that "the novel's idea" has. He further argues the social evolutionary viewpoint where proletarian literature originates from bourgeois literature, and along with the positive prospect that proletarian literature would mature, he argues the objectivity of Marxist criticism.[8]

8 Kim Ki-jin, "Peulolletalia Mun-ye Jakpum-gwa Peulolletalia Mun-ye Bipyeong"[Proletarian literary works and proletarian literary criticism, 무산문예작품과 무산문예비평], *Joseonjigwang* [조선지광],

The dispute that started from two novels' advances into very specific theorization about aesthetic understanding of proletarian novels and representation of teleological class consciousness. Moreover, the focus on the turnover debated on literary and artistic grounds is whether to see bourgeois literature before proletarian literature as the origin of proletarian literature or not, and this dispute expands into the debate of "class sense of purpose" and "romanticism."

The debate on the turnover of the literature and arts movement develops dramatically due to the difference of critical understanding on Cho Myung-hee's *Nakdonggang*. In his article "Theory of Purposefulness of Literature and Arts Movement" (문예운동의 목적의식론), Park Young-hee said, "the establishment of literature and arts theory – a struggle over theory – in the turnover period is not trying to divide literature and arts individually from literature and arts itself. Rather, in the unionist literature and arts theory, the establishment of theory for advancement to the front or the turnover of literature and arts movement – winning of purposeful consciousness – is the reason why they cannot advance without this theoretical struggle."(Park Young-hee : July 1927). Since it is not possible to reach Marxist objectives just by simple realistic representation, it means that people should carry contents with political purpose within a literature and arts movement.

On this matter Kim Ki-jin comments "the second phase of the Joseon Pro-

---

February 1927.

"In studying Russian literature, I believe that there is a need to think by combining the results of formalist and the opinions of Marxists. The reason is that we should not only master the ways in changing actual/real phenomenon into artworks, but also the ideology of the artists that maintains the connection with our class. (re-quoted from Lyubov Rogachevsky, Russian Artists Association)

letariat Proletarian literature movement is in the development from literature of poverty novels so far to new sense of purpose," and argued "Cho Myung-hee leapt from 'Jeogiap' [Low Pressure, 저기압] to *Nakdonggang*." It seems like our writer that presented the previous part in the second phase appeared." Kim Ki-jin highly appreciated the value *Nakdonggang* has as proletariat literature, and reads the possibility of proletariat revolution in *Nakdonggang*.

On such argument, Cho Jung-gon asserts, "what is the second phase and second phase literature? It is neither the 'novel full of inspiration,' as Kim said, nor is it a 'touching novel with impressive expressions.' Moreover, neither 'Joseon public's truthful life record' can become the works of the second phase, nor the depiction of 'dawn of life that shines with passion and not the life of despair.'"(Cho Jong-gon : October 1927) As a result, he re-analyzes *Nakdonggang* under 5 different standards.[9] He criticizes the representation of the national reality in the work, and finds that the fact that Rosa left for another place besides Joseon is a result of the Marxist sense of purpose not being re-recognized as nationalist consciousness. Above all, he denigrates the lyrics at the beginning of the novel as "sentimental verse about affection for one's hometown." He also finds character Park Sung-un's behavior to be not politically active, and the naturalistic technique used in the novel is ineffective for such political purpose. Strictly speaking, *Nakdonggang* does not comprise a Marxist tendency in the work, and cannot be evaluated as an appropriate 'text' for the second phase activity of KAPF. The argument that says "sensibility" or "romanticism" expressed in the work cannot go along with proletariat prole-

9 "1. Exact recognition of present level, 2. Marxists objectives, 3. Work action, 4. Have political struggle as content, 5. Expression." (Cho Jong-gon : October 1927)

tarian revolution demonstrates the status of *Nakdonggang* that is within the debate of KAPF literature.

The key to the debate of *Nakdonggang* is in the question can "the model of socialist movement" be realized in a literary work, and if so, in what way is this possible? *Nakdonggang*'s plot, which is structured in "recognition of reality-class-proletarian revolution" clearly demonstrates the political objective of socialist literature (novel) that Park Young-hee declares. Kim Ki-jin greatly appreciates the process where the main character, through the experience of bourgeois life, recognizes reality through poverty and leads others of the proletariat to be aware, and to move forward into class battle. The process of change from bourgeois life experience to proletarian class consciousness clearly realizes Kim Ki-jin's proletarian literature theory.[10]

Though Park Sung-un was the grandson of a fisherman, and a son of a farmer, he lived a life of a petit bourgeois working as a farming assistant in the county office after graduating agricultural school. However, as the independence movement broke out, he was imprisoned as a passionate independence fighter and was released. After he was released from prison he left for the north-west of Gando, and was active moving around from Manchuria, to Russian territory, to Beijing, to Shanghai and so on, and changes from pas-

10 Kim Ki-jin claims that Proletariat literature is of course literature, however it is difficult to eliminate bourgeois ideology completely in the literature sense, and the proletariat art was born from the results and the development of bourgeois literature that has a rich history. "The most crucial standard of Proletariat literature is the unimpaired context and form. Moreover, we can find the harmony of form and context its description, technique, and form that are outstanding in its times, and that we must learn. It doesn't mean that the past things are bound to be good. But dissecting and analyzing could become the motivation to destroy old literature."(Kim Ki-jin : Jan 1927)

sionate nationalist to a socialist. It is similar with Rosa, who was the daughter of a butcher, attended an all girls' high school in Seoul, and when she came home for the break from the school in Hamgyeong-do, where she was a regular teacher, she participated in an alliance for young women's association, became aware of class, and became a socialist.

The realistic pain and the class conflict that Cho Myung-hee experienced is reflected in the characterization like this. In an autobiographical article ("A Side of Life Record- From the Times of Aspiring for Literature and Art" [생활 기록의 단면 – 문예의 뜻을 두던 때부터], *Joseonjigwang* March 1927) that Cho Myung-hee wrote a couple of months before *Nakdonggang* was written, someone tells him, "You are definitely suffering from bourgeois ideological disease," or even tells Rosa "you still have the petit bourgeois mind." To such comments, Cho Myung-hee sometimes consented and later torments himself by saying "(I) still have a bourgeois spirit" However, as discussed earlier, Cho Myung-hee was seriously poor when he came back from Japan, and that was also the reason why he left for Yeonhaeju (Maritime Province of Siberia). Experiencing the gap between a realistic environment and the ideological world, Cho Myung-hee says, "Let's dissect and criticize reality and build ideological basics over experience and knowledge,"(Kim Ki-jin : Jan 1927) and he wrote a social tendency novel *Nakdonggang*.

Cho Myung-hee's creative writing theory of "Let's dissect and criticize reality" was influenced by naturalist theory of art, but we could also find its reason in the argument on the relationship between life and art centered around Park Young-hee, Kim Ki-jin, and Yeom Sang-Seop. Park Young-hee continuously emphasized that "rather than literature and art creating our life, our lives create our literature and art," and Kim Ki-jin claims "if literature generally comes out of life consciousness, it is not possible without basing it on the reformation of social organization, which decides life consciousness," and argues that art of literature should begin from proletarian life consciousness. (Hong Jung-sun 1989 : 416) Yeom Sang-Seop suggests "life, lifestyle is always serious to anyone... lifestyle is the first significance (第一義). People do not live in literature. We can artistically manage our lifestyle, but art is something that grows and develops within lifestyle." With 1926-1927 as its starting point, the KAPF debate changes from the point of life and life-ism (pro-life) to class consciousness and revolutionary will. It was influenced by the Soviet socialist movement and literature and art movement, it had a definitive influence on pursuit of spontaneous public consciousness and art theory accepting socialist literature and art movement as new knowledge or an ideological system.

Another issue that *Nakdonggang* has is about romanticism. Cho Jung-gon points out the inherent perception of reality in the literary work is at its limits in aesthetics as well as politics, and reasons for it are in the scene where *Nakdonggang* is depicted as a post-historical and romantic space,[11] and the attitudes of the characters that are not actively responding to nationalistic reality. By focusing on the inherent romanticism in *Nakdonggang*, Lee Hwa-jin evaluates that the debate on romanticism about Cho Myung-hee was not

11 "700ri (around 280km) of Nakdonggang, when the water that flows reaches here, it combines the branches of the river into one body and moves forward to the sea. The fields along the river that looks like a go board are opened up endlessly towards the sea, and in them graveyards of villages are placed here and there. Humans that live in the river here, the field there, and over there — the rivers have flown and so have the humans lived. Couldn't this river and this human forever be not separated now? (In *Nakdonggang*)

elaborately discussed by pursuing its traits, and analyzes the romanticism of *Nakdonggang* in relation to the literary and ideological experiences that Cho Myung-hee had when she was studying literature abroad. (Lee Hwa-jin 2013 : 257-258)

Literary imagination and representation about sense of life that promotes communication and coexistence through human sensitivity and intelligence that recognize universal and natural phenomenon are abundantly found in the poems, novels, and critiques that Cho Myung-hee wrote[12] "Natural space – *Nakdonggang*'s sanctification and glorification of its life force or optimistic prospect on construction of new society" and so on – "are based on anarchism, which he experienced while studying abroad, and the Daisho [大正] ideology that is deeply related to him, and strongly influenced by Tagor-like [類] Neo-romanticism[13] and the Neo-idealism that arose due to the theory of reformation,' which was popular in Japan and colonial Joseon because of the Russian Revolution and World War II." (Lee Hwa-jin 2013 : 253) In the midst of comprising such 1920s tendencies (life-ism and romanticism) of the Joseon

12 "If we compare the Universe that walks the road of infinity of space to a phoenix, what is different from the universe itself and a bird, or a soul of a person. In the functioning of a life, there is always a good, light, and sound."(In "On a spring lawn")
"From infinite to infinite is the shed of light. The wave of life that flows from eternity to eternity. The one that fought as a mere red piece of flesh in such a fierce sea, isn't that life solely?" (in "Death of Kim Young Il")

13 Jo Myeong-hee, "Saenghwal Danpyeon-ui gilok"[Record of the Life Fragment, 생활 단편의 기록], Lee Myung-jae ed, *Nakdonggang(Oe)* [Nakdonggang(other), 낙동강(외)], Bumwoo Publishing Co., 2004, 411.
"The steps of one's thought keeps going into the ever more gray fog. Never walk into the world of solitude alone. Lets meditate with our eyes closed and knee knelt in the world of vast solitude. Lets pray while listening to the sighing of solitude that is pushed out from deep within the heart. Recite the song of the prayer. Then I could also go into the state of "Tagore"."

literary circle, Cho Myung-hee wrote *Nakdonggang*.

The dispute on romanticism provides an important point in understanding the bourgeois origin of KAPF literature. In 1926, Yeom Sang Sup claims that the "proletariat has passion as a proletariat. There are tears. There is laughter. There is hope… and that innocent and humble passion ignites the desire for liberation, and will to fight, and the beautiful sentiment about that exercise of will stimulates as an energy source, and fosters the abundant convulsions of passion,"(Yeom, Sang-sup(2013), 447) and on the characteristics of proletarian literature, he defines it as "literature that emerges from the holy movement in search for the humanity that was lost in proletariats, and its spirit." Such remarks are in the same vein as the statement "there is happiness, brilliance, and strength of art in one's new life (all) unified and in expressing newly oneself (all)" in Kim Sa-guk's "What is art?" (「예술이란 무엇인가」, *A-sung* [아성], 1921.5), and "Spirit of Free Criticism" ([자유비평의 정신], *Shinsaenghwal* [New Life ,신생활], 1922.9)(Choi Byeong-goo 2013 : 17). Expressing the perception of the subject and the inner emotions are key aesthetic characteristics of early proletarian literature. Up until the materialism dispute in 1927, the socialist thought "it is not the repetition of proletariat/bourgeois dichotomy, but the conscious and awakening of a proletariat as a common human being," to be important, and "the attitude that a human should have towards reality, in other words ethics or morality are the important emotions that encourages life changes." (Choi Byeong-goo 2013 : 26) Proletarian literature was born from the influence of socialist cultural discourse in the early 1920s, but was divided into bourgeois and proletarian literature under the standard of economic determinism in 1926 over a span of 27 years. Yeom Sang Sup and Kim Ki-jin were evaluated bourgeois when it came to the method of global awareness and theory of art. The dispute about turnover was a problem of setting the direction of the proletarian literature and art movement, and on the other side, it was a proocess of contextualizing how to separate from bourgeois sensibility and the nature of Joseon literature in the 1920s.

The reason that Kim Ki-jin could be amicable towards *Nakdonggang* was due to the internalized characteristic of bourgeois literature. In depiction, *Nakdonggang* paints the prominent history of the Nakdong River through romantic views of nature, and through a petit bourgeois character promotes the discovery of a new human being as well as the will for revolution that class consciousness has.

In the process of going through such debate, KAPF presents "An Overview on the Proletarian Art Movement" (무산계급예술운동에 대한 논강) on *Yesul-undong* [Arts Movement, 예술운동].

> The Union of Joseon Proletarian Arts should undergo this process of the proletarian movement's turnover and achieve the sight of the national political fight.
>
> Therefore, the Union of Joseon Proletarian Arts should not limit the mission of proletarian art to the act of creative work, and should understand that our art must become weapons in order to proceed to the fight that the organization leads. Hence, we aim to save proletarian art from self-isolation of class.
>
> With such meaning, the arts movement of the Union of Joseon Proletarian Arts is wielded as a weapon in the struggle of art for political fights (*Yesul-undong* [Arts Movement, 예술운동], 1927.11).

In developing Joseon's national political movement KAPF clearly declares that literature is a tool for political fights. On such a development, Lee Buk-man "stresses that for a true turnover, they are organizing the proletariat against the oppression of the controlling class, and literature must become literature that can make them move forward to fight, in the article "Is the Turnover Theory of the Arts Movement a True Turnover Theory" [예술운동의 반향전환론은 과연 진정한 방황전환론이었던가] (*Yesul-undong*, 1927.11). With this KAPF develops an arts movement with the political objectives of proletarian literature.

So far, we have observed the origin and the development of KAPF literature in relation to *Joseonjigwang* and Turnover theory. *Joseonjigwang* was not just a journal but an important field of intelligence that created and distributed discourses in the formation and development of socialist ideology in the 1920s. It was a stage to theorize and newly recognize Western arts discourse (theory of public life, life-ism, thoughts of Western art) that was introduced by students, who studied in Tokyo, Japan in the 1910s and 1920s, in socialism, and it is significant in attempting to form socialist class literature closely connected to the reality of colonial Joseon through a global contemporary intellectual sense (politicizing and conversion into arts of the socialist movement). In this vein, we can ascertain that the criticism of the creation of socialist literature and its theorization is was contemporary, and that it was happening within a dynamic literature-field.

The debate on KAPF in 1926-1927 regarding Turnover theory was a process of critiquing the short story *Nakdonggang*, an attempt to theorize proletarian literature, and to attempt ideological artistic reorganization within

KAPF literature. In such dispute, *Nakdonggang* has a KAPF literary characteristic (class consciousness, possibility of proletarian revolution), and demonstrates the realistic relationship between class consciousness and the structured poverty of colonial land through realistic experience, and universal view of the world based on modern life and life discourse. Consequently, we can observe that the characteristics of KAPF literature and the aesthetic traits of novel representation not only end in one-time controversy, but also problematizing the search for the discursive origin of KAPF literature and political practice.

Works Cited

"*Joseonjigwang* Magazine Launched" [*Joseonjigwang* Chang-gan, 조선지광 창간], *Donga-Ilbo* [Dong-A Daily Newspaper, 동아일보], 5 Nov 1922.

"Jubo *Joseonjigwang* Balgulgwa Myeoch Gaji Munje" [Excavation of Weekly Magazine *Joseonji gwang* and Some Problems, 주보 조선지광의 발굴과 몇 가지 문제], *Geundae Seoji*[Modern Bibliography, 근대서지], 2011.12.

Cho, Jong-gon, "Nagdonggang-gwa Je-2-gi Jakpum" [*Nakdonggang* and its Second Period], *Joseonjigwang* [조선지광], Oct 1927.

Choi, Byeong-goo, "Sinche-ui Yumullongwa Pro-Munhak – 1927nyeon *Joseonjigwang*-ui Yumul Nonjaeng-eul Jungsim-eulo" [The Materialism of the Body and Proletarian Literature – Focused on Materialism Controversy of the *Chosunjigwang* in 1927, '신체의 유물론'과 프로문학 – 1927년 조선지광의 유물논쟁을 중심으로], *Minjok Munhaksa Yeongu* [Research on the History of Korean Literature, 민족문학사연구], Vol.53, 2013.

Han, Ki-hyeong, "Sigminji Geom-Yeol Geongchaeggwa Sahoejuui Gwanlyeon Jabjiui Jeongchi Yeokhak – Gaebyeokgwa *Joseonjigwang* Yeoksajeog Wisang BunseoKgwa Gwanlyeonhayeo" [The Political Dynamics of Colonial Censorship Policy and Socialist-Related Magazines : In Relation to the Historical Phase Analysis of *Joseonjigwang* and Gaebyeok, 식민지 검열정책과 사회주의 관련 잡지의 정치 역학 – 개벽과 조선지광 역사적 위상 분석과 관련하여], *Hanguk Munhak Yeongu* [Journal of Korean Literature, 한국문학연구], Vol. 30, June 2006.

Han, Ki-young, "Gaebyeok-ui Jong-gyojeog Isangjuuiwa Geundaemunhag-ui Sasanghwa" [Religious Idealism of Gaebang and Ideology of Modern Literature, 개벽의 종교적 이상주의와 근대문학의 사상화], *Sangheo Hakbo* [Sanghwak Society, 상허학보] Vol. 17, 2006.

Hong, Jung-sun ed, *KimFalbong munhak Jeonjib* [The Complete Works of Kim Falbong Literature, 김팔봉문학전집], Vol.4, Munhakgwa Jiseongsa [Literature and Intellectual History, 문학과지성사], 1989.

Im Hwa, "Jabji-Munhwalon" [Culture Theory of Magazines, 잡지문화론], *Bipan* [Criticism, 비판], Vol. 6, No. 5, May 1938.

Im Hwa, "Mun-ye Jabjilon" [Literary Magazine Theory, 문예잡지론], *Joseon Munhak* [Korean Literature, 조선문학], April – June 1939.

Jang, Sin, "Jubo *Joseonjigwang* Balgulgwa Myeoch Gaji Munje" [Excavation of Weekly Magazine *Joseonjigwang* and Some problems, 주보 조선지광의 발굴과 몇 가지 문제], *Geundae-Seoji* [Modern Bibliography, 근대서지], Dec 2011.

Jo, Myeong-hee, "Saenghwal Danpyeon-ui Gilok"[Record of the Life Fragment, 생활 단편의 기록], Lee Myung-jae ed, *Nakdonggang(Oe)* [Nakdonggang(other), 낙동강(외)], Bumwoo Publishing Co., 2004.

Kim, Ki-jin, "Peulolletalia Mun-ye Jakpum-gwa Peulolletalia Mun-ye Bipyeong" [Proletarian Literary Works and Proletarian Literary Criticism, 무산문예작품과 무산문예비평], *Joseon-jigwang* [조선지광], Feb 1927.

Kim, Sa-guk, "Jayu Bipyeong-ui Jeongsin" [Spirit of Free Criticism, 자유비평의 정신], *Shin-saenghwal* [New Life, 신생활], Sep 1922.

Kim, Sa-guk, "Yesul-ilan mueos-inga" [What is Art, 예술이란 무엇인가], *A-sung* [A-sung, 아성], March 1921.

Lee, Buk-man, "Yesul Undong-ui Banhyang Jeonhwanlon-eun Gwayeon Jinjeonghan Bangh-wang Jeonhwanlon-iessdeonga" [Is the Turnover Theory of the Arts Movement a True Turn-over Theory, 예술운동의 반향전환론은 과연 진정한 방황전환론이었던가], *Yesul-undong* [Arts Movement, 예술운동], Nov 1927.

Lee, Hwa-jin, "Jo Myeong Hui-ui Nagdong-ganggwa Geu Sasangjeog Giban" [The Jo Myeong Hui's *Nakdonggang* and its Ideological Foundation, 조명희의 낙동강과 그 사상적 기반], *Gukjee Omun* [International Language and Literature, 국제어문], Vol.57, 2013.

Park, Sang-joon, "Singyeonghyangpa Damlon-ui Hyeongseong Gwajeong Nongo" [A Discus-sion on the Formation Process of the New Socialist Discourse, 신경향 담론의 형성 과정 논고], *Hanguk Hakbo* [Korean Studies, 한국학보], Vol.24, No.4, 1998.

Park, Young-hee, "Munye Undong-ui Mokjeok-uisiklon" [Awareness of the Purpose of the Liter-ary Movement, 문예운동의 목적의식론], *Joseonjigwang* [조선지광], July 1927.

Park, Young-hee, "Tujaeng-gie Issneun Munye Bipyeongga-ui Taedo" [Attitudes of Literary Crit-ics at the Time of the Struggle, 투쟁기에 있는 문예비평가의 태도], *Joseonjigwang*[조선지광], Jan 1927.

Song, Min-ho, "KAPF Chogi Munyelon-ui Jeongaewa Gwahakjeog Isang-juui Yeonghyang" [The Development of KAPF's Early Literary Theory and the Influence of Scientific Idealism, 카프 초기 문예론의 전개와 과학적 이상주의 영향], *Hangukmunhak-yeongu* [Korean Litera-ture Studies, 한국문학연구], Vol. 42, 2012.

Yeom, Sang-sup, "Gyegeubmunhag-eul Nonhamyeo Sowi Singyeonghyangpa-e Malham" [Dis-cuss class literature and talk to the so-called new socialist literary wave, 계급문학을 논하며 소위 신경향파에 여함], Han Ki-Hyung & Lee Hye-Gyeong ed, *Yeomsangseob Munjang Jeonjib* [The Complete Sentences of Yeom Sang-sup Literature, 염상섭 문장 전집], Vol. 1, Somyeong Publishing Co., 2013.

Human Rights Education in the Japanese Cultural Context

Which Type of Rights Theory Can Provide a Better Guide?*

Teruhisa Se (Kyushu University)

1. Introduction

In the modern world, no society denies, at least officially, the importance of the norm of human rights (Bell 2000 : 3). Human rights education is needed in all areas of the world. However, almost all theories of human rights are based on assumptions strongly affected by modern Western culture. It is difficult to say that such theories offer justifications of human rights that can be readily accepted in any time and any place. This difficulty in theories of rights is particularly serious in human rights education, since the main target of human rights education is children and teenagers, who tend to be weak in handling abstract arguments which are unfamiliar in their daily lives.

In recent years, the demand for human rights education has increased even in non-Western societies. For effective human rights education in a society, it is necessary to explain the values of human rights in such ways that children

* This paper is an English, revised version of Se (2002; 2006).

in that society can understand easily (Bell 2000 : 80). Namely, it should be explained, in words and logic that pupils in the society can understand without problems, that human beings have a series of inviolable and inalienable interests and that those interests should be guaranteed to all people equally. Researchers in political theory or jurisprudence in a society (particularly, researchers in a non-Western society) have to take on the following role if they sincerely try to give back fruits of their academic activity to general people : i.e. the role to clearly show arguments that can help children in a society relate the values of human rights to their moral sense nurtured in daily lives in the society and realize the significance of human rights without difficulty. Researchers are expected to either select such arguments from existing rights theories or develop them by themselves.

The aim of this paper is to discharge the social responsibility of political theorists in the Japanese cultural context. I explore which type of existing human rights theories can give elementary or secondary school teachers appropriate guidance in demonstrating the importance of human rights in classrooms in Japan. I also show a method of explanation suitable for human rights education in Japanese classrooms by refining arguments offered by one type of rights theory.

As stated above, effective human rights education requires the values of human rights to be explained in such a way that children can understand the values, associating them with their moral sense acquired in daily lives. In addition, it is better that the explanation is consistent with and connected to the aims and values stressed in moral education or other instructions in school. This paper aims to clarify the type of human rights theory that can give proper directions in teaching the importance of human rights in Japanese classrooms. In order to make it clear, I examine which rights theory presupposes conceptions of self and morality that are familiar to Japanese pupils, or which one can explain the significance of human rights consistently with other purposes and values emphasized in family and school education in Japan.

The structure of this paper is the following. In the next section, I show the views of self and morality with which Japanese pupils are familiar, with reference to findings in comparative social psychology. I also indicate a general tendency of family and school education in Japan, and the values usually stressed in the education. In the third section, I argue that it is difficult for Japanese pupils to accept basic assumptions of mainstream human rights theories mainly developed in Western societies and that those theories cannot provide appropriate guides for human rights education in Japan. The forth section refers to indirect consequentialist theory of human rights based on fallibilism and claims its suitability as a guide theory for rights education in the Japanese cultural context. This kind of theory has also been developed according to Western political thought, but it can provide a way of explanation that is easily accepted by Japanese pupils. The fifth section summarizes the arguments of this paper and shows a way of teaching that is considered to be effective in making Japanese pupils understand the values of human rights. This concluding section also claims the necessity for further investigation about the methods of human rights education which are appropriate in non-Western cultural environments.

2. Cultural Features in Moral Consciousness and Moral Education in Japan

2-1. Views of self, morality, and self-actualization

1) An interdependent construal of the self

A large number of studies have pointed out that there are some differences in the culturally dominant view of the self between Japan and Western societies (Rosenberger 1992). Hazel R. Markus and Sinobu Kitayama (1991; Kitayama 1998), American and Japanese social psychologists respectively, recently treat just such a difference in a more academically sophisticated way with reference to many empirical findings. They term the view of the self dominant in Western culture (particularly in the main culture of the United States) 'independent construal of the self', and the one prevailing in East Asia, including Japan, 'interdependent construal of the self'. The most significant difference between the two construals is the extent to which the self is assumed to be separated from others and the surrounding situation (Markus and Kitayama 1991 : 245-246). With an independent construal of the self, the degree of subjective distance a person takes from others and the situation is relatively great. Namely, the person tends to perceive his self as a self-contained entity separated from others and the situation. On one hand, a person with an independent self is likely to define himself in relation to some internal attributes considered to be relatively invariable, such as his abilities, talents, motivations, desires, and character traits. On the other hand, the extent to which a person with an interdependent construal of the self subjectively takes distance from others and his surrounding situation is less. The self tends to be recognized as being closely tied to other selves and the situation. It is defined with reference to relationships to others and encompassing circumstances. The situation and relationships are perceived by a person with an interdependent construal of the self to be important elements that constitute his self.

2) Situation-based morality

There is a view of morality that is closely tied to an interdependent view of the self (Kitayama 1998 : 57-60). It is situation-based morality : a moral view that places stress not on abstract moral principles, but on matters embedded in the surrounding situation such as concrete social relationships, the feelings of others, and social roles. An independent construal of the self interprets a person as intrinsically separated from contingent human relationships and social roles. Thus, in a society where an independent construal of the self is dominant, the moral responsibilities of a person, transcending the given social context, are conceived to be independent of human relationships or social roles. They are considered to be determined by abstract moral principles (Shweder et al. 1984 : 168). On the other hand, a person with an interdependent construal of the self tends to regard morality primarily as keeping on good terms with others or fulfilling social roles smoothly (Markus and Kitayama 1991 : 227). Namely, being moral is likely to be understood as acting properly in a given social situation. Hence, it is said that situation-based morality prevails in a culture where an interdependent construal is dominant.

In contrast to the moral view prevailing in Western societies, which emphasizes the importance of ethical principles like fairness, equality or rights in moral thinking, it has been reported by many studies on Japanese culture that the morality widespread in Japan is one which takes contingent, situational matters seriously (Benedict 1954 : 224-227; Lebra 1976 : ch.1). This moral orientation has been also verified by many empirical surveys in social psychology and developmental psychology.

In a culture with a situation-based morality, a person is required to have the ability for empathy to sense the expectations, feelings and ideas of others acutely, even if they are not verbally expressed (Markus and Kitayama 1991 : 229). The reason why a person must be aware of the expectations and feelings of others in this view of morality is that, in order to act appropriately in a situation, it is necessary for him to be watchful of other people's interpretations about the particular situation and their responses to his acts. A considerable number of works on Japanese culture indicate that Japanese society puts special emphasis on empathy as an essential virtue which people have to acquire (Lebra 1976 : 38)

3) self-actualization

According to Kitayama and Markus (2000 : 113-116), these views of self and morality have a strong influence on the view of the process to self-actualization. According to them, in a culture where an independent construal of the self pervades (e.g. the United States), the process to self-actualization tends to be regarded as one in which a person discovers, confirms and expresses his positively valued inner attributes (e.g., abilities, talents, or personality traits). On the contrary, in a culture where an interdependent construal of the self is widespread (e.g. Japan), the process to self-realization tends to be understood in terms of relationships with a situation. Namely, self-actualization is regarded as a process in which a person internalizes other people's expectations toward him, discovers, through self-reflection, his own shortcomings *vis-a-vis* their expectations, eliminates the shortcomings, and attunes himself to the surroundings.

2-2. Features in Child-Rearing and Education

According to empirical findings in developmental and educational psychology, these cultural features are not only observed as existing characteristics, but also supported by social systems such as child-rearing practice and school education. Through such systems, this conspicuous moral orientation is transmitted in Japanese society from generation to generation.

1) Paying attention to other people's feelings and views

Comparative studies in developmental psychology report that mothers in Japan tend to refer to the feelings of other people when they instruct their children or control their behaviour (Hess et.al. 1986 : 155-157; Azuma 1994 : ch. 4). Similar tendencies can be seen in other settings in child-rearing practice. As anthropological studies often point out, a conspicuous feature in the method of Japanese child-rearing is that the parent often makes the child conscious of how others see him in order to improve his behaviour. Using this method, the parent generally places more stress on the perspectives of remote others rather than those of intimate others. It is said that the parent tries to make children internalize those perspectives and acquire the ability to check and revise their own behaviour from the internalized perspectives (Lebra 1976 : 153).

2) Empathy

In Japan, empathy is stressed not only in the family, but also in school education (Azuma 1994 : 103-108). One of the main features of Japanese school education, in comparison to its counterpart in Western countries, is that the development of empathic skills is considered to be an indispensable aim (Tsuneyoshi 1992 : ch. 2-3; 1998).

3) Making use of a 'good-child' identity

In Japanese child-rearing practice, more physical contact between the mother and the child is observed than in Western child-rearing practice. It is said that Japanese child-rearing stresses a sense of 'oneness', or a sense of a deep intimate relationship, between the mother and the child that is experienced through having frequent physical contact and spending a long time together (Lebra 1976 : 138-142). This tendency to stress a sense of oneness is interpreted as having the function of encouraging the child to internalize the mother's views. In addition, it is reported that, both in the family and school education in Japan, parents and teachers often try to make children have a 'good-child' or a 'good-student' identity (Azuma 1994 : ch. 3; Lewis 1995 : 130-133). These identities can serve to promote the internalization of the expectations of parents and teachers as well as the collective goals in classrooms or schools. This method of making good use of a 'good-child' identity and encouraging the internalization of others' expectations and collective goals is regarded as a feature of Japanese education.

4) The importance of self-reflection and flexibility

Stressing the importance of self-reflection is another feature of Japanese child-rearing practice and school education (Lewis 1995 : 120-122). Self-reflection (or *hansei* in Japanese) in this context means the activity of internalizing the viewpoints of diverse others and examining the validity of one's own behaviour and thinking in terms of those internalized viewpoints. Kitayama (1988 : 92) points out that 'Japanese child-rearing tends to encourage children to engage in self-reflection and put emphasis on the importance of making efforts to improve themselves, learning from the results of self-reflection.' A similar tendency is seen in school education in Japan. According to studies in comparative educational sociology (Lewis 1995 : 90-91, 120-122), an outstanding characteristic of Japanese school education is that students have a lot of opportunities of 'self-reflection' or 'self-criticism' in classroom meetings where they are required to think about their own conduct and their feelings about others. Such classroom meetings for 'self-reflection' or 'self-criticism' constitute a normal component of the school day and an important element of the curriculum in Japanese schools (Tsuneyoshi 1991 : 123-127).

The results of cross-national research on the contents of national-language textbooks used in elementary schools are interesting in that they highlight half-implicit features of moral education in Japanese schools. It is said that textbooks of a country's national language (e.g. textbooks of Japanese in Japan, or those of English in the United States) used in elementary schools usually contain a lot of stories that depict behaviour generally regarded as moral ideals in the country. The behaviour displayed by characters in those textbooks is thought to reflect conduct that each culture regards as morally suitable (Imai 1990 : 2; Tomo et.al. 1998 : 97). Yasuo Imai's analysis indicates that textbooks in Japan typically describe warm human relationships in which people try to delicately sense each other's feelings and flexibly revise their own behaviour in order not to harm the emotions of each other. In contrast, the themes which American textbooks are likely to stress are personal autonomy, self-assertiveness, fairness, equality, and strong willpower. Textbooks in the United States often deal with the conflicts among individuals having different interests and their fair solutions (Imai 1990 : chs. 5, 7). In addition, according to a study comparing textbooks in Japan and Britain (Tomo et.al. 1998), textbooks in Japan are likely to set flexible conduct as model behaviour. Namely, Japanese society tends to highly evaluate a style of conduct in which, when facing a new situation that may conflict with his existing views and acts, a person acutely discerns changes in the situation or senses surrounding people's feelings. Furthermore, a person is also expected to spontaneously reshape his own views and behaviour in order to adapt himself to the new situation or keep harmonious relationships with others (Tomo et.al. 1998 : 103-104).

5) The view of self-actualization and the features of child-rearing and education in Japan

I have referred to several cultural features of Japanese child-rearing and school education so far. These features can be interpreted in a consistent way if the above-mentioned view of self-actualization or personal maturity which Japanese people generally assume is understood. That is to say, we can interpret that, behind those features, there is the view that regards self-actualization or maturity as a process in which a person continuously revises and refines his thinking and conduct to truly fit the situation, by making use of empathic ability, internalizing the perspectives of a variety of others (including those both intimate and remote others), and reflectively examines himself from a variety of internalized perspectives. It can be surmised that the half-latent wish of parents and teachers of countless generations in the past for children to advance this process to self-actualization or maturity has formed the characteristic way of Japanese child-rearing and education (Lewis 1995 : 120-122).

3. The Difficulties in Human Rights Education Guided by Mainstream Rights Theories

The views of self and morality reported to be prevalent in Japan do not have affinity with the views of self and morality that dominant human rights theories, i.e. rights theories considered to be orthodox in Western political thought, generally assume. In addition, some basic assumptions, such as about human relationships or moral priorities, which underlie Japanese child-rearing and education, are also considerably different from those assumptions underlying the mainstream human rights theories.

Two types of human rights theory can be mentioned as being in the mainstream.[1] One is the theories sometimes called 'deontological' or 'rights-based'

1 The categorization of human rights theories in this paper is basically based on Sumner (1987).

theories.[2] Deontological rights theories regard some moral principles such as of human dignity, fairness or equality as self-evident and foundational. (See, e.g., Dworkin (1977 : 180-3)) This type of rights theory derives some list of human rights and their inviolability from those ultimate principles assumed to exist transcendentally. Namely, in this kind of theory, the value of human rights is explained by the logic that assumes the transcendental existence of the principles such as of human dignity, fairness and equality, and identifies a conception of rights in relation to these principles. Then, in this logic, the importance of the conception of rights is advocated.

The other orthodox type of rights theories is modern contractarian human rights theories based on the argument of mutual advantage. Modern contractarian human rights theories derive the basis of human rights only from the mutually advantageous convention that is assumed to be concluded among prudential, self-interested individuals (Gauthier 1986 : 1-6, 55-59; Narveson 1989 : 110-121). In this theory, human rights are understood as the products of strategic compromise among individuals essentially having separate, different interests.

These two mainstream types of rights theories do not provide proper guidance for the teachers engaging in human rights education in elementary or secondary schools in Japan. As stated above, the reason for this judgement is that the basic assumptions of these theories are radically different both from the views of self and morality prevalent in Japanese society and from the assumptions underlying Japanese child-rearing practice and education. If those

2 For the fact that deontological theories have been occupying the mainstream position in rights theory since 1970s, see Hart (1979 : 77).

rights theories are used as guidance for human rights education in Japan, it is feared that pupils may have problems in understanding the importance of human rights since they cannot easily associate the importance of rights with moral sense developed in them in everyday lives. It is also of concern that pupils might experience unnecessary confusion concerning the views of self and morality.

For example, on one hand, deontological rights theories employ the logic which posits the existence of some abstract principles such as those of fairness and equality as self-evident and argues for the value of human rights in relation to the presupposed principles. On the other hand, the prevalent view of morality in Japan, to which pupils are likely to be exposed, is the view that places emphasis on the importance of adequate responses to the feelings and the expectations of others in a situation, rather than on the observance of such abstract principles.

To take another example, the assumption of mutual antagonism among individuals, which underlies modern contractarian human rights theories, conflicts with the model of human relationships that Japanese child-rearing and education basically assume. According to a study in educational sociology comparing child-rearing practices in Japan and the United States (Tsuneyoshi 1992 : 2-19), the parent in the United States traditionally tends to regard the child as a separate individual, i.e. an independent agent holding his own desires, some of which may be antagonistic to the parent's or other children's desires. In contrast, as mentioned above, the parent in Japan tends to use the method to encourage the child to form a 'good-child' identity or a 'good-student' identity and makes him feel that he is a good member of a family or a classroom community. Such an identity has a function of promoting the internalization of other people's expectations or collective goals in the child (Azuma 1994 : 70-74). In order to make good use of this function and advance the internalization, it is reported that, in Japanese child-rearing and education, the parent or the teacher tends not to assume bad intentions in the child, and tends to try to make the child believe that he almost always keeps on intimate terms with the parent, the teacher and other children (Azuma 1994 : 70-89; Lewis 1995 : 130-133). This assumption in Japanese education markedly differs from the basic assumption of modern contractarian theories.

We have seen the inconsistencies between the assumptions of the mainstream human rights theories and several cultural views and features of Japan. We may, on these grounds, reasonably conclude that deontological rights theories, which presuppose the existence of transcendental moral principles, and modern contractarian rights theories, which start from the assumption of mutual antagonism among individuals, cannot offer good guidance for human rights education in Japanese classrooms.

4. The Merits of Indirect Consequentialist Theories of Human Rights Based on Fallibilism

Is there any type of rights theory that can properly guide human rights education in elementary and secondary schools in Japan? In this section, I would like to introduce a type of human rights theory as a candidate : indirect consequentialist rights theory based on fallibilism.[3] First, I briefly demonstrate the basic structure of this type of theory. Second, I explain why it is suitable as a guide theory for human rights education in the Japanese cultural context.

4-1. The Logic of Indirect Consequentialist Theories of Human Rights Based on Fallibilism

The phrase 'indirect consequentialism' might not be well-known and needs to be explained.[4] 'Consequentialism' means the moral position which evaluates states or actions only in terms of the value of their consequences. In other words, non-consequentialist theories appraise states or actions, at least in part, in terms of some aspect of them other than their consequences, for example, their intrinsic nature or their motivations. Consequentialism does not adopt these criteria of evaluation and appraises states or actions solely in terms of their consequences. Utilitarianism is a representative version of consequentialism.

Consequentialist theory generally has a basic principle which functions as the fundamental criterion of judgement on actins or states, like the principle

3 It must be difficult to say that indirect consequentialist theories of human rights are currently in the mainstream of rights theory. However, the logic of indirect consequentialism can be found in the tradition of Western political thought. According to Gray (Gray 1989 : 121-128), we can find it in the theories of J. S. Mill, Sidgwick, Hume, and Hayek.

4 For theoretical but concise account of indirect consequentialism, see Sumner (1987 : 178-180) and Gray (1989 : 122).

of utility in utilitarianism. On the one hand, ordinary (direct) consequentialist theories think that this basic principle consistently serves as the criterion of appraisal of every aspect of states or actions. Thus, it considers the basic principle can serve as the guide for practical actions. On the other hand, indirect consequentialism confines the application of the principle. It divides the levels of evaluation of states or actions into two : the critical or abstract level and the practical level. While indirect consequentialism thinks that the basic principle works as the general criterion of appraisal of states or actions at the critical level, it does not think so at the practical level. That is to say, indirect consequentialism does not regard the basic principle as a guide for practical actions, because, in order for a moral agent to make a prescription for his practical actions, various empirical (concrete) facts which are contingent on his situation have to be taken into account. The basic principle of a consequentialist moral framework could show what an agent should do even at the practical level if all necessary information about contingencies could be taken into account. However, because of a moral agent's fallibility, his weakness of will, or the variability of a situation, it is extremely difficult for him to specify what he should do in practice in terms of the basic principle. Therefore, indirect consequentialism recommends a moral agent to adopt not direct policy but indirect policy, in order to achieve a goal set by the basic principle. That is to say, indirect consequentialism considers that a moral agent can do better if he takes up some indirect policy such as the obedience of a rule or a custom, or the cultivation of a virtue. It recommends a moral agent to adopt such an indirect policy, rather than a more direct strategy which seems to him to be prescribed by the application of the basic principle of a moral system to his concrete problem situation.

An indirect consequentialist human rights theory employs this kind of logic and tries to clarify the need to respect the principle of human rights as an indirect policy that must be indispensably adopted. What has to be noted here is that the main reason why an indirect strategy, not a more direct policy, needs to be adopted is the fact of human fallibility. Scholars who deploy an indirect consequentialist theory of human rights generally refer to the inevitable fallibility of human-beings as they explain why the indirect policy, i.e. the observance of the principle of human rights, should be selected (Gray 1989 : 132 ; Sumner 1987 : 192).

Jeremy Shearmur (1990; 1996 : ch. 6), a political theorist in Australia, develops a human rights theory which is based on an idea of indirect consequentialism. His arguments also refer to human fallibility as the reason for adopting an indirect policy. I would like to show the typical way of arguments of indirect consequentialist theory of human rights based on fallibilism, along the lines of Shearmur's arguments.

Shearmur begins his human rights theory with assuming a utilitarian picture of an individual; a person is presupposed to be interested in the relief of his suffering and the promotion of his happiness. However, Shearmur thinks that, because human cognitive ability is unavoidably limited, a person frequently misjudges what he should prefer in practice in order to achieve that goal. If a person blindly adheres to his uncertain judgment and directly pursues his existing preferences, he cannot gain happiness in most cases. Instead, it is better for a person to adopt an indirect policy in order to achieve the ultimate goal. Namely, a person should be aware of his fallibility, respect others, and try to examine the validity of his preferences in the process of social interaction. Thus, the point of Shearmur's indirect derivation of human rights is that it is more likely to lead to happiness for a person if he respects the human rights of others, learns from their views, and intersubjectively scrutinizes his preferences, rather than blindly sticks to his judgment of preferences and directly pursues happiness on that judgment.

In other words, the logic of an indirect consequentialist theory of human rights based on fallibilism can be outlined in the following. Though any person hopes for and pursues one's well-being or self-actualization, he often makes mistakes in judging what constitutes his well-being because of human fallibility. It is uncertain that the pursuit of a person's existing conception of the good life leads to the achievement of the good life that he truly seeks. If a person blindly sticks to his current conception of the good life, it does not necessarily mean that he can achieve his self-actualization even when he managed to realize the state which the conception dictates. The conception of the good life which he presently pursues might turn out to be an insignificant life plan. Thus, it is better for a person to adopt an indirect policy so as to achieve his well-being. Namely, a person should be conscious of the limitations on his cognitive ability, respect the existence of others, learn from a variety of opinions and ways of life shown by other people, and critically examine his own existing thinking and conduct. Taking up such an indirect policy deepens his self-recognition and enables him to understand better what constitutes his well-being. Thus any given person needs opportunities for examining his existing conception of the good life in social interaction. That is to say, a person needs to equally admit not only to himself but also to all others a series of basic conditions for shaping one's own conceptions of the good life, trying out those conceptions, and learning from each other's opinions and ways of life. Therefore, it can be said that what has the function of protecting such conditions, i.e. human rights, should be ensured to all people equally. An indirect consequentialist theory of human rights based on fallibilism derives the necessity for human rights, in this way, from the wishes of individuals to achieve their best ways of life and the indispensable significance of intersubjective examination of their existing life plans.

4-2. The Effectiveness in Human Rights Education in Japan

It is considered that an indirect consequentialist theory of human rights, particularly its version based on fallibilism, is adequate as a guide theory for human rights education in Japan. There are several reasons. First, the views of self and morality underlying this type of rights theory have similarities to the views of self and morality predominant in Japan. An indirect consequentialist rights theory based on fallibilism understands that the self of a person needs to be interpreted by the person himself, since it is so complexly constituted by many attributes, such as ends, affections, social roles, and relationships, that even he himself cannot fully grasp all aspects of his self at once. It is considered in this kind of rights theory that a person has to gradually acquire the knowledge of his self and discover what constitutes his good life through a trial and error process in society. Such a view of self in an indirect consequentialist rights theory based on fallibilism has more affinity with the interdependent view of the self that is reported to be predominant in Japan, compared to, for example, an atomistic view of the self underlying a modern contractarian theory of rights. In addition, the logic of indirect consequentialism may be more easily accepted in Japan than that of deontological theories, since indirect consequentialist rights theories do not need to assume the existence of transcendental moral principles.

What is also important is that there is a similarity in the view of the process to self-actualization between indirect consequentialist rights theories based on fallibilism and Japanese cultural assumptions. The former puts stress on human fallibility and argues that, in order for a person to realize his self, he must widely learn from the opinions of others and their ways of life, and continuously examine his own conceptions of the good life. On the other hand, as stated above, the predominant view of self-realization in Japan regards the process to self-actualization as the process in which a person internalizes other people's expectations and perspectives by making use of his empathetic ability, discovers, through self-reflection, his own shortcomings in terms of the internalized expectations and perspectives, and constantly revises his thinking and conduct.

Furthermore, the values which an indirect consequentialist theory of rights based on fallibilism emphasises in explaining the necessity for human rights are considerably consistent with the values stressed in Japanese child-rearing and school education. An indirect consequentialist rights theory based on fallibilism argues that it is important for a person to learn from other individuals' opinions and conduct in order to examine his current life plans. Since this type of theory derives the necessity for the protection of human rights from this importance, i.e. from the conditions which enable a person to learn from others, mutual learning is a value strongly stressed. In addition, this type of theory argues for the importance of self-criticism, frank admission of one's errors, and their flexible correction. As mentioned in section 2, similar matters are emphasized in Japanese child-rearing and school education : the development of empathic ability, the internalization of other people's expectations and perspectives, self-reflective or self-critical attitudes to check oneself from the internalized expectations and perspectives, and personal flexibility to change one's thinking and behaviour, if necessary. Pupils are often made aware of and taught the importance of these matters in class (e.g. through reading the textbooks in which 'model' characters often appear), or in non-academic school activities (e.g. through participating in daily classroom meetings).

If explained by the logic of indirect consequentialism based on fallibilism, it is expected that pupils can understand smoothly the value of human rights. They can understand it consistently with the views of self and morality developed in everyday life and with the other moral values often emphasized in school education.

5. Concluding Remarks

To put it briefly, it can be said that the following explanation of the value of human rights, which is drawn from the logic of indirect consequentialism based on fallibilism, is most easily understandable to Japanese pupils.

Nobody's cognitive ability is perfect. Although any given person hopes for his self-actualization, he often makes mistakes in judging his own identity and what constitutes his truly good life. In order for a person to deepen his self-knowledge and seek his self-actualization, he has to cultivate his empathic ability and learn from other people's perspectives and ways of life. Then he also has to self-reflectively see himself in terms of the perspectives of others, and continuously revise, if necessary, his thinking and ways of life. The social conditions enabling a person to do these things must be arranged. Thus, it can be said that, in order for any given person to advance a process to self-actualization described above, the opportunities to freely form one's unique perspectives, try out diverse ways of life, and to learn from each other in social interaction, need to be guaranteed not only to the person himself but also all other people equally. A system of human rights functions to create and protect these opportunities. Therefore, human rights have an inviolable and inalienable value.

The merits of indirect consequentialist rights theory are not limited to the arguments of cultural affinity. Here, in order to show a rich potential of indirect consequentialist rights theories based on fallibilism, I would like to mention another merit in teaching the value of human rights in a classroom. This type of theories has superiority in that it can instruct pupils not to commit discrimination persuasively. Unlike other types of rights theories, this type of theories can appeal not only to the disadvantages from which discriminated people must suffer, but also to the disadvantages which people who commit discrimination must face. According to the arguments of indirect consequentialist rights theory, people who commit discrimination lose precious opportunities to make their lives fruitful by learning from others with different views and life styles. For instance, people who discriminate against race or gender cannot learn from the members of other racial groups or of other gender groups. Consequently, they abandon many priceless chances to reflect on their ways of life and make their life fecund. In this way, from a standpoint of indirect consequentialist rights theories based on fallibilism, it is possible to make it clear that discrimination or prejudice may bring disadvantages not only to people who are discriminated or prejudiced, but also to those who commit discrimination or hold prejudice. Hence, this type of rights theories is able to teach the harm of discrimination and prejudice extensively and is expected to curb them more effectively.

***

I have considered the question as to which type of rights theories should be selected as a guide theory for human rights education in Japanese classrooms, with reference to some cultural features in Japan. Only few studies have so far been made at problems concerning the cultural applicability of rights theories in terms of their effectiveness for human rights education. The need for human rights education in the non-Western cultural contexts has been increasing. Further investigation into these problems would be needed to enhance rights education in non-Western countries.

Works Cited

Azuma, H., *Nihonjin no Shitsuke to Kyoiku : Hattatsu no Nichibei Hikaku ni Motozuite* [*Discipline and Education in Japan : Comparative Studies on Human Development between Japan and the United States*], Tokyo : Tokyo University Press, 1994.

Bell, D. A., *East Meets West : Human Rights and Democracy in East Asia*, Princeton : Princeton University Press, 2000.

Benedict, R., *Chrysanthemum and the Sword : Patterns of Japanese Culture*, Boston : Tuttle Publishing, 1954.

Dworkin, R., *Taking Rights Seriously*, Guildford : Duckworth, 1977.

Gauthier, D., *Morals by Agreement*, Oxford : Oxford University Press, 1986.

Gray, J., "Indirect utility and moral rights," In his *Liberalisms : Essays in Political Philosophy*, London : Routledge, 1989.

Hess, R. D., Azuma, H., Kashiwagi, K., Dickson, W. P., Nagano, S., Holloway, S., Miyake, K., Price, G., Hatano, G., and McDevitt, T., "Family influences on school readiness and achievement in Japan and the United States : an overview of a longitudinal study," In Stevenson, H., et al. (eds.), *Child Development and Education in Japan*, New York : W. H. Freeman and Company, 1986.

Imai, Y., *America Jin to Nihon Jin : Kyokasho ga Kataru "Tsuyoi Kojin" to "Yasashi Ichiin"* [*American and Japanese : "Strong Individuals" and "Gentle members" in School Textbooks*], Tokyo : Soryusha, 1990.

Kitayama, S., *Jiko to Kanjyo* [*Self and Emotions*], Tokyo : Kyoritsu Shupan, 1998.

________, and Markus, H. R., "The pursuit of happiness and the realization of sympathy : cultural patterns of self, social relations, and well-being," In Diner, E. and Suh, E. M. (eds.) *Culture and Subjective Well-Being*, Cambridge, MA : The MIT Press, 2000.

Lebra, T. S., *Japanese Patterns of Behavior*, Honolulu : The University Press of Hawaii, 1976.

Lewis, C. C., *Educating Hearts and Minds : Reflections on Japanese Preschool and Elementary Education*, Cambridge : Cambridge University Press, 1995.

Markus, H. R. and Kitayama, S., "Culture and the self : implications for cognition, emotion, and motivation," *Psychological Review*, 98-2, 1991.

Naito, T., "A survey of research on moral development in Japan," *Cross-Cultural Research*, 28-1, 1994.

Narveson, J., *The Libertarian Idea*, Philadelphia : Temple University Press, 1988.

Rosenberger, N. R., "Introduction," In Rosenberger (ed.) *Japanese Sense of Self*, Cambridge : Cambridge University Press, 1992.

Se, T., "Jniken riron to nihon ni okeru jinken kyoiku : kabyushugi ni motozuku kansetsu teki kiketsushugi no jinkenron no yukosei" [Human rights theories and education : the applicability of an indirect consequentialist theory based on fallibilism to the Japanese cultural context], *Komin Kyoiku Kenkyu [Japanese Journal for Civic Eduation]*, 10, 2002.

________, "Jinken kyoiku : nihon no jinken kyoiku ni tekisetuna mitibiki wo ataeru jinken riron no tanakyu" [Human rights education : what type of human rights theory can provide an appropriate guidance for human rights education in Japan], In Citizenship Kenkyukai (ed.), *Citizenship no Kyoiku gaku* [Educational Studies of Citizenship], Kyoto : Koyo Shobou, 2006.

Shearmur, J., "From dialogue rights to property rights : foundations for Hayek's legal theory," *Critical Review*, 4 (1-2), 1990.

________, *Hayek and After : Hayekian Liberalism as a Research Program*, London : Routledge, 1996.

Shweder, R. A. and Bourne, E. J., "Does the concept of the person vary cross-culturally?" In Shweder, R. A. and LeVine, R. A. (eds.), *Culture Theory : Essays on Mind, Self, and Emotion*, Cambridge : Cambridge University Press, 1984.

Sumner, L. W., *The Moral Foundation of Rights*, Oxford : Clarendon Press, 1987.

Tomo, R., Majima, M., and Nomoto, T., "Nichiei no kokugo kyokasho ni miru taijinteki taishokodo" [An analysis of styles of behaviour found in text books in Japan and Britain], *Kyoiku Shinrigaku Kenkyu* [The Japanese Journal of Educational Psychology], 46 (1), 1998.

Tsuneyoshi, R., *Ningen Keisei no Nichibei Hikaku : Kakureta Karicyramu [A Comparative Study on Human Development between Japan and the United States : Hidden Curricula]*, Tokyo : Chuokoronsha, 1992.

________, "Small groups in Japanese elementary school classrooms : comparisons with the United States," *Comparative Education,* 30-2, 1994.

________, "Teaching empathy : family and education in Japan," *Journal of Japanese Trade & Industry,* 17 (5), 1998.

•• Contributors ••

Byeong-jin Kim is research professor at Ewha Womans University and is the author of "Awareness of Freedom and Life Consciousness in the 20th Century"(2017). His research field is Japanese thought history and east-asia modern knowledge.

Sun-hee Kim is research professor at Ewha Womans University and is the author of "The Challenge of Western Learning as Heterodoxy : Re-reading the Sŏngho School's Controversies and Conflicts Over Western Learning in Chosŏn"(2016). Her research field is Korean philosophy and east-asia modern knowledge.

Yeon-soo Kim is assistant professor at Ewha Womans University and is the author of "Die Modernisierung der deutschen literarischen Welt und Goethes 'Weltliteratur'"(2016). Her research field is German literature, world literature, and comparative literature.

Jin-hee Kim is associate professor at Ewha Womans University and is the author of "A Study on Kim Kirim"s Surrealism and Modernism"(2016) Her research field is Korean modern literature, east-asia modern knowledge and translation studies.

Youn-ho Oh is assistant professor at Ewha Womans University and is the author of "The Boundary space of The Empire and The Location of Diaspora"(2017). His research field is Korean modern literature, comparative literature, and diaspora literature.

Inhye Han is research professor at Ewha Womans University and is "Chinul's Chan Hermeneutics Beyond Historicism and Internal Dynamics"(2017) Her research field is English literature and east-asia comparative literature.

Tsunehiko Matsumoto is professor at Kyushu University and is the editor of *Meiji Document Novels*(2007). His research field is Japanese modern literature and especially Akutagawa Ryunosuke, Dazai Osamu, Matsumoto Seitcho.

Noriko Matsunaga is professor at Kyushu University and is the co-editors of *Introduction to Knowledge Processing Studies : Techniques for Accepting, Processing and Sending Knowledge in Japan*(2011). Her research field is history of education, history of cross-cultural communication, Japanese language teaching, and multicultural relations studies.

Elnoby Mohamed was research assistant staff at Kyushu University and is the author of "The imapct of One Thousand and One Nights on the Early Works of Mishima Yukio"(2016). His research field is translation studies, comparative literature, Japanese modern literature

Tsuyoshi Namigata is professor at Kyushu university and is the author of

The Expansion of the Japanese Avant-garde(2005). His research field is Japanese modern literature, comparative literature, and modernism in east asia.

Teruhisa Se is associate professor at Kyushu university and is the co-author of "A Conception of Human Rights Based on Japanese Culture : Promoting Cross-Cultural Debates"(2004). His research field is political theory, political philosophy, human rights theory.

Daniel J. Wyatt was graduate school student at Kyushu University and is the author of "Translation as 'Bakemono': Shapeshifters of the Meiji Era (1868-1912)" (2017). His research field is translation studies, comparative literature, and Japanese modern literature.